Disenfranchised Grief

Disenfranchised Grief

Recognizing Hidden Sorrow

Edited by
Kenneth J. Doka
Graduate School
College of New Rochelle

Lexington Books
An Imprint of Macmillan, Inc.
New York

Maxwell Macmillan Canada
Toronto

Maxwell Macmillan International
New York   Oxford   Singapore   Sydney

Lexington Books
An Imprint of Macmillan, Inc.
866 Third Avenue, New York, N. Y. 10022

Maxwell Macmillan Canada, Inc.
1200 Eglinton Avenue East
Suite 200
Don Mills, Ontario M3C 3N1

Macmillan, Inc. is part of the Maxwell Communication Group of Companies.

Printed in the United States of America

printing number
3 4 5 6 7 8 9 10

Library of Congress Cataloging-in-Publication Data

Disenfranchised grief: Recognizing Hidden Sorrow / editor, Kenneth J. Doka.
  Includes index.
     p.   cm.
  ISBN 0–669–17081–X (alk. paper)
  1. Grief.   2. Loss (Psychology)   3. Bereavement — Psychological
aspects.   I. Doka, Kenneth J.
  [DNLM: 1. Grief.   BF 575.G7   D611]
BF575.G7D57   1989
155.9'37 — dc20
DNLM/DLC
for Library of Congress   87–45967

To my parents, Frank and Josephine, and to my brother, Frank, and my sister, Dorothy, for their patience, love, and support; and to my son, Michael, who taught me how to share that patience, love, and support.

Contents

Figures and Table

Figures

Table

Acknowledgments

I n any book, one of the most difficult and enjoyable tasks is to acknowledge those who in one way or another have helped. It is difficult because there are often so many people to thank for assistance or encouragement that it is easy to miss someone inadvertently. The task is enjoyable because it is truly pleasurable to recognize colleagues and friends who have in one way or another, in a narrow or broad sense, contributed to this work.

First and foremost, I'd like to thank all those who have contributed their chapters and expertise. I hope they will forgive my constant reminders and varied deadlines. I'd also like to thank Daniel Leviton, the late Richard Kalish, Carol Selinske, and John Stephenson for recommending authors.

In a broader way I would like to acknowledge and recognize teachers and colleagues who encouraged my interest in the field. Two early teachers, Rosita Augusta and Ed Lipton encouraged me to aspire and challenged me to think. Paul Gabbert and Ted Westerman introduced me to sociology and encouraged me to attend graduate school. Throughout my graduate education I had gifted teachers such as Eva Kahana, Clement Mihanovich, Thomas McPartland, William Monahan, and Zev Harel. Robert Fulton, Robert Kastenbaum, Dan Leviton, and Eugene Knott all contributed to developing my interest in death studies. I owe thanks to Hannelore Wass, Robert Kastenbaum, and Austin Kutscher for encouraging me to write. Edie Stark, Jane Nichols, Joe Adams, Betty Murray, Howard Raether, and Roberta Halporn constantly challenged me to explore the clinical and practical implications of my work.

I would also like to thank all my colleagues in The Association for Death Education and Counseling for their continuing stimulation, support, and friendship. Two deserve special mention. Van Pine has been a teacher, mentor, friend, and taskmaster. I have much appreciated his help. Therese A. Rando is also a valued colleague and special friend who not only insisted I write this book but even put me in touch with her editor.

Finally, I'd like to recognize all those who worked to make this book a reality: the Faculty Fund of the College of New Rochelle for financial support;

my colleague and program director, Dr. Denise Smith-Fraser, for constant encouragement; my secretarial help, Joyce Griffith, who labored in this project even in the midst of personal crisis, and the ever cheerful, always helpful Vera Mezzaucella; Rosemary Stroebel, our departmental secretary, who effortlessly handled correspondence and calls while making sure I had my memos, messages, and umbrella; and finally, Margaret Zusky, my editor, and the staff at Lexington Books.

Introduction

In the movie *Torch Song Trilogy* there is a dramatic scene in which Arnold, the gay protagonist, raises his mother's ire by saying kaddish for his dead lover. "How," she demands, "can you compare your loss to mine?"

This scene is enacted countless times each day, as people experience the deep loss of someone they love. In some cases it may be the loss of a lover, homosexual or heterosexual. In others it may be the loss of an ex-spouse, a colleague, co-worker, or friend. Sometimes the loss is through a divorce, breakup, or through the experience of significant change in the other. Sometimes the loss may even be that of a pet.

But in each of these situations a person has experienced the loss of a meaningful and significant attachment. And in each situation this loss may not be recognized or validated by others. The grief subsequently experienced is then disenfranchised: the loss cannot be openly acknowledged, socially validated, or publicly mourned.

There is both an intersocial and an intrapsychic aspect of disenfranchised grief. Disenfranchisement can occur when a society inhibits grief by establishing "grieving norms" that deny such emotions to persons deemed to have insignificant losses, insignificant relationships, or an insignificant capacity to grieve. But as Kauffman points out, there is an intrapsychic dimension as well. The bereaved may experience a deep sense of shame about the relationship or they may experience emotions, perhaps reflecting societal norms, that inhibit the grieving process.

The concept of disenfranchised grief is also particularly suited to more complex societies. In less complex societies, deaths are marked communally, providing the opportunity for all members to express and experience grief. In more complex societies, funeral rituals are no longer communal but familial, and as a result the right to express grief is limited to those in recognized kin roles. The grief of others is disenfranchised.

The chapters in this book reflect five years of developing and exploring the concept of disenfranchised grief. In my work, the origins of the concept go back to a paper presented in 1984 which compared the grief experienced by homosexual and heterosexual lovers. After that presentation, others began to talk of the similarity between those losses and other losses that they had experienced personally or professionally. In each case the common denominator was the inability of the grievers to receive social support and validation.

Since that time, especially because of the AIDS crisis, there has been increased recognition of the need to explore the grief reactions that have been variously referred to in the literature as unsanctioned, unrecognized, or disenfranchised. I hope this book will facilitate that task.

The chapters in the introductory section seek to delineate the concept of disenfranchised grief. The first chapter defines it, describing the contexts in which it can occur. Pine's chapter roots the concept of disenfranchised grief in general theoretical treatments of grief. Kauffman provides an exploration of the intrapsychic dimensions of disenfranchised grief. Subsequent chapters then explore the nature and the clinical implications of varied disenfranchised grief situations, as well as professional responses and reactions to such losses. But at the core of each chapter is the hope that, by helping people to recognize such losses, support may be made more available to the bereaved, and their pain understood and thereby lessened.

Part I
Introduction

1
Disenfranchised Grief

Kenneth J. Doka

Introduction

Ever since the publication of Lindemann's classic article, "Symptomatology and Management of Acute Grief" (1944), the literature on the nature of grief and bereavement has been growing. In the few decades following this seminal study, there have been comprehensive studies of grief reactions (for example, Glick, Weiss, and Parkes 1974, Bowling and Cartwright 1982, Parkes and Weiss 1983), detailed descriptions of atypical manifestations of grief (for example, Volkan 1970), theoretical and clinical treatments of grief reactions (for instance, Bowlby 1980, Worden 1982), and considerable research considering the myriad variables that affect grief (for example, Raphael 1983, Rando 1984). But most of this literature has concentrated on grief reactions in socially recognized and sanctioned roles: those of the parent, spouse, or child.

There are circumstances, however, in which a person experiences a sense of loss but does not have a socially recognized right, role, or capacity to grieve. In these cases, the grief is disenfranchised.[1] The person suffers a loss but has little or no opportunity to mourn publicly.

Up until now, there has been little research touching directly on the phenomenon of disenfranchised grief. In her comprehensive review of grief reactions, Raphael notes the phenomenon:

> There may be other dyadic partnership relationships in adult life that show patterns similar to the conjugal ones, among them, the young couple intensely, even secretly, in love; the defacto relationships; the extra-marital relationship; and the homosexual couple . . . less intimate partnerships of close friends, working mates, and business associates, may have similar patterns of grief and mourning. (p. 227)

Focusing on the issues, reactions, and problems in particular populations, a number of studies have noted special difficulties that these populations have in grieving. For example, Kelly (1977) and Kimmel (1978, 1979), in studies of aging homosexuals, have discussed the unique problems of grief in such relationships. Similarly, studies (Heinemann et al. 1979, Geiss, Fuller, and Rush 1986) of the reactions of significant others of AIDS victims have considered bereavement. Other studies have considered the special problems of unacknowledged grief in prenatal death (Corney and Horton 1974, Wolff, Neilson, and Schiller 1970, Peppers and Knapp 1980, Kennell, Slyter, and Klaus 1970, Helmrath and Steinitz 1978), ex-spouses (Doka 1986, Scott 1985), therapists' reactions to a client's suicide, and pet loss. Finally, studies of families of Alzheimer's victims (Kay et al. 1985) and mentally retarded adults (Lipe-Goodson and Goebel 1983, Clyman et al. 1980, Edgerton, Bollinger, and Herr 1984) also have noted distinct difficulties of these populations in encountering varied losses which are often unrecognized by others.

Others have tried to draw parallels between related unacknowledged losses. For example, in a personal account, Horn (1979) compared her loss of a heterosexual lover with a friend's loss of a homosexual partner. Doka (1987) discussed the particular problems of loss in nontraditional relationships, such as extramarital affairs, homosexual relationships, and cohabiting couples.

This chapter attempts to integrate the literature on such losses in order to explore the phenomenon of disenfranchised grief. It will consider both the nature of disenfranchised grief and its central paradoxical problem: the very nature of this type of grief exacerbates the problems of grief, but the usual sources of support may not be available or helpful.

The Nature of Disenfranchised Grief

Disenfranchised grief can be defined as the grief that persons experience when they incur a loss that is not or cannot be openly acknowledged, publicly mourned, or socially supported. The concept of disenfranchised grief recognizes that societies have sets of norms—in effect, "grieving rules"—that attempt to specify who, when, where, how, how long, and for whom people should grieve. These grieving rules may be codified in personnel policies. For example, a worker may be allowed a week off for the death of a spouse or child, three days for the loss of a parent or sibling. Such policies reflect the fact that each society defines who has a legitimate right to grieve, and these definitions of right correspond to relationships, primarily familial, that are socially recognized and sanctioned. In any given society these grieving rules may not correspond to the nature of attachments, the sense of loss, or the feelings of survivors. Hence the grief of these survivors is disenfranchised. In our society, this may occur for three reasons.

1. The Relationship Is Not Recognized

In our society, most attention is placed on kin-based relationships and roles. Grief may be disenfranchised in those situations in which the relationship between the bereaved and deceased is not based on recognizable kin ties. Here the closeness of other non-kin relationships may simply not be understood or appreciated. For example, Folta and Deck (1976) noted, "While all of these studies tell us that grief is a normal phenomenon, the intensity of which corresponds to the closeness of the relationship, they fail to take this (i.e., friendship) into account. The underlying assumption is that closeness of relationship exists only among spouses and/or immediate kin" (p. 239). The roles of lovers, friends, neighbors, foster parents, colleagues, in-laws, stepparents and stepchildren, caregivers, counselors, co-workers, and roommates (for example, in nursing homes) may be long-lasting and intensely interactive, but even though these relationships are recognized, mourners may not have full opportunity to publicly grieve a loss. At most, they might be expected to support and assist family members.

Then there are relationships that may not be publicly recognized or socially sanctioned. For example, nontraditional relationships, such as extramarital affairs, cohabitation, and homosexual relationships have tenuous public acceptance and limited legal standing, and they face negative sanction within the larger community. Those involved in such relationships are touched by grief when the relationship is terminated by the death of the partner, but others in their world, such as children, may also experience a grief that cannot be acknowledged or socially supported.

Even those whose relationships existed primarily in the past may experience grief. Ex-spouses, past lovers, or former friends may have limited contact or they may even engage in interaction in the present. Yet the death of that significant other can still cause a grief reaction because it brings finality to that earlier loss, ending any remaining contact or fantasy of reconciliation or reinvolvement. And again these grief feelings may be shared by others in their world such as parents and children. They too may mourn the loss of "what once was" and "what might have been." For example, in one case a twelve-year-old child of an unwed mother, never even acknowledged or seen by the father, still mourned the death of his father since it ended any possibility of a future liaison. But though loss is experienced, society as a whole may not perceive that the loss of a past relationship could or should cause any reaction.

2. The Loss Is Not Recognized

In other cases, the loss itself is not socially defined as significant. Perinatal deaths lead to strong grief reactions, yet research indicates that many significant others still perceive the loss to be relatively minor (Raphael 1983). Abortions too can constitute a serious loss (Raphael 1972), but the abortion can take place without the knowledge or sanctions of others, or even the recognition that a loss has occurred. It may very well be that the very ideologies of the abortion controversy can put the bereaved in a difficult position. Many who affirm a loss may not sanction the act of abortion, while some who sanction the act may minimize any sense of loss. Similarly, we are just becoming aware of the sense of loss that people experience in giving children up for adoption or foster care (Raphael 1983), and we have yet to be aware of the grief-related implications of surrogate motherhood.

Another loss that may not be perceived as significant is the loss of a pet. Nevertheless, the research (Kay et al. 1984) shows strong ties between pets and humans, and profound reactions to loss.

Then there are cases in which the reality of the loss itself is not socially validated. Thanatologists have long recognized that significant losses can occur even when the object of the loss remains physically alive. Sudnow (1967) for example, discusses "social death," in which the person is alive but is treated as if dead. Examples may include those who are institutionalized or comatose. Similarly, "psychological death" has been defined as conditions in which the person lacks a consciousness of existence (Kalish 1966), such as someone who is "brain dead." One can also speak of "psychosocial death" in which the persona of someone has changed so significantly, through mental illness, organic brain syndromes, or even significant personal transformation (such as through addiction, conversion, and so forth), that significant others perceive the person as he or she previously existed as dead (Doka 1985). In all of these cases, spouses and others may experience a profound sense of loss, but that loss cannot be publicly acknowledged for the person is still biologically alive.

3. The Griever Is Not Recognized

Finally, there are situations in which the characteristics of the bereaved in effect disenfranchise their grief. Here the person is not socially defined as capable of grief; therefore, there is little or no social recognition of his or her sense of loss or need to mourn. Despite evidence to the contrary, both the very old and the very young are typically perceived by others as having little comprehension of or reaction to the death of a significant other. Often, then, both young children and aged adults are excluded from both discussions and rituals (Raphael 1983).

Similarly, mentally disabled persons may also be disenfranchised in grief. Although studies affirm that the mentally retarded are able to understand the concept of death (Lipe-Goodson and Goebel 1983) and, in fact, experience grief (Edgerton, Bollinger, and Herr 1984), these reactions may not be perceived by others. Because the person is retarded or otherwise mentally disabled, others in the family may ignore his or her need to grieve. Here a teacher of the mentally disabled describes two illustrative incidences:

> In the first situation, Susie was 17 years old and away at summer camp when her father died. The family felt she wouldn't understand and that it would be better for her not to come home for the funeral. In the other situation, Francine was with her mother when she got sick. The mother was taken away by ambulance. Nobody answered her questions or told her what happened. "After all," they responded, "she's retarded." (H. Goldstein, private communication)

The Special Problems of Disenfranchised Grief

Though each of the types of grief mentioned earlier may create particular difficulties and different reactions, one can legitimately speak of the special problem shared in disenfranchised grief.

The problem of disenfranchised grief can be expressed in a paradox. The very nature of disenfranchised grief creates additional problems for grief, while removing or minimizing sources of support.

Disenfranchising grief may exacerbate the problem of bereavement in a number of ways. First, the situations mentioned tend to intensify emotional reactions. Many emotions are associated with normal grief. Bereaved persons frequently experience feelings of anger, guilt, sadness and depression, loneliness, hopelessness, and numbness (Lindemann 1944, Worden 1982). These emotional reactions can be complicated when grief is disenfranchised. Although each of the situations described is in its own way unique, the literature uniformly reports how each of these disenfranchising circumstances can intensify feelings of anger, guilt, or powerlessness (see, for example, Kelly 1977, Geis, Fuller, and Rush 1986, Peppers and Knapp 1980, Doka 1985, 1986, Miller and Roll 1985).

Second, both ambivalent relationships and concurrent crises have been identified in the literature as conditions that complicate grief (Worden 1982, Raphael 1983, Rando 1984). The conditions can often exist in many types of disenfranchised grief. For example, studies have indicated the ambivalence that can exist in cases of abortion (Raphael 1972), among ex-spouses (Doka 1986, Scott 1985), significant others in nontraditional roles (Doka 1987, Horn 1979), and among families of Alzheimer's disease victims (Doka 1985). Similarly, the literature documents the many kinds of concurrent crises that can trouble the disenfranchised griever. For example, in cases of cohabiting couples, either heterosexual or homosexual, studies have often found that survivors experience legal and financial problems regarding inheritance, ownership, credit, or leases (for example, Kimmel 1978, 1979, Doka 1987, Horn 1979). Likewise, the death of a parent may leave a mentally disabled person not only bereaved but also bereft of a viable support system (Edgerton, Bollinger, and Herr 1984).

Although grief is complicated, many of the factors that facilitate mourning are not present. The bereaved may be excluded from an active role in caring for the dying. Funeral rituals, normally helpful in resolving grief, may not help here. In some cases the bereaved may be excluded from attendance. In other cases they may have no role in planning those rituals or in deciding whether even to have them. Or in cases of divorce, separation, or psychosocial death, rituals may be lacking altogether.

In addition, the very nature of the disenfranchised grief precludes social support. Often there is no recognized role in which mourners can assert the right to mourn and thus receive such support. Grief may have to remain private. Though they may have experienced an intense loss, they may not be given time off from work, have the opportunity to verbalize the loss, or receive the expressions of sympathy and support characteristic in a death. Even traditional sources of solace, such as religion, are unavailable to those whose relationships (for example, extramarital, cohabiting, homosexual, divorced) or acts (such as abortion) are condemned within that tradition.

Naturally, there are many variables that will affect both the intensity of the reaction and the availability of support. All the variables—interpersonal, psychological, social, physiological—that normally influence grief will have an impact here as well. And while there are problems common to cases of disenfranchised grief, each relationship has to be individually considered in light of the unique combinations of factors that may facilitate or impair grief resolution.

Implications

Despite the shortage of research on and attention given to the issue of disenfranchised grief, it remains a significant issue. Millions of Americans are involved in losses in which grief is effectively disenfranchised. For example, there are more than 1 million couples presently cohabiting (Reiss 1980). There are estimates that 3 percent of males and 2–3 percent of females are exclusively homosexual, with similar percentages having mixed homosexual and heterosexual encounters (Gagnon 1977). There are about a million abortions a year; even though many of the women involved may not experience grief reactions, some are clearly "at risk."

Disenfranchised grief is also a growing issue. There are higher percentages of divorced people in the cohorts now aging. The AIDS crisis means that more homosexuals will experience losses in significant relationships. Even as the disease spreads within the population of intravenous drug users, it is likely to create a new class of both potential victims and disenfranchised grievers among the victims' informal liaisons and nontraditional relationships.[2] And as Americans continue to live longer, more will suffer from severe forms of chronic brain dysfunctions (Atchley 1985). As the developmentally disabled live longer, they too will experience the grief of parental and sibling loss. In short, the proportion of disenfranchised grievers in the general population will rise rapidly in the future.

It is likely that bereavement counselors will have increased exposure to cases of disenfranchised grief. In fact, the very nature of disenfranchised grief and the unavailability of informal support make it likely that those who experience such losses will seek formal supports. Thus there is a pressing need for research that will describe the particular and unique reactions of each of the different types of losses; compare reactions and problems associated with these losses; describe the important variables affecting disenfranchised grief reactions;[3] assess possible interventions; and discover the atypical grief reactions, such as masked or delayed grief that might be manifested in such cases. Also needed is education sensitizing students to the many kinds of relationships and subsequent losses that people can experience and affirming that where there is loss there is grief.

Notes

1. A term suggested by Austin Kutscher (private communication).

2. One can also speak of "disenfranchising deaths." In some cases the cause of death creates such shame and embarrassment that even those in recognized survivor roles (such as spouse, child, or parent) may be reluctant to avail themselves of social support or may feel a sense of social reproach over the circumstances of death. Death from a dreaded disease like AIDS and certain situations surrounding suicide and homicide are illustrations of disenfranchising death. Each carries a stigma that may inhibit even survivors in recognizably legitimate roles from seeking and receiving social support.

3. As has been stated, some of these variables will be common to all losses. Others, such as the degree to which a loss is socially recognized, publicly sanctioned, openly acknowledged, or replaceable, may be unique to certain types of disenfranchised grief.

References

Atchley, R. 1985. *Social Forces and Aging.* 4th ed. Belmont, Calif.: Wadsworth.
Bowlby, J. 1980. *Attachment and Loss: Loss, Sadness and Depression.* vol. 3. New York: Basic Books.

Bowling, A., and A. Cartwright. 1982. *Life After a Death: A Study of the Elderly Widowed.* New York: Tavistock.

Clyman, R., C. Green, J. Rowe, C. Mikkelson, and L. Ataide. 1980. "Issues Concerning Parents After the Death of Their Newborn." *Critical Care Medicine* 8, 215–18.

Corney, R.J., and F.T. Horton. 1974. "Pathological Grief Following Spontaneous Abortion." *American Journal of Psychiatry* 131, 825–27.

Doka, K. 1985. "Crypto Death and Real Grief." Paper presented to a symposium of the Foundation of Thanatology, New York, March.

———. 1986. "Loss upon Loss: Death After Divorce." *Death Studies* 10, 441–49.

———. 1987. "Silent Sorrow: Grief and the Loss of Significant Others." *Death Studies* 11, 455–69.

Edgerton, R.B., M. Bollinger, and B. Herr. 1984. "The Cloak of Competence: After Two Decades." *American Journal of Mental Deficiency* 88, 345–51.

Folta, J., and G. Deck. 1976. "Grief, the Funeral and the Friend." In *Acute Grief and the Funeral,* edited by V. Pine, A.H. Kutscher, D. Peretz, R.C. Slater, R. DeBellis, A.I. Volk, and D.J. Cherico. Springfield, Ill.

Gagnon, J. 1977. *Human Sexualities.* Glenview, Ill.: Scott, Foresman.

Geis, S., R. Fuller, and J. Rush. 1986. "Lovers of AIDS Victims: Psychosocial Stresses and Counseling Needs." *Death Studies* 10, 43–54.

Glick, I., R. Weiss, and C.M. Parkes. 1974. *The First Years of Bereavement.* New York: Wiley.

Heinemann, A., et al. 1983. "A Social Service Program for AIDS Clients." Paper presented to the Sixth Annual Meeting of the Forum for Death Education, Chicago, October.

Helmrath, T.A., and G.M. Steinitz. 1978. "Parental Grieving and the Failure of Social Support." *Journal of Family Practice* 6, 785–90.

Horn, R. 1979. "Life Can Be a Soap Opera." In *Perspectives on Bereavement,* edited by I. Gerber, A. Weiner, A. Kutscher, D. Battin, A. Arkin, and I. Goldberg. New York: Arno Press.

Kalish, R. 1966. "A Continuum of Subjectively Perceived Death." *The Gerontologist* 6, 73–76.

Kay, W.J. et al., eds. 1984. *Pet Loss and Human Bereavement.* New York: Arno Press.

Kelly, J. 1977. "The Aging Male Homosexual: Myth and Reality." *The Gerontologist* 17, 328–32.

Kennell, J., M. Slyter, and M. Klaus. 1970. "The Mourning Response of Parents to the Death of a Newborn Infant." *New England Journal of Medicine* 283, 344–49.

Kimmel, D. 1978. "Adult Development and Aging: A Gay Perspective." *Journal of Social Issues* 34, 113–31.

———. 1979. "Life History Interview of Aging Gay Men." *International Journal of Aging and Human Development* 10, 237–48.

Lindemann, E. 1944. "Symptomatology and Management of Acute Grief." *American Journal of Psychiatry* 101, 141–49.

Lipe-Goodson, P.S., and B.I. Goebel. 1983. "Perception of Age and Death in Mentally Retarded Adults." *Mental Retardation* 21, 68–75.

Miller, L., and S. Roll. 1985. "A Case Study in Failure: On Doing Everything Right in Suicide Prevention." *Death Studies* 9, 483–92.

Parkes, C.M., and R. Weiss. 1983. *Recovery from Bereavement.* New York: Basic Books.

Peppers, L., and R. Knapp. 1980. *Motherhood and Mourning.* New York: Praeger.

Rando, T. 1984. *Grief, Dying and Death: Clinical Interventions for Caregivers.* Champaign, Ill.: Research Press.

Raphael, B. 1972. "Psychosocial Aspects of Induced Abortion." *Medical Journal of Australia* 2, 35–40A.

————. 1983. *The Anatomy of Bereavement.* New York: Basic Books.

Reiss, I. 1980. *Family Systems in America.* New York: Holt, Rinehart and Winston.

Scott, S. 1985. "Grief Reactions to the Death of a Divorced Spouse." Paper presented to the Seventh Annual Meeting of the Forum for Death Education and Counseling, Philadelphia, April.

Sudnow, D. 1967. *Passing On: The Social Organization of Dying.* Englewood Cliffs, N.J.: Prentice-Hall.

Volkan, V. 1970. "Typical Findings in Pathological Grief." *Psychiatric Quarterly* 44, 231–50.

Wolff, J., P. Neilson, and P. Schiller. 1970. "The Emotional Reaction to a Stillbirth." *American Journal of Obstetrics and Gynecology* 101, 73–76.

Worden, W. 1982. *Grief Counseling and Grief Therapy.* New York: Springer.

2

Death, Loss, and Disenfranchised Grief

Vanderlyn R. Pine

Introduction

Throughout human history, the occurrence of death has given rise to social ceremonies and commemorative activities to note the death, to recognize the place the dead person occupied in society, and to assist the bereaved through the process of grief. Each culture faces death with its own definition of "appropriate" social-emotional reactions, ranging from resignation to hysteria, and when death occur, it provides the occasion for socially conditioned grief reactions and mourning practices (Pine 1972).

Funeral rites allow the bereaved to pass through the period of adjustment after a death with a defined social role; they also delimit the period of mourning, allow the bereaved to release grief emotions publicly, and aim at helping to commemorate an individual's death. Furthermore, funeral rites provide an opportunity for group assembly, reaffirm social values, and attempt to provide relief from the guilt that is often part of grieving (Pine 1972).

Most of the activities surrounding funeral rituals have emerged from long-standing community practices. Historically, such practices have incorporated a set of interrelated, knowledgeable people, the majority of whom were very familiar with the customs and their purposes. In such a setting, it was possible for close kin, friends, distant kin, and acquaintances to come together to share their grief. In our modern, compartmentalized society, funeral practices tend to be limited primarily to the "proper" bereaved people. This has helped create an underclass of grievers whose legitimacy may not even be recognized and whose needs are not addressed. Such people may go begging for assistance and suffer from what is called disenfranchised or unsanctioned grief.

It is important to understand that the term *disenfranchised* implies that some right or privilege was possessed in the first place. For our purposes, the original enfranchisement is conceived as having been both a right and a privilege uniformly granted to all members of a community or society. This more accurately describes the earliest human societies in which a tight-knit, cohesive, and mutually interrelated group openly expressed and shared their common life experiences.

The analytical importance of this concept is that there have been major social organizational, social structural, and social psychological changes to our modern social system. As a result of these changes, certain categories of grievers have been shunted out of the mainstream. This has created an underclass of grievers whom we describe as disenfranchised by society from the normal grieving process.

Those experiencing disenfranchised grief may be from three general types of grievers. One type includes people whose relationships are socially unrecognized, illegitimate, or in other ways unsanctioned. Another type includes people whose loss does not fit the typical norms of appropriateness. A final type of griever includes people whose ability to grieve is in question or who are thought not to be legitimate grievers.

Theories about Grief

To understand the complexities of disenfranchised grief, it is helpful first to understand the typical patterns, reactions, and manifestations of normal grief. The writings of several noted death scholars can be integrated to form a general theory that helps us to understand the complications of unsanctioned grief.

In "Mourning and Melancholia" (1959, p. 153), Freud identifies grief as a "painful" state of mind and refers to it in terms of the "economics of the mind." Using the concept of economics allows Freud to treat grief as part of a psychological exchange process, with tasks and activities being carried out as "labor" in exchange for a kind of psychic "freedom" from the dead person. In our present analysis, the problem is even more intense because the griever has to be connected legitimately before he or she can begin to attempt some kind of freedom.

The goal of what Freud (1959, pp. 156–61) referred to as "the work of grief" is to free the bereaved person from the attachments to the dead person, the inhibitions of becoming a separate being, and conflicts of ambivalence over the lost love relationship. Therefore, "the work of mourning" is a temporal process over time. Again the rub is intensified because much work must be done on not just time present but also time past. The disenfranchised griever has the difficult task of reconciling simultaneously that which is and that which was.

According to Freud's theory (1959, p. 163), after "normal grief" accomplishes the "labor" of freeing the bereaved from the dead person, it does not leave "traces of any gross change" in the bereaved person. This has led some to believe that completed grief work represents a cured condition. Freud did not intend this interpretation to be used by clinicians, who view grief as "curable" in the medical sense, implying that it is an "illness." His point was that the human psyche has the *ability to cope naturally* with loss. The assumption, of course, is that the griever can *return* to some appropriate (but altered) state of being. However, the disenfranchised griever is one who "should not" (by social convention) show traces of any change, gross or otherwise.

Freud did not use a time limit to describe the duration of "normal" grief. Freud's view is that completing the *process* of grief work determines the time limit of the duration of "normal grief." Hence, when the process has occurred, then, enough time will have passed for the griever to complete the three essential tasks of grief work: freedom, separation, and coping with ambivalence (Osterweis, Solomon, and Green 1984). All of these are difficult tasks for someone who is a disenfranchised griever.

In the "The Symptomatology and Management of Acute Grief" (1944), Lindemann distinguishes between normal and pathological grief, delineating ways of dealing with repressed and delayed grief, both of which he believes are common problems. Lindemann points out that grief may be an *acute* psychosocial condition that is characterized by a rapid onset, serious conditions, and treatable symptoms.

Lindemann explains that acute grief is an observable syndrome with psychological and somatic symptoms that may appear immediately, be delayed, exaggerated, or apparently absent. Furthermore, distorted reactions may occur and can be viewed as a specific aspect of the grief syndrome. All his observations are relevant to disenfranchised grievers.

Lindemann believes that with appropriate psychiatric intervention, distorted grief may be transformed into normal grief with the possibility of resolution. In other words, he thinks that with understanding *and* clinical intervention, unresolved grief is manageable. But Lindemann had foremost in mind the distorted grief of a normally grieved person. Though many of his points may be applicable to disenfranchised grievers with distorted symptoms, it is likely that the standard assessment and treatment modalities will be of limited value. As a case in point, how does one easily recognize symptoms when there is no apparent link to some traumatic death event?

Lindemann (1944, p. 143) points out that the duration of grief reactions depends on how well the bereaved person performs "grief work." The resolution of grief may be subverted when bereaved people try to avoid carrying out grief work because of the distress and emotional energy required to complete it. As was stated previously, the disenfranchised griever has many potential reasons for avoiding the grief work, and most of them are linked to the unsanctioned or unrecognized relationship.

By resolution, Lindemann (1944, p. 143) means achieving "emancipation from the *bondage* to the deceased," readjustment to the environment, and the ability to form new relationships. The idea that the dead person holds the bereaved "in bondage" refers to the interpersonal relationship between people. In this sense, bondage emerges from power so dominant that the dead person remains not only in the bereaved person's memory but also in control of the bereaved person's life. For most disenfranchised grievers the bondage matter is a nonissue, for many gladly would have entered into "bondage" if given the opportunity for a public relationship.

According to Lindemann, it is possible to predict the type and severity of a distorted grief reaction from information and knowledge about the premorbid personality of the bereaved. For example, the extent of the affective (love/hate) relationship to the deceased is an important factor in determining the severity of the grief reaction. Also, Lindemann found that patients with obsessive or depressive personalities often experience agitated depression after bereavement. Once again, and in addition to personality traits, the power of the community over the sanctioning of a relationship influences the affective conditions of the griever.

One of Lindemann's major contributions to grief studies involves the concept of management. Lindemann explains that with proper management severe psychosomatic and/or medical problems stemming from distorted grief can be avoided, ameliorated, or eliminated. Among other things, the psychiatrist, psychologist, or other professional can help "share" the grief work by helping the bereaved person extricate him- or herself from overattachment to the dead person. Lindemann (1944) states that the bereaved need to accept the pain of their loss, review their (past) relationship with the deceased, and realize that there will be changes in their expressions of emotional reactions. The bereaved need to "talk through" their sense of loss and sorrow. Moreover, the professional care provider should encourage new patterns of conduct for the bereaved in his or her new life without the deceased person. Such steps are sensible and potentially effective for disenfranchised grievers, but enormous initial problems remain with recognition, identification, and diagnosis.

It is noteworthy that Lindemann states that these techniques for grief reaction management "can be done in eight to ten interviews." This creates the impression that there is a standard number of sessions or interviews needed for accomplishing management of grief reactions. This particular element of Lindemann's study appears to be at odds with the point that each person's uniqueness and special needs must be taken into consideration in order for the bereaved person to deal with death in a healthy fashion and in order for the caregiver to help the bereaved person manage his or her grief reactions. Lindemann was concerned with trying to break through the barrier of *not* attempting to assuage grief by psychiatric intervention. Thus, the focus should not be on his time or session estimate but on the idea of addressing such needs in a timely, direct manner. Furthermore, for disenfranchised grievers, it is important to strive to attain positive goals through therapy using a reasonable time frame in light of all important factors.

In *Bereavement: Studies of Grief in Adult Life* (1972), Parkes presents two elements that he believes influence bereavement. One of these elements he calls "stigma," and it suggests the social attitude of ostracism in the treatment of the newly bereaved person. People often avoid the bereaved person or feel uncomfortable in his or her presence. The not-so-hidden meaning is that the bereaved person is viewed by others as tainted by the death of a loved one. For someone who is disenfranchised the flip side of the stigma coin is the "search for connection syndrome." Paradoxically, while being isolated because the stigma of death is difficult to handle, many disenfranchised grievers secretly yearn to be recognized and thereby stigmatized. In reality, it is not likely that a disenfranchised griever would welcome being ignored or isolated, but for many at least it would be a connection.

Parkes calls the other element "deprivation," referring to the absence of those psychosocial supplies such as love and security which were provided by the dead person. By identifying the deprivation factor, Parkes provides a critical link between grief and bereavement. Bereavement is equivalent to deprivation in the objective sense because it represents a measurable or actual loss. Grief, on the other hand, is a psychosocial response to loss. This distinction helps in recognizing the observable elements of a particular bereavement and its losses and then in treating the attendant psychosocial grief reactions.

Parkes notes that the effects of ambivalence, the inability to communicate, and the absence of understood social expectations and acceptable rituals for mourning are likely to foster pathological reactions to bereavement. He believes that therapists dealing with grief reactions should assume an accepting attitude in order to enable the bereaved person to feel free to express feelings of anger, guilt, despair, and anxiety. This should promote the transformation of pathological grief into normal grief, and then the bereaved can be directed toward resolution. Clearly, these matters are even more difficult to resolve for the disenfranchised grievers.

The Role of the Funeral in Resolving Grief

In analyzing funeral rites and mourning behavior in *The Elementary Forms of Religious Life*, Durkheim (1915, p. 435) points out that funeral rites are ceremonies that designate a state of "uneasiness or sadness." The implication is that death produces personal anxieties that are addressed by the funeral ceremony, which in turn is indicative of a society's feelings and beliefs about death. Durkheim points out that funeral rites mirror a particular society's death concepts, and that they provide a particular interpretation of life and death.

According to Durkheim, mourning behavior is neither a natural reaction nor a spontaneous release of emotions. He argues that the bereaved are actors who feel obliged to "play out" their emotions through gestures that are sanctioned by society. In other words, if a bereaved person does not display his or her grief in an acceptable manner, the community will show its disapproval or impose some sort of punishment. Hence, Durkheim posits,

> Mourning is not a natural movement of private feelings wounded by a cruel loss; it is a duty imposed by the group. One weeps, not simply because he is sad, but because he is forced to weep. It is a ritual attitude which he is forced to adopt out of respect for custom, but which is, in a large measure, independent of his affective state. (1915, p. 443)

Although Durkheim exaggerates the influence of society over the individual's actual emotional reactions, the point is a perceptive one regarding the public functions of mourning. Moreover, the person's affective state does fit into a general community attitude scheme in which social expectations help facilitate the individual expression of grief. Unfortunately, the disenfranchised griever generally is not granted such an opportunity. For that matter, the worst part is that in all likelihood there are *no* expectations at all. It is as if society says, not only do we not recognize your need to grieve, we also do not recognize your relationship in the first place. It is reminiscent of the double slap routine of vaudeville in which the victim is hit both ways, once coming and once going.

In *Magic, Science, and Religion* (1948), Malinowski notes the strong impact on and the ways in which *society* is affected by death. He observes, "(Death) . . . threatens the very cohesion and solidarity of the group . . . (and the funeral) counteracts the centrifugal forces of fear, demoralization, and provides the most powerful means of reintegration of the group's shaken solidarity and of reestablishment" (1948, p. 53).

Malinowski (1948) explains that the despair, the funeral ceremonies, and the mourning behavior all serve to demonstrate the emotions of the bereaved and the loss experienced by the whole group. These aspects of death reinforce as well as reflect the natural feelings of the survivors. The death rites create a social event out of a natural act, for it is only natural to die. In this sense, then, the rites become rights for those who *should be* grieved. By its inverse, this means that some members of society have their personal dyadic solidarity shaken but that there may be no group to which they can turn for support, and in that sense they are disenfranchised.

In most societies, it is during the funeral ceremony that death reactions become visible (Pine 1972, Rando 1984). Funeral rites provide bereaved people with a defined social role that functions to help them pass through a period of adjustment following the death. Funeral rites also intend to put a limit on the period of immediate mourning and aim to provide the bereaved with a public forum in which to release their grief emotions.

However, there are those whose mourning is not delimited because its presence has not been acknowledged. Furthermore, it is likely that disenfranchised grievers have difficulty releasing their emotions privately, let alone publicly. The road back to an accepting society has to be difficult when the group does not even know that a loss has occurred for the disenfranchised griever.

In *Elements of Social Organization* (1964), Firth emphasizes that there are societal elements that usually help the bereaved resolve their ambivalent feelings about death:

> A funeral ritual is a social rite par excellence. Its obstensible object is the dead person, but it benefits not the dead, but the living . . . it is those who are left behind—the kinsfolk, the neighbors, and other members of the community—for whom the ceremony is really performed (p. 63).

Firth (1964, p. 63) observes that the funeral supplies three necessary elements to the living. The first element is the resolution of uncertainties in the behavior of the immediate kin. The funeral provides relatives with an opportunity to publicly display their grief, and it sets a limit on the time of their (public) mourning. As such, it is a ritual of closure. Closure can only occur when something has been opened in the form of a community relationship. In the close-knit communities studied by Firth, there tended to be an inherent sense of community loss after most deaths. Thus, public mourning behavior at least allowed those who were in some way disenfranchised the opportunity to feel a sense of mourning, even if it were not legitimitaly theirs to begin with.

Firth describes the second element as the fulfillment of social consequence, which means that the ceremony helps to reinforce the appropriate attitudes of the members of society to each other. Although stressing the dead, the funeral points out the value of the services of the living. As has consistently been the case, the disenfranchised griever is at a great disadvantage here. In most instances the services of the living are only acknowledged for those who are thought of a legitimate or sanctioned by society.

The third element is the economic aspect. Every funeral involves the expenditure of money, goods, and services. Analytically, this ties in with Freud's reference to the concept of economics and the exchange process in relation to grief and mourning. Freud (1959) notes that the bereaved feel they must "compensate" in some way for the death. He was referring here to the psychological exchange process. Firth, on the other hand, states that the exchange process is important to the bereaved on a tangible social and economic level as well. Bereaved people may feel the need to make restitution to the deceased by purchasing such nonabstract items as funeral feasts, funeral merchandise, religious services, and so forth. For the majority of disenfranchised grievers, there is little, if any, opportunity to compensate by expenditure, either monetary or symbolic. In our relatively materialist society, this denies disenfranchised grievers of yet another outlet generally afforded to those seen as legitimate.

Practical Grief Concerns

Many of the theoretical perspectives can be integrated with practical concerns into a coherent framework through which we can gain a fuller understanding of death and grief. The following discussion is a synthesis of the works already cited, plus personal observations on the critical issues noted in them.

Evidence indicates that grief can be resolved. Resolution does *not* mean that the bereaved person will actually "get over" the pain of grief, not does it mean that the bereaved will never again experience pain in connection with the death. Rather, it means that the bereaved person reaches a point at which the pain of a particular death can be accepted and can be "lived with." When this occurs, the bereaved person feels that life can continue without the one who has died.

Most clinicians have found that death and grief should be shared openly with other people. One difficult aspect of this issue is timing, for different grievers of the same dead person experience different grief reactions at different points in time. Although such reactions may not be shared easily, it is beneficial when they are mutually understood and accepted.

The implications of these observations are especially difficult for disenfranchised grievers. Time often has little or no meaning in relation to their public social selves. The recognition factor is part of the problem, but even more troublesome is the mutuality issue. Perhaps the dead person represents the only truly significant other for the disenfranchised griever. This renders the sharing dimension out of the realm of possibility, thereby heightening the problem.

Another aspect of shared grief is the communication process itself. *Open* communication allows for and promotes differences in style, intensity, and depth of grief. Open communication is essential in attempting to cope with these and other differences in people. Again, the very fact of disenfranchisement generally compromises the ability to have open communication.

Most writings confirm that anticipatory responses to a potential death should be recognized as a form of actual grief. The so-called anticipatory grief process should be considered a beneficial and necessary step toward resolution. Although anticipatory grief generally can be a positive experience, there is a potential problem—namely, *too much* anticipatory grief may be detrimental. Excessive anticipation can result in people's emotionally and physically distancing themselves from the dying person "too soon," causing the dying person to feel abandoned and isolated. Thus, the unsanctioned or unrecognized griever may be led into deeper grief. Unfortunately, there are no guidelines to determine the correct amount of anticipatory grief that is beneficial for a so-called normal griever, let alone one who is disenfranchised.

The evidence indicates that professional intervention can be helpful in the death-related grief process and should be initiated when it is warranted. Assistance can be given by those in many different care-providing occupations, including physicians, nurses, clergy, social workers, funeral directors, hospice workers, family therapists, and grief counselors.

There are self-help groups to help the dead person's family cope with death, as well as self-help groups to assist care providers in dealing with the deaths of their patients or clients. The self-help groups that deal with death concerns include such organizations as the Compassionate Friends, Widow-to-Widow, SIDS Support Groups, Candlelighters, volunteer hospice groups, and others. These organizations offer interactive membership, with participatory activities and peer counseling.

For disenfranchised grievers, there generally are no coherent, well-organized, or readily available self-help groups. Moreover, even though each self-help organization has a special constituency, most of them do not have a section for people who can be considered disenfranchised grievers. The result is that this potentially beneficial source of social and emotional support is typically not available for disenfranchised grievers.

Conclusion

The matter of disenfranchised grief is complex and multifaceted, and it involves numerous psychological, social, and cultural dimensions. Furthermore, people develop various methods of coping with life and death events in accordance with their beliefs, values, sociocultural backgrounds, *and* the general expectations of society.

The ideas of great thinkers are useful as a springboard for further advancement in the field of disenfranchised grief. The essential clarity, logic, and believability of their writings make their ideas so beneficial in establishing the present perspective. Their works blend into a design of themes woven into patterns of coping strategies for dying, death, bereavement, and grief. One hopes that some new ideas will be generated from the grief studies discussed in this chapter.

Questions abound regarding how best to assist disenfranchised grievers. Several general ideas come to mind. First, there is the educational process.

Cognitive awareness of the unique elements for such people may foster a greater degree of understanding in the general population. Given this possibility, it seems essential to develop a more public view of this exceptionally personal grief reaction. In this vein, educational efforts ought to be made to improve overall cognizance of the problems of disenfranchised grief.

Another area ripe for serious attention is the therapeutic setting. Grief counselors and others would do well to develop strategies for facilitating disenfranchised grief. In light of the success of self-help groups in addressing more common forms of grief, it may be useful to develop concrete suggestions about the nature and likelihood of disenfranchised grief. Then, with aggressive community information programs and the formation of a volunteer focus group, the subject can be thoroughly explored and discussed. If the need exists, it is reasonable to expect that an ongoing group of people who feel disenfranchised in their grief will emerge.

For some, just the opportunity for public expression and/or recognition of the situation may suffice to propel them into more therapeutically sound grieving modalities. For others, more action may be necessary, and the group meetings can serve as the starting point for them. Given the evidence of other self-help programs, group participants may feel less threatened about seeking personal assistance if they have already witnessed the benefits of the self-help group model.

Clinicians must be mindful of the possibility of loss that is not readily observable. This awareness can be useful in assessing any (and all) clinical relationships, since the presence of disenfranchised grief can easily complicate and compromise many other situations. It is very useful to understand that many subclinical states of being can exacerbate a readily observable condition *in addition to* the condition itself. Appropriate probing about other, less obvious losses can open up new productive avenues of therapeutic intervention if disenfranchised grief can be uncovered.

Disenfranchised grief is an increasingly prevalent condition. In a highly mobile society with limited avenues for effective leave-taking in ordinary, everyday life and very few avenues when death does occur, the dilemma for those with suspect or nonexistent rights and privileges will be even more difficult.

One hope is that this book can open up the lines of communication and awareness so that disenfranchised grievers will at least have a legitimate opportunity to express their deep feelings. At the most hopeful level, such grievers will find new and unique means to resolve their grief. If this can occur, then, some of modern society's most poignant examples of loss will have a place in the open. This place is one where all grievers have the right to resolve the pain of loss.

References

Bowlby, J. 1969. *Attachment and Loss, vol. 1; Attachment.* New York: Basic Books.

Durkheim, E. 1915. *The Elementary Forms of Religious Life.* New York: Free Press.

Firth, R. 1964. *Elements of Social Organization.* Boston: Beacon Press.

Freud, S. 1957. "Mourning and Melancholia." In *A General Selection from the Works of Sigmund Freud,* edited by J. Richman. New York: Doubleday, 1957.

Lindemann, E. 1944. "The Symptomatology and Management of Acute Grief." *American Journal of Psychiatry* 101, 141–48.

Malinowski, B. 1948. *Magic, Science, and Religion.* Garden City, N.Y.: Doubleday.

Osterweis, M., F. Solomon, and M. Green, eds. 1984. *Bereavement: Reactions, Consequences, and Care.* Washington, D.C.: National Academy Press.

Parkes, C.M. 1972. *Bereavement: Studies of Grief in Adult Life.* New York: International Universities Press.

Pine, V.R. 1972. "Social Organization and Death." *Omega* 3:2, 149–53.

Rando, T.A. 1984. *Grief, Dying, and Death: Clinical Interventions for Caregivers.* Champaign, Ill.: Research Press.

3
Intrapsychic Dimensions of Disenfranchised Grief

Jeffrey Kauffman

Self-disenfranchising Grief

Disenfranchisement is a sociological concept and may be most obvious to us in its sociological dimension, but there is also an intrapsychic dimension of disenfranchisement. Wherever social disenfranchisement is operative, there are corresponding phenomena taking place on the intrapsychic level. Furthermore, an individual may disenfranchise himself or collaborate in his own disenfranchisement—that is, the *source* of the disenfranchisement may not necessarily be societal but may arise from within the self. The psychological and sociological sources of disenfranchised grief may sometimes tend to blur together or may be undifferentiated. These two dimensions also influence each other. The distinction between psychological and sociological disenfranchisement is in some ways fraught with problems. Nevertheless, I hope to show that the distinction is meaningful and useful, and that *the concept of self-disenfranchisement brings to light important aspects of disenfranchised grief.*

In self-disenfranchised grief, incipient grief is not recognized or is covered over, much the same as in socially disenfranchised grief, except that the source is oneself. While in societal disenfranchised grief the source of the disenfranchisement is the failure of others to acknowledge and recognize the grief, in self-disenfranchised grief the source is one's *own* lack of acknowledgment and recognition of it. The specific psychological phenomenon operating in disenfranchised grief is shame. For example, an individual may be embarrassed over his grief at the death of a pet. He will then be inclined to inhibit the expression of this grief and be denied his due grief process, regardless of whether his family, friends, or colleagues think this ridiculous and devalue him for it or not. In other words, he can just as well impose sanctions against himself, regardless of what his immediate social environment may think. In self-disenfranchisement the source of the shame and inhibition of the grief process is not in the actual views of others, but in the imagined views of others or the intrapsychic dynamics of the individual. The intrapsychic grief–inhibiting phenomenon is shame; in *self-disenfranchised grief one is disenfranchised by one's own shame.*

Shame is sometimes called the social emotion, in part because our awareness of ourselves in the company of another is regulated by shame. Social support, which is available when grief is sanctioned, provides not only an environment that helps to hold one up but also recognition and legitimization in the eyes of one's community which is crucial to facilitating the mourning process. When an emotion is not acceptable to the norms of a society, as in disenfranchised grief, the intrapsychic function that inhibits the experience and expression of emotion is shame.

Etymologically, shame means both exposure *and* cover. Today, we have nearly lost touch with the sense of shame as cover. This is the protective sense of shame, as in discretion and modesty (Schneider, 1977). We have virtually lost touch with the idea of shame as the cover that safeguards and nurtures the experience of our humanness, realized in the "meeting place" between self and other. It also safeguards and nurtures our relationship to the sacred. The very differentiation of the sacred and the profane exists by virtue of shame, for without it, the profane would destroy the sacred and then destroy itself. The protective function of shame operates in the sanctioning of grief to secure a human and sacred space for the experience and expression of grief.

Nietzsche wrote that "shame exists everywhere where there is mystery" and that "the feeling of shame seems therefore to occur where man is merely a tool of manifestations of will infinitely greater than he is permitted to consider" (Nietzsche 1911).

Grief that is shame covered may have far-reaching consequences for our relation to other persons, ourselves, and our humanness, and for the realization of the sacred within us and our community. Bertha Simos has written that "shame sets off an unconscious fear of abandonment" (Simos 1979). In this function as a trigger for unconscious fears of abandonment we may consider the possibility that feelings of abandonment in bereavement may be intensified by shame.

Intrapsychic Disenfranchisement

In approaching the diverse kinds of situations in which self-disenfranchised grief exists, it may be helpful to create some categories. First, we should distinguish between those situations in which there really are social sanctions against the grief of an individual and those in which there really are not social sanctions disenfranchising the grief of an individual. Instances where social disenfranchisement is in force always involve, on an intrapsychic level, the operation of the shame-related forces described here. It is the second type, in which social disenfranchisement of grief is really not operating as a shame-inducing force to inhibit the experience of grief that we will now categorize and examine.

Shame over One's Own Emotions

The first type of situation in which grief may be disenfranchised by one's own shame is where one is *ashamed of one's own emotions*. The most common example of this intrapsychic dimension of disenfranchised grief is for one to feel shame in the face of normal guilt. The guilt thus being inhibited leads to complications in the mourning process. Guilt that is unsanctioned and shame covered in the mourning process will have consequences commonly associated with guilt complications in grief—recurrence of the unresolved guilt conflicts in other relationships, self-destructive behaviors, and anger—plus complications caused by the need to enforce the shame inhibitions. An even more common occurrence, though less recognized, is for shame to conceal one's sense of utter helplessness in the face of the death of another. Helplessness and powerlessness are closely linked to feeling ashamed, inferior, and inadequate. When the grief-stricken sense of helplessness is severely inhibited, disorders in one's sense of self may occur, such as losing touch with one's feelings, a sense of self-alienation, a weakened sense of self, or a damaged sense of ego-mastery. Panic attacks also may occur.

There are many grief-related intrapsychic states of which one may feel ashamed. As well as particular states—such as guilt, helplessness, feeling out of control, rage, loneliness, and so on—one may feel ashamed of the *very exposure of the self* in grief. Highly tender, vulnerable, valuable, private parts of oneself are normally hidden even from one's own awareness. The self is secured against exposure of the deepest layers of its existence by protective shame, or else, if this integrity of the self is in danger of being violated, one's relationship to one's own being will be threatened. It is not only in the experience of being exposed to the eyes of others that this fundamental disenfranchisement may occur. One may also be in the position *simply in relation to oneself* of being either violated or nurtured by the opening of deeper layers of the self which tends to occur in grieving.

One may feel shame about the hallucinatory processes generated in grief. Hallucinatory experiences in grief are not only not abnormal, but they may also be a vital and profound part of the mourning and healing process. Extremely significant intrapsychic communications are taking place in the hallucinations and the dreams about the deceased which are experienced by the bereaved. Our society tends to disenfranchise and delegitimize this extraordinary intrapsychic process. Even in the privacy of one's own experience, one may be fearful and ashamed of the powerful hallucinatory presences and adumbrations that emerge in consciousness. When the hallucinatory dimension of grief is disenfranchised, needed realizations of the death and of the meaning of the death, and resolutions of the relationship to the deceased may be blocked. An opening to a sense of spiritual reality that may be fostered in the power and personal significance of hallucinatory grief processes will be sealed off if one devalues or hides from this profound intrapsychic grief language.

The Memory of Past Unsanctioned Grief

Another source of self-disenfranchised grief is the persistence of a previous experience of unsanctioned grief. In this instance, the effects of the earlier sanctions and the consequent unprocessed grief have become part of one's present grief reaction; the experience of the new grief is disenfranchised by intrapsychic forces brought into being by an earlier disenfranchisement, despite the absence of any significant social disenfranchisement in the present situation. Disenfranchised childhood grief is a very powerful and widely shared example of this. Someone whose grief over the death of a parent or a sibling was unsanctioned is at risk, in subsequent losses, for self-disenfranchised grief. Although this is only one of a number of possible outcomes, the sense that we may not, cannot, and need not grieve may persist. Unsanctioned or disenfranchised grief does not evaporate over time—it is there. And when a new loss occurs, the old disenfranchisement will affect the new situation, and may enforce a repetition of the earlier inhibited grief pattern. The new bereavement may also provide an opportunity for a grief that was disenfranchised many years earlier to emerge and be acknowledged.

Shame-Prone Personality Traits

Another frequently encountered type of self-disenfranchised grief is noted in shame-prone personality traits. Shame-proneness is a far more common factor inhibiting the experience and expression of grief than is recognized. The very failure to recognize shame-proneness as a common aspect of grief (a socially determined refusal to recognize shame) is very curious, for it seems to be indicative of that very shame-proneness.

The shame-prone personality is likely to feel overwhelmed in grief by feelings of self-consciousness, failure, inadequacy, inferiority, abandonment, and exposure. He is even likely to feel ashamed of his shame, and sometimes to disenfranchise himself profoundly. While this shame and its related feelings are likely to be pervasive in the shame-prone personality (except for feelings of self-consciousness, which usually do not occur in persons who are not shame-prone), nearly all persons, in the face of their deepest and most private grief feelings, are subject to some degree of disenfranchisement. Our society generally does not sanction or value deep grief and so disenfranchises people from the deeper emotional and spiritual healing and growth that are possible.

Shame-prone personalities are likely to present shame-determined, complicated grief, in which the mourning process is severely inhibited. For these individuals, social disenfranchisement of grief will squelch the experience of grief more completely than it will for those who have a strong source of identity, a well-developed sense of autonomy, and a healthy sense of self-esteem. However, it takes a special and rare courage to acknowledge and adequately mourn when the grief is not socially recognized. Persons with shame-prone traits, by experiencing a recognition and sanctioning of their grief, will grow especially in their identity, autonomy, and sense of self-esteem.

Intrapsychic Dimensions of the Loss of Community

One of the profoundly disturbing consequences of disenfranchised grief is that because of a lack of social sanctioning and social support, the bereaved may become disillusioned with and alienated from their community. Community is the natural support network in which one's basic sense of *identity* and *belongingness* are realized. The space of family, friends, church, neighbors, and colleagues in which we live is the arena in which we experience the human reality of our existence. When bereavement needs are disenfranchised by one's community, those parts of oneself where the unrealized, unrecognized, unsatisfied, disenfranchised pain exists are negated. This pain in an especially meaningful way defines who one really is, and so the value of one's bond to the community can be damaged. Our basic sense of belonging, the shelter of being in a community, our realization of ourselves as community-dwellers, the touchstone of our being as a social animal—this sense is disenfranchised. The loss of community that may occur as a consequence of disenfranchised grief fosters an abiding sense of loneliness and abandonment. Communities that sanction and support the grief of their members, that have norms that are flexibly responsive to the needs of their members by recognizing and sanctioning the suffering that exists within the community—these are sane and healing communities.

References

Nietzsche, F. 1911. "Early Greek and Other Essays." In *The Complete Work of Nietzsche,* edited by O. Levy, translated by M. Mugge. London: George Allen and Unwin.

Schneider, C.P. 1977. *Shame, Exposure and Privacy.* Boston: Beacon Press.

Simos, B.G. 1979. *A Time to Grieve: Loss as a Universal Human Experience.* New York: Family Service Association.

Part II
Disenfranchised Relationships

I n one sense it is fitting that a discussion of disenfranchised relationships
should begin with AIDS. For although the phenomenon of disenfranchised grief has a long history, AIDS is the Great Disenfranchiser. AIDS
has left in its wake hundreds of thousands of bereaved persons who are bereft
of any recognizable role or opportunity to acknowledge and share their grief
publicly. Certainly, as Fuller, Geis, and Rush review, there are the bereaved
lovers of homosexual victims of the disease. But this discussion may also, by
inference, have application to the heterosexual lovers of IV-drug users, many
of whom may have had long-lasting liaisons.

But these lovers are not the only ones disenfranchised. Lois Dick
acknowledges that medical staff, particularly nurses, are often drawn into
the AIDS patient's battle for life. That AIDS patients may be of the same
age group as the staff, with care often taking place over long, intermittent
periods, perhaps in a crisis atmosphere, contributes to what Fulton (1987) has
called the "Stockholm syndrome." Taken from the psychology of hostages,
this concept reminds us that in times of great emotional upheaval strong
bonding can take place very quickly. Thus, medical staff may often experience
real grief over the loss of a patient, a grief that may not be recognized or
acknowledged by others or even by themselves.

Another significant type of caregiver, foster parents of pediatric AIDS
children, may also feel both bereft and bereaved. Anderson, Gurdin, and
Thomas, pioneers in the foster placement of "boarder babies" (children with
AIDS who do not have viable homes), argue that foster parents are by the very
nature of their role disenfranchised. For although foster parents are encouraged to develop warm and supportive relationships with their foster children,
they have very limited legal rights over these children and ambivalent social
support and recognition.

But AIDS is doubly disenfranchising. Beyond even the many bereaved
who are disenfranchised through an unrecognized role, AIDS is a disenfranchising death. Certain deaths are in themselves disenfranchising when they
carry associations and perceptions that inhibit survivors from acknowledging

grief and seeking support. Many cases of suicide and some of homicide are examples of disenfranchising deaths. Here the conditions of the loss may make survivors reluctant to share the loss and fearful of public opprobrium. For example, in the case of suicide there may be a public perception that survivors share responsibility for the act. And in certain types of homicide, the victim (and, by inference, those around him or her) may be blamed for his or her fate.

AIDS is also a dreaded disease, deeply feared by a panicked public. The fear is understandable even if the panic is unwarranted. Two types of diseases have historically been dreaded: those great pandemics, such a bubonic plague or typhus, which have devastated communities; and the "shameful stigmas" such as cancer, leprosy, and syphilis, which were feared because of the insidious and painful process of individual death.

AIDS is the archetype of the "dread disease," for it contains all the worst elements of earlier dreaded diseases. It is infectious, chronic, fatal, painful, disfiguring, and morally stigmatizing. Since AIDS is such a dreaded disease, even those survivors with recognizable roles, such as parents, may feel (and have the experience) that public acknowledgment of their loss can lead only to communal disapproval and social withdrawal. Hence, many parents may choose to keep their loss hidden.

One thing AIDS has done is to make us very aware that most members of society have significant relationships with others outside the kin system. The person with AIDS affirms a "chosen family" as important as the biological family, which is leading to a general social recognition of the special roles that others beyond the family have in one's life. As the authors in this part of the book note, sometimes sexual relationships, such as those of cohabiting partners or lovers in extramarital affairs, may be involved. Continuing relationships with ex-spouses are discussed. The strong bonding of friends is celebrated in our literature and media but is rarely acknowledged in times of loss. And one may spend twenty-five years working side by side with a colleague for forty hours a week and yet be expected to work the same way in that colleague's absence. In all of these cases, there are human relationships that are strong even if only partially acknowledged or perhaps unacknowledged. With the loss of these relationships, there is grief—but it is often disenfranchised.

Reference

Fulton, R. 1987. "Unanticipated Grief." In *Death: Completion and Discovery,* edited by C. Corr and R. Pacholski. Lakewood, Ohio: ADEC.

4

Lovers and Significant Others

Ruth L. Fuller
Sally B. Geis
Julian Rush

I n our society the word *lover* connotes a relationship that is more intense than *friend* but much more tenuous than *spouse*. A relationship between friends is implicitly asexual and not exclusive. Any one person may have many friends. The spousal relationship is assumed to be sexual and primarily monogamous. The relationship between lovers is seen as explicitly sexual. Monogamy is often assumed but is not a necessary condition for the lover relationship. The mental image of lovers is usually that of a young man and a young woman conveying a sense of enchantment with each other.

The AIDS crisis jolted average Americans by forcing them to face the fact that not all lovers are heterosexual pairs. The initial emergence of this contagious, incurable, and fatal disease in the United States' gay population precipitated a confrontation between two conflicting views of our society. The dominant view is that we are a heterosexual society with a few deviant homosexuals. The conflicting view that AIDS forced us to confront is that we are a society of diverse sexual life-styles: heterosexual, bisexual, and homosexual. (Geis and Fuller 1985, Albert 1986, Shilts 1987).

An awareness of this new view has come through our understanding that during the first years after its appearance in the United States, AIDS was transmitted primarily by homosexual contact (Geis and Fuller 1985, Geis, Fuller, and Rush 1986). This realization has been a painful discovery for heterosexuals and homosexuals. However, for the dominant heterosexual population, this combination of homosexual sex with fatal, contagious disease has created a profound reaction of fear, disgust, and outrage targeted at the gay and lesbian population (Albert 1986, Shilts 1987). It is our view that using a conceptual frame of reference about minority experience is helpful in understanding our society's intense negative response to persons with AIDS and their loved ones (Fuller, Geis, and Rush 1988).

Like other minorities, gays and lesbians were largely ignored by the dominant society as long as they remained invisible—that is, the closeted, gay artist who can be likened to the helpful black handyman. The dominant society was offended by an increasingly visible gay and lesbian subculture that was perceived as blatantly sexual. Society's disgust toward persons with AIDS and their lovers was exacerbated by the perception that the sexuality of this group was also blatantly promiscuous. A small subculture of highly visible, extremely promiscuous gays became equated with the entire homosexual population. Society was outraged by their "bathhouse" culture and political activism in cities like San Francisco and New York (Albert 1986, Kotarba and Lang 1986). The appearance of AIDS as a diagnosable illness afflicting this population allowed much of society to define the illness as a plague created by the will of God to punish sinners: "They got what they deserved" (Lattin 1986). Members of the dominant society could feel justified in ignoring the disease and ostracizing the dying patients and their loved ones, particularly their "new families" within the gay community (Tavares and Lopez 1984, Geis and Fuller 1985).

This cultural phenomenon of the mid-1980s led to our initial observations concerning the disenfranchised grief of those persons close to gay AIDS patients. Commonly it is the lovers and friends of those in the gay community who care for and mourn the death of a gay AIDS patient (Barbuto 1984, *Service* 1987). Sometimes significant others include wives, former wives, children, siblings, parents, and other friends. However, let us focus first on the lovers who have formed the relationship of a couple.

Loss and Grief Prior to Death

The diagnosis of AIDS has a profound impact on the person who is ill and on the loved one (Barley 1988). Although no one can predict either the exact course of the illness or the precise time of death, the couple knows that AIDS is the most severe manifestation of HIV infection and that there is no definitive cure for the disease (Forstein 1988, Koop 1988, "Update AIDS" 1988). As the patient's illness progresses, the lovers describe some of the feelings they experience. One such feeling is that of isolation (Langone 1987). A poignant description of loss of support was given by one young man: "One of the hardest things to see is how empty and quiet the house has become. A faithful few are here, but the dozens of people that we had called close friends just disappeared. They don't even call. Maybe they think that you can get AIDS through the phone." The isolation from a community family was doubly devastating because each of these young men was estranged from his biological family. The lover went on to explain, "I left home as a kid and I rarely even talk to my family. I had found a new family, but now I'm losing that one too." Limited or no contact with one's biological family is not unusual.

The central support for many gay AIDS patients comes from segments of the gay community organized to fill the need (Barbuto 1984, Tavares and

Lopez 1984). Organizations such as the Colorado AIDS Project provide volunteers for direct care, research, education, and political activity ("Update" 1988). Concerted efforts such as this project bring to the couple and their significant others affirmation of their humanity.

However, the patient's relationship with the biological family in general and parents in particular needs to be addressed. The lack of contact between the patient and his family is usually painful for the patient. In preparing for death, the patient and the family may attempt a reconciliation. Before a successful reconciliation can occur, the family must work through their feelings about their son's (or brother's, and so forth) sexual relationship with another man (Tiblier 1986). Parental aspirations for sons usually do not include hopes for a homosexual relationship. Although familial support of gay or lesbian lovers is growing, it is not a societal norm. The lover and the biological family may be "in opposite camps," and the lover may become the target of the biological family's wrath. He may be denounced as the cause of the patient's "waywardness." In order to effect a familial reconciliation, the patient may denounce himself as "evil" and, either by implication or directly, the lover too. Without support, few lovers can cope with the profound feelings of betrayal, pain, grief, and hopelessness that such a denunciation evokes. Here is a description of one such reconciliation:

> Phillip had an impossible choice to make. But—I was there for him, day and night, month after month. Then his parents came and cried and told him how much they loved him and wanted to take him home, if he would repudiate evil and evil-doing (being gay). Finally he said that he repented his sins and would turn his back on evil. They swooped him up and he was gone, without a word.

We do not know how often reconciliation combined with rejection occurs, but it is not rare. The conflicting views of society are presented and one possible resolution is reached. The patient joins with the dominant culture in denouncing homosexuality as a sinful deviation from the cultural norm. This method of reestablishing the biological family unit leaves the now former lover to process grief that arises from several sources: rejection by and isolation from the loved one, ambivalence about the outcome of the relationship, and assault upon his sense of worth. The feelings are passionate, and it is with concern that support groups continue work with former lovers.

Grief Following Death of the Loved One

The grieving process may have begun prior to the loved one's death (Carr 1985, Fuller and Geis 1985). The acute grief following the actual death is described as being even more intense. One survivor described his feelings in this way:

> I wander around the apartment and there are so many things that remind me of him. I don't know if I can stay there even though this has been my home for years. I must admit that I am drawn to the medicine cabinet. I have not cleaned out all of Carl's medicine. I keep thinking that it would be so easy to just take everything that is left, and not wake up.

Among others, Forstein (1988) reminds us of the suicidal risk in persons who have recently lost someone to AIDS. Lovers consider their own risk and mortality. They may be among the "worried well"—that is, those who do not have AIDS but are anxious (Forstein 1984, Tavares and Lopez 1984). Numerous authors, including Buckley (1988), point out that not everyone exposed to HIV becomes infected and not everyone infected develops AIDS. The potential source of infection is not the day-to-day care given to a seriously ill or dying loved one, but in risky sexual activity, sharing IV needles, blood transfusion, or similar transmission (Lyles 1987, Forstein 1988, Koop 1988).

The sources of support for the grieving lover continue to be those resources that have been in place prior to death. As noted earlier, helpful persons still come from primarily the gay community (Tavares and Lopez 1984, Geis, Fuller, and Rush 1986). The dominant society is more likely to extend to the lover its permission to grieve the loss of the beloved, if the relationship has (a) demonstrated devotion but not blatant sexuality; (b) fulfilled the expectations of the biological families; (c) received familial support as exemplified by an engagement; and (d) ended with an illness or accident viewed as an unfortunate occurrence (Fuller and Geis 1985).

The relationship between gay lovers does not meet these criteria of society and therefore would not be sanctioned for grieving and mourning. Albert (1986) discusses the "three judgmental options" associated with homosexuality, namely, "alternative lifestyle, illness or deviance." The view of homosexuality as deviant makes it unlikely that the biological family of the dead lover will embrace the survivor in a common sharing of grief and mourning.

The grief work begun by the couple prior to death becomes even more poignant because the preparation for separation resembles that of a married couple. The two discuss funeral plans, disposition of shared possessions, even the future life of the partner who will be left alive. However, the status of lover has some striking differences from that of spouse. The lover has no legal right to make decisions about such matters as funeral or burial arrangements. The lover cannot prove his legal rights to property unless there is a carefully drawn will. Frequently, biological family members appear during the last few weeks of the patient's life. While he is alive, they may not be able to force the patient to reject his lover and life-style, but immediately following the death, they often take over and assert their legal prerogative to make decisions.

For the lover who has been struggling, often alone and usually for many months or even years, this disenfranchisement is devastating:

> Greg and I talked over everything. In those last months he'd really gotten into Zen meditation. We planned a simple service with some poetry and chants and everything. We were going to put his ashes under the willow tree in our back yard.
>
> But that last week his parents swooped in and took over. Greg tried to stop them, but he was too weak. I tried to stop them, but I didn't count. They called some preacher from the church they belong to back home. And suddenly he and Greg's mother were in charge. They decided everything, the words and music. Everything. They had the service in a funeral home. Of course they didn't want me to sit with the family. They really didn't even want me to come. Greg would have hated the whole thing, that was the hardest part.
>
> One thing his mother didn't get her way about, though. She wanted to take his body back to their hometown. But the funeral home people were too scared, they wouldn't do it for her. So at least he was cremated the way he wanted to be. They took the ashes.
>
> Then they got a court order and took everything they thought was Greg's out of the house, all the furniture and art and stuff that we had collected. They acted as if they deserved it for all the pain Greg and I had caused them. It wasn't the money so much, though some of the artwork was fairly valuable. It was the idea. They left me with nothing to remember him by. It was as if they wanted it that way.

We have speculated that several factors come together, leading the couple to a state of legal unpreparedness. First, human beings find it difficult to confront their own mortality, especially when young, so wills are not common. Second, gay couples are not allowed to make their relationship legal through marriage contracts; they have become accustomed to the nonlegal status of their relationship. Third, prior to the patient's death, neither partner anticipates the possibility that the patient's biological family might change their behavior.

Young gay couples may not consider the power of intense feelings, such as regret, fear, guilt, or greed, which are operating in family members and motivating precipitous actions. The family that has ostracized the gay person for years is not expected to change.

Another interviewee described the aftermath of his lover's death:

> John died with our dearest friends nearby. He wanted his family to see that we were really a couple, even before he got sick. They never did.

> What happened after he died was unbelievable. His parents appeared and came rampaging through our house and just packed up everything except my clothes. They came in like vultures and took everything, saying that it had been John's and was now theirs. They were his heirs. They looked at me as if I were dirt. I talked with an attorney. I don't have any rights. Spouses have rights. Children have rights. But legally, I don't exist.

Attempts to help avoid this new devastation can be seen in the very practical help of having the gay couple look at the state of their legal affairs prior to *he patient's death. One counselor shared what he had experienced while working with a couple in his support group:

> Mike knew that Sam was concerned about the very comfortable home they had made together and the successful business that they had developed but all in Sam's name. It was hard for me to bring it up but we (the group) had talked about how unprepared some survivors have been when they find out that they have no legal rights. I asked Mike and Sam about the arrangements for Mike. It turned out that nothing was in place. Over several weeks, they worked with an attorney who got titles changed and a will made so that Mike could continue as Sam wished him to do. It did work out well.

This couple benefited from the painful experiences of other grieving survivors.

The Current Social Climate

Our society continues to struggle in the process of addressing its fear of, anger with, and rejection of persons with AIDS and their loved ones (Des Jarlais, Friedman, and Sturg 1986, Matthews et al. 1986). In the struggle, some social institutions appear to be moving toward position that a society is responsible for its members. For example, the surgeon general's office sent its brochure an AIDS to every American household (Koop 1988). The Rev. Kenneth Barley (1988) is one of a growing number of clergy acting on an ethical commitment to this group. The press reflects the shifting in our society's stance, appearing to focus to some extent on the place for reasonable, humane treatment of these families (Friedman and Shaw 1988).

Biemiller (1988) reports on a conference, during which Anthony Quinton, a philosopher, succinctly described what has been presented to us by the appearance of a new plague: "There is surely no doubt that if AIDS were caused by some absolutely morally neutral activity, like eating cod's roe or drinking goat's milk, most people would feel differently about it." Other studies (Geis, Fuller, and Rush 1986, Tiblier 1986) describe the disorganizing effect of AIDS as an unfamiliar, contagious, life-threatening illness associated with homophobia. This combination of factors has contributed to the ease with which the AIDS patient and loved ones have been moved into a feared and hated minority group (Fuller, Geis, and Rush 1988). The task of addressing and resolving our fears is ongoing (Wendler 1987), for we fear a new plague for which medicine has no cure (Biemiller 1988). Another fear stems from society's relatively recent confrontation with diverse sexuality as a norm.

Approaches for Psychosocial Interventions

The ability to provide adequate psychosocial support of persons with AIDS and their loved ones can be enhanced by two combined approaches: one conceptual design for dealing with groups, and one set of practical guidelines for working with individuals. The conceptual approach that we offer can be used by any outsider approaching any minority group. It assumes that the outsider's intent is to learn more about the group and to be helpful to the group. The ten-step approach is as follows:

1. Complete some "homework" before meeting by reading about the group and having conversations with knowledgeable resource persons concerning the language and vocabulary of the group, issues, values, and protocol requirements.

2. Engage a liaison person who will facilitate an introduction to the group or representatives of the group. The liaison must be a person known to and accepted by the group as a proven friend.

3. Meet at a time and place that is convenient for the group (the group's territory).

4. Maintain the stance of a guest while clearly presenting your background and purpose for being present.

5. Listen carefully and respond thoughtfully but spontaneously.

6. Prepare to be seen as a representative of the enemy camp and therefore a target of rage. It may be necessary to apologize for the inhumanity of the system you represent while giving the group an experience that supports your claim that individual members of that system can be "okay."

7. Summarize what you have learned from the group, then what you hope the group has learned from you.

8. Commit yourself to that which is guaranteed—that is, to return one or more times or mail a reference, and so forth.

9. Extend a realistic invitation for the group to visit you at your home base in a context that is meaningful to group members—that is, address a small group of students in an informal seminar, for example.

10. Prepare to receive individual calls for assistance in furthering the purposes of the group—for example, the name of the key person to contact in your setting for distribution of the group's written material. If you are the key person, say so and complete the task (Fuller, Geis, and Rush 1988).

The practical approach to offering support to persons with AIDS is one that Langone (1988) attributes to the New York–based Chelsey Psychotherapy Associates. We think this approach offers psychosocial intervention for the loved ones also. We have summarized the essential elements:

1. Be physically present and involved
2. Remember physical touch
3. Share crying or laughter
4. Ask about the illness and be prepared to listen
5. Be honest (but not tactless)
6. Support decision making
7. Keep any promises you make
8. Be prepared for anger
9. Control your own expectations about what the person or loved ones "should" be doing
10. Do some concrete helpful things *after* asking for permission
11. Draw upon religious commitments with the loved ones, if you are so oriented
12. Write
13. Support hope for the future.

This approach to changing anxious, cerebral concern into alive and tangible care of suffering fellow human beings has been extremely helpful to couples and other loved ones.

In 1985 we asked whether our society should be judged by how it treats the members declared to be unwanted (Geis and Fuller, 1985). Now we add this question: Isn't it clear that those considered unwanted might include any one of us? In any given era, we might be the wrong age, sex, skin color, or religion, but we may also be in the wrong state of physical, emotional, or financial health. As individuals who might find ourselves among the unwanted, how do we wish our society to respond?

References

Albert, E. 1986. "Illness and Deviance: The Response of the Press to AIDS." In *The Social Dimensions of AIDS: Methods and Therapy*, edited by D.A. Feldman and T.M. Johnson. New York: Praeger.

Barbuto, J. 1984. "Psychiatric Care of Seriously Ill Patients with Acquired Immune Deficiency Syndrome." In *Psychiatric Implication of Acquired Immune Deficiency Syndrome*, edited by S.E. Nichols and D.G. Ostrow. Washington, D.C.: American Psychiatric Press.

Barley, K. 1988. "AIDS: A Gospel Response." Sermon, Jan. 31, Montview Boulevard Presbyterian Church, Denver, Colo.

Biemiller, L. 1988. "Plagues: How People Responded to Them in the Past Is Studied by Scholars as a Guide in AIDS Crisis." *The Chronicle of Higher Education*, Jan. 27, pp. A6–A8.

Buckley, R.M. 1988. "AIDS in Office Practice: Workup for Patients Who May Have HIV Infection." *Medical Aspects of Human Sexuality* 22, 104–12.

Carr, A.C. 1985. "Grief, Mourning and Bereavement." In *Comprehensive Textbook of Psychiatry/IV*, edited by H.I. Kaplan and B.J. Sadock. Baltimore: Williams and Wilkins.

Des Jarlais, D.C., S.R. Friedman, and D. Sturg. 1986. "AIDS and Needle Sharing within the IV-Drug Use Subculture." In *The Social Dimensions of AIDS: Methods and Therapy*, edited by D.A. Feldman and T.M. Johnson, New York: Praeger.

Forstein, M. 1984. "AIDS anxiety in the 'worried well.'" In *Psychiatric Aspects of Acquired Immune Deficiency Syndrome*, edited by S.E. Nichols and D.G. Ostrow. Washington, D.C.: American Psychiatric Press.

———. 1988. "Suicidal Concerns of Patients Who Test HIV-Positive." *Medical Aspects of Human Sexuality* 22, 112A.

Friedman, J., and B. Shaw. 1988. "The Quiet Victories of Ryan White." *People*, May 30, pp. 88–96.

Fuller, R.L., and S.B. Geis. 1985. "Communicating with the Grieving Family." *Journal of Family Practice* 21, 139–44.

Fuller, R.L., S.B. Geis, and J. Rush. 1988. "Lovers of AIDS Victims: A Minority Group Experience." *Death Studies* 12, 1–7.

Geis, S., and R.L. Fuller. 1985. "The Impact of the First Gay AIDS Patient on Hospice Staff." *The Hospice Journal* 1, 17–36.

Geis, S.B., R.L. Fuller, and J. Rush. 1986. "Lovers of AIDS Victims: Psychosocial Stresses and Counseling Needs." *Death Studies* 10, 43–53.

Koop, C.E. 1988. *Understanding AIDS*. HHS Publication No. (CED) HHS–88–8404, pp. 1–8.

Kotarba, J.A., and N.G. Lang. 1986. "Gay Lifestyle Change and AIDS: Preventive Health Care." In *The Social Dimensions of AIDS: Methods and Therapy*, edited by D.A. Feldman and T.M. Johnson. New York: Praeger.

Langone, J. 1988. *AIDS: The Facts*. Boston: Little, Brown.

Lattin, D. 1986. "AIDS: A Sign of God's Wrath, Baptist Leader Claims." *Rocky Mountain News,* Jan. 18, p. 119.

Lyles, J.C. 1987. "AIDS Workers Criticize Statement." *Methodist Reporter,* June, p. 1.

Matthews, W.C., M.W. Booth, J.D. Turner, and L. Kessler. 1986. "Physicians' Attitudes toward Homosexuality. Survey of a California County Medical Society." *Western Journal of Medicine* 144, 106–10.

Service of Celebration to Honor the Dead and Support the Living. 1987. Denver, Colo.: Iliff School of Theology.

Shilts, R. 1987. *And the Band Played On: Politics, People, and the AIDS Epidemic.* New York: St. Martin's Press.

Tavares, R., and D.J. Lopez. 1984. "Response of the Gay Community to Acquired Immune Deficiency Syndrome. In *Psychiatric Implications of Acquired Immune Deficiency Syndrome,* edited by S.E. Nichols and D.G. Ostrow. Washington, D.C.: American Psychiatric Press.

Tiblier, K. 1986. "Intervention with the Family of the Patient with Acquired Immunodeficiency Syndrome: A Clinical Sociological Perspective (Research Brief)." *Social Oncology Network* 2, 1.

"Update." 1988. "Colorado AIDS Project News, Spring, pp. 1–8.

"Update on AIDS." 1988. *Medical Aspects of Human Sexuality* 22, 101–2.

Wendler, K. 1987. "Ministry to Patients with Acquired Immunodeficiency Syndrome: A Spiritual Challenge." *Journal of Pastoral Care* 41, 4–16.

5
Dual Disenfranchisement: Foster Parenting Children with AIDS

Gary R. Anderson
Phyllis Gurdin
Ann Thomas

T he middle-aged black woman quietly cracked the door and entered the sleeping child's room. Before moving to the young child's bedside, she tiptoed to the window and lowered the shade to stop the mid-morning sun from flooding the room with light and awakening the child from his hard-won sleep. The boy was moving from side to side and breathing with some difficulty, although his eyes remained closed. The woman slid to a plastic chair near the bed and held the child's hand, softly singing a song whose words were inaudible to the medical personnel who preferred to remain outside the hospital room door. Hovering near the child, she kept singing and soothing him all day.

This woman was not the young boy's mother or aunt or grandmother. He was not her biological child. And she was not a nurse or hospital volunteer who would count this child as a temporary patient, or client, or assignment. She had been his foster mother since shortly after his birth, and beginning at age two he had lived with her for more than half of his life. She did not know that he was HIV positive—that he evidenced the virus that causes AIDS in children and adults. She had been surprised by his frequent symptoms: stubborn infections, fevers, diarrhea, and an increasing shortness of breath. Her pediatrician sent her to a specialist who, after testing, diagnosed the child as having AIDS. Any professional misgivings that this foster mother would abandon the boy to the hospital or call her caseworker demanding his removal were quickly set aside as the foster mother firmly stated her affection for the child and her commitment to see him through this illness. And if he was going to die, a possibility that was dawning on her, she was determined to give him the best possible life in the days or weeks or months that remained.

This woman is one of a growing number of diverse adults becoming substitute parents for children in need of a home. Foster parents are single adults, single parents, or married adults who have volunteered or been recruited by child welfare agencies. They provide a temporary home for a child or children who need a caregiver other than their parents for a variety of reasons: (1) the parent is unable to care for the child because of such circumstances as illness or hospitalization, and no relative or family friend is available or able to care for the child; (2) the parent has physically abused the child, necessitating a change of environment for protection; (3) the parent has neglected the child, thus endangering his or her health and well-being; or (4) the parent has abandoned the child. Foster parents provide the physical and emotional home environment for a child who has experienced a separation from his or her parents and often additional trauma as well:

> Three children were being transported to a foster home by a social worker because their stepfather had sexually abused them and their mother stated she could not care for them or protect them. No friend or relative was willing or able to care for the children while their mother sought help. The children were confused by their stepfather's actions, baffled by his disappearance, and upset at being separated from their mother. They huddled together in the car and literally clung to the social worker. Upon arrival at the foster parents' home, the children dutifully entered. The foster mother appeared warm and friendly. She carefully approached the youngest child, a four-year-old girl, and asked her if she understood the word "foster parent." The girl shook her head "no." The woman explained, "'Foster' means 'friend'; I will be your friendly parent until you can return home to your mother." This explanation satisfied the children.

However, this position of substitute parenting is an ambiguous one at best. With paradoxical expectations that are often less than satisfying to foster parents, the emotional challenge and commitment seems to require heroic translation and implementation by foster parents. Sometimes the foster parent chooses and is able to adopt the foster child. Generally, foster parents are told that their place in the child's life is temporary, that they must be prepared for separation from the child, who will be moved in accord with a plan for permanency, often a reunion with rehabilitated parents or to an adoptive home. Yet it is evident that the children require the emotional involvement and commitment of the foster parent—in simple terms, the love of a parent. Foster parents must juggle this commitment with the knowledge that this relationship will not last and may end suddenly. Foster parents are not completely replacing the parents, but they often develop the care, concern, and hopes for their foster child as parents do for their children. At times this foster parent loyalty to the child may be very strong as the foster parent witnesses the effects of past traumatic situations for the child.

Nevertheless, the foster parent–foster child relationship is viewed and defined as something less than completely legitimate by social agencies. Foster parents are given a meager governmental stipend to cover the financial needs of the child—to pay for food and clothes, and for personal items. This stipend is inadequate for addressing most children's needs and is often supplemented by foster parents' personal funds, and because of the foster parents' quasi-employee status with the child welfare agency, a role and a relationship are created that looks different from a parent-child relationship. In fact, the agency remains ultimately responsible for the child's well-being, and foster parents' decisions are reviewed, amended, or approved by monitoring case-workers. Consequently, this strange status of parenting but not being recognized as a parent may minimize or ignore a foster parent's emotional ties to the foster child. It also potentially deprives foster parents of certain rights and privileges that because of their long-term commitment to a child they may deserve.

This lack of legitimization extends into society as a whole. Foster parenting may be conceptualized as "baby-sitting" or as a "boarding arrangement," or criticized as "warehousing" of children. Foster parent motives are treated as suspect. Foster parents are often perceived as "getting rich" by taking children into their homes. More ominously, cases of sexual abuse or child abuse in foster care homes may lead to overgeneralizations about exploitive motives among those caring for children. The care of foster parents for children and the grief upon separation or tragedy is underestimated if not undermined by such stereotypes.

So, in the context of an open-ended, "temporary" placement, foster parents are asked to provide a child with security and a context in which to trust an adult relationship. In a confused or underestimated role, foster parents' feelings and attachments may be undiscovered, ignored, or misinterpreted. A caring foster parent is in a vulnerable position.

Foster Parenting and Children with AIDS

These general concerns about the disenfranchising of foster parents are magnified in situations involving children with AIDS. More than a thousand children with AIDS have been reported to the Centers for Disease Control in the United States. Thousands more suffer from AIDS-related illnesses that can be fatal in childhood. The precise number of children who have the HIV infection is unknown, but estimates reach into the tens of thousands. The percentage of infected children who will become ill or will progress to AIDS is high; often it is more a question of when symptoms will appear or worsen than if they will develop. Early cases of children with AIDS were first spotted among hemophiliacs and children who had received blood transfusions. However, for the great majority of children who have been infected, transmission occurred in utero from infected mothers who shared unclean IV-drug needles or had sex with partners who had AIDS. As the number of AIDS cases among women of child-bearing age increases, the number of infected children is expected to continue to multiply.

The diagnosis of AIDS is often made after infected children become ill and are brought to hospitals. A number of these children require substitute home care, since their parents are dead or sick with AIDS or a related illness; cannot care for their children because of their disorganization resulting from drug habits and life-styles; or have abandoned the child upon learning of his or her serious illness. The challenge for the foster parent is formidable: to provide a loving home for a medically at-risk child who, although unlikely to return to the natural parents, will most likely be with the foster parent temporarily, as the illness is life threatening, resulting in death. The challenge is compounded by the foster parent's potential fears and necessary precautions concerning infection. There is also an increased need for agency support since often the illness of the child cannot be disclosed to relatives, friends, or neighbors, whose reaction to the child and foster parent may be negative and harmful.

Description of Foster Parents

In the last several years a number of adults have volunteered to care for a child with AIDS through a specialized AIDS foster care program developed by one of the owners at Leake and Watts Children's Home. More than forty children are cared for in twenty-five foster homes. Foster parents range in age from thirty-two to seventy-two, with the majority over the age of forty. Most have a high school education, although some did not graduate from high school, and others have graduated from college. More than half of the foster parents are married, nearly one-third have been married more than once. A number of divorced, separated, widowed, or never-married adults are caring for children with AIDS. The majority of the foster parents are black and Latino parents. The average number of their own children at home is one. The majority of foster parents do not work outside the home. Most care for either one or two foster children.

Project staff have assumed that these foster parents are similar to foster parents who care for "normal" children. However, there are several distinctive traits: (1) these foster parents were well informed about AIDS before beginning foster parenting an AIDS child, and they were convinced that they were not endangering themselves or their families by caring for an infected child; (2) a number of foster parents had medical training or life-experience in caring for someone who was very ill or dying. These foster parents are not strangers to serious illness or to the social and psychological challenge and stress of caring for an ill person.

The foster parents reported that they have given a great deal of consideration to death but that their outlook on life focused on the present day. They know that a high percentage of children with AIDS die in a relatively brief period of time, and they know there is no cure for the illness. They said they could accept this prognosis. Their motivation is to give the children the highest quality of life as long as possible, believing that all children deserve this opportunity to live their lives to the fullest.

One foster parent described her concern:

> Two years ago I saw a newspaper story about children who had been born with AIDS. It showed pictures of the kids, and my heart went out to them. The only home these kids had ever known was a hospital room, because nobody wanted them . . . I hate to think that any of those kids may have to live without knowing the love of a real family like ours.

Another foster parent noted, "They give us an excuse to be kids again . . . basically they are healthy and playful. We just have to hope they continue to respond to medication. We know the prognosis isn't good, so we feel we have to live for today and make their lives good today."

These foster parents were offered a "normal" foster child rather than a child with AIDS or AIDS-related complex (ARC), but they preferred to care for a child with the disease.

This illustrates the experiences and challenges facing foster parents of children with AIDS:

> Mrs. S. is a single woman who is trained as a licensed practical nurse. She has two biological children, ages twelve and fourteen. She is the sole support of the family. Her husband deserted her when the children were toddlers. Mrs. S. worked as an LPN on the night shift in a large general hospital. Often her assignment was to care for AIDS patients. She decided to leave her job and applied to be a foster parent for two HIV-infected children. She chose to be a foster parent as it provided her with the same income she was earning as an LPN in the hospital. She felt in the hospital she was not able to provide the level of care her patients needed. At home she felt she could make a difference in the lives of two children.
>
> A little girl of fifteen months was placed in the home of Mrs. S. The child has been hospitalized for most of her life. Her mother is an IV-drug user, HIV-infected, who could not care for her. In the hospital the child had numerous illnesses such as thrush, ear infections, and diarrhea.
>
> She has neurological damage and is developmentally delayed. The child exhibits very disturbed behavior in the hospital and on placement in the foster home. She had violent temper tantrums that did not respond to intervention by the caring person. She was sullen, moody, and most of the time she would not interact with another person or child.
>
> After ten months in the home, she is making progress in meeting developmental milestones. She is still developmentally delayed, especially in the area of speech development and fine motor coordination. She is a sullen, difficult child who is often cranky. Her temper tantrums have decreased. She is in the process of a full neurological work-up to determine if her symptoms

are related to the progression of the disease. Six weeks after placement of the first child, a second child was placed. This was a seven-month-old girl who was born prematurely and who lived in the hospital for seven months as no home could be found for her. The child at seven months weighed seven pounds. She could not smile or turn over. It was felt the child's prognosis would be greatly improved if she had one constant maternal figure. At seventeen months, after ten months of living in a foster home, she has more than doubled her weight. She has had infections and illnesses, but none have required hospitalization. She has made remarkable developmental progress. At sixteen months she walks and says simple words. She is a friendly, cheerful, and responsive child.

Mrs. S. is aware of the fact that AIDS is a fatal disease. The fact that the children have done so well in her home has convinced her in spite of the prognosis that they will survive. She focuses on the present for her children and provides them with an excellent quality of life, and feels she can handle their illness and even their deaths.

Besides the medical issues and the developmental challenges, the foster parent faces potential discrimination because of the stigma associated with AIDS. Some foster parents reported they were shunned by neighbors, their children were isolated, and they were isolated in the community. Because of these negative reactions to caring for AIDS children, foster parents are advised to be very careful about telling other people about the nature of the child's condition. This concern for confidentiality is important for the child's protection but also for the foster parent's. The result of this caution is an isolation of the foster parent from natural support networks. If it is potentially dangerous to talk about your concerns and your joys with relatives, friends, and neighbors, who can you share with and from whom will you gain support and legitimization? This isolation is particularly threatening because of the medical risk and the life-threatening nature of AIDS and because of the need of foster parents for support when coping with these serious concerns.

Professionals working with AIDS are trying to bring about social acceptance for foster parents caring for AIDS children by going public at every available opportunity. Courageous foster parents have been on television and on the front page of newspapers such as the *New York Times*. In these forums, foster parents have discussed their confidence in infection control and their freedom from fear of disease transmission, as well as the emotional rewards they obtain from caring for HIV-infected children.

Foster parents receive crucial support from a variety of sources: first, from their own immediate family and understanding relatives and friends; second, from the child welfare agency—specifically, Leake and Watts—through the provision of supportive and educational counseling from social workers and nurses, and also from the range of specialty medical and diagnostic services the agency mobilizes to serve the child and foster parent; third, from other foster parents who are also caring for children with AIDS; and fourth, from a number of medical and social agencies developing in the community to provide respite care and day care for children with AIDS.

The extreme needs of the children, the compassion of the foster parent, and the sense that these children are doubly victimized by illness and social stigma combine to produce a close bond between foster parent and child. As foster parents note the dramatic changes in the children's health and developmental states resulting from their consistent care, they take pride in their achievement and build a strong commitment to the child's well-being. Weathering medical crises also enhances bonding even while surfacing the foster parent's fear for the child's health and life. There is little likelihood that these children will return to their natural parents since many of these parents have died from AIDS, are very ill, or are active IV-drug users. The foster parent recognizes that he or she is the primary person for this child and that without the foster parent the child may not have a home. This awareness and the sense of responsibility and importance further heighten the foster parent–child tie. Since many of these children are infants and have been in hospitals for their early months without bonding to another adult, the child's response to the foster parent also enhances their relationship.

This closeness and commitment, at times almost a sense of "mission" on the part of foster parents works to provide a special setting for children. It also poses the problem of separation through a serious illness that leads to hospitalization and death. There may be some magical thinking by parents that says, "If I care enough and am superattentive, I can prevent my foster child from getting ill." Consequently, the grief of the foster parent may involve a special pain as a sometimes anticipated but usually denied event is not prevented by their conscientious care. Again, to the extent that this grief cannot be shared or expressed to others because of the stigma attached or is misunderstood or not appreciated because of the nature of a foster parent role, the grief is further compounded.

Foster Parenting and Grief

As was noted earlier, inherent in the foster parent role is coping with separation. For foster parents this initially means greeting and caring for a child who has been separated from a natural parent. In some cases of a child with AIDS, the child may not have known this parent for long—the primary caregivers may have been hospital personnel. The removal of a child from the hospital and placement into a home environment may appear to pose minimal separation pain for a child. However, it illustrates for the foster parents their lack of personal control: the child is placed in the home through an agency decision and may be removed from the home by an external decision-making process or circumstances. Again, with AIDS, the child's leaving the home is more often precipitated by illness and hospitalization, which is followed by a return to the natural parents, and then a move to another foster care home. So, the first and primary grief is the sadness related to the separation from and loss of a child whom you have loved, cared for, suffered for and with, and defined as part of your family.

Another aspect of grief is the sadness one experiences upon first witnessing a child who is ill or has been neglected or has endured a long hospitalization because there was no other home. There is a pain that accompanies witnessing these circumstances, even though this pain has motivated the person to become a foster parent and to attempt to improve the child's quality of life.

There is also the grief of not only witnessing but trying to respond effectively to the pain and suffering of a child: The helplessness that initially accompanies rising fevers, continuing diarrhea, or stubborn recurrent infections. The frustration with illness, and with the medical interventions that are uncomfortable and, at times, painful for young children. The sadness when a child cannot comprehend what is happening to him or her and no amount of skill or patience can clearly communicate or verbally comfort. The worry that even when things appear to be going well they will not remain that way for long.

It can be shocking and sad when people whom you have counted on to help or understand have difficulty accepting your decision to care for a child with AIDS. Foster parents who should be receiving praise and recognition are instead receiving rejection and condemnation. It can hurt when the television news reports on a bombed trailor, an excluded child, an isolated family because of AIDS. These events are not impersonal or distant. This type of sadness can turn to anger, indignation, and resolve to care for one's child despite a sometimes ugly, ignorant world.

A rarely identified aspect of the foster parent's grief and a challenge to her or his ability to care for the child is helping the foster child understand his or her terminal condition. This problem is currently somewhat uncommon, perhaps because of either the early age of infant death or the continuing survival of many ill children through ongoing intervention.

Children who are diagnosed with a terminal disease go through emotional stages of dying that must be viewed in relation to their developmental stages. In particular, their disease needs to be discussed in words understandable to the child when the child indicates an interest in knowing. It is important not to give information to the child until he or she is ready to hear it. Assistance with guilt feelings associated with an undue sense of responsibility for their illness (or their parent's illness) is necessary. Children may use anger as a defense to cope with their illness. They may project their angry feelings onto foster parents. Children will need help with understanding hospital stays and treatments, and they need a foster parent to be available as much as possible. Responses to direct questions about death need to be answered as honestly as possible, bearing in mind that time is a difficult concept for children under the age of five to comprehend. An atmosphere that provides for nurturance and caring, open communication in response to the child's request for information, and the emotional availability of the foster parent will assist the child in dying without fear and unnecessary agitation.

However, to be able to assist children requires some degree of understanding and acceptance on the part of the foster parent. Even to say or think "assist the child in dying" is at some level unnatural and difficult. Foster parents treasure a hope that their child will survive the illness, that their foster child will live long enough for a medical cure to be discovered. Nevertheless, with a bleak prognosis and no cure soon available, the foster parent must balance a realism about the child's condition with a positive attitude that communicates hope, peace, and energy to the child. So again the foster parent is asked to act out a paradox: to anticipate death but live hopefully.

The anticipation of serious illness or grief may be difficult, for foster parents practice a high degree of denial. Helping professionals often practice the same defensive blocking of a cruel prognosis from conscious thought and memory. This blocking is supported by Leake and Watts's foster care experience in which no children in care have died yet. This experience has been noted by other programs serving children with AIDS. This denial can be viewed, conversely, as a belief in hope and an act of faith that preserves an optimism and a present-day perspective on caring for a child with AIDS.

Anticipatory grief—picturing and thinking about the separations, illness, or death that are highly probable if not a certainty—may help some foster parents cope with their fears and sadness. Anticipatory grief may evidence a number of stages, including depression, heightened concern for the ill child, rehearsal of the illness or death, and an adjustment to the consequences of the loss. This process may be guided or supported by appropriate helping professionals.

The death of a child is a trauma. It is difficult to deal with a child's death since a child is not offered the experiences an adult has over his or her lifetime, and this strikes one as unjust. Foster parents feel responsible for the child, and the death may create feelings of guilt or inadequacy—"If I had been a better parent, could have given more, he might not have died!" Feelings of helplessness and powerlessness are common, particularly when a terminal illness leaves no hope for recovery.

Assisting foster parents to anticipate and manage a serious illness or death of a child with AIDS is a vital task of the child welfare agency. As was stated earlier, the natural support systems of the foster family may be alienated from the family, unwilling or unable to help, misunderstanding or misinterpreting foster parent grief. So the child welfare staff must provide support, sounding boards, and shoulders for grieving foster parents. This involves a commitment of time and energy beyond that normally invested in working with a foster family, and it requires a relationship with the foster parent that predates the crisis of illness, a relationship that has been tested and can be trusted through the loss of the child. This process will be risky and challenging for helping people who will probably share a foster parent's grief and will have to rely on their personal and professional experience with grieving to support the parent genuinely.

In addition to such staff, parent groups are helpful in assisting with feelings associated with the death of a child. Foster parents caring for children with AIDS have an existing group forum through agency training sessions and recognition events that could be modified to address group concerns related to the serious illness or death of a child. To date, in the Leake and Watts program there have been no deaths of children, so grief work has focused primarily on education and individual anticipatory grief, but also on maintaining an attitude of hopefulness and living for the day rather than waiting for illness and death.

When a child dies, a child welfare program could make grief counselors available to foster parents and their families (not forgetting the children of foster parents who develop a relationship with the foster child). However, this program will depend on those workers who have built long and intense involvement with the foster family. This also raises the issue of the grief work of staff who cherish both the child and the foster family. When the time comes, participation in funeral arrangements and memorial services should be shared by staff and foster families. This may help the caring professional to acknowledge, think through, and constructively work on her or his own grief. Furthermore, the death of a child should not precipitate the closing of a foster home because there is not a child in placement. The agency will follow up and maintain a relationship with the foster family for some time after the loss of the foster child.

Conclusion

The grief of a foster parent may result from any number of separations and losses, as well as from witnessing and responding to the trauma of a child. These losses and this trauma are magnified and certain when the foster parent is caring for a child with AIDS. A foster parent's grief is often misunderstood and ignored when he or she is discounted for not being the child's "real" parent, or when he or she is perceived as a paid employee boarding a ward of the court. This downplaying or discounting of foster parent grief is exacerbated for those foster parents caring for children with AIDS because they face general prejudice, stigma, and perhaps specific discrimination and loss of friendships and family support. These harmful reactions from those who normally could be relied on for understanding have led to great caution in discussing a foster child and to not identifying specific issues or AIDS-related information. This secrecy may shield the foster parent from some criticism or abuse, and it respects the child's right to confidentiality, but it also removes a primary means for working through one's grief—talking it out with caring, understanding friends and family.

This constriction of a supportive network adds additional incentive and responsibility for professionals working with these foster parents for them to be supportive, encouraging listeners. An aloof, stereotyped "professional" attitude or distance is inappropriate because the child welfare worker becomes a crucial part of the foster parents' world. The foster parents must create, or have created for them, a new network of understanding and support. This network is composed not only of agency personnel, but also of other foster parents who are in similar circumstances, or other individuals who understand AIDS and have been moved to respond with compassion to people in need. Support groups should continue for foster parents after the death of their foster child.

Society has failed in general to understand or appreciate the role of foster parents. Caring for someone else's biological children but caring for them with the special love of a parent needs to be appreciated by helping professionals and by the community. This recognition of foster parents and the validation of an inevitable grief process because of separation and loss are particularly needed for the growing number of families who have opened their homes and hearts to children with AIDS.

6

An Investigation of the Disenfranchised Grief of Two Health Care Professionals Caring for Persons with AIDS

Lois Chapman Dick

> Death is indeed a fearful piece of brutality; there is no sense pretending otherwise. It is brutal not only as a psychical event, but far more so psychically: a human being is torn away from us, and what remains is the icy stillness of death.[1]
>
> —Carl Jung, Psychologist

> I go out to my club up the street to work out. To try to work it out on the weights and all I hear is . . . Did you hear so-and-so is sick? . . . Did you know that so-and-so is dying? I just walk out of there. I can't stand it. Sometimes I just want to move to a different town . . . and sell shoes.
>
> —Mark Dion, M.S.W., Social Worker

> There's no end in sight. The overwhelmingness of not being able to solve the problem. I think of that as I go to funerals. About all these people dying. We are going to lose all these people. You look backward more than you look forward. You don't want to look forward in this job sometimes.
>
> —Margo Bykonen, R.N., Nurse

For Carl Jung, the Swiss psychologist who died in 1961, death with its myths and mystery was to be a recurring theme in his lifelong exploration of the unconscious. During his lifetime two world wars were to show him the scope of its horror and pain, and he was to experience it intensely upon the death of his mother. In his autobiography, *Memories, Dreams, Reflections,* he wrote of being thrown back and forth between the contrasting emotions of warmth and joy, and terror and grief.[2] Today, in Seattle, Mark Dion and Margo Bykonen are being buffeted by the same storm of emotions. This time it is not the scourge of war but the pandemic of AIDS that afflicts their days and dreams.

Mark and Margo are grieving, and they are grieving primarily alone. Throughout the world other health care professionals share membership in their fraternity of pain and isolation. To be alive is to grieve, as no one of us is immune to the loss of those we love. Why is their grief different? It is different because it is not sanctioned, it is disenfranchised. Through the words of Margo and Mark, poets and sociologists, philosophers and theologians, this chapter will attempt to answer these questions.

Margo Bykonen, married and twenty-eight years old, is the AIDS outpatient coordinator for a large Seattle hospital. One of her roles is to make contact with each patient diagnosed with AIDS or ARC who comes into the hospital. She evaluates their current needs based on where they are in the disease process and refers them to community service agencies or individuals. She may, in some cases, act as a resource person to prevent unnecessary hospitalization, to improve continuity of care, and to support patients living in the community between hospitalizations. She also acts as an educator for hospital staff, providing training on AIDS caregiver and treatment issues.

Prior to her work as AIDS outpatient coordinator she was a primary care nurse and then a member of the hospital's home-care hospice team. Although her interest in working with AIDS patients started when Margo was working as a primary care nurse, it was not until she became a hospice nurse that she experienced following patients from first diagnosis through the whole disease process to their deaths. Her recognition of the multitude of problems faced by the person with AIDS or ARC led her to accept her current position.

Mark Dion came to his work by a different route. Mark, thirty-eight and a gay man, began working with people with AIDS and ARC in 1984 as a volunteer with Shanti (an organization devoted to caring for the terminally ill). He acted as an emotional and spiritual support person, becoming a part of people's lives through their illness, their dying, and their death. It was in this capacity that he met his first person with AIDS. Mark perceived a much greater need for social work involvement than was available in the community. He was able to convince the Northwest AIDS Foundation to establish a social service outreach program to deliver direct services to people with AIDS. Mark became the director of social services. His staff provided case management and referral, systems negotiation, housing and emergency shelter, and psychosocial support to persons with AIDS.

Mark continued to work with the Northwest AIDS Foundation until the summer of 1987.

> I can deal with it [AIDS] in terms of volunteer work. I can deal with it in terms of clients . . . in the community in general. You know, my own denial stuff . . . never allowing myself the reality that people I've known for years and assumed will be there for me the rest of my life are also going to be dealing in a real way with this disease. Last spring, I mean within a month, I was getting phone calls and being invited to dinner and hearing "I'm sero-positive," "I have shingles," "I have Kaposi's," "I have pneumocystis." By late summer I felt I needed a change. To do social work all day and go home

to AIDS stuff with my friends drove me nuts. I very much wanted to be present in their lives and still do . . . while we still have the time.

Mark knew he wanted to teach, and when he heard that the University of Washington had received grant money from the National Institute of Mental Health to fund an AIDS training project, he applied for and got the position of associate director. In this capacity he is charged with the teaching of psychosocial and neuropsychiatric issues in AIDS to other social workers, physicians, nurses, home care personnel, nursing home staff, and others who may be involved in providing care for AIDS and ARC patients. In addition, Mark does a considerable amount of community education.

In his study of death-related behavior, *Sociology of Death,* Glenn M. Vernon refers to the loss nurses experience when a patient dies.[3] He discusses the theory of Barney Glaser and Anselm Strauss which identifies three types of loss: a personal loss, a work loss, and a social loss. Glaser and Strauss state that work loss is incorporated into the nursing role. In working with patient after patient the nurse adjusts to work loss as an expected aspect of her job. Work loss is anticipated and expected. They acknowledge that when a nurse develops a social awareness of her patient her reaction is different from that to a work loss. The implication is that her reaction will be more intense.

Margo's interactions with her patients have increased her social awareness of them.

> AIDS is different. They [persons with AIDS] are young and their lives are just beginning to get good . . . People dying of cancer in their sixties and seventies—they've had good times and a chance to be of value to society and AIDS patients aren't getting a chance . . . And often they do life reviews. What have they accomplished? Sometimes they haven't accomplished a lot in terms of society's values. They don't feel they have made a difference.

Mark and Margo work with a population that is highly stigmatized by our society—gay men and IV-drug users. The preponderance of AIDS patients are to be found in either or both of these groups. In his definitive study of stigmatization, Erving Goffman describes those whom society stigmatizes:

> If there is to be a field of inquiry called "deviance" it is social deviants as here defined that would presumably constitute its core. Prostitutes, drug addicts, delinquents, criminals, jazz musicians, bohemians, gypsies, carnival workers, hobos, winos, show people, full time gamblers, beach dwellers, homosexuals . . . and the urban poor . . . these would be included.[4]

Not only are gay men and IV-drug users "deviants" and therefore stigmatized by society, but those who associate with them are also stigmatized:

I have considered one set of individuals from whom the stigmatized person can expect some support: those who share his stigma and by virtue of this are defined and define themselves as his own kind. The second set are—to borrow a term once used by homosexuals—the "wise," namely persons who are normal but whose special situation has made them intimately privy to the secret life of the stigmatized individual . . . Wise persons are the marginal men before whom the individual with a fault need feel no shame nor exert self-control, knowing that in spite of his failing he will be seen as an ordinary other.[5]

Goffman, writing in 1963, chose to separate out certain members of society and label them "deviant" and to characterize the rest of society as "normal." This "we/them" view is, unfortunately, still all too prevalent in our society.

Margo is now a "wise" person and, to use Goffman's term, suffers "courtesy" stigmatization. Goffman further warns that the person with the "courtesy" stigma may make the normal uncomfortable by confronting them with "too much morality":

People ask me why I do this job . . . and that's another frustration. To me that's a social statement. What they are really saying is "Why do you want to work with *those* people? . . . People don't want to hear anybody telling them about the problems of AIDS patients . . . They kind of go: "Oh no, not somebody who's a caseworker talking about this." Or "Why should *those* people get special treatment?"

Mark has experienced this dramatically time and time again:

You're with someone in a grocery store and his face is marked with the purple lesions of Kaposi's. You are standing in the checkout line and you see people stare and they all move to the next line. God, how that feels!

Margo and Mark, "privy to the secret life" of AIDS patients and their families, are seldom able to escape the reality of the personal devastation occurring around them. Indeed, Mark confronts the effects of AIDS everywhere he turns. Not long ago a friend asked Mark to accompany him to the Social Security office (to file a claim for disability due to AIDS). Mark was not surprised to find that he went through the experience on "automatic," having done it dozens of times with his AIDS clients. It was only upon returning that it occurred to him that it had *not* been automatic for his friend and when asked, his friend responded that he had hated it and felt out of control. For Mark this incident signified the merging of his work world with his private world.

It's feeling like a lot again. Another [friend] is very sick. Lives alone. We're running hard to pull in support. Tough stuff. I saw him last night and he was actively hallucinating, and I had to pull out all my resources to be there. I didn't realize how hard it was until this morning. I got up with a horrible headache and I've been wrought all day. This is a man who watched his lover die of the disease in the same way. He experienced major dementia and that's what is happening to him. And he knows it. And he looks at me and says, "Is this what I have to look forward to, months of in and out of restraints?" And, goddammit, what do I tell him?

The inability to escape:

I go out with friends for a beer . . . which I don't usually do because I'm not a bar person . . . or we go dancing . . . or just to go and socialize . . . two years ago nobody wanted to hear me talk about AIDS. Now, nobody says, "What did you do last weekend? Did you have a great time? They say, "Who's sick, who's dying, who's dead?"

The inability to play:

Sometimes I park my car and stare at people playing soccer at Green Lake [a park in Seattle]. And I'll think, God, that's incredible. They are playing just to play. I miss being in a place where I can do that. I bet AIDS and death never even enter their minds. *I* can't take off the damn coat [of knowledge].

The inability to be comforted by attending funerals of those who have died:

Going to funerals? For a while there I really had to watch it . . . all I was doing was going to funerals. A man who had ARC told me, "You need to be careful because if you hang around people who are dying you are going to feel old fast." He was right. I'm facing forty and suddenly I'm dealing with issues around age that I never looked at before.

Margo's inability always to find comfort at the funerals of her clients:

I don't enjoy going to funerals. I don't get a lot out of them. I don't like the formality, I guess. It's not how I remember people. Sometimes it leaves me feeling worse. People up there doing services that didn't know the person. Not getting the sense of what the person's life was about. I might have more sense of that and want to keep the memories intact. I have been to some great funerals where the person who died has designed their own service. That makes it more meaningful.

And for Mark when there is no funeral there is the loneliness of his grief:

He [an AIDS patient] had specifically requested no service. And I left after he died and only then did I learn the meaning of the old cliché: services are for the survivors . . . I had no way of letting go . . . my own goodbye . . . it felt abrupt for me, not finished . . . My feeling after the death was, how do I get from here to there [back to life]?

The difficulty Margo was finding solace from grief in religion:

And people say, "Well, their suffering is over." Certainly their suffering is over, but that does not make it any easier that the person isn't here anymore. It's not a comfort for me to think that they are somewhere else. That doesn't make it okay.

The magnitude of the losses visited upon Mark and Margo and the intensity of their grief cannot be overstated. One of the most debilitating losses may be having to acknowledge to themselves their inability, in spite of training, to assist the person with AIDS. Margo's nursing expertise, at times, is not enough:

You're constantly making an effort to keep this person comfortable at the end, and sometimes you are not succeeding . . .the swelling . . . the tumors . . . with medication you can't make them go down. I'm used to being able to take away pain. If I can't control their pain, why am I there?

After a death Margo may have to offer comfort to a friend or partner for whom this most recent death is just one of a constant stream of deaths:

Those who have seen thirty of their friends die . . . what can I do for people experiencing that? I don't feel very useful and capable of dealing with that person's grief. I don't know how to be therapeutic in that situation. I'm seeing it a lot. Patients die in the spring and now we are dealing with their partners dying. It's like watching a family die one by one from this illness. I tend to just throw up my hands and go, "Oh, yeah!"

Earlier, reference was made to a warning given to Mark about the aging that comes from attending too many funerals. If we had no calendars or clocks the only way we would know we were aging and nearing death would be to witness the dying of our peers. Avery Weisman alludes to this in his book *On Death and Dying* when he writes: "Death and time are inseparable portions of our personal presence. Clocks and calendars are convenient amulets that lull us into believing that time ends when death begins."[6] Indeed, loss and death have prematurely aged both Mark and Margo. Their spiritual and existential issues are those of people many years their senior: issues of death, dying, morality, ethics, joy, sexuality, values.

On societal values:

Margo: Our age group, people twenty-five to forty-five, are dying . . . mortality . . . people who are young are dying. Society has never been known to focus on death and dying. It's interesting, when all these people are dying from AIDS [no one cares] . . . but when it's infants in New York or wherever there's sympathy. What is valued in society? It isn't young, gay men or a person with a substance abuse history.

On Personal values:

Margo: When you look at someone, you are looking at a person: a human being. A couple of patients I cared for in the hospital I got to know as persons, not by their sexual orientation. It just hit me that there are some wonderful people that just happen to be gay and the people in this group just happen to be the ones affected first by this illness.

Mortality:

Margo: Our lives are not infinite and it's important to take advantage of what we have each day. That's reaffirmed to me every time somebody I have cared about dies. And it frustrates me when people treat the death as a number. This is not just a number, but someone who could have been a very important part of this society.

Mark: There is some kind of archetypical sense of my own consciousness around a point we move to, that we anticipate, and are heading toward, and a point from which we move away. A beginning, and a creating, and an expectation, and you reach a certain point and all the energy shifts to a letting go, and a passing away, and it is closure time rather than beginning time. And suddenly I find myself on the other side of the metaphor and I don't like it. I'm not ready to be dead. There are things I still want to create in my life.

Mark's poignantly expressed awareness of his own existence and mortality, and sense of the shortness and fragility of his life attest to the aging effect of the dying that surrounds him daily. He unknowingly echoes the words of Paul Tillich, who, in speaking of humanity's eternal quest for meaning in the face of death, wrote, "We move toward something that is not yet, and we come from something that is no more."[7]

Sexuality and love:

Mark: One of the things that people really underestimate is the loss to gay men, in particular the changes around their sexuality. So much of our identification was around sexual expression, a broad range of freedom in sexual expression, pleasure and delight in our sexuality . . . Where will we find joy, pleasure, spontaneity, playfulness, nurturence, and all that stuff that was so primarily focused in a certain way of being sexual? It's hard to have any romance, because romance is based on fantasy, when you are living in such reality. And for me the loss is manifold. How will I meet people and have fun when everyone is coming at me, seeing me as the AIDS person?

Can the ability to love survive in the face of the stigmatization Mark experiences by both "courtesy" *and* group membership? The philosopher Maurice Merleau-Ponty has said, "We weigh the hardihood of love which promises beyond what it knows, which claims to be eternal when a sickness, perhaps an accident will destroy it."[8] Love and sexuality are inseparable, and Merleau-Ponty has argued that sexuality has its basis in affectivity and that affectivity is essential for human life. Sexuality uses one's body, soul, thoughts, and emotions. Mark is anticipating the diminishing opportunities to express himself fully as a sexual being. We may choose, as humans, to deny or forgo sexuality as a means of human expression. But surely the choosing should be ours alone.

Where do Margo and Mark take their wounded hearts and tortured minds for comfort? Who will listen? Who can reassure them of their survival in the face of their agonizing awareness? Has their journey with the dying taught them truths about their existence which allow them some joy, some freedom?

Margo receives support from her husband, even though he doesn't understand to the degree that she would like him to understand.

> He hears me talk and he's very good about listening . . . he listens all the time, but sometimes he listens and it isn't active listening where he responds back, and that's not as helpful as someone who has been there as a co-worker.

Margo feels less isolated now that a social worker has been hired by the Northwest AIDS Foundation to be based at the hospital where she works. It is with this social worker that she can share her frustration and anger at the limited resources available to her clients. She still misses the peer support she experienced working on a hospital unit. Even with peers there are times when it is more permissible to share feelings of loss.

> If I have had a long-term relationship with a patient it's more okay to talk about the loss. Length of time with a patient can give legitimacy to grieving.

Acknowledgment of her loss and her sadness comes occasionally from the partner of a patient who has died or his family.

I've had partners or family members come up to me at a funeral and say, "You were more than just a nurse." I've had patients who introduced me as a friend, and I prefer that to "This is my nurse."

It is more difficult for Mark both to grieve and seek out comfort. When asked to whom he turned for support he replied,

It's funny. I don't think I'm very good at it [turning to others for support]. It's something that's very hard for me to admit. I give a great lecture on it! I was thinking about that the other day. I do a lot of grieving alone. I've gotten better at grieving and that feels good to me.

Mark recounted that he went on a spiritual retreat several years ago that he found very healing despite his skepticism about participating in such an event. He described his experience as a "tremendous gift" to himself that resulted in a change in how he viewed his own grieving. He began to look at his grief as another form of meditation and not as a dysfunctional behavior.

It didn't mean that I was doing something wrong because I was crying all the time. It was a way, in fact, that I could get clear and move to a greater sense of life and understanding. I'm a lot better now. When it happens I take time for it [grieving]. I don't walk away from it. Friday nights are standard grief nights for me. Because I go at a pretty strong pace all week and there it is. So, I try on Friday nights and Saturday mornings to be a little gentle with myself.

Mark has learned to accept his private grief, but he struggles with asking for comfort. He can talk about his sadness but admits that the asking for and taking of comfort from another is uncomfortable.

There must be something scary about that for me. Part of it is that it's hard to ask for comfort when everyone is dealing with the same thing. Where do you go to grieve when everyone is grieving? Because I don't know anyone who isn't [grieving].

Paradoxically, in the midst of his almost unrelenting anguish, Mark has achieved a certain peace, learned a profound lesson. He has lost the fear of personal death.

If I found that I had two years or something [to live], I'd feel ready. I wouldn't feel that this was the worst thing in the world. I don't feel that way about death. It wouldn't be all that wrenching. There's been a lot of letting go already. Does that make sense? Sometimes I feel like it might almost be a relief.

With Mark's acceptance of the possibility of his own life ending has come the ability to be fully committed to the present.

> I now have the ability to be present with the living. I experience a lot more now. There are periods lately where that's really been clear. And I've felt this incredible sensation of ebullience. This is incredible. I really love what I am doing and yet I am not attached to it.

This new sense of being which Mark articulates is perhaps best reflected in his words about a trip to Hawaii that he took with a friend a year ago:

> It was really a lark. And I had an exquisite, extraordinary time . . . sensate pleasure and spiritual highs. We were on a hike and my friend was going to continue on and I was going to turn back, and I said goodbye and it was a gorgeous day. And I said to my friend, "You know, bliss is a spiritual truth, too."

Mark, in the awareness of that moment and in the millions of moments since, discovers his humanity. The existentialist Albert Camus, on a different beach decades before, spoke of the same discovery:

> Here I understand what is meant by glory: the right to love without limits . . . In a moment, when I throw myself down among the absinthe plants to bring their scent into my body, I shall know . . . that I am fulfilling a truth which is the sun's and which also be my death's. In a sense, it is indeed my life that I am staking here, a life that tastes of warm stone, that is full of the sighs of the sea and the rising song of the crickets . . . I love this life with abandon and wish to speak of it boldly: it makes me proud of my human condition . . . learning patiently and arduously how to live is enough for me.[9]

Why is the grief of Mark and Margo different? It is different because it is disenfranchised. Their grief is solitary, unrecognized and uncomforted. The persons for whom they grief are deemed by society to be unworthy of concern and deserving of their fate. Except on rare occasions neither families of origin nor families of choice include Mark and Margo in the comforting embrace of shared sorrow. In the face of overwhelming, unending death they have come to question their deepest values, the meaning of their existence, their belief in a deity who visits such pain upon humankind. Yet they continue to search for joy and to display unceasing dignity. Perhaps they share the feelings of Albert Camus when he wrote of his own loss of the death of André Gide: "Those deprived of grace simply have to practice generosity among themselves."[10]

Those of us who know Margo and Mark and those of us who know others doing similar work have a responsibility to them. That responsibility should include the public acknowledgment of their contributions to society and the private offer of our love and devotion to their humanity.

Notes

1. C.G. Jung, *Memories, Dreams, Reflections* (New York: Vintage, 1963), p. 314.
2. Ibid.
3. G.M. Vernon, *Sociology of Death* (New York: Ronald Press, 1970).
4. E. Goffman, *Stigma* (Englewood Cliffs, N.J.: Prentice-Hall, 1963), p. 29.
5. Ibid.
6. A.D. Weisman, *On Dying and Denying* (New York: Behavioral Press, 1972), p. 216.
7. P. Tillich, *The Meaning of Death* (New York: McGraw-Hill, 1959), p. 33.
8. M. Merleau-Ponty, *The Primacy of Perception* (Evanston, Ill.: Northwestern University Press, 1964), p. 27.
9. A. Camus, *Lyrical and Critical Essays* (New York: Vintage, 1970), pp. 68–69.
10. Ibid.

7

The Left Lover: Grief in Extramarital Affairs and Cohabitation

Kenneth J. Doka

S tudies of grief and bereavement have long recognized that relationship and attachment to the deceased are critical determinants of the intensity of grief. Yet most studies only examine the effect of death on the immediate family or close kin. Recently there has been a recognition that there is a need to include non-kin relationships in studies of grief. As early as 1976 Folta and Deck noted,

> While all of these studies tell us that grief is a normal phenomenon, the intensity of which corresponds to the closeness of the relationship with the deceased, they fail to take this (i.e., friendship) into account. The underlying assumption is that "closeness of relationship" exists only among spouses and/or immediate kin. (p. 239)

Similarly, Raphael (1983) in her comprehensive review of grief reactions considers that

> there may be other dyadic partnership relationships in adult life that show patterns similar to conjugal ones, among them the young couple intensely, even secretly, in love; the de facto relationship, the extra-marital relationship and the homosexual couple. (p. 227)

One of the most neglected areas is the study of grief in nontraditional heterosexual relationships such as extramarital affairs and heterosexual cohabitation. Although these relationships do differ, they may be defined as "nontraditional" in that they both are multidimensional (including sexual) dyadic relationships that exist outside the traditional institution of marriage and therefore have limited public acceptance, some degree of negative sanction, and tenuous legal standing.

Sections of this chapter were published earlier in "Silent Sorrow: Grief and the Loss of Significant Others," *Death Studies* 11, 453–69.

These relationships are, however, relatively common in contemporary society. While Hite (1987) (in a study that has been criticized as methodologically flawed) found that as much as 70 percent of her sample had had at least one extramarital affair, most researchers believe the figure is somewhere between 40 percent and 50 percent (Reiss 1980, Thompson 1984). Researchers also estimate that more than 1 million couples are presently cohabiting (Reiss 1980).

The problem of grief in these relationships has not been much studied; the very secrecy of the relationship inhibits research. Horn (1979) offered a personal account of her reaction to the death of a heterosexual live-in lover and compared that loss to a friend's loss of a homosexual lover. Doka (1987) studied a small sample of bereaved who had been involved in both heterosexual and homosexual nontraditional relationships. Some implication may also be drawn from the study of the grief problems of homosexual lovers. And although this material is limited, there is at least some research (Kimmel 1978, 1979, Kelly 1977, Heineman et al. 1983, Geis, Fuller, and Rush 1986).

Dimensions of Nontraditional Relationships

Before discussing the particular problems of grief in nontraditional relationships, it is important to recognize that these relationships can vary in very significant ways and that the different ways in which the relationships were perceived by the survivors can influence the intensity and resolution of grief. Though these same variables can influence bereavement in marriage as well, the range in these dimensions is likely to be greater in nontraditional relationships.

One critical dimension is the degree to which a person is invested in a relationship. As Reiss's (1980) typology of extramarital relationships shows, these may range from defining the relationship as a casual fling to more serious and sustained commitments. Extramarital relationships can be sexual, emotional, or both (Thompson 1984). Studies of cohabitation show similar variations in investment. Tanfer (1987) found that some cohabiting couples viewed their relationship as a trial marriage, while others perceived it as a permanent alternative to marriage. Similarly, Kurdek and Schmitt (1986) found that many cohabiting partners saw few barriers to leaving the relationship. One can assume that the greater the commitment, the more intense the grief.

This leads to another dimension—the meaning that the relationship has for the parties. Every relationship supports some sense of self. It is essential to consider what aspects of self are supported by the relationship and how they will be maintained in the absence of the relationship. Some of the attributes may be very positive. For example, the relationship may support attributes of desirability or importance. But there may be negative effects as well.

In cases in which there is more meaning in the relationship and/or more ambivalence, resolution of grief would be more difficult.

The opportunity to find replacements for new relationships is another variable in nontraditional relationships. In some cases there may be many opportunities to reinvest in new roles and relationships, while in others such opportunities might be risky or limited. The less opportunity to replace a relationship, particularly one that is defined as meaningful, the more difficult it is to reinvest and thus complete the tasks of grief.

Then, there is the dimension of acceptance-rejection. To what degree is the relationship accepted or rejected by others? When the relationship is accepted, there is greater potential for social support by family and friends which facilitates the resolution of grief.

Finally, one dimension is somewhat particular to nontraditional relationships. Some of these relationships may be very open, while others are quite secret (Thompson 1984). That is, the knowledge of the relationship can be limited to the involved parties, shared only with intimates, or generally known within a larger circle of family, friends, co-workers, and the community. The more open the relationship, the more opportunity there is to acknowledge grief and receive social support.

Nontraditional relationships then may be viewed as being part of a continuum. At one end might be relationships that are open and accepted, and involve heavy degrees of commitment and affect, yet will provide opportunities for replacement. In contemporary American society, some cohabiting heterosexual relationships would fall closer in this range. In these cases, grief may approximate that experienced by many spouses, albeit without some of the traditional sources of support. Other cohabiting or extramarital relationships may be at other points on this continuum. Here the myriad combinations may complicate grief considerably.

A number of factors complicate grief in nontraditional relationships. Five are particularly significant.

1. Intense Negative Affect

Many emotions are associated with normal grief. The bereaved frequently experience feelings of anger, guilt, sadness, depression, loneliness, hopelessness, and numbness (Worden 1982, Glick, Weiss, and Parkes 1974, Lindemann 1944). Often these emotions are intensified in nontraditional relationships. Research has reported that the bereaved have strong feelings of guilt, shame, anger, embarrassment, loneliness, and isolation (Doka 1987). Because these relationships are negatively sanctioned, feelings of guilt may be particularly evident and may be manifested in three ways. First, in some cases, the bereaved person may believe that the relationship itself was a factor in the death. Doka (1987) reported a case in which a woman was mourning the loss of a man with whom she had had an affair for a number of years. Though the affair had terminated almost a year prior to the death, she still had strong feelings of guilt. She wondered how much the strain of the affair—the secrecy, the excitement, and the added tension at home—had contributed to his fatal attack.

Second, the general nature of the relationship may contribute to feelings of guilt. There may be a moral sense that the nontraditional relationship was wrong and that the death was a punishment for that loss. This may be compounded by a strong sense of alienation from sources of solace such as religion. Both relationships mentioned here exist outside of church-sanctioned marriage. While denomination and clergy may differ in the degree or intensity with which they accept or condemn relationships, and bereaved may differ in their perception of morality, the bereaved may experience a sense of separation from their denominational heritage. They may be reluctant to worship, hesitant to contact clergy, and disinclined to participate in religious organizations or church-sponsored grief support groups.

Finally, the very condition of the death can lead to a great sense of embarrassment, shame, and subsequent guilt. Bereaved may have to explain to strangers such as police, medical personnel, funeral directors, and even family members the nature of the relationship and the circumstances of death.

Other emotions may be intensified as well. Survivors may exhibit considerable anger over being deserted in such an untenable situation. Survivors may also experience extreme isolation, loneliness, and even a deep sense of persecution.

In addition, some of these relationships may be highly ambivalent. This is particularly true in extramarital relationships. Thus bereaved may have very mixed feelings toward the relationship. On the one hand, the relationship may meet certain affective and sexual needs; it may provide a sense of excitement. On the other hand, the bereaved may resent the constraints of the relationship (for example, limited freedom to call, restrictions of liaisons) and may be troubled by issues of morality. They may be torn by desires to continue and to end the relationship. The death of the partner then resolves a problem, perhaps causing both relief and guilt.

This degree of ambivalence may not be as evident in more stable and open relationships. Here any ambivalence is more likely related to the history and interaction of the personalities involved. But in the more secretive and transient relationships, the ambivalence may be a built-in aspect of the relationship itself.

2. Exclusion from Care and Support of the Dying

In addition to the intense negative effect, those in nontraditional roles are also inhibited from behaviors that are therapeutic.

Often, care of the dying person by the significant other can facilitate later grief adjustment (Hamovitch 1964). But frequently, those involved in non-traditional relationships are excluded from an active role in the care of the dying. In some cases the exclusion may be physical. Often intensive-care units limit visiting to the immediate family. In other cases, bereaved may be reluctant to visit for fear of an embarrassing encounter with family members.

In still other situations, the constraints of the nontraditional role can inhibit signs of care or emotional leave taking that would later facilitate grief resolution. Bereaved may feel inhibited from publicly expressing their emotions, finishing business, or leave taking.

3. Lack of Social Support

One of the factors critical in facilitating bereavement is the presence of social support (Parkes 1980), yet this too is often lacking in nontraditional relationships. The grief may have to remain private. Few may know of the relationship and the family of the deceased, even in cases of cohabitation, may not feel any responsibility toward the bereaved partner.

This lack of social support can continue even after the death. When a spouse dies, the surviving spouse undergoes a transition to the role of "widow" or "widower." That role, however vague, has a certain status that is recognized by the larger community. It carries legal and social rights. For example, bereaved spouses may be permitted time off from work, be excused from certain social responsibilities, and be permitted a wider range of emotional expression. The survivor in a nontraditional relationship has no such role. In a nontraditional relationship, persons lose significant roles when their partner dies, but there is no defined transitional role for them to assume. There is no formal recognition that they are "bereaved," little support or sympathy for emotional reaction, no personnel policies that cover time off from work.

4. Exclusion from Funeral Rituals

Participation in planning funeral rituals can also facilitate grief adjustment (Doka 1984). Yet often persons in nontraditional relationships may be denied any role in planning or participating in funeral rituals. Sometimes the secrecy of the relationship inhibits any role.

At other times, the exclusion may be unintentional. Often the family "circles the wagons" at the time of a death. Those outside clear and immediate kinship can easily be forgotten. Folta and Deck (1976) found that friends were frequently not consulted at a death.

Often too the bereaved person is excluded from any recognition in the funeral. The relationship, even if long-lasting and relatively open, may not be acknowledged by the family in the funeral, in the funeral orations, or in the death notices. The family may simply be embarrassed and confused as to how they may explain the relationship to others.

In cases in which the relationship is secret, there naturally is no recognition or even knowledge of grief within that relationship. In some cases, the exclusion is total. Sometimes because of the clandestine and sporadic nature of the relationship, the survivor may not even become aware of the death until weeks after the event.

5. Practical and Legal Difficulties

Finally, bereaved may experience legal and practical problems related to the death. There may be problems of inheritance, such as dying intestate, or legal battles with relatives, problems of ownership when one party in joint ownership dies, and difficulties that arise from the fact that the survivor has no legal standing and therefore cannot sue in cases of wrongful death.

Even when legal problems are absent, there may be practical problems that complicate the death. As Horn (1979) notes, such nontraditional couples may not be carried under each other's medical insurance, or have the shared financial resources (such as credit cards, joint accounts) that can provide emergency reserves. Other problems may seem minor but still create considerable difficulties. Roberta Horn (1979) in her personal account of the death of her lover describes the difficulty of returning her lover's tools to his family:

> I decided to contact H's brother, but what story should we tell him? I was nauseous by this time from the subterfuge. A young male neighbor of mine finally called the brother for me, claiming H had been helping him fix his apartment, and offered to bring the things back to the brother, since we certainly didn't want the brother to pick them up at my home. (p. 144)

These legal and practical difficulties create additional stress or concurrent crises, such as legal barriers, that impede the resolution of grief. This points to the central paradox of disenfranchised grief: the grief is complicated, but the normal sources of social support in grief are often not as available.

Implications for Grief Resolution

All of these special difficulties combine to complicate grieving in nontraditional relationships. Worden (1982) suggests that the resolution of grief involves four tasks:

1. Accepting the reality of loss
2. Experiencing the pain of grief

3. Adjusting to an environment in which the deceased is missing
4. Withdrawing emotional energy from the deceased and reinvesting it in others

When one experiences the loss of a significant other in a nontraditional relationship, it is more difficult to complete these tasks. It is harder to accept the reality of loss if one is excluded from the dying process, restricted from the funeral rituals, inhibited from acknowledging the loss, or even given delayed news of the death. The intense, complicated, and ambivalent emotions associated with nontraditional relationships can constrain effective progress. The sensitive, sometimes secretive, and exciting nature of the relationship may make replacement difficult. In addition, traditional sources of solace such as ritual and religion may complicate rather than facilitate grief work. Formal and informal systems of support may be neither available nor helpful.

Given these circumstances, it is not unusual to expect atypical manifestations of grief. Often, since the resolution of the tasks of mourning is impaired, grief can become chronic. In other cases, the secretive nature of the relationship and the lack of social support may lead to delayed or masked grief reactions. Sometimes the latter might emerge in physical illness or unusual behaviors. In one case a woman who had been very careful to maintain a discreet affair with a married man who had died began to engage in openly provocative and flirtatious actions in her office. Bowlby (1980) suggests that sometimes the bereaved may become so euphoric that it can be described as a manic episode. Although I have not observed such reactions, and Bowlby (1980) does not find it common, it is logical to be aware that it could occur in nontraditional relationships.

In assisting clients in resolving such a loss, counselors and caregivers should be aware of the unique context of such losses. First, the counselor has to be extremely sensitive to the moral ambiguity that may surround such relationships. Clients may be highly defensive. In some cases, they may actively seek the counselors' approval of the relationship. In others, they may seek condemnation. This defensive and ambivalent context suggests caution.

It is also especially important to define the nature of the relationship. How committed were both parties? What did the relationship mean to the survivor? How many people knew of the relationship? As part of grief resolution, it is important to find meaning and purpose in the relationship. The counselor should try to have clients affirm, within their own beliefs and ethics, the value of the association. Often it helps if they can consider how they or the significant other changed and developed through that relationship. In that context, even painful events can be reinterpreted as part of an experience in which one learns and grows. Where appropriate and needed, and again within their own religious and ethical convictions, clients may accept and extend forgiveness. Rituals, such as confession and absolution and readings from their religious traditions, as well as pastoral counseling from empathic clergy, may assist in exploring moral issues and resolving grief.

It is particularly important to assess the circumstances of the death. How did it occur? Where was the surviving partner during this process? How was the surviving partner informed of the illness, hospitalization, and/or death? To what degree was the surviving partner involved in the decisions and care of the dying partner and/or in the postdeath rituals?

This naturally leads to a discussion of the degree of social support that the surviving partner received during any illness as well as at and after the time of death. Who knew of the relationship? How supportive were people? Did the family of the deceased support the partner, and in what ways?

These discussions provide the basis for assessing and exploring any particular factors that may be impeding the resolution of grief. Counselors may need to explore with clients the degree to which the circumstances of the death, the nature of the relationships, or any legal or other difficulties associated with the loss of the relationship have created concurrent crises, emotional blockages, or unfinished business. In dealing with these difficulties, counselors may first need to help clients affirm the reality and legitimacy of their grief. Often because that grief is disenfranchised, it may be masked, and it is not unusual to see the client initially focus on another issue. Once that is completed, counselors can assist clients in verbalizing effective responses to the loss, attempting to frame and test solutions to problems generated by the loss, and bringing closure to any unresolved issues. The latter difficulty is often an issue in nontraditional relations since these relationships are often ambiguous and, in the aftermath of death, unfinished. A few techniques are especially helpful. Often a letter to the deceased or a discussion with an empty chair can provide needed closure; assisting the client in developing alternative rituals may facilitate grief resolution by allowing the resolution of unfinished business and reaffirming a sense of involvement and control.

Counselors may also need to review with clients other losses they have sustained at the death of a partner. The relationship may have provided a sense of excitement or supported an aspect of self. There may be a loss of dreams, perhaps of eventual marriage. And there may be, particularly in cases of cohabitation where the partner was politely tolerated but the relationship never accepted by the deceased's family, a loss of ties to that family.

It is also important to explore whether anyone else in the survivor's environment was affected by the loss. In cases of cohabitation and even extramarital affairs, the lover may have had a relationship with other family members, such as children of the surviving partner. Their reactions to that loss may very well affect the grief of the partner.

Counselors may also need to assist clients in developing a "story" that explains both the relationship and grief. The story is an account of the history and significance of the relationship, and of the impact of the loss. The development of the story has three therapeutic functions. First, it affirms the value of the relationship and the normalcy of grief. Second, it provides an opportunity for the client to review any remaining issues or difficulties that may impair an ability to reinvest in any future relationship. Third, it provides the client with a rehearsed explanation that mitigates any lingering discomfort caused by the ambivalent status of the left lover. For although being a widow offers both socially recognized status and a clearly outlined past relationship, the remaining partner has no such role. The story then provides an explanation of the role of the deceased in his or her life to future lovers, spouses, or children.

Finally, it should be recognized that other variables that affect the intensity of grief, such as the characteristics of the bereaved, affect grief in nontraditional relationships as well. Grief in nontraditional relationships is but one aspect of grief as a whole. The loss of a significant other, in whatever role, is painful. But only when we recognize and understand the reality and unique nature of the pain can we begin to help ease it.

References

Bowlby, J. 1980. *Attachment and Loss: Loss.* Vol. 3. New York: Basic Books.

Doka, K.J. 1984. "Expectation Death, Participation in Funeral Arrangements, and Grief Adjustment." *Omega* 15, 119–30.

———. 1987. "Silent Sorrow: Grief and the Loss of Significant Others." *Death Studies* 11, 455–69.

Folta, J., and E. Deck. 1976. "Grief, the Funeral, and the Friend." In *Acute Grief and the Funeral,* edited by, V. Pine, A.H. Kutscher, D. Peretz, R.C. Starer, R. De Bellis, R.J. Volk, and D.J. Cherico. Springfield, Ill.: Charles C. Thomas.

Geis, S.B., R.L. Fuller, and J. Rush. 1986. "Lovers of AIDS Victims: Psychosocial Stresses and Counseling Needs." *Death Studies* 101, 43–54.

Glick, I., R. Weiss, and C.M. Parkes. 1974. *The First Year of Bereavement.* New York: Wiley.

Hamovitch, M. 1964. *The Parent and the Fatally Ill Child.* Duarte, Calif.: City of Hope Medical Center.

Heineman, A., G. Soucy, D. Richards, and H. McMillan. 1983. "A Social Service Program for AIDS Clients." Panel presentation to the Annual Meeting of the Forum for Death Education and Counseling, Chicago, Oct.

Hite, S. 1987. *Women in Love.* New York: Knopf.

Horn, R. 1979. "Life Can Be a Soap Opera." In *Perspectives on Bereavement,* edited by I. Gerber, A. Weiner, A. Kutscher, D. Battin, A. Arkin, and I. Goldberg. New York: Arno.

Kelly, J. 1977. "The Aging Male Homosexual: Myth and Reality." *The Gerontologist* 17, 328–32.

Kimmel, D. 1978. "Adult Development and Aging: A Gay Perspective." *Journal of Social Issues* 34, 113–31.

———. 1979. "Life History Interviews of Aging Gay Men." *International Journal of Aging and Human Development* 10, 239–48.

Kurdek, C., and J.P. Schmitt. 1986. "Relationship Quality of Partners in Heterosexual Married, Heterosexual Cohabitating, and Gay and Lesbian Relationships." *Journal of Personality and Social Psychology* 51, 711–20.

Lindemann, E. 1944. "Symptomatology and the Management of Acute Grief." *American Journal of Psychiatry* 101, 141–49.

Parkes, C.M. 1980. "Bereavement Counseling: Does It Work? *British Medical Journal* 281, 3–6.

Raphael, B. 1983. *The Anatomy of Bereavement.* New York: Basic Books.

Reiss, I. 1980. *Family Systems in America.* 3d ed. New York: Holt, Rinehart and Winston.

Tanfer, K. 1987. "Patterns of Premarital Cohabitation among Never Married Women in the United States." *Journal of Marriage and the Family* 49, 483–97.

Thompson, A. 1984. "Emotional and Sexual Components of Extramarital Relations." *Journal of Marriage and the Family* 46, 35–42.

Worden, W. 1982. *Grief Counseling and Grief Therapy.* New York: Springer.

8
The Friend-Griever

Edith S. Deck
Jeanette R. Folta

Introduction

In the decade that has passed since the first publication on friends and grief (Folta and Deck 1976) little attention has been given to this issue. The major comprehensive studies on grief continue to focus on spouse and kinship grief. Bowling and Cartwright's (1982) study of elderly widows and Parkes and Weiss's (1983) study on recovery from bereavement allude to friends as support givers but not as grievers. The newer studies of the treatment for grief (Bowlby 1980, Worden 1982, Raphael 1983, Rando 1984) do not address the possibility of the friend as a bereaved person. Even the studies of special groups such as homosexuals (Kelly 1977, Kimmel 1978, Horn 1979) and AIDS (Saunders and Valente 1987, Goldmeier 1987) focus on the dying or their lovers and not on friends. The latest book on AIDS (Corless and Pittman-Lindeman 1988) refers to bereavement overload and heightened anxiety among members of the homosexual community, yet does not list friends nor grief in the index, and it gives no attention to friends as grievers in the text.

During this same time period several comprehensive books have been written about friends. These books (Bell 1981, Derlega and Winstead 1986, Pogrebin 1987) devote between one paragraph and three and a half pages to friends experiencing loss or grief. They focus on the definition of friends, establishment and break-up of friendship groups, and differences in friendship patterns by gender and number of friends. The absence of consideration of friends and grief is surprising since by most calculations we average three to five close, intimate friends, and therefore grief from the death of friends affects between 6 and 10 million Americans annually.

Although we have entered a conservative period that emphasizes the idea of a return to a traditional family structure, social change moves us forward not backward in time. We decry the seemingly lessening importance of the family and the seeking of gratification from nonimmediate kin. Yet from cradle to grave we place our family members in the care of nonfamily institutions (Folta and Deck 1976). More individuals than ever before are choosing the single life-style, and those who marry are postponing first marriages to age twenty-five for women and twenty-four for men (U.S. Census Report 1985). One in four Americans lives alone or with nonrelatives (Levine 1984). Seventy million of us are single, divorced, or widowed (Pogrebin 1987). Within this framework there is a shift of primary group relationships from family to friends.

Throughout the life cycle, peers are often more significant in importance than kin. For both young people and early middle-age adults, whether single or married, and living near or far from immediate kin, friends often provide the most meaningful and psychologically close relationships. In the increasing geriatric population, friends or nursing home roommates again play the role of intimate group kin (Folta and Deck 1973). Among the elderly, as with young people, the primary group relationship is shifting from kin to friend. More and more elderly as well as young people are living together outside wedlock and finding primary group relationships among non-kin. Even outside this type of relationship, especially among those elderly who are on the periphery of the family group, the fellow inmate or old-time friend is the most important person in one's life.

This chapter is about friends. In particular, it is an exploration of the meaning and consequences of the loss of friends through death. We examine both the individual and social aspects of the process of grief resolution by the friend-griever. Finally, we consider possible implications for social change.

The Nature of Friendship

Since Georg Simmel (1950) first used the concept of "sociability" to describe the purest form of interaction among equals, scholars have attempted to describe and refine the concept of friendship. Long ignored as an area of serious study by social scientists, it has recently been called the "mystique of the '80's" by Pogrebin (1987) who claims "we've always valued our friends, but never before have we prized them as we do today" (p. 126).

Although the definition of a friend is highly personal and individualized, there are consensual meanings attached to the concept. Friendship refers to voluntary, enduring social relationships. It involves choice, sharing, valuing, trust, loyalty, and pleasure. Friends differ from acquaintances in many ways. Acquaintances are people we know by name or face and like kin are not chosen by us. Friendship relationships are more significant. They involve self-revelation and disclosure, exchange of confidences, a willingness to accept the other "as it," a sense of "we" group and mutual identification.

Friends tend to be homogeneous (Verbrugge 1977). They are chosen from similar demographic backgrounds. Most often they are of the same or similar age, sex, religion, race, and class. They represent similarity in personal characteristics, interests, values, and attitudes. Friends are expected to treat each other as persons of real significance in their own right as well as in their relationship to each other. From friendship we derive a sense of self-confirmation, a sense of who we are, of self-worth and self-esteem.

Friendships vary in intensity and importance throughout the life cycle. Around age three, the child begins to form friendships, and by age five to seven these friendships begin to mimic the adult version (Rubin 1980). Some of these friendships remain stable over a lifetime and are valued as special relationships. As each ensuing year passes, the importance of friendship grows. With adolescence comes the intense need to be accepted by peers and to develop close relationships. This is a period of need for sharing feelings, emotions, intimacy, private experiences, and affection. Friends often become more important than kin. However, as Bell (1981) noted, "The adolescent's shift from family to peer influences is not easily accepted by the family . . . Intense competition between parents and peers to influence the adolescent intensifies as they move through the years of adolescence" (Bell 1981, p. 45)

This conflict continues through marriage. Lopata (1975) indicates that marriage results in an expectation that in the ideal marriage, friendship should be exclusively between husband and wife, and no other relationships should interfere in the marital system. Friendship in adult life is viewed as a subversion of the value of kinship, especially for women, who are expected to receive all their emotional gratification from an attachment to their spouse, children, and relatives. In reality, friends play a significant role in the life of the adult. The women's movement itself has been instrumental in making women aware of the value and significance of their friendships.

In the past, the traditional family met the needs of the elderly. With the growth of industrialization, urbanization, and nuclear families, the care of the elderly has been transferred to other institutional structures. Retirement communities, elderly housing projects, home-sharing programs, and nursing homes have replaced the family home. These changes have created a shift in interpersonal relationships from the extended kin to friend. The elderly have fewer options available for close family relationships. Many who have never married, are estranged from spouses, widowed, have no children or have outlived them, or moved away have no or limited intimate kinship relationships. Shulman (1975) claims friends and neighbors are three times more likely than family to be identified by adults as sources of emotional bonding and support. The majority of the elderly who have friends see them almost every day and interact with them more frequently than with kin.

From the point of view of the kin, there are four possible reactions to friendships. Often because we are geographically, socially, or emotionally detached from our families, they are unaware of our friends. While they may have heard names, they have never met these significant others. In some cases friends are both known and acknowledged by family or close friends. As stated earlier, kin may perceive friends as competition for their affections and time and hence may try to exclude them from important family events. In other cases friends may be elevated to the position of honorary kin. This tends to occur in two situations. When family are especially attracted to a member's friend, they may accord him or her special privileges ordinarily reserved for kin. When "friends" are lovers as opposed to "only friends," as in the case of unwed or homosexual couples, family members who cannot or will not acknowledge the relationship tolerate it by redefining it to friendship or even honorary kinship. Hence such friends may be accorded the title of "my adopted child," aunt, or uncle. The manner in which the kin react to friends affects both the living relationship and the grief responses.

Grief and the Friend

Since the publication of Freud's classic work *Mourning Melancholia* (1917), scholars have continued to interpret grief as an individual problem that is linked to personal inner psychological reactions to loss. The approaches to both normal and pathological grief are almost exclusively from the framework of the intrapersonal or microscopic level of analysis. Some have tried to define grief as a set of symptoms or a syndrome (Lindemann 1944), while others have viewed grief as a series of tasks. Patterson (1969) states, for example, that "grieving is the gradual process of destroying the intense emotional ties to the dead person . . . and making restitution for the loss" (p. 75). Clayton et al (1968) and Allistair (1970) tell us that the most difficult emotional experience an individual faces is the severing of close relationships to the deceased, yet neither includes relationships beyond the spouse and immediate kin. Others have attempted to identify various stages in the process of bereavement. The number of stages varies from three (Bowlby 1961), to five (Kübler-Ross 1969), to six (Engle 1964). All imply that failure to resolve grief resides in the individual and requires private or group therapy in order to prevent or cure the pathology.

While we do not deny the importance of the microscopic, individualistic interpretations of grief, no analyses of friends in grief can be complete without an examination of several macroscopic social structural variables that contribute to the problem. Grief is not exclusively an intrapersonal problem, although it has been redefined as such. It is not the individual who is the cause of the problem but rather the social structure. As death happens to us all, so grief is a part of our lives. The study of grief is more than the study of symptoms and possible pathology; it is the study of people and their most intimate relationships. While dealing with the individual is necessary, it is not sufficient for understanding non-kin grief.

The fact that society structures family and other relationships, legal responsibilities, and institutions in certain ways creates problems. This becomes increasingly apparent when analyzing the friend-griever. Although family structures, roles, and relationships have changed dramatically over the past few decades, social protocol still assumes that kin are the most important relationships even when the members are isolated or estranged from each other. There appears to be a cultural lag between the social definition of rights and responsibilities of family members, and the reality of social relationships. Even in successful "palimony" cases, the legal rights of kin appear to outweigh the intimate personal concerns.

Many claim that prior preparation (that is, knowing that death is imminent) helps to decrease grief at the time of death. Those closest to the patient deserve some kind of adequate warning, say some physicians. Health care workers claim to espouse the holistic philosophy of care, yet in practice there are policies that negate that possibility. Upon admission to a health care facility, patients are asked to state their nearest of kin. When admissions officers are asked why, patients are told the hospital must have someone to notify in case of emergency. No one seems to consider the fact that the patient may prefer that a non-kin person be notified. In order to name someone else, the patient must lie and state that he or she has no living kin. Hospital personnel are reluctant to discuss the patient's condition with non-kin even when the patient makes such a request, and rarely are non-kin notified of a death.

Many units, including ICU, coronary care, and critical care units have policies that prohibit visitation by nonimmediate kin. It is of course understandable that limitations need to be placed on the number of visitors, but it must be understood that the policy benefits the hospital or nursing home and not necessarily the patient. The latter is rarely consulted in the matter and may be required to see family even if his or her preference is to see someone else. The friend who wishes to visit is forced to lie and become a "family member." It is amazing but understandable to nurses how large the sibling population grows in critical times.

Not only does the health care facility exclude friends during the dying process, but family rights to exclusive visitation outweigh the patient's right to self-determination. Pogrebin (1987) summarizes the situation most eloquently when she describes one man's experience with the dying of his best friend. He says, "When Josh was dying, his wife and children monopolized every last minute for themselves; they couldn't share him" (p. 107). He describes being pushed aside and kept at a distance: "Someone from the family was always around the hospital bed. I wanted to ask them to leave us alone for a minute, but they seemed to resent that I was there at all. I wasn't able to tie up the loose ends before he died. . . . People should realize that friends too need to say good-bye" (p. 107).

At the time of death health care professionals not only do not notify friends but often take special precautions to prevent friends from knowing that death has occurred. In the case of death of the elderly, family often refuse to allow public notification through newspapers, and friends may only discover the fact days or months after the death has occurred. When family members are in competition with friends or disapprove of a friendship, they often take drastic steps to prevent the friend from discovering the death until after all funeral or body disposal activities have been completed.

Society dictates who is a legitimate griever. While numerous studies of grievers, including Jackson (1966), Covill (1968), Durkheim (1915), and Folta and Deck (1973), all demonstrate the importance of the funeral as an integral aspect of grief resolution, family maintain the right to determine whether or not such a ceremony will be held and who may attend. By custom, the accepted definiton of who is bereaved is reserved for spouse and immediate kin. Consolation is often not given to the person closest to the deceased who may be experiencing the highest level of grief. Even that person must defer to the nearest of kin since society expects the latter to experience the greatest grief, with decreasing concern and interest as one moves to distant kin and friends. In fact, society often considers interest in the deceased by non-kin as an infringement upon family rights and prerogatives, and any say in funeral or burial arrangements is considered an intrusion on the sanctity of the family. The legal inheritance rights and financial responsibilities of kinsmen explains some but not all of the concern over "kinship priority" and kin notification.

The decision to hold either no funeral or a private one leads to potential difficulties for both friends and family. Viewing the body presents the moment of truth and allows for no denying of reality. Our studies show that the lack of a funeral or memorial prevents the development of awareness and leads to feelings of disbelief for months and even years after death. For the friend, the only opportunity for mutual sharing of the loss is in his or her peripheral role at the funeral. The private funeral disallows the rights of all except the immediate kin to grieve.

Even when a funeral is planned and public, the social structure of the workplace may prevent participation. Schools, especially colleges and universities, do not recognize the death of a friend as a legitimate cause for absenteeism. Personnel policies in most places of employment rarely allow time off for someone to grieve for a friend, although some will grant time off for a few hours to attend a funeral. Even the airlines have a definition of acceptable grievers. Tickets may be exchanged or refunded only for the death of "a spouse, parent, child or sibling," and then "only with a notarized death certificate and notarized letter stating relationship" (Continental Airlines 1988). Extended kin are eliminated from their acceptable list of grievers.

Social Features of Bereaved Friends

We have terms or labels that signify most types of grievers. Wives and husbands become widows and widowers; children become orphans; brothers and sisters are said to experience sibling loss; but there is no term to describe those who grieve friends. Titles give rise to identity and normative structures, and prescribe expectations for role behavior. The friend who is grieving has no identity, no role recognition, and no function with respect to the deceased. In effect, the grieving friend is in a state of anomie.

The social meaning of the grief period is that the recognized griever is not able, expected, or allowed to function in a normal manner. The family is expected to behave as mourners, experiencing sadness and crying in amounts deemed appropriate. They are expected to perform a variety of functions such as planning the funeral, greeting guests, dealing with funeral directors or clergy. They are prescribed, socially acceptable rules on clothing, places to sit, things to do. These mourners are released from the usual daily tasks of work and play. Not so the friend.

There are no normative arrangements for lovers or friends who are dependent upon or who had strong attachments to the deceased. There are no social expectations that one behave as a mourner and no clearly defined roles or functions with respect to the deceased. Each situation is dependent upon the immediate family's wishes, regardless of the strength or nature of the friendship relationship. Society has accorded the family the power to determine the role of the friend-griever on an individual basis.

Friends may be shunned, ignored, or even met with open hostility by the family who dislike the friend or disapprove of the relationship. It is not uncommon that in situations where friends live together outside the legal bonds of matrimony, are extramarital friends, or are members of the gay community (friends or lovers), the stigma attached to the relationships leads to ostracism by the family. In a recent situation involving two college students who lived together despite family disapproval, when one was killed in an auto accident on holiday break, her parents refused to allow public notification of the death and forbade family, clergy, and the funeral director to notify the young man. Only when he returned to college did he learn of his lover's death. Members of the gay community often report being met with hostility from the families of their deceased friend. Widows, widowers, and children have behaved similarly toward opposite-sex, extramarital friends of the deceased spouse or parent. In the case of the elderly, family often fail to recognize friendship relationships and therefore ignore friends and their grief.

There are, of course, situations in which friends of the deceased are liked or even accorded honorary family membership. In these cases, family often include the friend in the planning of activities and/or recognize the right to grieve. Even in the best of situations, however, the role of the friend-griever is prescribed for the individual by the family. These "rights" are not automatically accorded the friend-griever as they are the kin. This dependence upon the sufferance of kin deprives the friend-griever of formal, and often informal, social resources to assist him or her in grief resolution.

When death occurs in a family, we assume a crisis. Even when kin do not grieve, we rally to their support. A crisis in the family requires the reorganization of roles, functions, and interactive patterns so that it will continue to function as a unit. Such a crisis is believed to be critical but of short duration. No such concern is registered in the case of friendship groups. There is neither an assumption of crisis nor an expectation of the need for reorganization.

Legal constraints further complicate the picture. Friends have no legal status. They enjoy no rights to be notified of illness or death, to make life/death decisions, or to plan or attend funerals, no matter how close the relationship. Among a large number of friends who live together, it is not uncommon practice to purchase material goods jointly. At the time of death, kin not uncommonly either lay claim to the goods or require the friend to purchase the deceased's share. Unless the survivor can prove ownership, even items that she or he owns may be confiscated by kin. In the absence of legal proof of ownership or a will, the friend has no legal rights except as the court may determine. Frequently the level of grief is so intense or the friend is so upset by the perceived lack of respect for the deceased on the part of the family that he or she acquiesces and does not pursue legal redress through the courts. In any event, a dispute over material goods invariably results in a threat to self-esteem.

Consequences

The level of intimacy among friends is higher than in many other social relationships. The demand of friendship for mutual trust, openness, self-disclosure, concern for each other's interests, affection, and warmth leads to intense identification among friends. Thus the death of a friend is a profound loss. Since the identification is so great, the sense of loss of self and the threat to self is very intense. There is both the fear that "it could have been me" and the relief that "it wasn't me."

The death of a friend confronts us with our own death. In the case of young people, it is seen to violate the ideals of fairness, goodness, and justice. With adolescents, the three leading causes of death—accident, suicide, and homicide—occur quickly without warning or preparation. Death of the young appears to be out of the order of life. The violence of the death compounds the problem, and mourning is intense. Even the elderly, for whom the death of friends is more common, experience intense grief and a need to deal with the question of the quality of their remaining life.

It may be that accepting the death of a friend is even more difficult than accepting the idea of one's own death. The death of peers destroys the social network in which the individual is a member. Most friendship groups are dyads. Therefore the death of one means the demise of the group and hence the absence of a social support system.

In multiple friendship groups, death calls for the rearrangement of the group. If the group is to continue, it must reorganize its roles and system of interaction. Because friends are one of the most important sources of information and of social approval and because we test our own opinions, attitudes, and values on them, their loss leads to a search for substitutes but none may be found.

Social institutions often enact social policies that in effect negate the deceased in relation to the friend. This is accomplished by prohibiting open discussion of the deceased and/or the circumstances surrounding the death. This commonly occurs in schools and nursing homes. In one local high school, students were forbidden to discuss or mention by name on the school grounds five students who, after skipping school and consuming alcohol, were killed in a head-on speeding accident that also took the lives of two prominent citizens. Nursing homes frequently attempt to hide death by not mentioning the name of the deceased to other residents and by ignoring questions or falsifying answers about the death.

The public display of emotional responses such as crying and expressions of sadness by the friend-griever is discouraged or misinterpreted. The experience, common among family members, of anger that may erupt in feelings of failure, impulsive acting-out, or even self-destructive behavior is perceived as part of the normal grieving process. When friends have the same experience, it is rarely attributed to grief, and punishment for such behavior is more severe because our society lacks any socially recognizable state of grief for friends.

The expression of strong emotional reactions or prolonged crying or sadness results in the belittling of the meaning and significance of the friendship. Society labels this behavior as unusual and unacceptable. Guilt is superimposed on the remorse, and society implies that the intensity of the reaction to the friendship loss is pathological. This often leads friend-grievers to distance themselves from others, which leads to isolation. Some even break ties with other friends and refuse to enter new friendships for fear of future loss and threat to self-esteem.

All grievers attempt to deal with the painful void caused by the death. This void may be felt as a defect in the sense of intactness and wholeness of self. It may be manifested in the individual by various bodily sensations or pain that is identical to that experienced by the deceased. In the case of the friend-griver, the strong identification with the deceased friend increases the projection of self into the deceased. Not uncommonly the grievers experience extreme concern with their own state of health, make frequent visits to physicians, and become preoccupied with their own possible death. Physicians and other health care workers do not routinely examine for the relationship between health problems and grief. When they do, there is a tendency to make light of the problem and assume that since the loss is not of kin the symptoms will soon disappear. If they do not, the griever may be labeled neurotic.

The family can acceptably talk about and rehash old relationships and receive some comfort and validation from others to resolve their loss. The friend who attempts the same tactics may be ostracized from the group or may even be considered "a little weird" (Folta and Deck 1976). The friend, who may feel remorse, guilt, or regrets about certain aspects of the relationship, has no way to resolve the feelings.

Because friendship is such a unique type of relationship, with shared feelings, secrets, and self-disclosure, after death these experiences cannot be shared or validated. Even the meaning of social events changes. Many joint activities were in large part enjoyable and pleasurable because they were engaged in with a friend and not because of the intrinsic value of the activity itself. Friends help us to define and accept ourselves. Their death creates a loss of our identity and a threat to our self-esteem, and it renders our role as friend meaningless.

Implications

As was stated earlier, with approximately 2 million deaths a year in the United States and three to five friends per person, the magnitude of the problem for friend-grievers is great. Grief is not only an intrapsychic problem, it is also an interpersonal problem. Its resolution is dependent upon the nature of the social structure and context.

Currently there is a beginning awareness of the role of friends in society, but there remains a need for more research to identify systematically the nature of friendship loss through death and its impact on individuals and society. Clearly, we need to investigate the similarities and differences between kin and friend; the long-lasting effects of the death of a friend; the components of social structure that influence the role of friends; and the consequences of social response to friend-grievers. Such research could provide a framework for planning and implementing needed changes in our social structure.

If in fact, prior awareness of death, continuing participation in the social life of the dying, and recognition of death are important determinants of grief resolution for friends, then clearly the health care system must institute change. Ill and dying patients need to have the opportunity to choose the persons whom they wish to have notified, to participate in their care, and to visit them while they are ill or dying. The acknowledgment of the importance of a close friend would enable both the dying and the griever to complete unfinished business and to make their farewells. Further, the inclusion of friends in the care of the dying may reduce pain and fear for the patient and increase self-esteem for the friend.

Nursing homes, retirement communities, and housing projects for the elderly could be effective in assisting friends in grief. Rather than hiding death, the death should be acknowledged to the residents. Special memorial services can be designed by those staff and residents who wish to engage in such activity. Such services can be held in chapels or dining halls where even bedridden patients may have access, and this would acknowledge the significance of the deceased and the rights of friends to mourn. Being able to disclose and display grief publicly provides a setting for social support and may even decrease symptoms commonly experienced by grievers. Not only would this be beneficial for friends but it would serve as a reaffirmation of life. Such memorial services do not require the permission of family, although they too might be invited to participate. For those patients who are physically able and wish to attend customary funerals, staff should make arrangements for attendance. Likewise, in situations where staff have developed a close friendship with a patient, some mechanism should be developed to allow for public recognition of the loss and/or attendance at the funeral.

School systems need to implement similar policies. Classroom teachers need to acknowledge the death of students and provide a milieu in which students can discuss the death and publicly mourn. Assemblies might be held for memorial services designed by the students and teachers. At minimum, special allowances need to be made for students to be absent from class to attend funerals. In certain situations, such as sudden, unexpected deaths, special sessions for close friends are necessary for group support. This presupposes that teachers be adequately prepared to deal with death in the classroom or have access to consultants for this purpose.

Acknowledging the importance of friends by employers would create an awareness of the possibility of the need for extended time off in the case of emergency. Organizations need to develop flexible personnel policies that would allow sufficient time off for employees to participate in caregiving for dying friends and/or for grief resolution upon the death of a close friend. Such policies could result in lower rate of employee illness and absenteeism.

Without changes in the social structure, the friend-grievers will remain a high-risk population. They will continue to be treated as if they caused the problem. This is not merely a personal problem, however, it is a social problem. Grief must be public to be shared and shared to be diminished.

References

Allistair, M. 1970. "Bereavement as a Psychiatric Emergency." *Nursing Times,* July 2, 841–843.

Bell, R.R. 1981. *Worlds of Friendship.* Beverly Hills, Calif.: Sage Publications.

Bowlby, J. 1961. "Process of Mourning." *International Journal of Psychoanalysis* 42, 317–40.

———. 1963. "Pathological Mourning and Childhood Mourning." *Journal of the American Psychoanalytic Association* 11, 500–41.

———. 1980. *Attachment and Loss: Loss, Sadness and Depression*. New York: Basic Books.

Bowling, A., and A. Cartwright. 1982. *Life After a Death: A Study of the Elderly Widowed*. New York: Tavistock.

Clayton, P., L. Desmaraus, and G. Winokus. 1968. "A Study of Normal Bereavement" *American Journal of Psychiatry* 125, 168–178.

Continental Airlines, 1988. Personal communication, March 22.

Corless, I.B., and M. Pittman-Lindeman. 1988. *A.I.D.S.: Principles, Practices, and Politics*. New York: Hemisphere.

Covill, F.J. 1968. "Bereavement—A Public Health Challenge." *Canadian Journal of Public Health* 59, 170.

Derlega, V., and B. Winstead, eds. 1986. *Friendship and Social Interaction*. New York: Springer.

Durkheim, E. 1915. *The Elementary Forms of Religious Life*. Glencoe, Ill.: The Free Press, 1947.

Engle, G.L. 1964. "Grief and Grieving." *American Journal of Nursing*, 64; 93–98.

Folta, J.R., and E.S. Deck. 1973. "Reconstruccion Social Después de la Muerte." *Tribuna Medica*, 26 Oct., pp. 20–21.

———. 1976. "Grief, the Funeral and the Friend. In *Acute Grief and the Funeral*, edited by B. Pine, A.H. Kutscher, D. Peretz, R.C. Slater, R. De Bells, R.J. Volk, and D.J. Cherico. Springfield, Ill.: Thomas.

Freud, S. 1951. "Mourning and Melancholia." In *A General Selection from the Works of Sigmund Freud*, edited by J. Richman. New York: Doubleday, 1957.

Goldmeier, D. 1987. "Psychosocial aspects of A.I.D.S." *British Journal Hospital Medicine* 37. 232–240.

Horn, R. 1979. "Life Can Be a Soap Opera." In *Perspectives on Bereavement*, edited by I. Gerber, A. Weiner, A.H. Kutscher, D. Battini, A. Arkin, and I. Goldberg. New York: Arno Press.

Jackson, E. 1966. *The Christian Funeral*. NY.: Channel Press.

Kelly, J. 1977. "The Aging Male Homosexual: Myth and Reality." *The Gerontologist* 17, 328–32.

Kimmel, D. 1978. "Adult Development and Aging: A Gay Perspective." *Journal of Social Issues* 34, 113–31.

Kübler-Ross, E. 1969. *On Death and Dying*. London: Macmillan.

Levine, S.B. "Single Living: The Growing Population of Women Who Are Changing Our Attitudes and Our Lives." 1984. *Ms.* (Nov.).

Lindemann, E. 1944. "Symptomology and Management of Acute Grief." *American Journal of Psychiatry* 101 (Sept.), 141–48.

Lopata, H.Z. 1975. "Couple-Compassionate Relationships in Marriage and Widowhood." In *Old Family/New Family*, edited by N. Glazer-Malbin. New York: Van Nostrand.

Pogrebin, L.C. 1987. *Among Friends*. New York: McGraw-Hill.

Patterson, R.D. 1969. "Grief and Depression in Old People." *Maryland State Medical Journal* 18, 75–79.

Rando, T. 1984. *Grief, Dying and Death: Clinical Interventions for Caregivers*. Champaign, Ill.: Research Press.

Raphael, A. 1983. *The Anatomy of Bereavement*. New York: Basic Books.

Rubin, L. 1980. *Children's Friendships*. Cambridge: Harvard University Press.

Saunders, J., and S. Valente. 1987. "Bereavement in Survivors of A.I.D.S." Paper presented to symposium on grief, King's College, London, Ontario.

Shulman, N. 1975. "Life-cycle Variation in Patterns of Close Relationships." *Journal of Marriage and the Family* (Nov.), 817–19.

Simmel, G, 1950. *The Sociology of George Simmel*. Trans. Kurt Wolff. New York: Free Press.

U.S. Census. 1985. *Census Report*. Washington, D.C.: Bureau of Census.

Verbrugge, L.M. 1977. "The Structure of Adult Friendship Choices." *Social Forces* (Dec.), 577.

Worden, W. 1982. *Grief Counseling and Grief Therapy*. New York: Springer.

9

Monday Mourning: Managing Employee Grief

Alexis Jay Stein
Howard Robin Winokuer

L oss is an integral part of life. Unfortunately, no one is immune. From the instant of birth until the moment of death, every individual will struggle with the pain that accompanies a loss. Psychiatrist George Engel postulates that loss and the ensuing grief is "psychologically traumatic to the same extent as being severely wounded or burned is physiologically traumatic" (Engel 1961). Engel argues that the equilibrium, health, and well-being of the individual is severely compromised, and it is the mourning process that allows the individual to heal. Although the nature of the impairment varies with the individual and the type of loss, all human beings will experience a period of bereavement. While loss is a universal experience, individuals who are employed are at significant risk: death, divorce, relocation, being laid off, passed over for a job, or being forced into early retirement create additional burdens for the employee.

Approximately 2.5 million people die annually in the United States. For each death, another three lives may be affected. That means that 7.5 million people per year face some form of grief because of death. Since half of that number is employed, it is easy to see the enormous effect grief has on the business environment. Add an additional 1 million people who are coping with separation and divorce and another 4 million people who are dealing with such work-related losses as transfers, job changes, or being passed over for promotion, and you have more than 8.5 million employees, or 16 percent of the workforce, coping with a major personal loss each year (Bolyard 1983, Sprague 1984).

Bereavement following a loss is often a devastating experience. A grieving person is faced with an emotionally rocky journey. While the process is normal and unavoidable, it is nevertheless troublesome and often leaves the individual unable to function within acceptable limits at the workplace. The individual's productivity may be significantly affected, and the cost to business is conservatively estimated in the billions of dollars (Bolyard 1983, McClellan 1985, Myers 1984). Decreased productivity, increased health care costs, absenteeism, and accidents are the primary indicators of a troubled employee.

Loss is an affair of the heart. It is an emotional as well as a psychologically traumatic experience. Work is intellectual, concrete, production oriented, physically and sometimes mentally mechanical. In his exploration of capitalism in the twentieth century, Braverman (1974) examined the nature of the work environment. Building on the works of Marx and Weber, he states that

> the animating principle of motion-time studies and other scientific investiga-
> tions is the view of human beings in machine terms. . . . Since management
> is not interested in the person of the worker, but in the worker as he or she
> is used in office, factory, warehouse, store or transport processes, this view
> from the management point of view [is] not only eminently rational but the
> basis of all calculation. The human being is here regarded as a mechanism
> articulated by hinges, ball-socket-joints, etc. . . . a man may be regarded as
> a chain consisting of the following items: (1) sensory devises . . . (2) a com-
> puting system which responds . . . (3) an amplifying system—the motor-nerve
> ending and muscles . . . (4) mechanical linkages . . . whereby the muscular
> work produces externally observable effects. In this we see not merely the
> terms of a machine analogy used for experimental purposes, nor merely a
> teaching metaphor or didactic device, but in the context of the capitalist
> mode of production the operating theory by which people of one class set into
> motion people of another class. It is the reductive formula that expresses both
> how capital employs labor and what it makes of humanity.

Thus the rules of twentieth-century work are built on a foundation of norms that see the employee as machinelike, devoid of human emotions, and unaffected by personal experiences.

The vision of man as a machine is diametrically opposed to human needs. This kind of work experience fosters an environment in which the expression of feelings is taboo. Loss is a feeling experience, and a period of mourning and bereavement must follow in order for an individual to heal (Worden 1982). A conflict therefore emerges between the needs of the bereaved individual and the goals of the workplace. This conflict leads to disenfranchised grief.

Doka (1986) defines disenfranchised grief "as the grief that persons experience when they incur a loss that is not or cannot be openly acknowledged, publicly mourned, or socially supported." In the norms of the world of work, all losses then become disenfranchised because emotions and feelings are discounted, discouraged, and disallowed. The exception to this unstated rule is loss due to death. However, even mourning as it relates to death is severely constrained by narrowly defined policies that govern acceptable behaviors.

On reviewing personnel policies from a wide range of organizations, including international employers, city government, large national manufacturers, nonprofit agencies, professional firms, and small and medium-sized local manufacturers, the investigators found remarkable similarities.

All companies recognized loss due to death as an acceptable cause for leave or absence from work. However, there was a marked difference in the policies of white-collar and blue-collar workers. For example, although all companies recognized absence from work due to death, blue-collar workers most often had to take leave without pay. An exception was in large companies with unionized workers. White-collar employees seemed to fare a little better, with more benefits and clearly defined guidelines. Listed under such headings as "Funeral Leave," "Emergency Personal Leave," "Authorized Absences with Pay," and "Special Leave," these policies spell out how many days a person can be absent from work and what relationships justify leave with pay. Most companies recognize death of a parent, spouse, sibling, or child; others also recognize grandparents, stepchildren, in-laws, and other kin relations. Though some companies leave time off up to the discretion of the manager, the majority of the companies reviewed provided three days leave with pay for funerals. Several companies spell out in elaborate policies details regarding acceptable leave. Most leave is based on the nature of the relationship. Here is an example of one such policy:

1. Four (4) days in the event of the death of a wife, husband, any legal children, stepchildren, and one (1) male parent or stepparent, and one (1) female parent or stepparent.

2. Three (3) days in the event of the death of a brother, sister, grandfather, grandmother, any grandchildren, or one (1) mother-in-law and father-in-law as defined as the mother or father of an employee's current living spouse.

3. The day of the funeral only in the event of the death of a brother-in-law and sister-in-law who shall be defined as the brother or sister of a current living spouse, or the husband or wife of a sister or brother. The day of the funeral in the event of the death of a son-in-law or daughter-in-law. Son-in-law and daughter-in-law are defined as the current spouse of a current living son or daughter.

In summary, many companies give three days off to help employees cope with the death of a loved one. None of the organizations reviewed had policies on leave for death of a colleague or co-worker. Most companies, however, do have informal policies to address such deaths—that is, time off for the funeral or to visit the family. The investigators also found that other informal responses to the grieving individual or the families of the deceased included the sending of flowers, food, or memorials of one kind or another. Employer responses to grief center on the early days of bereavement. Yet grief research indicates that people are initially in a state of denial and disbelief after a loss and most manifestations of grief often do not begin to show until weeks or months after the event. Bereaved people experience over time impaired decision making, lack of motivation, inability to concentrate, confusion, higher accident rates, and a wide range of other normal but dysfunctional responses. As a result, grieving employees have a higher absentee and sickness rate for many months following a significant loss.

Working individuals spend almost 50 percent of their awake time in the office or factory where they are employed. Often the relationships that develop between co-workers have an intensity and a life all their own, even when the relationship is not carried over into their personal lives. Colleagues working together can develop an emotional dependence upon one another. They may see each other daily; they may work as a team—feeding work one to the other—they may encourage creativity and be motivators for each other; and they may become a support system that enhances their productivity. When this bond is broken, the employee who is left behind is often thrown into a state of anger, confusion, sadness, and helplessness. There is no way for the individual to avoid the absence of his or her co-worker. Work is a constant reminder of the loss. The emptiness and feeling of powerlessness may continue for months, rendering the employee far less productive than normal. The intensity of the feelings depends upon both the nature of the lost relationship and the cause of the separation. For instance, a co-worker who leaves by choice produces different feelings than does a colleague who dies. In addition, the nature of the death plays a major part in the emotions of the remaining co-worker. Thus, stigmatized death such as suicide, murder, or AIDS may evoke great anxiety and guilt, as well as intensified anger, whereas death by natural causes may be somewhat less painful to cope with. Whatever the cause of the loss, the remaining employee is left in a vulnerable state.

The previous discussion outlines the general extent of businesses' stated response to death and of employees' reactions. In a society that has such difficulty dealing with death, which is considered the ultimate loss, other losses, such as divorce, violence, fire, rape, and so on, are hardly even recognized. A review of the literature found it nearly devoid of studies on grief in the workplace. Most references, when available, dealt with death. The investigators' interviews with grieving employees, managers, and bereaved co-workers also centered on death-related grief and the company's response.

Case Studies

Bill

Bill, a twenty-two-year employee with a national insurance company, had an exemplary work record and had earned numerous promotions during his career. At the age of sixty, his wife died suddenly. Bill seemed to adjust well at first, but even he underestimated the emotional toll the death would take. Initially, co-workers were extremely supportive and management was flexible. He returned to work less than a week after his wife's death. He looks back on that time and describes a period of mechanical, robotlike functioning, doing all of his necessary tasks in a satisfactory but perfunctory manner. His co-workers and supervisors seemed relieved that he was in "control" of himself and his situation, and within weeks all mention of his loss, his wife, and his adjustment ceased. For the first six weeks, Bill appeared "normal." However, during the next three months Bill's absentee rate increased 300 percent and his ability to handle his work load became impaired. Over the next six months Bill's performance continued to decline. He had trouble concentrating, making decisions, and managing his time. His productivity was negatively affected but did not become noticeable until months later. He was having an extremely difficult time adjusting to life without his spouse of thirty-eight years. Life seemed meaningless, and the loneliness was unbearable. Bill became socially withdrawn and depressed, he lost weight, and his appearance suffered. His boss kept asking him, "What's wrong Bill? When are you going to be your old self?" Nine months after the death, Bill's supervisor no longer associated his poor performance with his loss. Pressure was brought to bear on Bill, and he was warned that he must improve his output. Bill felt further isolated and abandoned, not only in his personal life but at work too. The next six months were "pure hell." A year and three months after his wife's death the expectation was that he should be fully functioning. Unfortunately, his performance showed little change. He was placed on probation for the next two months and told that he would need to improve or be terminated. Seven months short of early retirement, Bill was let go after twenty-three and a half years of service. Bill went into a deep depression. Under his doctor's direction Bill joined a bereavement group and for the first time he had an opportunity to deal with his grief. Shortly thereafter Bill began his healing journey back into life and living, but he and his company had paid a heavy price. The company lost a valued employee long before it needed to, and Bill was emotionally, intellectually, and financially penalized because of forced early retirement.

Claire

Claire at forty-two was a vice president in a large bank. She had been with the company three and a half years when her fiancé died suddenly of a heart attack. Because she wasn't married, the death was not recognized as one with funeral leave privileges. Claire took several days off, using her "sick leave," and returned to work by the end of the week. Support from co-workers and management consisted of flowers being sent and initial words of caring and concern. Of course, once back at work it was business as usual. Claire found herself crying on and off during the days that followed, and so she kept more and more to herself, keeping the door to her office closed most of the time.

She worked hard to make sure people didn't know she was having a difficult time. Her immediate staff was aware of her pain. They seemed supportive, and her secretary did her best to lighten Claire's load when possible. During a particularly difficult week three months after Paul's death, Claire had to make a major presentation to bank officers and key board members. It took all the energy Claire could muster. Her immediate bosses were unaware of just how hard it was for her to make her report. In fact, since the week Paul died there had been no mention of her situation by any of her fellow officers. The presentation went well, and Claire was pleased with the response. By the time she got home, however, she was extremely depressed and could not stop crying. She stayed out of work the next two days, calling in sick. On her return to the office, she tried to pick up where she had left off, but everything she did became a major effort. In spite of her emotional situation, Claire's department continued to produce at a significant rate. While her performance at work did not suffer, personally Claire experienced extreme pain and turmoil. Her social network at work also suffered because, in Claire's words, "people just don't understand what I'm going through." At her regularly scheduled review, which came six months after Paul's death, her ratings as usual were all excellent. Her supervisor, though, added the following:

> Your personality has changed. You used to be bubbly, outgoing, and smiley—a team player. Now you're quiet and aloof. You're not a team player, you're not holding the team together. Lately I haven't seen you in the role of the leader. You seem at times cynical. I'm not complaining, it's just that I'd hate to see you turn into this kind of person. I'm not being critical. I understand . . .

Her supervisor never mentioned Paul's death or made the connection between her changed behavior and her grief. Instead of acknowledging the quality of her team's performance, he focused on the symptoms of her grief. He missed a golden opportunity to provide a much-needed source of support at a very critical time in her life. The insensitivity and untimeliness of his remarks began a process of alienation for Claire. A year and a half after Paul's death Claire chose to leave her promising future and seek work in a more congenial environment.

Susan

In a metropolitan hospital, Susan worked as part of a team of twelve nurses. Many of them had been together for more than three years. One rainy evening, Susan was involved in an automobile accident. She was rushed to the hospital in critical condition. The following day her co-workers were shocked to learn that Susan had been admitted. The team really pulled together, with the head nurse's supportive direction. Nurses covered for each other so that they could each spend some time with Susan. She died two days later. The nurses continued to perform their duties but in a state of shock. The hospital worked hard to staff the unit in order for some of the nurses to attend the funeral and to be with the family. Several days later a memorial service was held at the hospital, and people were given a chance to remember Susan. A grief counselor was brought in to work with the staff as a group, as well as to provide individual counseling for three nurses who were having a particularly difficult time. The team approach to nursing compounded their grief. The nurses were constantly reminded of their loss and of Susan's absence from the floor. With the help of the grief counselor, four of the nurses set up a support group to help them through the following months. The head nurse's understanding of the grief process helped establish a supportive environment. By acknowledging and dealing with the nurses' grief the hospital averted a potential crisis, and the unit was able to function with a minimal amount of disruption.

Bruce

Bruce had been experiencing depression for the last year and a half. He had taken extended sick leave on a number of occasions. His work was severely affected, and while his co-workers tried to pick up the slack, several colleagues were beginning to resent the added pressure. One day when Bruce was out sick, he committed suicide. The office was astounded. People were walking around in disbelief. For days the department was at a virtual standstill. Bruce's closest friend at work spent most of his days with Bruce's wife and children. The funeral was held on a Saturday, and most of the staff attended. Work in the following weeks looked normal from the outside. However, upon closer examination the aftermath of Bruce's death became more evident. Co-workers experienced anger at Bruce for taking his life; guilt at themselves for their past resentments; feelings of sadness and helplessness over their lack of power to make a difference; and confusion over how it could have happened. It tooks weeks before Bruce's secretary would enter his office. Other people had to go in and clean his desk out. At the regular planning meetings, Bruce's absence was a painful reminder of his death. He had been such an integral part of the process that people was constantly confronted with their loss. Months later, an audio tape with Bruce's voice was inadvertently discovered. For days after it haunted those who had heard it. The staff supported one another in the best way they knew how, but Bruce's death left a painful mark upon them all.

Implications

In the beginning of this chapter the point was made that each year grieving or troubled employees cost management billions of dollars in lost productivity.

This is in direct contrast to the hoped-for vision of the employee as a machine, busily churning out work at a constant pace, impervious to personal experiences. "The 'scientific management' of Frederick Taylor, with its 'time and motion' studies, rote routine and inhumane, machine-like efficiency are no longer the dominant management style of the American industry" (McClellan 1985). Gradually over the last forty years business had begun to address the personal needs of employees. Business could no longer ignore the effect a troubled employee had on productivity and the bottom line. Because of the prevalence of alcohol abuse among many in the work force, the economic costs of alcoholism forced employers to respond. The dramatic rise since the 1950s of employee assistance programs (EAP is used here as a generic term denoting company-approved assistance designed to meet the needs of troubled employees) can best be attributed to economic issues such as decreased productivity and rising health care costs. While humanitarian concerns may also be a motivator, "the preponderance of literature on the subject suggest that economic issues are the major factor in the increased attention that EAP's are receiving" (Myers 1984). In the last ten to fifteen years EAPs have greatly expanded their forms of assistance to employees in need.

As EAPs have ballooned, so have the services and types of problems addressed. It is no longer strange for an EAP to work with such issues as drug abuse, emotional, marital, family, and financial difficulties, as well as alcoholism (Wrich 1988). Unfortunately, only the largest employers generally provide such services: "An estimated 60–70% of all employers with 3,000 or more employees offer EAP's" (Hellan 1986). That still leaves a sizable work population without the benefit of assistance. The other major concern that emerges is that employees are only referred to EAPs when their performance is suffering. Although many programs may encourage self-referral, it is the exception rather than the rule. EAPs can play a significant role in helping an employee cope with personal loss, but it is the work environment itself that must become more accommodating to the needs of grieving employees. A grieving employee is not mentally ill or guilty of aberrant behavior except as defined by the workplace. The range of normal grief includes mental lapses, decreased energy, difficulty in making decisions, anxiety, helplessness, inability to concentrate, preoccupation, social withdrawal, memory gaps, crying, and other seemingly inappropriate (to the work environment) emotional responses. According to Sprague (1984) nearly 16 percent of the work force is going to experience a loss during any given year. Although most grieving people experience some or all of the aforementioned grief reactions, most will not experience long-term debilitating effects or long-term diminished job performance— especially if they are supported by an environment that understands the nature of the grief process and allows for healing to occur over a long period of time. Three to five days of funeral leave cannot begin to address the grieving individual's needs. Healing goes on over a lengthy period of time, with anniversaries, birthdays, and holidays acting as triggers for less productive times. Managers, employers, and knowledgeable co-workers can do much to support grieving employees through this stressful time and thus drastically reduce nonproductive behaviors.

Recommendations

According to one researcher, "There isn't a manager or executive who will not be confronted eventually with death in the workplace" (Kaplan 1985). Companies need to provide training in grief to both managers and employees. For managers this training will provide the information necessary to understand the grief process and so understand grieving employees. For employees it can be a road map through a difficult time. When a co-worker or colleague dies, it is usually left to the supervisor or manager to notify other employees. Managers who have been trained to understand what grieving employees may be experiencing are more sensitive to the needs of their staff. They also learn how to handle their own grief better while supporting those they manage. Managers can do more for a grieving employee by appreciating "what is involved in the process and realizing that the expression of feeling—even during working hours—is a healthy sign that the grieving process is taking place. In fact, managers should worry more about those employees who do not show any signs of emotion after experiencing a loss" (Deffand 1986).

Managers must also understand the time frame of grief. It all too often has a tendency to show up long after the employee is expected to have learned to cope or adjust to his or her loss. It is not strange for a grieving individual to be hardest hit by grief six to nine months after the initial death.

Employers need to understand that grief takes time. It would be helpful for managers to have access to consultants and professionals who are knowledgeable about the grief process. Managers who show interest and understanding in the grieving employee's situation create an atmosphere of trust, helpfulness, and loyalty. It is also extremely important that managers encourage employees to reach out and get the help they need from professionals early in the process. When managers do this, employees get the message that they are important to the company and that the company is willing to intervene and assist them in working through their grief.

The following are recommendations for handling grief in the workplace for employers and managers.

Recommendations for Employers

Broader definition of relationships in personnel policies. "In 1980, there were approximately 1.56 million unmarried heterosexual couples living together, a three-fold increase over 1970. Government statisticians expect that the number of heterosexual cohabiting couples will double in the 1980s" (Katz 1988). Traditional policies limit the definition of significant relationships, ignoring liaisons such as fiancés, cohabiting lovers, lovers, co-workers, friends, and so on. These relationships should also be recognized.

Training and workshops for supervisors, managers, and executives on characteristics of bereavement and support for grieving individuals.

Lunchtime seminars for interested employees on loss as part of life and coping with grief.

Support groups for individuals in the midst of death, divorce, and other loss-related issues.

Bereavement counseling for those recovering from a significant death.

Recommendations for Managers

Private individual meetings when possible to inform co-workers of a colleague's death. This gives staff a chance to express feelings openly and time to adjust to the shock before going into the work situation.

Flexibility in interpreting personnel policies, recognizing that many significant relationships exist outside of traditional definitions (see above explanation).

With sudden or violent death of a co-worker, provide small-group time for people to express themselves. When possible have a mental health professional facilitate the meeting to help employees vent feelings. This act can go a long way toward stabilizing the work environment. Several meetings may be necessary.

Times of crisis require sensitivity and understanding in dealing with employees. Being flexible with schedules, deadlines, and time off helps the employee heal.

Release time for colleagues to visit and support the grieving family.

Acknowledgment of employee death through memorial services, newsletter articles, scholarships, and so forth.

Periodical check-ins with individuals to ensure that they are managing their grief in a healthy manner. This follow-up is a means of support and an affirmation of the employee.

Encourage workers to use outside resources in working through their grief: employee assistance programs, mental health-centers, grief professionals, and so on.

Resources

To Life
P.O. Box 9354
Charlotte, NC 28299
(704) 332-5433

American Association for
  Suicidology
2459 South Ash
Denver, CO 80222

Association for Death Education
  and Counseling
638 Prospect Avenue
Hartford, CT 06105

Foundation of Thanatology
Columbia—Presbyterian Medical
  Center
630 W. 168th Street
New York, NY 10032

Hospice National Office
1901 N. Fort Myer Drive
Suite 307
Arlington, VA 22209

National Sudden Infant Death
  Syndrome Foundation
310 South Michigan Avenue
Chicago, IL 60604

Parents of Murdered Children, Inc.
1739 Bella Vista
Cincinnati, OH 45237

Community Resources

> Widow to Widow groups
> Funeral homes
> Hospice chapters
> Mental health centers
> Employee assistance programs

Conclusion

Grieving employees cost organizations billions of dollars a year. Not only is productivity adversely affected but the quality of the work environment can be vastly impaired. Therefore, the ability of managers to identify employees experiencing grief and loss and to refer them to appropriate resources can be critical to the well-being of the work climate as well as to the individual.

Loss is an integral fact of life. Grief is the outcome of loss and must be experienced by the individual so that he or she can heal. Most people do not have the luxury of taking extended leave. They must keep on working while they put their lives back together. Managers can play a critical role in helping bereaved employees mend as they work through the grieving process (Deffand 1986, Bolyard 1983).

References

Bolyard, C.W. 1983. "Rescuing the Troubled Employee." *Management World* 12, 15–16.

Braverman, H. 1974. *Labor and Monopoly Capital: The Degradation of Work in the Twentieth Century.* New York: Monthly Review Press.

Deffand, M. 1986. "Coping with Personal Loss." *Supervision* 65, 51–54.

Doka, K.J. 1986. "Disenfranchised Grief." Paper presented at the Eighth Annual Meeting of the Association for Death Education and Counseling, Atlanta, Ga.

Engel, G.L. 1961. "Is Grief a Disease? A Challenge for Medical Research." *Psychosomatic Medicine* 23, 18–22.

Hellan, R.T. 1986. "Employee Assistance." *Personnel Journal* 65, 51–54.

Kaplan, G.M. 1985. "A Death in the Office." *Nation's Business* 73: 77.

Katz, J.N. 1988. "Civil Liberties." *American Civil Liberties Union* (Winter), 22.

McClellan, K. 1985. "The Changing Nature of EAP Practice." *Personnel Administrator* 30, 29–37.

Myers, D.W. 1984. "The Troubled Employee." In *Establishing and Building Employee Assistance Programs,* edited by D.W. Myers. Westport, Conn.: Quorum Books.

Sprague, R.L. 1984. "Helping Employees Cope with Personal Loss." *Management World* (Oct.), 26–29.

Worden, J.W. 1982. *Grief Counseling and Grief Therapy.* New York: Springer.

Wrich, J.T. 1988. "Beyond Testing: Coping with Drugs at Work." *Harvard Business Review* 66, 120–28.

10
A Later Loss:
The Grief of Ex-Spouses

Kenneth J. Doka

> For the first time in our history, two people entering marriage are just
> as likely to be parted by divorce as death. (Weitzman 1985, p. 17)

I t is almost unnecessary to remind readers that the divorce rate in the
United States has climbed during the last three decades. Increased
economic opportunities for women, an emerging psychological sense of
entitlement, and changes in divorce laws have all transformed the norms of
marriage and separation. "Till death do us part" has become "as long as our
love lasts." Each year approximately 1.2 million American marriages are dissolved by divorce. Of every ten marriages, close to five will end in divorce.

Yet Weitzman's comment is incomplete. A marriage may end in divorce,
but at some point one ex-spouse will have to face the death of the other, and
this kind of grief is often unrecognized, disenfranchised. For although people
recognize the grief of a spouse, they may very well assume that an ex-spouse,
particularly if the divorce was some time ago, will have no grief reaction.

Relationships do not necessarily end with divorce; they continue to evolve
and change. Ex-spouses are still tied by considerable bonds. They may have
children in common. They may share friends. They may maintain contact
with in-laws, particularly but not exclusively when children are involved.
They may be bound by economic interests and issues of alimony, child support, or joint property.

Beyond these interactional and economic bonds, there may be emotional
ties as well. Ex-spouses may still have strong, albeit highly ambivalent, feelings toward one another. They may be seeking to resolve powerful feelings
of anger and guilt. They may even harbor a fantasy of eventual reconciliation.

Thus even after divorce it is important to remember that a multifaceted
and often conflicted relationship is likely to continue. An earlier study of
divorced spouses found that most divorced couples did form a new, relatively
stable, though not necessarily cordial, relationship (Doka 1986). These rela-

tionships often require continued readjustment and reworking. A recent study of divorces found that while most maintained contact with their ex-spouse, 43 percent were dissatisfied with the new relationship. A similar percentage also expected new issues of conflict to arise, particularly in regard to coparenting concerns (Lyons et al. 1985).

Divorce, then, ends a marriage, not a relationship. The relationship, modified by divorce and the subsequent events in the life of each partner, continues. The forms this relationship can take differ widely. One can envision a series of intersecting continuums, such as the degree of contact and the extent of emotional investment. The content of interaction in each relationship then may have its own place in that field. Figure 10–1 demonstrates how this works.

For example, "A" would represent a divorced couple that parted as "friends," feeling generally positive about each other even after the separation and maintaining high levels of contact and emotional investment. "B" would be a divorced couple that harbors strong negative affect even as constraints

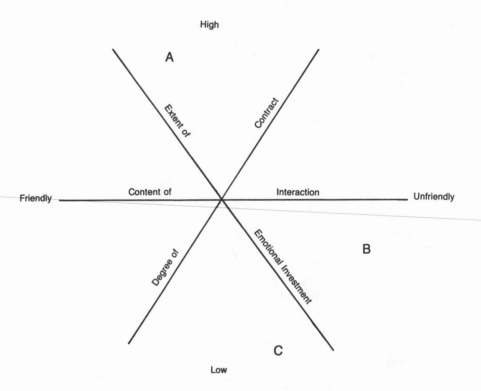

Figure 10–1. Points of Intersection in the Divorced Relationship

maintain them in fairly constant interaction. "C" would represent ex-spouses who have become disengaged. Finally, it should be noted that ex-spouses may define their place in the field differently and that these relationships may change over time.

The fact that relationships continue in some form after a divorce does not imply that ex-spouses do not experience a profound sense of loss at the time of divorce. The experience of divorce can create great grief. Researchers (Kitson et al. 1980) have found that the divorced experienced more mental and physical health disturbances than even widows.

The loss of a divorce may be particularly hard to resolve for a number of reasons. First, grief reactions are often complicated by high levels of guilt, anger, perceived desertion, and ambivalence (Kitson et al. 1980, Raphael 1983, Doka 1986). Second, the divorced tend to have less social support and sympathy than do widows (Kitson et al. 1980, Doka 1986). Third, the fact that the person remains alive may make it difficult to accept the finality of the loss. The divorced and their children may sustain and support fantasies of reform and reconciliation (Raphael 1983, Doka 1986). Finally, continued interaction with the ex-spouse can create additional complications that exacerbate the resolution of grief. As Raphael notes,

> The special difficulty in divorce is that the "bereaved" must mourn someone who has not died and may have to mourn one type of relationship with the partner to reestablish a different one. This is difficult to do at the best of times and the more so when guilt and anger are pronounced. (1983, p. 228)

Nonetheless most people do resolve the loss of a divorce, though this may take many years (Wallerstein and Kelly 1974, Lyons et al. 1985). At this point, as was previously mentioned, a new relationship is formed and the divorced person is able to adjust to a life in which the ex-spouse has a different, often less significant, role. Time certainly is a factor in resolving that loss. And while most divorced people over time do resolve the loss, some do not resolve it even years after the divorce (Doka 1986).

Death After Divorce

What occurs then when people experience a loss upon a loss, when death follows divorce? Both Doka (1986) and Scott (1987) studied this issue and reported similar results.[1] Primarily two patterns of response were found.

In the first pattern, the spouses had resolved their prior loss of the divorce. These spouses described the divorce as a major loss, creating intense grief. Over time, though, they were able to resolve that loss and create a new relationship with the ex-spouse. Generally, the relationship formed was one in which there was not great emotional commitment. In this pattern the impact of the subsequent death of the ex-spouse was minimal. The loss did not seem to cause either long-term psychological trauma or severe social dislocation. Some, however, were troubled by their lack of emotion.

In the second pattern, the ex-spouses reported that they had not resolved the loss of divorce prior to the death of the spouse. Here strong grief reactions, similar to those of widows, were evident. These ex-spouses reported that they often broke down and cried at the news of the death, feeling numbness and surprise. Respondents had difficulty accepting the finality of loss. There were strong affective responses here. Emotions such as guilt and regret were particularly prevalent. In this pattern many of these marriages and divorces were tempestuous. Respondents felt that they may have contributed to the death by the stresses that the relationship and its dissolution created. They sometimes felt that if they hadn't gone through with the divorce the person may not have died. They may have felt moral guilt, regretting words or any wishes that their ex-spouses would die. There was often much unfinished business. And many respondents in their pattern felt a deep sense of anger: against the ex-spouse for placing them in this untenable position; against the ex-spouse's new mate for any role in the dissolution and the usurpation of the spouse role; and against medical staff, friends, clergy, in-laws, or anyone who contributed to their deep sense of discomfort. These feelings of guilt and anger were often exacerbated by the responses of others. For example, in one case a mother-in-law at the funeral publicly accused the ex-spouse of killing her son with the divorce (Doka 1986). Some of Scott's (1987) respondents reported similar angry accusations from children.

Even though there were two patterns of responses, both groups of ex-spouses noted unique problems that can occur when an ex-spouse dies. First, an ex-spouse has an ambiguous role. There was, and perhaps still is, a significant relationship with the former mate, yet they are no longer married. Ex-spouses experience this ambiguity at the time when their former mate is hospitalized. They may feel a desire or an obligation to visit, yet they may also experience discomfort and confusion. There are no norms to guide how long one visits, what one says, or how one interacts with others, such as friends, former in-laws, and even the new spouse, at bedside. They lack legal privilege to medical information and may not be fully informed about the nature, seriousness, and course of the treatment and condition.

The time of death was also very difficult for ex-spouses. They tended to feel slighted at the death notice that ignored them. And they often felt out of place at the funeral. Again, they often did not know how to behave at the funeral—where to sit or what to say. They perceived that their presence created discomfort and confusion for others. Eulogies tended to be stressing. Ex-spouses reported annoyance at not being recognized and anger at any positive reference to a current spouse and present marriage.

This sense of ambiguity often continued after the death. Scott (1987) found almost half her sample did not find friends to be supportive or helpful. Respondents reported that friends often did not know what to say, sometimes even joking about the death. And ex-spouses were unclear on how to respond. There was a lack of social support. They had few people with whom they felt comfortable enough to discuss their reactions (or their lack of feeling). They could not publicly mourn the death without explaining the divorce. Because of the stigma of divorce, they often were reluctant to draw on other sources of support such as clergy. Personnel policies that did not accord time off from work for such loss added to a sense of disenfranchisement.

There were other complications as well. If the surviving ex-spouses had remarried, they faced the difficulty of sharing that grief with the new spouse. Many found their children's reactions difficult. Some were the focal point of their children's anger. Some felt a sense of anger and betrayal if the child expressed grief, while others were concerned by the child's lack of response.

The type of response that any given ex-spouse experiences will depend on many variables. Rando (1984) notes that the intensity of grief reaction is affected by variables such as the circumstances of the death, the relationship and nature of attachment to the deceased, reactions to previous loss, the personality of the bereaved, social variables such as the degree of formal and informal support, cultural practices and beliefs, and the general life-style practices of the bereaved. These variables can be expected to affect the responses of ex-spouses as well. But it is important to consider that the very nature of loss in this situation can create conditions that can complicate grief. For example, Parkes and Weiss (1983) and Rando (1984) affirm that factors that discourage the expression of grief such as lack of meaningful rituals or family support cause problems in grief reactions. And Rando (1984) and Raphael (1983) also state that ambivalent relationships, concurrent crises, and previous losses can negatively influence the course of grief. Many of these circumstances are present in situations in which divorce precedes death.

A critical variable, though, does seem to be the degree to which the ex-spouse has worked through the previous loss of the divorce. Both Doka (1986) and Scott (1987) found that time is a necessary but not sufficient condition for this to occur. In both studies those who experienced a death of an ex-spouse within five years of the divorce tended to have more severe reactions. Most of the respondents whose spouse died following a divorce that occurred more than five years earlier tended not to experience intense grief. The key issue did not seem to be time per se but only time insofar as it allowed the resolution of the earlier loss of the divorce. Both Doka (1986) and Scott (1987) found cases in which there was intense grief at the death of an ex-spouse decades after the divorce. Further research will need to clarify the factors that inhibited earlier resolution of the loss at the time of the divorce.

Considerable research will also need to be done on other variables that might complicate or facilitate the resolution of grief. Differing conditions of divorce, ages at the time of divorce and death, relationships with the ex-spouse prior, during, and after the divorce, relationships with any new spouses, responses of children and significant others—these are all areas that seem fruitful for further exploration.

Before closing this section, it is important to recognize that the ex-spouse is not the only person affected by both the loss of divorce and subsequent death. There has been little research on the grief reactions of children to the loss of a noncustodial parent. But both Doka's (1986) and Scott's (1987) research suggest problems that may complicate the resolution of grief. While children's (including adult children's) reactions tended to be highly idiosyncratic—depending upon their age, coping style, relationship with the noncustodial parent prior to the divorce, relationship after the divorce, and response to the divorce—their reactions (or even lack of response) often did trouble parents. It may very well be that children in such cases receive ambivalent messages from the surviving parent. If they mourn the loss, they may feel or be made to feel disloyal to the custodial parent (and, perhaps, to the new step-parent). If they do not mourn the loss, they may think that they are ungrateful or unfeeling. Grief responses such as anger or guilt can cause renewed stress and tensions with the surviving parent. In addition, the loss of the non-custodial parent may leave feelings over the divorce still unresolved, eliminate fantasies of reconciliation, create anxiety about the health of surviving parent, and remove the respite (and perhaps an alternate option) that visits with the noncustodial parent provided.

Implications for Counselors

In general, dealing with cases of disenfranchised grief may become increasingly common for counselors. Certainly the very nature of disenfranchised grief means that bereaved who experience it may be less likely to receive informal social support and thus be more dependent on formal sources of support. And the experience of losing an ex-spouse will become more prevalent as cohorts with higher divorce rates age.

In the past decade there have been some excellent treatments of the nature and principles of grief counseling (see, for example, Rando 1984, Raphael 1983, Worden 1982). While the paradigms presented there provide a foundation for grief counseling, counselors will need to be sensitive to specific concerns that may be evident in this type of loss. Five concerns will be considered here.

Clients may need, first, to recognize that a loss in fact occurred. Since the loss of an ex-spouse is generally not socially recognized, bereaved ex-spouses may internalize a belief that they have no right, role, or reason to grieve. Counselors may need to help bereaved clients recognize that they may have experienced a real loss and subsequently are reacting with grief. Specifically counselors may wish to

Explore the history and nature of the relationship with the ex-spouse. By exploring the relationship prior to, during, and after the divorce, bereaved ex-spouses may be moved to recognize the commitment and affect that was, and may still be, invested in the relationship, thereby validating their sense of loss.

Examine their sense of and response to loss at the time of divorce. This has dual function. First, it may indicate ways in which bereaved ex-spouses cope with loss. Second, it may evidence a need to resolve the prior loss of divorce.

Review any physical, cognitive, emotional, or behavioral changes that clients may have experienced in reaction to the anticipation or reality of loss. The counselor's goal here is to help clients recognize and identify any symptoms of grief. Since clients may deny any grief reaction, it is perhaps best to explore such reactions in a way that is independent of the loss. Questions such as "Have you experienced any differences in the way you feel over the past six months (or at any time encompassed by the loss)?" are open-ended enough to minimize denial while providing a basis for evaluating factors that might have caused such change.

Second, clients may need to verbalize and explore any affective responses to the loss of an ex-spouse. Since bereaved ex-spouses may have limited social support, they may have a great need for an opportunity to vent their feeling in a supportive and nonjudgmental environment. Specifically counselors may wish to

Examine and begin to resolve the range of emotional responses that bereaved ex-spouses experience. Counselors will need to be particularly sensitive to unresolved anger and guilt.

Explore any unresolved feelings from past losses, particularly the divorce.

Examine any ambivalent feelings toward the ex-spouse and the divorce.

Normalize and assist clients in interpreting affective responses to the loss, including any lack of affect. Bereaved often need to hear and understand that their affective responses to the loss are indeed normal and understandable. Since knowledge about the nature of grief is often limited, the bereaved generally lack a clear set of norms on how and what they're supposed to feel, complicating any interpretation of response. This is particularly true in cases of disenfranchised grief. The bereaved ex-spouse may believe that any emotional response to the loss of the ex-spouse is incomprehensible or deviant. Conversely, the lack of any response may cause the ex-spouse to question his or her own emotional capabilities and original commitment to the relationship, perhaps even exacerbating feelings at the time of the divorce. Yet both types of responses are typical and understandable in the loss of an ex-spouse.

Review the reactions of children and significant others and examine the ex-spouse's responses to those reactions. The ex-spouse is not only reacting to the loss but also to the reactions of others in the environment, such as children, relatives, in-laws, friends, the new spouse or significant other, and perhaps even the deceased's present spouse. It is helpful then to explore with ex-spouses how these people are responding both to the loss and to them, and to examine the ways in which these reactions are facilitating or complicating their grief, as well as the reactions ex-spouses are having to both these responses. Ex-spouses may need to be encouraged to develop strategies for dealing with responses that they find destructive to their grieving, such as friends who "congratulate" them on the loss.

Examine any unresolved tensions or difficulties that emerged in the course of the illness or funeral. In addition to any difficult responses to friends or family, ex-spouses may still have unresolved anger resulting from problems experienced during the course of illness or at the funeral. There may be anger at medical personnel or hospitals for policies and procedures that excluded the ex-spouse. There may be anger resulting from their treatment at the funeral or toward responses of clergy. They may feel personnel policies that did not recognize a right to grieve were unfair. Since these types of experiences are not uncommon among ex-spouses, it is worthwhile to trace their role and reactions during the illness (for example, how did they find out about the illness? Did they visit? How were they treated? What were they feeling? What factors led them not to visit?), and at the funeral (What were they feeling? How did they make the decision to attend or not to attend? How did people respond to their presence? What do they remember of the eulogy/ homily? How comfortable were they at the funeral? Did they receive time off from work?)

Identify and work to resolve unfinished business. In the loss of an ex-spouse there may be a considerable amount of unfinished business. There may be things ex-spouses need to do, such as ventilate feelings, forgive or ask forgiveness, say a final goodbye. Thus, assisting the bereaved ex-spouse in identifying and resolving such business can be critical. Letters to the deceased ex-spouse, talks at the graveside, diaries, and talking to empty chairs are standard and effective ways of resolving such unfinished issues. Rituals too remain a powerful tool in completing unfinished business and in resolving grief (Rando 1984, Hart 1988). Since the ex-spouse is often excluded from planning, participating, or even attending funeral rituals, the counselor may find it helpful to assist ex-spouses in developing meaningful alternate rituals.

Third, clients should explore the ways in which the death of an ex-spouse may affect their lives. The divorced and the widowed experience a great sense of change at the time of loss. The death of an ex-spouse may effect profound or subtle changes the surviving ex-spouse's life as well. Counselors then may wish to explore with clients

Financial implications of the death. The death of an ex-spouse ends any alimony or child support. Children, or perhaps even ex-spouses, may receive insurance or a legacy, complicating feelings of gratitude or guilt.

Changes in the patterns of their own lives. If there was an ongoing relationship with ex-spouse, this will mean that the survivor's life will change. It may be as subtle as lacking a person to call to discuss common problems with children or as profound as now becoming the custodial parent.

Changes in the patterns of lives of any children. The children's lives may change as well. There may no longer be a place to go on weekends or holidays. Children may lose a meaningful relationship or even the fantasy of one. The response of the child to such changes may affect the life of the surviving ex-spouse.

Changes in the relationship with others. Most ex-spouses in an earlier study (Doka 1986) reported that the death of an ex-spouse changed their relationships with others. In many cases a last link with ex-in-laws was severed, but in a few, the death of an ex-spouse led to reconciliation with in-laws. In all of these areas, counselors should explore with clients both the ways in which the death will affect the nature of their lives, and their reactions to such changes. By assisting clients to identify prospective changes in their lives, counselors facilitate the clients' sense of coping and control.

Fourth, the counselor should allow the ex-spouse the opportunity to withdraw emotionally from the deceased. One of the major tasks of grief is to withdraw emotional energy from the deceased and reinvest it in others (Worden 1982, Rando 1984). The ex-spouse may still have emotional energy invested in the deceased ex-spouse that will need to be released. Specifically, counselors will wish to

Explore with the ex-spouse any remaining emotional ties.

Work through any fantasies of restoration and reconciliation that are ended by the death.

Develop creative ways to say goodbye, if there is a need. Rituals are an extremely effective way to deal with grief. As was stated earlier, the lack of rituals surrounding divorce and the possible inability of the ex-spouse to participate in a meaningful way in the funeral may limit the therapeutic role of such rituals for the ex-spouse. If there is a need, the counselor can assist the client in developing a meaningful way to say goodbye. Perhaps it will be a private mass, a small memorial service, or even a letter read and burned at graveside.

Explore the ex-spouse's attitudes toward the development of other relationships. Some ex-spouses may have experienced such pain at the time of divorce (and the subsequent death) that they are reluctant to develop new relationships. The counselor can assist the client in assessing how these events affected their attitudes toward relationships and in developing appropriate engagements with others.

And fifth, the counselor and the client will want to explore the implications of the experience for the ex-spouse's faith and philosophy of life. A loss may deeply challenge our beliefs about both God and the nature of the world. Therefore the counselors will wish to explore just how this loss has affected the ex-spouse's belief structure. The goal here is to assist the ex-spouse in achieving a sense of reconciliation with the self, the deceased ex-spouse, and, if meaningful, God. This may be an effective area for resolving any bitterness that still exists. A view that the deceased ex-spouse received his or her "just desserts" may be emotionally satisfying, but it can lead to delayed grief reactions and complicate later loss.

Conclusion

It is important to reaffirm that not every ex-spouse will experience a grief reaction to that loss. Just as there are multiple variables that affect any individual's response to loss, so there are many variables that frame an ex-spouse's response. And in many cases, a sense of loss may be mitigated by an earlier, effective resolution of the divorce. Yet the very recognition that ex-spouses can, will, and do grieve will ease the sense of disenfranchisement that minimizes and negates such loss.

Note

1. Both studies have very limited databases. Doka conducted intensive in-depth interviews with eight volunteers from the New York–New Jersey region. Scott used mailed questionnaires on a sample of seventy-one volunteers from fifteen different states. While this database is very limiting, the fact that their conclusions converged gives one greater confidence in the findings. A basic principle in the interpretation of research is the principle of "triangulation"—that is, the more that dissimilar methods yield similar results, the more confidence you can have in those results.

References

Doka, K.J. 1986. "Loss upon Loss. The Impact of Death After Divorce." *Death Studies* 10, 441–50.

Hart, Orno Van der. 1988. *Coping with Loss: The Therapeutic Value of Leave-Taking Rituals.* New York: Irvington Press.

Kitson, G.C., H.Z. Lopath, W.M. Holmes, and S.M. Meyering. 1980. "Divorcées and Widows: Similarities and Differences." *American Journal of Orthospychiatry* 50, 291–301.

Lyons, G., M.L. Silverman, G.W. Howe, G. Bishop, and B. Armstrong. 1985. "Stages of Divorce: Implications for Service Delivery." *Social Casework* 66, 259–67.

Parkes, C.M., and R.S. Weiss. 1983. *Recovery from Bereavement.* New York: Basic Books.

Rando, T.A. 1984. *Grief, Dying, and Death.* Champaign, Ill.: Research Press.

Raphael, B. 1983. *The Anatomy of Bereavement.* New York: Basic Books.

Scott, S. 1987. "Grief Reactions to the Death of a Divorced Spouse." In *Death: Completion and Discovery,* edited by C. Corr and R.A. Pacbolsk. Lakewood, Ohio: Association for Death Education and Counseling.

Wallerstein, J., and J. Kelly. 1974. "The Effects of Parental Divorce: The Adolescent Experience." In *The Child in His Family,* edited by J. Anthony and C. Koupurnik. New York: Wiley.

Weitzman, L.J. 1985. *The Divorce Revolution: The Unexpected Social and Economic Consequences for Women and Children in America.* New York: Free Press.

Worden, J.W. 1982. *Grief Counseling and Grief Therapy.* New York: Springer.

Part III
Disenfranchised Loss

I n some cases, grief is disenfranchised because the loss is simply not recognized as significant or important. Hence, any experience of grief is simply not considered legitimate.

Peppers, Ryan, and Nichols discuss losses that occur prior to or soon after birth. Nichols's chapter on perinatal loss affirms that individuals can and do develop significant attachments to a child prior to birth, and as a result they will mourn the death of that child. But that mourning is often complicated by the social perception that since the parents have had only minimal contact with the baby, any loss is slight. Writing from a personal perspective, Ryan affirms that the loss is experienced by fathers as well as by mothers. Moving from a similar perspective on human bonding, Peppers asks whether there is grief when the loss is elective, as when women choose to terminate the pregnancy by abortion. Peppers concludes that there is grief and that the extent of grief is affected by a number of variables, and he suggests clinical implications for grief and family planning counselors.

Stewart, Thrush, and Paulus extend this notion of bonding. Humans are also capable of developing bonds with other species, and the human-pet bond is often rich, complex, and therapeutic. Thus, the loss of a pet can cause grief. The authors emphasize that loss in one vulnerable population, the elderly, where pets may also be daily companions; the conclusions may be extended to other vulnerable groups as well. Children, for example, are often especially attached to their pets, and although they are often supported when they experience such loss, adults need to be aware that as they respond to their child's loss, they have an excellent opportunity to teach the child healthy ways to grieve. Other especially vulnerable people may be those for whom the pet is a significant living link to an earlier loss, or in those in the rare situation in which they and the pet share a similar condition, and thus the death of the pet presages the mortality of the owner. While these examples highlight particular vulnerabilities, they do not mean to deny that anyone who is attached to an animal will experience grief at the loss of that pet.

The concluding chapters in this section make an important point. Most of the losses we experience are not due to physical death. Martin points out that divorce is a significant loss and that in some ways, because it lacks the social support and rituals that surround death, it may be more difficult to resolve. LaGrand addresses the issue of the loss of significant love relationships, noting how these losses are often deeply mourned and generally discounted. Finally, Doka and Aber consider "psychosocial losses," in which the person is still physically present but so changed that others may mourn the person "as he or she previously existed." These chapters then remind us of the many, often multiple losses that people experience in their daily lives, such as the loss of or change of friends, jobs, situations, and homes, all of which may be, in their own particular ways, mourned.

11
Perinatal Death

Jane A. Nichols

"You're lucky you never took him home."

"You're young; you can have another."

"He would have been a vegetable."

"You're lucky it happened now; she would have been such a burden."

"At least you don't have to get up with her in the middle of the night."

"You have your other children."

"Well, it happens in life."

Clichés like these are commonly heard by parents whose newborn infant has died. They are clichés that write off the experience of other human beings; statements that discount grief; remarks that say "never mind"; words that sear into the heart and create chasms in relationships. They are statements of disenfranchised loss.

When a newborn dies, parents grieve (Benfield, Leib, and Reuter 1976). Yet the world that surrounds them tends to discount their loss, and emotional and cultural supports that are normally available to grievers often are not present for this group of parents. For example: newborn death notices are prohibited by many newspapers; there are no sympathy cards on the market for this specific loss, as there are for "father" or "mother"; clergy are often unwilling to baptize dying babies, so it feels as though these infants "don't count"; funeralization, public visitation, and viewing are frequently discouraged; some hospitals take on the responsibility of burial, using common, unmarked graves; few books address the unique issues of newborn death; many counselors and therapists are among the ranks of those who do not recognize the potential for grief, or the need for emotional support and the therapeutic process. In these ways, bereaved parents get the message that

Preparation of this chapter was supported in part by the Ohio Department of Health, Maternal and Child Health Grant 523-E8.

"nothing *really* happened here," are deprived of validation, and are left on their own to do the work of mourning.

Circumstances

The term *perinatal death* refers to the death of infants after the twentieth week of gestation and through at least the first month after birth.[1] The most common cause of newborn death is premature birth—that is, birth prior to the time when the baby's lungs and other organs are mature enough to sustain life. In the Regional Neonatal Intensive Care Unit (NICU) of Children's Hospital Medical Center of Akron, Ohio, about half of the deaths occur within the first three days of life when mothers are still confined to the hospital of birth. Since the United States has regionalized systems of care for sick newborns, many infants are separated from their mothers during the few days of their lives and at the time of death. Fathers, in this scene, are caught between the need to be with the mother at the hospital of birth and the desire to be with the baby in the NICU, which is often several miles away.

There are other circumstances in which newborn death occurs and which can complicate the grief of parents. Some of these include:

The death of one twin, with the other twin surviving or dying at a later time

Death after many weeks or months of care in the NICU—weeks in which family members ride on a roller coaster of emotion and thought between hope for life and fear of death

Sudden, unexpected death in utero after which the mother must labor for the dead-birth of her baby

Anticipated death due to a genetic flaw or a handicapping condition detected in utero by prenatal testing

Death due to a prenatal infection caused by a bacteria that is normally present and unharmful but for unknown reasons suddenly becomes overwhelmingly lethal to a particular baby

Death as a result of a parental decision to remove the infant from respirator support or to induce labor prematurely because of an irreversible, fatal condition of the baby. In this case, parents and caregivers alike may presume that the parents have no "right" to grieve; an element of shame about the decision may also be present, and grief, therefore, may be hidden.

These circumstances, and others, influence the grieving patterns and post-death needs of family members and should be taken into account when dealing with surviving parents.

Parent Response

> My baby, my child,
> The child of my dreams.
> The dream of my dreams.
>
> Where are you?
> Why can't I have you?
> Why must you stay away beyond my grasp?
> No one knows you but me.
> I love you.
> —Mom (Anonymous)

When a baby dies, parents respond with a natural collection of reactions similar to those observed in other mourners: shock, disbelief, anger, bewilderment, guilt, yearning, and others. Physical, mental, emotional, and spiritual grief reactions noted in traditional grief literature (Kübler-Ross 1969, Parkes 1974, Rando 1984, Worden 1982) are also present in parents of newborns. There are, however, some unique distinctions that affect postdeath needs as well as parental grief.

As indicated previously, our culture is highly ambivalent about the value of a newly born or defective infant. There is often an erroneous assumption that because the relationship between a newly born infant and a parent is one that is expected to exist primarily in the future, that the bonds that are joined throughout pregnancy are thus negated or nonexistent. Those who hold these attitudes are apt, then, to be unresponsive toward both the loss and the grieving parents.

Second, although there may be strong spiritual, physical, and emotional bonds with the baby, many parents have not had the opportunity to "get to know" their child in this world, nor have they had the opportunity to move into their parenting role with him. The extended family has also not had the opportunity to know this child, and therefore may not share in the parents' grief, or even recognize it. These circumstances may present a special need for parents to "introduce" the child, to talk about her, to show pictures of him, to help command a spot for this baby within the family circle.

Next, newly delivered mothers may be physically weary or sedated. They may also be influenced by postpartum hormonal changes and the emotional flux that frequently accompanies them. Postdeath decision making, then, may need to be delayed until the mother has had a chance to restore her balance somewhat. Further, labor and delivery have chemically prepared the woman to mother her baby, to nurture and care for her newborn. Separated at birth, the mother may be physically and emotionally aching to be with her infant. Additionally, breast milk may be an unpleasant and physically painful reminder that there is no baby. Health care personnel need to be attentive to this special need in more creative ways than just administering the traditional "shot" to prevent lactation. Some mothers are reluctant to receive that kind of treatment, hoping that the baby will survive and need her nutrition. Furthermore, for many mothers stopping lactation prior to the baby's death is like sending a "die" message to her child, so that that approach is not acceptable.

Cause of death, guilt, and self-blame can be particularly major issues for parents and an especially heavy burden for the mother, since the baby was so recently created by the two, and nurtured and borne by the woman. Additionally, as the abortion rate increases, there is a growing number of mothers for whom perinatal death triggers old wounds and regrets about decisions made in the past. Issues of feelings of lowered self-worth may thus emerge.

The terminal illness or death of a baby also appears to trigger spiritual and religious issues in parents much more quickly than with deaths of older people. These issues tend to focus on questions such as, "Why would God do this to an innocent child?" "What kind of God would do this?" "How can this be fair?" "Do we reap what we sow?" Many caregivers respond to these questions with pat answers or by ignoring them rather than engaging in an exploratory process. In this way, parents may be left with a sense of spiritual amputation and yet another loss to grieve. Further, the sense that a baby's death is unfair, "not right," and undeserved elicits prompt and powerful anger in grievers. Caregivers frequently misunderstand this kind of anger, are put off by it, and parents can be further isolated.

Another issue for bereaved parents is how to relate to their other children. The cliché "you have your other children" suggests that the other children are a source of comfort and perhaps could even take the place of the one who has died. Frequently nothing could be further from the truth for grieving parents. No other child replaces the one who died. Further, children can interrupt and intrude upon the grief of parents simply because they are naturally being themselves. In addition, many parents do not know how to tell their children about the baby's illness or death, nor do they know how to help the children. Parents are usually confused and frightened that they may "do harm." Supportive care combined with adequate information about how children grieve and the nature of their needs can be extremely helpful to parents.

Relationships can add difficulty to the course of grief for parents of newborns. Many grandparents, themselves grievers, seek to protect their "children" and may not have relinquished their role of parenting their now adult offspring, thus adding an unusual dynamic to parental grief. Frequently grandparents interfere with or attempt to take over decision making. "Children" may be reactive to good advice or may passively follow well-meant but poor advice. One mother described it this way: "It's amazing how much our family had always been interfering with our lives! Grief wasn't destroying us; it was us allowing them to destroy us." Aftercare often involves a process of *unlayering* grief, with parents first needing to deal with issues about the grandparents before they can get to their grief issues.

Many bereaved parents discover that their young social friends, unskilled in ways of being supportive and caught up in being young adults and building fresh lives, find it particularly difficult to take time out to stand quietly alongside the grieving parents; parents may feel deserted. Many young friends are having babies of their own; grieving parents can feel jealous and hateful. Young friends, focusing on which car to buy or fussing over "whether we go to his family's party or hers," may seem inane and trite to bereaved parents; they may question their ability to select friends.

The relationship between mother and father can be strained also. The cliché "you have each other" is not necessarily true. On the surface it may appear that they have been through so much together that their bond is strengthened. But the emotions of grief do not necessarily create a tighter bond. Parents grieve differently; and grieving differently, they may not have the energy or skill needed to minister to one another. Parents grieve different things. A father, for example, may be grieving a "namesake," whereas a mother may be grieving "something of her own." Additionally, parents do not experience the same feelings at the same time—that is, they grieve incongruently. Further, men and women tend to use different coping skills with which to ease their pain and release their grief. He may decide to take a second job, whereas she may want to be held and cuddled. If parents do not understand these dynamics, they run the risk of losing the illusion about each other. One can easily see the potential for disruption.

Further, studies also indicate that men tend to have fewer symptoms of grief than do women, and that men tend to experience their symptoms of grief for a shorter period of time than do women when their baby has died (Nichols 1987a and 1987b). Having apparently recovered from their grief, fathers may join the ranks of others who urge mothers to "get over it" or who imply "there is something wrong with you" if the mother's grief persists. Mothers, on the other hand, may suspect that the father did not love the baby enough to grieve as long as she. She may even wonder if he loved the baby at all. Many factors other than love influence the duration and intensity of grief. Parents can benefit from knowing there are differences and can be coached in learning how to honor them in each other, rather than letting them become a source of additional grief and suffering.

A final unique aspect of the grief that parents experience following a perinatal death is that many parents are reluctant to complete their grief because, they say, to do so feels as though they are "abandoning" the baby. Since other people did not honor the life of their child, many parents feel they must "hold on," even when they are otherwise ready to "let go and move on."

All of the circumstances and unique aspects of perinatal death occur against the backdrop of two significant factors that influence grief in general in our society. First, there is an impatience with grief, especially when it has moved beyond the acute phase—that is, there is a cultural desire either to get grief over with or to avoid it altogether. Second, we tend to be unskilled or inhibited about expressing and releasing emotion in ways that are rich and full and cleansing; we tend to be wimpy about our expression of feelings. These two factors strongly repress the ways we grieve.

Caregiving Response

The therapy for unrecognized loss is to recognize it. Parental grief is facilitated when those people who are present honor the fact that something significant has occurred: A child was born, a child has died. Who was she? What gifts did he bring? What have we to learn? How do we go on?

Many caregivers have begun to acknowledge what parents have always known. They have known that when a baby is born, most (but not all) parents wish to see, touch, hold, talk to, comfort, sing to, snuggle, explore, and protect their baby. Whether the baby is normally formed, deformed, alive, or dead does not appear to alter significantly these desires for most parents. Caregivers have learned to facilitate parents' getting to know their baby before they must say goodbye and let him go. They have learned to do it by offering parents the opportunity to spend time with the child, by letting them know it is okay (but not mandatory) to be with the dying baby, by providing privacy, by showing their personal acceptance of the baby herself, and by trusting parents' intuitive wisdom about what they want and what they need at this poignant and powerful time in their lives (Down 1986, Nichols 1987a, 1987b).

As caregivers have become more skilled in engaging in the hello-goodbye process with parents, many have also learned that if they are quietly in the presence of parents as the parents interact with their dying or dead child, many spontaneous healing events occur and the moments can be transformational: sadness can turn into peace. As a co-worker said to me recently, "If parents are allowed to orchestrate the scenario during and after their child's death, it often becomes a lovely pageant . . . and it's often not sad."

Some parents bathe their baby, some shampoo her hair. Some dress the baby; others undress him. Some take the baby out into the sunshine; others have invited her brothers and sisters to sing to her. None of these behaviors is considered bizarre or unusual. They are considered spontaneous responses to legitimate needs of parents who want to "parent" this child and who are say-ing hello and goodbye at the same time. Many caregivers recognize that these responses are also creating memories and a concrete focus for parents who otherwise may not know who or what they are grieving. Although these behaviors do not end grief, they relieve it and meet many immediate needs.

If the mother is still confined to the hospital of birth, caregivers may need to arrange for a special pass or possibly ambulance transportation so that she can have the opportunity to be with her child. If that is not possible, one could consider taking the baby back to the mother in the hospital of birth after the death has occurred, prior to transport to the funeral home.

Other caregiving responses believed to honor the baby and recognize and respect the parents' grief include naming the baby and using the name; taking pictures, especially of parents holding the baby; providing footprints, a lock of hair, the hospital bracelet, and other memorabilia to parents. Many mothers and fathers view baptism as the only means of "protection" they can offer their baby. If clergy are unwilling to baptize the infant because they con-sider it theologically unnecessary, caregivers or parents can perform the rite at the hospital or the funeral home. Hospital rules regarding visiting hours and number of visitors can be made flexible at this time so as to accommodate grandparents, siblings, and other significant people (remember too that some-times friends are more significant than family) in "getting to know" the baby. This also provides hospital personnel with an opportunity to coach the extended family on the significance of the event and to suggest ways in which the family can be supportive.

Personally designed birth and death announcements can be sent to friends. Personalized, creative funeralization, in keeping with family tradition and taste, can be encouraged. Arranging for the funeral can be therapeutic for both parents; mothers should not be excluded, if they wish to be there. Partic-ipating in the funeral service can also be helpful. Some parents prepare special music or write a poem for the occasion. Siblings can take part. A ritual to name the baby can be incorporated into the service. Clergy can be helpful if, in the funeral service, they publicly acknowledge the legitimacy of parental grief. Additionally, using metaphors, such as "rosebuds" or "angels" instead of referring personally to the baby, should be done with discretion since met-aphors can add to the disenfranchisement of loss.

Memorialization may be particularly important when responding to dis-enfranchised loss. "The world must have tangible proof that my child lived and was cared for" seems to be the sentiment. For this reason, grave markers can be significant; many parents spend a great deal of time personally design-ing their baby's headstone. Others burn a special candle on holidays, create a memorial garden, or plant a tree. Some contribute money to a special char-ity; others provide a gift in their child's name to an organization. One father, a carpenter by trade, donated a whole summer using his skill to restore a sailing vessel for a museum and memorialized his baby son by placing his name plaque on the completed project. Frequently, it takes a considerable amount of time before parents identify just the "right" way to commemorate their child. Additionally, many communities now sponsor an annual remembrance service for bereaved parents and families as a special time to honor the child's memory.

Providing an opportunity for follow-up and long-term support is another avenue for caregiving response. Many physicians offer couples the opportunity to attend a follow-up interview to review the baby's clinical course, explore implications of this information for future pregnancies and other family members, and raise questions regarding possible genetic implications. The two questions most frequently asked by parents are, "Why did this happen?" and "Will it happen again?" For this reason, an autopsy followed by a discussion with parents may be highly desirable. Such a meeting may also greatly reduce the amount of blame and guilt which some parents carry.

Follow-up care also provides the opportunity for caring others to "bear witness" to the experience, pain, and grief of parents and may be especially important to the resolution of disenfranchised loss. Whether by parent support group, individual or group therapy, or any other means, sympathetic acknowledgment of a parent's distress can be healing.

Many parents also need and desire sympathetic comforting: the holding, rocking, cradling gestures exchanged between two human beings who care and who are willing to be present to each other without need of discussion. This presents a curious circumstance that is not unique to perinatal death but is still worthy of mention in this context. In our culture women have been assigned the major responsibility for nurturing, sustaining, and comforting. Women nurture and sustain their children, their men, their world. Although women are often each other's best friends, there is a cultural prohibition for women *openly* to minister to and comfort one another. Further, in a society that has become increasingly confused and anxious about sexuality, same-sex touching, regardless of gender, is also unsanctioned. If the woman, then, is the primary long-term griever of infant death, who "mothers" the mother? If she is the caretaker, who will take care of her? For many, the answer is "no one." Caregivers may need to challenge gently this potential deprivation among women, uncover the secret that most women *are* best friends, explore options, and perhaps (if the caregiver is a woman) provide the needed comfort.

Long-term support also provides an opportunity for parents to explore ways of gaining relief from and eventually releasing feelings and thoughts that are troublesome to them. Issues of guilt, jealousy, protectiveness of or coldness toward surviving siblings, anger with God and other religious-spiritual matters, and dealing creatively with anger are concerns that frequently surface in such sessions.

Parents often need to be taught how to express and release anger in ways that are safe to themselves and to others. They may need permission to be angry with God, to be coached in learning how to express their agony, and how to make peace with their Higher Source. Many need to learn how to forgive themselves and others. Others require assistance in identifying the gifts that the baby and the circumstances brought.

If parents have been deprived of the opportunity to see, touch, or hold their baby at the hospital or funeral home, they may experience a vagueness about who or what they have lost. Their grief may be shadowy and thus difficult to deal with. Creative therapy can help parents gain a focus for their grief (Panuthos and Romeo 1984). The use of imagery, gestalt-type therapy, or art can be used successfully by parents who need to create a more concrete image of their lost child. One mother drew a pencil-sketch of what she imagined her daughter had looked like, then framed the work and placed it among the school pictures of her other children on the living room wall, so as to complete the family circle and also to memorialize the baby.

Conclusion

It is difficult to understand why so many people do not acknowledge the death of a baby as a valuable loss. Perhaps it is because until recently childhood death was a common event. At the turn of the century, for example, *half* of the deaths were of children under the age of fifteen. Stillbirths and miscarriages were highly prevalent. People did not *expect* that all their children would live, much less that all their pregnancies would come to fruition. That is no longer true: most people in the United States have come to believe so strongly in the miracles of modern medicine that they expect all will live to a ripe old age. It is a shock to many couples "when it happens to them."

For whatever reasons perinatal death is not acknowledged as a legitimate source for mourning, the fact remains that when a newborn dies, parents *do* grieve. And if they grieve, they deserve the sympathy, support, encouragement, and steadfastness of those around them, lest they be left in indifference.

Note

1. There are two other groups of hidden grievers who are sometimes erroneously lumped into the same category with parents who have experienced perinatal death. They are parents of babies born prior to twenty weeks of gestation via spontaneous abortion, miscarriage, or induced labor; and parents who are infertile, who grieve the child who will never be born. Although their grief is legitimate and may be similar to that of parents who experience newborn death, little systematic study has been done with those parents. Assumptions about their grief and helpful responses to it should

not be automatically drawn from the realm of perinatal death and are not addressed in this chapter.

References

Benfield, D.G., S.A. Leib, and J. Reuter. 1976. "Grief Response of Parents After Referral of the Critically Ill Newborn to a Regional Center." *New England Journal of Medicine* 294, 975–78.

Down, M.L. (producer) 1986. *Some Babies Die.* Berkeley: University of California Extension Media Center. Film.

Kübler-Ross, E. 1969. *On Death and Dying.* New York: Macmillan.

Nichols, J.A. 1987a. "Newborn Death." In *Parental Loss of a Child,* edited by T.A. Rando. Champaign, Ill. Research Press.

——— .1987b. "Perinatal Death: Bereavement Issues." *Archives of the Foundation of Thanatology* 6: 1–13.

Panuthos, C., and C. Romeo. 1984. *Ended Beginnings.* Granby, Mass.: Bergin and Jarvery.

Parkes, C.M. 1974. *Bereavement.* Baltimore: Penguin.

Rando, T.A. 1984. *Grief, Dying, and Death: Clinical Interventions for Caregivers.* Champaign, Ill. Research Press.

Worden, W.J. 1982. *Grief Counseling and Grief Therapy.* New York: Springer.

12

Raymond: Underestimated Grief

Dennis Raymond Ryan

My first son, Raymond, died suddenly two weeks after he was born. As a young father I experienced what is now labeled disenfranchised grief—that is, grief that is not openly acknowledged or socially supported. In an attempt to contribute to the understanding of this kind of grief and to help others who are going through it and will go through it, I offer this personal reflection on the experience.

I did not recognize the intensity of my own grief. Surely, I was saddened by my son's death, but in a sense Raymond was a stranger to me. I had not carried him for nine months and had not felt him grow and move inside me. I had not cared for him much at all during those first two weeks of life because there were so many other details to be taken care of. Besides, I didn't know how to do baby things. Why then should I have felt much grief?

This lack of awareness of my feelings was due partly to my personality. I did not know myself well then, but since that time I have come to understand myself in terms of Carl Jung's personality theory. My tendency was to be both introspective and a thinker. I was very much at ease with my own thoughts but had difficulty relating to other people's feelings as well as my own. I also had difficulty communicating what was going on inside me to others. These were the liabilities of my type of personality.

I was also in shock over my wife's great grief, the magnitude of which surprised and scared me. Judy was a nurse and had worked for years in both the operating rooms and emergency rooms of hospitals. She always seemed to rise to the occasion when there was an emergency. Now she was numb and seemed to be sinking into the deepest possible depression. It was understandable. First there had been the sudden hemorrhaging caused by a placenta previa. She had been rushed to the hospital for an emergency caesarean. After the surgery she had been in shock, but she recovered and came home quite weak with the baby. Now the boy had died so suddenly. It was too much for her to bear.

Friends would drop in to convey their condolences. It was so clear how much Judy was hurting that the attention was focused primarily on her. I don't think I resented the attention, but now I know that I was needy also. But at that time, I preferred not to be in the spotlight, at least not as someone in need.

I had cast myself in the role of the strong one and was trying to live up to that role. Modeling is the most powerful teacher and both my parents had given me the models of strong people in adversity. At some time in my life I had accepted the goal of becoming a strong person in the sense of not letting adversity break me emotionally, or of never letting stress lead me to the point that I was out of control.

I knew I could hide my feelings very well. I had learned that and counted it as strength. People who thought similarly would never try to draw someone's feelings out unless they wanted to humiliate him or her. I was thankful to these, for there were times when I was very close to that fearful state of being out of control with sorrow. But I was spared the indignity.

My father had been my model for strength. He was a doctor and had seen a great deal of sorrow in his life. I used to love to listen to his stories of his days putting up with great adversity overseas during the Second World War and also as a young intern, while on ambulance duty would treat stab wounds on newspaper stands in New York City. I learned to be compassionate from the way he talked about and cared for his patients. And I learned always to be in control of my emotions, not to let things affect me. So it seemed.

I only once remember hearing him expressing great grief in an uncontrolled way. That was one time in the middle of the night when I woke because I heard the phone ring. My parents' room was close enough for me to hear my dad answer and then cry out, "No, no!" and let out great, sorrowful sobs as he struggled to ask questions. This was not the death of either his mother or father, which I did see face, but the death of his closest friend and medical colleague. I remember running to the door to witness this expression of great grief, but Mom shooed my sisters and me back to our rooms.

Now when they came to see us after Raymond had died, my father threw his arms around Judy and me and sobbed those same great, sorrowful sobs. This was over the death of the grandson who was named after him. Perhaps it was the experience of the fragility of our lives and biological immortality that compounded the grief; perhaps he was getting old and was less in control. All I knew was that I had to be strong for my father, my model and mentor of emotional strength.

Even if I had been in touch with my feelings, I would have been confounded by my ambivalence over the birth of my son. First there was the fact that I was still a struggling graduate student and living off the "sweat of my frau." We lived in a tiny, two-room apartment. The bedroom was so small that the queen-size bed just barely fit. My practical nature was concerned about where our new family member would fit. The added cost also loomed menacingly. I wasn't ready yet. I couldn't really provide. It would be easier without him. These were thoughts that had wandered in and out of my consciousness during the pregnancy and the days of his short life.

When he died, there was guilt over having thought these things at all. I don't think I consciously believed my thoughts could have contributed to his death, but to some extent maybe they had. In graduate school, I had studied Hinduism, and then as a part-time professor I had taught it and some of its teachings had affected me. Maybe I had generated bad effects with my negative thinking. Maybe I had created bad karma and contributed to this bad result. (The following year, Judy and I did go to India and had this interpretation verified. We had met a Hindu pundit who asked if we had any children; when we told him of the death of Raymond, he simply said, "Bad karma caused it.")

My guilt had even more foundation than just this. Raymond had shown signs of ailing to my wife early in the day. I dismissed her repeatedly stated misgivings throughout the day as unfounded and typical of the hyper state of new mothers. Even though my wife was a very competent emergency room nurse, I still put her off until evening. Then it was only her tears and near hysteria that convinced me to take her to the doctor. But I still did not believe. Was this denial or just pigheadedness?

When I heard the doctor's grave concern and wish to admit the baby immediately to the hospital, I was in shock. My memory of that night was that of being in an altered state of consciousness that I have never experienced since. We stayed at the hospital until late, when the doctor sent us home. We were home only a few hours when he called back to say how critical Raymond was. Emergency surgery was the only hope.

My wife wanted to assist but this was not acceptable. Instead we sat holding each others' hands so very tightly and sharing tears. It was the most intense grief I have ever felt, but I kept struggling to be strong for Judy. When the doctor, our friend, came out to say that the team had been unable to save the baby's life, we cried together. We had, by that time, some preparedness. Then Judy asked to see him. I remember that I had a strong aversion to doing this and tried to express it, but Judy asserted herself, and so arm in arm we walked into the recovery room to see our son's dead body.

It was a terrible sight and one that I shall never erase from my memory. His skin was all motted and blue. They had shaved his head, and there were intravenous needles sticking out from ugly blue veins in his scalp and attached to tubes running to hanging sacks of dark maroon blood. His eyes were open, staring up unfocused, and unreal. How I wanted to run from that nauseously green, sterile room. How I wanted to be anywhere but there. How I wanted to be anyone but me. But that was only inside. On the outside, I recall holding Judy tight as she cried and touched him. The staff, who were standing about, seemed to be judging how well I stood up to the ordeal. Is he strong?

I must have felt some of this at that time, but I don't think I allowed much of any of it to stay very long in my consciousness. It was much too threatening. I might lose control. I might appear weak. I might be weak. Besides, even if I wanted to express these feelings, I didn't have words. I didn't have any models. No one had ever taught me what to expect in such a situation, how to grieve, how to express these feelings.

As a result of Raymond's death and my lack of understanding of my responses, some relationships became ambivalent. For example, I had a cousin who had given birth to a son around the same time that Judy gave birth to Raymond. I didn't want to hear about that baby or visit my cousin and see him. There were other friends with sons around Raymond's age whom I also resented but never openly. I just would not want to visit them or even hear about them.

One of the feelings I had was grief over what could have been. I remember holding him in my arm once and feeling how fragile he was—too fragile for a man to hold. When he was older, I thought, I could handle him without fearing that I would accidentally hurt him. Maybe I didn't hold him more because I thought that I didn't deserve such a beautiful child. I remember feeling very proud and possessive of my son. I recall humming the show tune from Carousel, "My Boy, Bill." As I hummed I let myself think of what he might become and how proud I wanted him to be of his old man. And when he died, I lost that with a tremendous thud. No one else heard it, but I did. A felled tree in a forest with no one to hear its great descent to earth. I didn't think a father's grief would be so severe.

When I returned to work, most of my colleagues were solicitous. There were the usual sympathy notes and inquiries about Judy. Some seemed to avoid me out of either awkwardness or some subconscious primitive taboo. I don't remember anyone reaching out to me in a way that might have given me a chance to express some of my own complex feelings. There may have been some, but I don't recall it. Others I guess thought that I wasn't hurting. Unless you have gone through something similar, I think that it's difficult to know what another may be feeling and, even more, what one should do in response. It's like someone who is suffering from some ailment, arthritis, for example; unless you have experienced it or something similar, you don't really understand or really know how best to respond.

Judy was also deeply grieved, and I tried to support her as best I knew how, but at that point in my life I knew very little about grief and how to support the bereaved. I wasn't a good listener, nor was I comfortable when she cried. I used to try to get her to stop, rather than letting her express her sorrow. Thank God for those who knew better.

Judy would talk about Raymond's death to her mother, to her friends, even to my mother and sister. I would overhear the conversations on the phone and even encouraged Judy to call them and them to call Judy. When they got together, I would see the intense expressions on their faces as they sat close together holding each other's hands. I saw and heard the tears, but I was mute.

I think I must have felt envy and anger over Judy's ability to express her feelings. But then I would count it as weakness and put up another wall of steel around my own. This generated more feelings of loneliness and the hopelessness that can devastate the strongest among us.

Of the three ways through which one can express grief, acting it out was the one that helped me. This happened just a year and a half later when my older sister, Marcia, died suddenly of a massive cerebral hemorrhage, at the age of thirty-three. In shock, I instinctively pulled out all the boxes of old family pictures and put together an album that showed my relationship with my sister. It started with a picture of us when I was a baby and she was three, and it ended with a picture of us together on the weekend before she died. I didn't understand what I had done, then. I remember I knew it was something that I had to do and that on finishing it, I had reached a point of acceptance or reconciliation with the reality of her death.

In the case of Raymond I did not create an album. There were only half a dozen pictures and no long relationship. This time it was the rituals around the funeral that provided me with some outlets for the expression of my grief. Because we were poor, I wanted to avoid an expensive funeral. We found that the funeral director whom Judy's family had used over the years was very understanding and charitable. He could see our condition and offered a casket and services for fifty dollars. No wake, no cremation, no embalming or fixing the body. The closed casket would be taken on the back seat of his car to the cemetary after a brief service at the funeral home. A priest friend of ours said some prayers. Raymond was only an infant, an unspoiled child of God, who had no need of a church service.

I wonder about that now. He didn't need the service, but I think we did. A service would have slowed down the disposition. As it was, my memory is that we hurried Raymond off a little too fast.

The funeral director did a wonderful thing. When we arrived at the home on the morning of the funeral, he asked Judy and me if we wanted to see the body. My memory from the recovery room was still fresh in my mind, and I shrank from another face-to-face encounter. He assured my wife that Raymond looked very peaceful. On his own, the funeral director had fixed him up in the baptismal robe and cap that Judy had knitted during her pregnancy. I still felt reluctant, but Judy pulled me gently to the table on which the small white casket rested. When the box was opened, the sight that greeted me filled me with a happiness that I could not help but feel. My eyes filled as I struggled to fix my whole consciousness on this vision of unearthly peace. I was liberated from the horrors of the old image in the recovery room. Raymond was no longer held to this earth: he was free; he was gone. That was a great gift, and I shall always be grateful to the funeral director, Mr. Blackley of Ridgefield, New Jersey, for such a gift. It was a gift with many dimensions, but the tears it allowed me to shed were the most valuable.

We buried Raymond in the plot of his great-grandparents who had died so long ago that we were allowed to use their plot again and avoid the expense of a new plot. This grave became another unexpectedly important focus for the expression of my grief.

We had not been a grave-visiting family, so again I had never learned the importance of gravesites for the expression of grief. Judy and I went back many times to this special place of shared sorrow, and expressed our grief in tears and prayers and manual labor. We would fix the plot, planting grass and flowers that would bloom during the different parts of the year.

Sometime soon after the funeral I started to read books about grief so I could understand what was happening to Judy and me. This was one time when books did help, especially books in which people shared their experiences and told what helped. I read about the importance of personalizing your grief. In one particular case, a couple had made their own tombstone for their child's grave. As soon as I read this, I knew that this was something I had to do for my son, even though I had never done anything like it before. It was the same feeling I had about making the picture album for my sister. This time I recognized that I had the same need as the couple in the reading. I inquired about how to go about the project from a teacher of sculpture at the college where I taught part-time. This teacher was sensitive to the idea and encouraged me.

But where to get a piece of granite? Three months after Raymond's death, my wife and I drove down to the western shores of the Chesapeake to visit her aunt. I took a walk down along the water where the authorities had erected a wall to protect the land from erosion during storms. To shore up the wall against the waves' impact, they had dumped large chunks of rock. I couldn't believe my eyes. It was granite! I spent hours searching for just the right-size piece. I hadn't even sketched the thing out or done any measuring at the gravesite, but I knew the piece when I first laid eyes on it.

Once I got it home, I carefully planned the engraving. I had a hammer and chisel and sunglasses to protect my eyes and a need that was more of a compulsion in my heart. I didn't fully understand why I had to do this to express my grief, but I felt the urgency of having to do it and knew it was right. I am grateful that no one blocked me or thwarted me by making me feel foolish. Those who encouraged me were effective supporters of my grief.

We took the completed piece to the cemetery on one of the first mild days in March. The ground was clear and had thawed. The earth seemed to receive the stone lovingly to its new home. That Saturday, when Judy and I placed the "pillow stone" before the large gravestone with her grandparents' names, I could feel that I had reached closure on something. It was still sad, but things were all right. I could rest more easily now about my loss. I hadn't been able to publicly acknowledge the grief, but I had felt it and I had expressed it in a way that was meaningful to me.

Grief is the reaction to a loss. The extent of the grief is proportional to the extent to which we valued the one lost. How do we know how valuable someone is to us? Our head can produce pages of analysis that either confirm or dismiss someone's value in a relationship. This kind of data is frequently handed down by parents and bandished about by friends and acquaintances. Now I think that this information is more often misleading than helpful when determining or estimating grief.

What we must teach our children and students to do is to learn to listen to their hearts and honestly acknowledge what it is that they hear. Before we can counsel people about how to express grief, we must teach them to be able to sense it honestly and courageously. Tools such as the Myers-Briggs personality study can help people understand themselves and their personality liabilities. Communication skills, especially reflective listening and the expression of feelings, are essential for human development.

We need to teach people how to be in touch with their feelings of grief and how to express these to others in words. Also, we need to teach them how they can express their grief by acting it out. This area is not only the most creative area but also the one most easily misunderstood. For the acts are often irrational, if not in their design then in the intensity with which they are executed. However, it is the nature of grief to be irrational. This fact needs to be repeated until everyone accepts it and allows it in themselves and others.

If we do this, if we educate people and free them from false judgments about values in relationships, if we empower them to express their grief and to help others to express theirs, then there may no longer be a need to deal with disenfranchised grief. Our goal, then, is a society where all grief may be openly acknowledged and socially supported.

13

Grief and Elective Abortion: Implications for the Counselor

Larry G. Peppers

Introduction

Maternal grief has been defined as "a mother's highly variable emotional, psychological, physical, and social response to the involuntary loss of her fetus or infant."[1] Since 1969 a rather large body of literature has developed documenting the grief reaction of women to miscarriage, stillbirth, and neonatal death.[2] Taken as a whole the research has demonstrated that, whether prepartum or postpartum, involuntary fetal/infant loss is a traumatic and significant life experience that elicits a strong grief response.

Peppers and Knapp[1] have reported data from women who experienced involuntary fetal/infant death and examined that data from the theoretical perspective of maternal-infant bonding.[3] Briefly stated, this theory argues that a mother's emotional attachment to her child begins to develop early in the prenatal period. Based upon the grief responses of sixty-five women who had experienced miscarriage, stillbirth, or neonatal death, Peppers and Knapp concluded that this basic contention of maternal-infant bonding theory was accurate.

Specifically, this chapter addresses the issue of involuntary versus voluntary loss: is there a grief reaction to voluntary abortion? If so, what is the nature of the response? How does it compare with involuntary loss? What are the practical, theoretical, and clinical implications of this grief reaction?

Previous Research

Behavioral research on elective abortion can be grouped into three general categories: (1) general survey or epidemiological studies; (2) studies that

The author acknowledges the administration and staff of Midtown Hospital in Atlanta, Georgia, for their suggestions and helpful cooperation during the course of this project.

A large part of this manuscript has previously been published in *Omega: Journal of Death and Dying*. I wish to thank Dr. Robert Kastenbaum and *Omega* for permitting the reprint and revision of the original article.

appear, by design, to support a particular political stance on abortion; and (3) studies that have addressed the decision-making process and the psychological effects of abortion.

Representatives of the first category include studies conducted by the U.S. Census Bureau, McAnarney, Kane, Bogen, and Brennan.[4-8] These investigations have indicated that three to four out of every ten pregnancies end in abortion; that one in three are performed on adolescents; that 40 percent of the women conceive again within three years of their abortion; and that approximately one out of three abortions is performed on married women. Although each of these studies has contributed to the literature, a complete sociodemographic profile of abortion remains unavailable. Furthermore, the data included within these reports may not represent present trends. Data collection in the majority of the studies in this category was conducted before elective abortion became a widely available alternative. It is now estimated that approximately 1.5 million abortions are conducted annually in the United States.

Perhaps because of the moral and/or emotional overtones associated with the topic of abortion, studies grouped within the second category must be read with skepticism. On one hand, there are the proponents of abortion who present evidence regarding the benefits of abortion over the delivery of unwanted children. On the other hand, there are the opponents of abortion who present their evidence to refute the findings of the latter. This thesis-antithesis nature of the literature is apparent in studies of abortion and child abuse. One side argues that child abuse is prevalent after an unwanted pregnancy; therefore, abortion is beneficial.[9,10] The other side, however, points to data that indicate the prevalence of child abuse in wanted pregnancies and adoptions, undermining the benefit of abortion.[11-13] This same "debate" is apparent in articles dealing with the pros and cons of rape and abortion[14] and incest and abortion.[15] Even though these studies have opened various avenues of investigation, a critical review suggests that they lack objectivity and, more often than not, are based on small clinical samples and case studies.

The final category of previous research focusing on the effect of abortion must be reviewed within the context of two historical periods: (1) studies conducted prior to 1973, and (2) studies conducted after the Supreme Court decision in 1973. Prior to the widespread legalization of abortions, research was focused on *psychiatric* sequelae, primarily because of the psychiatric requisites mandated for the conduct of "therapeutic" abortion.[16-19] These early studies encountered problems of inadequate sample size and were often biased by the authors' personal attitudes toward abortion.[20,21]

While the pre-1973 studies tended to be clinical and diagnostic, post-1973 studies have been more broadly descriptive of the aftermath of abortion. They have sought to delineate specific emotions emanating from the abortion experience. As one might expect, the incidence of the various emotions varies greatly from study to study. Demonstrated postabortion feelings include guilt, remorse, anger, denial, and depression.[14,19,20,22] Other studies have focused on the "happy satisfaction" with the abortion decision.[23,24]

To summarize, the literature on the social, emotional, and psychological sequelae of elective abortion, while growing in volume, can best be characterized as relatively sparse, unsystematic, and methodologically questionable. For the most part, data have been gathered from small, select clinical samples, have often been reported as case studies, and have frequently been biased toward the stated attitudes of the investigators. What is presently needed is a more consistent approach, larger samples, and a theoretical framework by which future research may be integrated. Perhaps the greatest shortcoming of the present body of literature is the lack of *any* theoretical underpinning. The study summarized in this chapter attempted to overcome this problem by testing hypotheses derived from maternal-infant bonding theory.

Mother-Infant Bonding

What is the nature of the mother-infant bond? How does it develop? Answers to these questions have been sought through study of both human and other animal species. Although the findings are voluminous, many of them have been integrated into the maternal-infant bonding theory articulated by Klaus and Kennell.[3]

In developing the concept of maternal-infant bonding, Klaus and Kennell attempted to document prenatal emotional attachment by examining the grief response of twenty women whose infants had died from one hour to twelve weeks after delivery.[3] They reasoned that length and intensity of mourning is proportionate to the closeness of the relationship prior to death. Observable grief in each of their respondents led them to conclude that "significant bonding had been established by the time of or soon after the birth of the child."[3] This conclusion has been substantiated by the work of others who have documented a grief response following miscarriage[25,26] and stillbirth.[27,28] In addition, data gathered by Peppers and Knapp provided direct evidence of early prenatal attachment. Data comparing the grief response of women who had suffered miscarriage, stillbirth, and neonatal death led the authors to conclude that the reaction to the loss was as great in the case of early miscarriage as it was in the loss of a neonate.[1]

Perhaps the greatest theoretical contribution of Klaus and Kennell was their articulation of the *process* through which attachment occurs. They outlined nine events that are thought to be important to the formation of the maternal-infant bond:

1. Planning the pregnancy
2. Confirming the pregnancy
3. Accepting the pregnancy

4. Fetal movement
5. Accepting the fetus as an individual
6. Birth
7. Seeing the baby
8. Touching the baby
9. Caretaking

The attachment of mother to infant begins long before conception occurs. Bonding, at least in fantasy, may begin as early as in childhood, when a young girl begins to fantasize about motherhood and to internalize the female sex role. Playing "house," mothering dolls and younger siblings—each is an activity that subconsciously begins to prepare her for the future real-life role of mother.

As many women approach adulthood their thoughts often center on marriage and a family. For some, starting a family immediately after marriage is the goal. Others may begin a career and take time to adjust to marriage before planning children. Planning may simply involve abandonment of contraception, or it may include a scheduled sex life. In either case the woman makes a decision to get pregnant; having a baby becomes a goal. The process of bonding has begun.

Am I or am I not? Whether the baby is planned or unplanned, this can be an anxiety-producing question. Some women fear an affirmative answer, others a negative one. In either case the confirmation of pregnancy is an important milestone. The initial realization of pregnancy under any circumstances can cause mixed feelings. The woman will review many facets of her life, ranging from her partner's projected reaction, to her personal life-style. Economic considerations, marital situation, career, reaction of parents—each thought gradually leads to another crucial stage, acceptance of the pregnancy.

The new mother experiences two important developmental changes during pregnancy: (1) physical and emotional changes within herself, and (2) growth of the fetus. Feelings about these changes vary from woman to woman, depending on her desire to be pregnant and her present life situation. For those who cannot accept their pregnancy, the bonding process ceases and abortion becomes an alternative.

Fetal movement and perception of the fetus as a separate individual often occur concurrently as "quickening," the sensation of fetal movement. The feeling of movement requires the woman to change her concept of the fetus from a being that is a part of herself to a living baby who will soon be a separate individual. According to Bibring,[29] this realization prepares the woman for birth and physical separation from her child. This preparedness in turn lays the foundation for a permanent relationship with the child.

Birth, seeing, and touching the baby completes the bonding process,

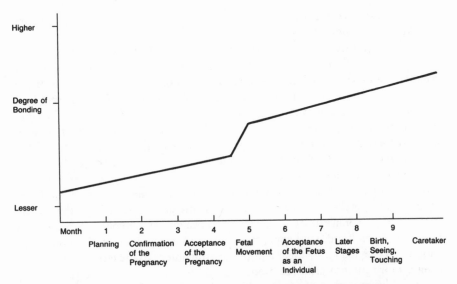

Figure 13–1. The Process of Maternal-Infant Bonding

and caretaking begins. This entire process is graphically represented in figure 13–1.

Bonding and Elective Abortion

Maternal-infant bonding theory, and particularly the first four stages outlined earlier, provides a framework for examining the psychoemotional reaction to elective abortion. Since research is so limited, it seems to describe extensively a research project considered relevant to the topic. A sample was selected consisting of eighty volunteers whose pregnancies were terminated during July, August, and September of 1982. Each of these women was a patient at Midtown Hospital, Atlanta, Georgia. During the preprocedure counseling session, the study was explained, questions were answered, and informed consent obtained. Each woman then completed a three-part questionnaire designed to obtain sociodemographic information, data related to the abortion decision, and responses to a grief scale. Approximately six weeks after the abortion procedure, each participant completed another questionnaire that included the grief scale and other questions regarding their abortion experience.

The following hypothesis was tested: *Women who elect to terminate their pregnancy will not experience a grief reaction.* Since this primary hypothesis had not been previously tested and was stated in a null form, two subhypotheses were formulated for testing in the event that the primary hypothesis was not accepted.

Subhypothesis 1: *The grief reaction experienced following elective abortion will vary depending upon the length of the pregnancy.* Ambivalent feelings about the pregnancy may cause a woman to delay her decision on abortion until after fetal movement occurs. As can be seen in figure 13–1, "quickening" brings with it a major increase in bonding. We expected a more intense reaction to the pregnancy termination among those women who delayed their decision beyond the perception of fetal movement.

Subhypothesis 2: *Women who voluntarily elect to terminate their pregnancy will have a less intense grief reaction than those women who involuntarily lose their pregnancy.* This hypothesis was designed as a means of determining the difference between spontaneous and elective abortion—that is, the variable of personal choice with respect to pregnancy outcome. Again within the context of bonding theory, planning and acceptance of the pregnancy should have yielded a stronger emotional attachment to the fetus, thereby eliciting a more intense grief reaction.

In addition to these three stated hypotheses, several variables were considered to be consequential to the abortion decision and its aftermath. Given the moral, legal, and social controversy surrounding the issue of abortion, it was thought that variables such as religiosity, age, income, sexuality, and social support might have an impact on a woman's feelings regarding her decision to terminate the pregnancy. Such variables could also impinge upon her subsequent reaction to the abortion.

Elective abortion was defined as the voluntary termination of a pregnancy during the twenty-four weeks subsequent to the last menstrual period (LMP). Specific medical procedures employed are based upon the number of weeks LMP. This study included three types of procedures.

1. Vacuum aspiration (VA), seven to twelve weeks LMP
2. Dilation and evacuation (D & E), thirteen to sixteen weeks LMP
3. Intrauterine induction (IND), seventeen to twenty-four weeks LMP

The temporal sequence of these procedures denotes the length of the pregnancy, thereby allowing empirical testing of the first subhypothesis.

Involuntary fetal/infant loss included spontaneous abortion, stillbirth, and neonatal death. Losses of these types may occur at any point in the pregnancy through the fourth week postpartum. The important consideration for purposes of the present study was the involuntary nature of the loss.

Grief was defined as the emotional, psychological, physical, and social response to loss. Measurement of the grief reaction was accomplished using a grief scale developed in a prior study.[1] This scale included thirteen items representing selected symptoms of grief.[30,31] The symptoms included sadness, loss of appetite, irritability, sleeping problems, difficulty concentrating, preoccupation of thoughts, depression, anger, guilt, problems returning to usual activity, repetitive dreams, exhaustion, and lack of strength. Respondents were asked to rate themselves on a scale from 1 (no problem) to 9 (extreme difficulty) on each of these variables, yielding a score ranging from 13 to 117. The overall grief score was determined by summation of responses to each of the items.

Results

The results of the study answered certain questions, left others unanswered, and raised new issues. The discussion that follows addresses the data analysis pertaining to the three stated hypotheses.

The basic hypothesis was developed to test the idea that acceptance of a pregnancy is a necessary stage in the development of the maternal-infant bond. Assuming that the decision to terminate a pregnancy indicates a lack of acceptance, low grief scores were anticipated. The results proved interesting. The mean grief score for the preprocedure response was 60.98 (s.d. = 20.24), as compared to a postprocedure mean of 35.45 (s.d. = 16.52). Median scores were 60.00 and 33.00 respectively. Preprocedure scores ranged from 29 to 104, while postprocedure scores had a range of 14 to 77.

Is there a grief response to elective abortion? Generally speaking, the data suggested that a grief response occurs. Furthermore, given the fact that the intense response was present prior to the actual procedure, *the decision to terminate the pregnancy may initiate the grief reaction.* The fact that postprocedure scores were significantly lower indicated a relatively rapid resolution of the grief response. The wide variability of scores did indicate, however, that some women had little difficulty either prior to or subsequent to the procedure, while others suffered tremendous emotional trauma. Characteristics distinguishing these two groups will be addressed later.

With respect to the first subhypothesis, the grief scores clearly indicated that the intensity of the grief reaction was dependent upon the length of the pregnancy. Using the abortion procedure as a measure of the length of pregnancy, an analysis of variance and the grief scores was conducted. An F-ratio of 3.07 ($p < .05$) was calculated for the preprocedure scores, while the calculated F-ratio for postprocedure scores was only 0.74 (NS). More directly, the women were also asked the number of weeks that had passed since they had had their pregnancy confirmed. Statistically significant correlations were calculated between weeks since confirmation and pre- and postprocedure grief scores, $r = .45$ and $r = .39$, respectively. The longer the pregnancy continued, the more emotionally traumatic the termination was, and the more difficult it was for grief resolution to occur.

To summarize, the data led to the following conclusions:

There is a grief reaction to elective abortion

The grief reaction is most likely initiated when the decision to terminate the pregnancy is made

Some women experience a minimally dysfunctional grief reaction, while others suffer greatly

The intensity of the grief reaction is associated with the length of the pregnancy

Grief associated with elective abortion is symptomatically similar to that experienced following involuntary fetal/infant loss

Theoretical and Clinical Implications

As a "test" of maternal-infant bonding theory, the results of this earlier study were inconclusive. On the one hand, they appeared to indicate that planning and acceptance of the pregnancy are not necessarily important steps in the bonding process; grief did occur irrespective of planning and acceptance. On the other hand, the variability of grief scores and the correlation between length of the pregnancy and grief lent support to the process as presented by Klaus and Kennell.

Clarification of this difference may lie in the analysis of other factors that impinge upon the individual who seeks the abortion. Discussions with clinical staff members and patients themselves pointed toward three possible areas of investigation: (1) social control factors, (2) the patient's perception of the pregnancy, and (3) the social stigma attached to abortion.

Many factors play a role in a woman's decision to seek an abortion. Social control factors such as age, income, religious beliefs, the presence or absence of social support systems, partner attitude, and marital status could quite conceivably operate to heighten or lessen the psychoemotional response to the abortion. Where these control factors are minimal—that is, where there is a minimal amount of pressure because of age, income, and so forth—the decision to terminate the pregnancy may be made with relative ease, with self-interest as the only major consideration, and with little ambivalence or anxiety. On the other hand, where social control is strong, the decision may be laden with ambivalence, anxiety, and concern for the consequences. Indeed, these factors appear to be the most frequently mentioned reasons for delaying the abortion beyond the first trimester of the pregnancy. As the data clearly indicate, the longer the pregnancy continues, the greater the grief response. Clinicians should make themselves acutely aware of the social environment in which the abortion decision is made, particularly in those cases where the decision has been delayed beyond the first trimester. Has the decision been made because of pressures from "external" social factors? Is there undue ambivalence regarding the procedure as a result of emotional attachment to the fetus? Is the woman seeking the abortion because she wants it or because she perceives it to be the only alternative she has? Each of these questions should be pursued and resolved to the patient's satisfaction.

Another factor often alluded to by counselors that may affect the grief reaction is the patient's perception of the pregnancy. Does the patient perceive herself as "simply" pregnant or does she see herself as a potential mother? To illustrate, the woman who views herself as "going to have a baby" places a different subjective meaning on the situation than does the woman who says "I am pregnant." In the first case the fetus is recognized; in the second case the fetus is given little or no recognition. This difference in perception would obviously affect the development of the emotional bond and perhaps the abortion experience as well. If the counselor should detect a strong identification of the patient with the fetus, those feelings should be discussed and the potential consequences explored. To reiterate an earlier conclusion, the grief response may be similar to that of women who have experienced miscarriage or stillbirth. Clearly, certain symptoms of grief, such as guilt, might be heightened in this situation. The counselor should be knowledgeable of the uniqueness of maternal grief and its consequences.

The social stigma attached to an unwanted pregnancy and to abortion may also affect the patient's reaction. Stigma refers to an attribute that is deeply discrediting; the stigmatized individual is "reduced from a whole and usual person to a tainted, discounted one."[32] If a woman perceives herself as stigmatized because of her pregnancy and abortion, she might understandably isolate herself from established support systems. She may impose upon herself, or find imposed upon her, closed communication channels. Her decision will be made alone and her grief will be experienced alone. The importance of having open communication channels during times of crisis has been well documented. A woman who is isolated will certainly experience more difficulty than will a woman who has an available social support system. *By all means* clinicians should explore the support systems available to the patient and, if none are available, stress the availability of counseling within the clinic.

Additional implications of the study are found within the wide variability of the grief scores. While some women experienced minimal difficulty with their abortion experience, others found it to be extremely stressful and debilitating. While some women apparently come to a resolution of their grief rather quickly, others find it difficult, as evidenced by the high postprocedure scores. What social and/or psychological factors differentiate these two groups? Answers to this question can facilitate identification of the "high-risk" patient. Identification in turn can facilitate appropriate patient-clinic interaction.

A cursory examination of the data related to high pre- and postprocedure grief scores indicated that there were certain factors that may be important in determining the level of anxiety experienced as a woman faces the prospect of abortion and the way she copes with it afterward.

Characteristics of those respondents who scored high on the preprocedure scale included:

Those having a D & E induction procedure

Those who indicated frequent church attendance

Those who indicated infrequent sexual activity

Those who had discussed their decision with a minister

Those who had a family member who opposed the abortion

Those whose relationship with the partner had ended

Those who were seeking the abortion for financial reasons

Those who had had several weeks to consider the abortion

It should be noted that black women and those who had had less than a high school education demonstrated high preprocedure scores. It is important for the counselor to determine the extent to which these factors are operating with *each individual patient.* Counseling should be more than an explanation of the procedure itself. Although clinicians deal with abortion procedures on a daily basis, they should remember that for the patient this is an event in her life that is significant, highly anxiety producing, and one that can have consequences long after the procedure is performed.

Characteristics of those respondents who scored high on the postprocedure scale included:

Catholics

Those who had less than a high school education

Those who had had a prior live birth

Those who had had multiple abortions

Those who had had previous miscarriages

Those whose reason for seeking the abortion was either financial or because of their age

Those who had no one to talk to prior to the procedure

Interestingly, postprocedure scores were highly correlated with age. Counselors who detect these characteristics in the preprocedure interview should stress the importance of postprocedure follow-up with the patient. When possible they in fact should initiate follow-up with a call to the patient in the days or weeks after the procedure.

While further investigation is needed, it is hoped that this study will stimulate an evaluation of counseling programs in abortion clinics. What modalities are most appropriate? Though it is true that some patients find a "happy satisfaction" with their abortion experience, it is also true that many women have a difficult time as they face the abortion and an equally difficult time coping with it afterward. They feel a sense of loss and they do experience grief. Clinicians should be knowledgeable about grief and prepared to counsel their patients accordingly. With this sensitivity patient care can only be enhanced.

Notes

1. L. Peppers and R. Knapp, "Maternal Reaction to Involuntary Fetal/Infant Death," *Psychiatry* 43 (1980), 155.

2. E. Kirkley-Best and K. Kellner, "The Forgotten Grief: A Review of the Psychology of Stillbirth," *American Journal of Orthopsychiatry* 52:3 (1982): 420.

3. M. Klaus and J. Kennell, *Maternal-Infant Bonding* (St. Louis: Mobley Press, 1976).

4. U.S. Census Bureau, *Perspectives in American Fertility* (Washington, D.C.: U.S. Government Printing Office, 1975).

5. E. McArarney, "Adolescent Pregnancy—A National Priority," *American Journal of Disabled Children* 132 (1978), 125.

6. F.J. Kane, "Therapeutic Abortion—Quo Vadimus," *Psychosomatic Disease* 9 (1968), 201–7.

7. I. Bogen, "Attitudes of Women Who Have Had Abortions," *Journal of Sexual Research* 102 (1974): 97–109.

8. W.C. Brennan, "Abortion and the Techniques of Neutralization," *Journal of Health and Social Behavior* 358 (1974): 64.

9. M.B. Beck, "The Destiny of the Unwanted Child," in *The Unwanted Child*, edited by C. Reiterman (New York: Springer, 1971).

10. M. Dennis, "Life and Death in an Abortion Hospital," in *Necessity and Sorrow* New York: Basic Books, 1976).

11. E.F. Lenoski, "Translating Injury Data into Preventive Health Case Services: Physical child Abuse," unpublished paper, Department of Pediatrics, University of Southern California, 1976.

12. B.D. Schmidt and C.H. Kempre, *Child Abuse: Management and Prevention of the Battered Child Syndrome* (Basel: Ciba Geigy, 1975).

13. S.M. Smith, *The Battered Child Syndrome* (London: Butterworth, 1975).

14. S.K. Mahkorn, "Pregnancy and Sexual Assault," in *The Psychological*

Aspects of Abortion, edited by D. Mall and W.F. Watts (Washington, D.C.: University Publications of America, 1979).

15. G.E. Maloof, "The Consequences of Incest: Giving and Taking Life," in *The Psychological Aspects of Abortion,* edited by D. Mall and W.F. Watts (Washington, D.C.: University Publications of America, 1979).

16. A. Barnes, "Therapeutic Abortion: Medical and Social Sequelae," *Annals of Internal Medicine* 75 (1971), 881–86.

17. R. Kretschmer and A. Norris, "Psychiatric Implications of Therapeutic Abortion," *American Journal of Obstetrics and Gynecology* 98:2 (1967), 363–73.

18. S.L. Patt, R.G. Rappoport, and P. Barglow, "Follow-up of Therapeutic Abortion," *Archives of General Psychiatry* 20 (1969), 408–14.

19. A. Peck and H. Marcus, "Psychiatric Sequelae of Therapeutic Interruption of Pregnancy," *Journal of Nervous and Mental Disorders* 143 (1966), 417–25.

20. B. Sarvis and H. Rodman, *The Abortion Controversy* (New York: Columbia University Press, 1973).

21. N. Simon and A. Senturia, "Psychiatric Sequelae of Abortion: Review of the Literature," *Archives of General Psychiatry* 15 (1966), 378–79.

22. M.H. Liebman and J.S. Zimmer, "The Psychological Sequelae of Abortion: Fact and Fallacy," in *The Psychological Aspects of Abortion,* edited by D. Mall and W.F. Watts (Washington, D.C.: University Publications of America, 1979).

23. K.R. Niswander and R.J. Patterson, "Psychologic Reaction to Therapeutic Abortion," *Journal of Obstetrics and Gynaecology of the British Commonwealth* 29 (1967), 702–6.

24. H. Whittington, "Evaluation of Therapeutic Abortion as an Element of Preventive Psychiatry," *American Journal of Psychiatry* 126 (1970), 1224–29.

25. R.T. Corney and F.T. Horton, "Pathological Grief Following Spontaneous Abortion," *American Journal of Psychiatry* 131 (1974), 825–27.

26. N. Simon, D. Rothman, J.T. Goff, and A. Senturia, "Psychological Factors Related to Spontaneous and Therapeutic Abortion," *American Journal of Obstetrics and Gynecology* (1969), 789–806.

27. K. Kowalski and W. Bowes, "Parent's Response to a Stillborn Baby," *Contemporary Obstetrics and Gynecology* 8 (1976), 53–57.

28. J. Wolff, P. Nielson, and P. Schiller, "The Emotional Reaction to Stillbirth," *American Journal of Obstetrics and Gynecology* 108 (1970), 75–77.

29. G. Bibring, "Some Considerations of the Psychological Processes in Pregnancy," *Psychoanalytic Study of Children* 14 (1959), 113–21.

30. J.H. Kennell, K. Slyter, and M. Klaus, "The Mourning Response of Parents to the Death of a Newborn Infant," *New England Journal of Medicine* 283 (1970), 344–49.

31. E. Lindemann, "Symptomatology and Management of Acute Grief," *American Journal of Psychiatry* 101 (1944), 141–48.

32. I. Goffman, *Stigma* (Englewood Cliffs, N.J.: Prentice-Hall, 1963).

14

Disenfranchised Bereavement and Loss of a Companion Animal: Implications for Caring Communities

Cyrus S. Stewart
John C. Thrush
George Paulus

T he loss of attachment to significant objects may result from developmental advances or declines, by the choices individuals make, by the actions of others over whom one lacks control, or through the unavoidable winds of change that sweep across all sociocultural landscapes. However, disruptions occur, these alterations activate a transitional condition where substantial dislocations between the self and the social world are experienced. As the individual strives to adjust to these alterations, culturally patterned bereavement behaviors facilitate acceptance of an altered reality and support the redesign of life structures. The feelings resulting from grief (commonly perceived as abandonment, rejection, loneliness, resentment, anger, insecurity, and worthlessness) that accompanies significant-object loss enhances interpersonal affiliation, promotes social cohesion, and ensures group solidarity. The development of mourning rituals allows for the socially recognized expression of grief and creates mechanisms that dramatize the significance of the lost object. The more important and socially acceptable the relationship, and the greater the irreplaceability of the lost object, the more appropriate is the activation of social support and the institutionalization of bereavement.

This chapter is concerned with significant-object loss among the elderly. The mourning rituals that surround the loss of a human loved one encourage the expression of grief, communicate the supportive availability of others, and enforce emotional and affiliative ties are generally not activated by pet loss (Stewart et al. 1985, Rosenberg 1984). Quackenbush has observed that the situation of pet death contains "no socially sanctioned rituals or cultural mechanisms through which grief and mourning can occur" (1984, p. 97). Additionally, Sullivan and Fudin contend that "many people have continuing problems with the death of a pet because family, friends, and society in general do not judge it as an event worthy of much grief" (1984, p. 171). In fact Voith (1984) comments that the pursuit of social support under these conditions of loss may produce social ridicule. Consequently, pet death may lead to an intensified need for bereavement under conditions where resources for grief resolution through mourning are restricted.

The Disenfranchisement of Bereavement

Where the expression of grief and the enactment of mourning rituals are discouraged we may speak of disenfranchised bereavement (Doka 1986, 1987). Though the experience of loss is an unavoidable consequence of life itself, not all loss is socially recognized or legitimated. Society specifies what relations are meaningful and what losses are significant. Individuals will also define the importance of relations and loss.

When individual definitions are consistent with social labeling, bereavement behavior produces affiliations between the individual and society that may lead to enhanced personal well-being and social cohesion. Where the individual experiences significant loss but society does not legitimize the expression of grief, stress reactions can be intensified where social systems might provide the support necessary for the individual to work through his or her grief. The institutionalization of bereavement rituals is a means of establishing and reinforcing the normative expectations of a society, and the ritual behaviors may act as a means of social control. Recognizing that social reactions not only prescribe the ritualistic aspects of bereavement behavior but also specify the situations in which such behavior should be exhibited and by whom, Averill (1968) points to the precedence of society when a conflict with personality needs is encountered. The absence of or intolerance toward bereavement behaviors generally produces an intensification of grief, feelings of abandonment from and resentment toward nonsupportive significant others, and a potential devaluation of the self.

The case of pet death reflects those circumstances where an individual suffers significant-object loss but, because of disenfranchised bereavement, does not have a socially legitimized channel through which to express grief. Both the significance of the human-pet bond (Fox 1984, Friedmann et al. 1984, Harris 1984) and the stressful nature of its disruption and loss (Anteleys 1984, Levinson 1984, Ryder 1984) have recently been documented. Because of the superficiality of support available to the elderly, their specific vulnerability merits special attention (Lynch 1979, Elwell and Maltbie-Crannel, Bustad 1980, Paulus et al. 1984, Stewart et al. 1985).

People-Pet Attachment among the Elderly

The animal that most humans consider as "pet" is usually chosen for the innate capacity it has for consistently displaying and responding to attachment (Rynearson 1978). It is the pet's preverbal attachment attitude that satisfies the human's repressed need for nurturance. The pet's nonverbal acceptance and response to the human enables the development of trust (Corson et al. 1977, Levinson 1972, Archov 1977). The companionship of a pet and the resulting bond can contribute in a positive way to an individual's sense of self-worth (Bustad 1980).

When a pet owner's need for emotional fulfillment leads to psychological investment in a pet, separation from or loss of that pet can exact a price for those years of companionship in the form of complicated and enduring psychological reactions such as grief and mourning (Keddie 1977). When humans grieve the death of another human they are usually surrounded by others who share their grief. The loss is recognized as significant, and sympathy and support are offered to the grieving person. These same supportive conditions are not readily available when a person's pet dies (Quackenbush 1984, Thomas 1982).

In view of the theoretical significance of companion animals in the elderly's affectional attachment system, the loss of a pet can be an event that has an enormous impact. The stressful nature of these effects is directly associated with the extent of the elderly's attachment. The centrality of the pet in the individual's sphere of relationships and the intensity of involvement obviously influence the reaction to loss. The adjustment problems experienced by the elderly at times of separation can be greater when the social system places limited emphasis on the people-pet relationship. In this vein, special attention should be focused on the therapeutic role that the clinical veterinarian can play at pet death by enabling the development of franchised bereavement and the establishment of caring communities.

In order to examine these assumptions systematically, a survey of 220 respondants[1] from Florida and Michigan was conducted (Stewart et al. 1985). This study revealed that pet ownership tends to be less likely among older respondents, those with relatively few friendship networks, and those reporting lower associational and group involvement. Approximately 90 percent of the respondents reported that the personal value they receive from their pets is companionship. Further evidence of the dependent nature of the people-pet bond is revealed by the fact that 95 percent of the elderly owners treat their companions as family members and that 75 percent of the owners expressed the belief that "the death of an elderly pet owner's pet might result in ill health for the owner."

Our primary concern focuses on the exchange between the elderly pet owner and the veterinarian when a pet becomes seriously ill and dies. The goal of this exchange is facilitating the elderly's adjustment to the loss of the pet. An awareness of the social and psychological consequences of significant attachment loss is important for the veterinarian in understanding what expectations a pet owner may place upon him or her at the companion's death. Even if the pet owner does not make demands of the veterinarian, he or she should be sensitized to the potential adverse outcomes that may result from pet death in the elderly community and is in a position to legitimize the grief.

Veterinarians are critically situated to provide direct emotional support and referral assistance for the elderly pet owner at the time of loss. Because of the lack of opportunity to express grief experienced with the death of a pet, the veterinarian can play an important role in primary care through assisting the elderly owner to maintain emotional stability. Consequently, sensitivity of the veterinarian to the emotional impact of pet death on elderly owners and their acceptance of this intervention as a legitimate dimension of the professional role becomes an issue of critical importance.

In order to assess this question, a stratified purposive sample[2] of veterinarians in Florida and Arizona was collected (Paulus et al. 1984). The overriding conclusion of this research was that practicing veterinarians are sensitive to the psychological dependence of the elderly upon their pets and that irreversible loss can have significant health implications for the bereaved owners. Specifically, more than 90 percent of the veterinarians believe that elderly widows and couples have a moderate to strong emotional attachment to their pets, and more than 85 percent contend that the status of a pet is close to that of a family member. Regarding the bereavement reactions that attend the loss of a loved one, more than 60 percent agreed with the statement that "it is more difficult to tell an elderly owner than a younger owner that his or her pet has died." Our sample also recognized that "the death of an elderly owner's pet might result in a state of ill health for that owner." With these beliefs in mind, it is worthwhile to note that although 80 percent believe that the personal difficulties of elderly owners at the death of their pet is a professional issue for the practicing veterinarian, only 10 percent "follow up the death of an elderly owner's pet to see how they are adjusting to the loss." The discrepancy between avowed belief in the adverse psychological impact of the loss and the perception of professional responsibility to accommodate and support the owners is explained by a feeling of professional unpreparedness.

Clinical Strategies for Bereavement Intervention with Elderly Pet Owners

Though grief and mourning behaviors of the elderly resulting from the loss of a companion animal are real and pervasive, the disenfranchised nature of the bereavement process has been shown to result from the social denial of the human-pet bond as a significant relationship. The general impact of disenfranchisement is to disallow or devalue the public mourning and social legitimation of grief, which is prerequisite to successful adjustment to significant-object loss. The consequence is that those who lose their pets often are forced, by the lack of interest or empathy expressed by significant others, to engage in grieving in socioemotionally unsupported contexts. With the acknowledged restricted social networks of many of today's elderly, the disenfranchised nature of bereavement attendant to pet loss can intensify feelings resulting from that loss and increase stress.

Until society legitimizes the expression of grief and mourning as a result of the loss of a pet, interpersonal support for those who have lost a companion is likely to be restricted to those who share the legitimation of a people-pet bond and/or have been most directly involved with this attachment (that is, the veterinarian). Consequently, the structure of modern veterinary practice must include sensitivity to the human impact of pet death and understanding of various clinical strategies to enable the development of grief work in the elderly.

To facilitate this grief work, three distinct and critical periods during the death of a companion animal can be identified. The first period of the death process involves serious illness or injury where rehabilitative procedures are aimed at restoring the animal to a state of good health. Where the recognition of the terminal state of the pet is apparent, decisions regarding natural death or euthanasia will be made. The physical and emotional state of the pet owner is characterized by manifestations of somatic distress (for example, pacing, sweating, and heightened blood pressure) and emotional trauma (such as anxiety, anger, depression, disbelief, denial, and anticipatory grief). Interactionally, the pet owner intentionally limits outside social contacts and narrows his or her focus around the pet and the care provider. *Amelioration strategies* will reduce the intensity of grief by preparing the pet owner for the death of the pet. The second period refers to those events immediately contingent to the time of death. Physically and emotionally, the pet owner experiences intensifications of those experiences encountered during the illness or injury stage, and interaction becomes increasingly focused on the pet, the veterinarian, and the immediate death situation. *Deathwatch strategies* are employed with the purpose of enabling the pet owner to accept the finality of death. Intensified physical distress and emotional trauma accompanied by grief and mourning exemplify the third period in the death process. Interactionally, the pet owner's behavior is that of searching for understanding and support from others. *Recovery strategies* focus on styles of follow-up with the owner to assess how he or she may be adjusting to the loss of the pet. (See table 14–1).

Amelioration Strategies

During the death process, the veterinarian must keep in the forefront of awareness the reality that, in dealing with elderly clients, they may be encountering individuals who are losing an attachment that is personally defined as one of the most significant and meaningful relationships they have. Not only

Table 14–1
Clinical Strategies for Bereavement Intervention

Stage of the Death Process		Amelioration	Deathwatch	Recovery
Condition of Pet		Terminal Illness Critical Injury	Moment of Death	Dead
Condition of Pet Owner	Physical	Somatic Distress Reactions	Somatic Distress Reactions	Somatic Distress Reactions
	Emotional	Anxiety Concern Anger Depression Anticipatory Grief	Grief Feelings of Loss Anxiety Anger Depression Abandonment	Grief Mourning Anxiety Anger Depression Abandonment
	Interactional	Limited and Structured	Focused and Structured	Searching for Understanding
Intervention Goals		Preparation	Acceptance	Adjustment

is the client facing the imminent death of a deeply significant attachment, but the perception of death and dying may stimulate painful memories and other unresolved conflicts regarding loss and death in other significant contexts.

In order to avoid activating the client's defensive processes, the veterinarian should avoid any collusion with the client that would reinforce the development of shared fantasies that the pet can be cured if only enough personal commitment, professional skill, and financial resources are invested. Such shared beliefs and wishes may function to produce more intense and destructive reactions upon the occasion of death. As stressful as the loss of a companion animal is, the lack of adequate preparation will forestall the enactment of anticipatory grief and escalate an already stressful situation. Collusion may also activate the client's denial/avoidance defenses, inhibiting the acceptance of reality and undermining the expression of grief. Additionally, such alliances may produce hostile and demanding reactions that enable the pet owner to disregard or misinterpret clinical information (Sullivan and Fudin 1984, Link 1984).

Preparation of the elderly client for pet death requires full disclosure of all clinical information, thereby enhancing the client's willingness to understand and recognize the terminal situation. Although many clients may tend toward defensiveness, clarity and honesty will facilitate the ultimate acceptance of death and the activation of bereavement behaviors. Many elderly clients will express relief that their defenses may be released and energy redirected toward bereavement and final closure. Conscious verbalizations regarding the terminal quality of the pet's condition will facilitate the development of personal control and power by reducing the anxiety and depression often attendent upon the unknown. The veterinarian's explicit verbal recognition of the client's grief can produce the enfranchisement (that is, the accepting and supportive context) within which the client will be able to confront and express his or her feelings. Moreover, the client's recognition of the reality of death will also be enhanced by the clinician's remaining available to answer whatever questions the client may have. Such continued availability reinforces the accepting nature of the clinical environment and facilitates further reduction of anxiety and the beginning of grief work.

No matter how available the clinical staff or how supportive the environment, defenses organized around avoidance/denial and anger can be expected. When these defenses are encountered, it is imperative that the veterinarian recognize them as the various stages in the bereavement process. Therefore, it is strongly urged that both denial and anger be encouraged and allowed full responsible expression. To inhibit them would lead to an increased perceptual and behavioral rigidity, in addition to being a significant factor in the delay and complication of bereavement. When such defenses are encouraged, the clinician must be cautious not to become overly protective or to accept responsibility for the terminal situation. Such strategies may encourage narcissism and impede both the process of reality testing and the normal bereavement process (Quackenbush 1984). The ubiquitousness of these defensive responses has led Rosenberg (1984) to conclude that until the client has demonstrated an enhanced coping ability, it may be prudent to use whatever life-sustaining methods may be available for maintaining the pet. When combined with encouragement of the elderly client to visit his or her pet and offering of maximum opportunity to interact physically and verbally with the pet, these strategies have been successful in enhancing the acceptance of reality (Sullivan and Fudin 1984, Walshaw 1984).

Enhancing contact opportunity between the elderly client and pet should be a strategy of choice, not only at clinical offices but also in terms of treatment procedures of dying pets. Extending the pet care team into the client's home may not only be a cost-effective treatment decision, but may also help the elderly client to evaluate more realistically the pet's condition. Moreover, such outreach strategies will enable the achievement of emotional closure and anticipatory grief by allowing the client to spend meaningful time with the pet which might otherwise not be available. Sensitive observation of the elderly owner's vulnerability to pet death and the presence of available support systems for the owner may also be assessed at this time.

When home care is not the strategy of choice, visits are not the only way to enhance human-pet contact. Many veterinarians have found that the intensity of grief can be moderated if clients desire and are encouraged to participate meaningfully in care giving to dying animals in a manner of their choosing (Sullivan and Fudin 1984, Link 1984). Enabling the elderly client to become an integral part of the team may be clinically inconvenient. However, in terms of familiarity between client and clinical staff and the owner's resulting confidence in clinical procedures, along with the recognition that preserving and protecting a valued life is a cardinal value, the benefits more than outweigh the costs incurred.

It should be emphasized that an elderly client's grief reaction will be significantly affected by how the professional staff relates to him or her and to the situation. Staff members who relate to the client must be attuned to the fact that the client will be very attentive and sensitive to how he or she and the pet are being treated. Awareness, sensitivity, and compassion should be demonstrated in all contacts with the elderly client and the pet. Discussions should be conducted in person, and all vagueness and jargon should be eliminated, for this enhances anxiety and contributes to a sense of confusion and insecurity. Compassionate, candid, and assertive phrasing can enhance reality testing, enable emotional expression, and quicken the passage through denial. Walshaw (1984) suggests that attention be focused on the manner in which the pet is treated. The style of treatment becomes particularly crucial at those times when the elderly client is present and especially when death of the pet is imminent.

Deathwatch Strategies

These techniques are employed by the veterinarian immediately prior to and subsequent to the experience of death. The recognition of the traumatic impact of pet loss to elderly owners (Stewart et al. 1985) has led many clinicians to accept responsibility for dealing with an elderly owner's grief as the final obligation to the pet client (Rosenberg 1984, Walshaw 1984, Katcher and Rosenberg 1978). Compassionate and adequate preparation of the elderly owner for this event will be of decisive significance in facilitating acceptance, resolution, and the encouragement of the bereavement process.

Pet death may revive unresolved conflicts concerning loss and confrontations with one's mortality, not to mention the permanent loss of a valued other. However, we must be sure to realize that such situations may also highlight the veterinarian's own feelings of insecurity surrounding the death process. While the interaction between the veterinarian and owner are of great significance during the amelioration stage, at deathwatch such anxieties will interact with each other to produce a devastating situation for the elderly owner. When a brusque and authoritarian attitude develops and is combined with a triage mentality, client needs are grossly neglected (Sullivan and Fudin 1984). This situation becomes intensely pathogenic when compared with a prior condition of nurturant support. Consequently, it needs to be emphasized that those strategies that work during amelioration also work at deathwatch. However, in view of the crucial importance of deathwatch, additional strategies may be suggested that will enable the elderly client to engage in bereavement behaviors.

The overriding component in deathwatch strategies is the continuation of the humane and compassionate environment established during the amelioration stage. Whether pet death is by natural process or the result of euthanasia, it is not an event normally encountered by the elderly client. In addition, the death experience may generate unresolved conflicts, feelings of infantilizing dependency, and anxiety regarding prior and anticipated loss. The death process must be surrounded by decorum, dignity, and respect for the passing of a valued life and for the social dissolution of a meaningful relationship. Sullivan and Fudin speak directly of this atmosphere when they suggest that fears about death will be moderated when the client perceives the pet having "met death in a supportive environment with people who cared" (1984, p. 173).

To further enhance the solemnity of the moment of death, the presence of a quiet room has been successfully employed (Walshaw 1984). In this context, the elderly client may be encouraged to express feelings of loss and receive supportive interactions from the staff which will provide a sense of validation and legitimation for his or her feelings. Emotions will tend to be an ambivalent mixture. Guided expression can enable the elderly client to interpret the relations in terms of benefits rather than costs. Defining the perceptual universe in positive terms may enhance the probability of an enduring experience that can be reliably and pleasantly recalled. Verbal recognition of fears and angers, reassurance that one's pet did not suffer and a supportive review of the relationship with the pet are techniques that will enhance grief expression and facilitate mourning (Quackenbush 1984).

The reinforcement of bereavement should not be delayed after death but can be a meaningful aspect of clinical procedures for a "painless death." When euthanasia has been selected, three general procedures to facilitate bereavement can be instituted. It is certainly a wise strategy to provide the client with sufficient advanced notice of when the procedure is scheduled. The preparatory time will eliminate pressures and surprises by enabling the client to accommodate to reality and the finality of death. Such planning enables the clinician to assess realistically the client's emotional readiness and acceptance of the decision and to facilitate the process of closure by ensuring that the client has time to be alone with the pet. Such preparation recognizes the importance of the relation and reduce the anxiety felt by both pet and client (Link 1984).

The client's active participation in clinical procedures can also be actively encouraged. If this option is selected, the client needs to be more than a passive observer. It is suggested that the exact sequence of events be precisely detailed and explained. Knowledge, understanding, and involvement tend to reduce anxiety by enabling the client to see the procedure as a gentle and respectful process. Moreover, such involvement establishes the reality of death, thereby encouraging active grief work (Sullivan and Fudin 1984).

Often overlooked is the importance of the time of day. Euthanasia should be scheduled for a calm period. The lack of competing commitments allows the clinical staff a maximal amount of uninterrupted time with the client to answer any questions and provide whatever reassurance may be required. Such sensitive scheduling will maximize flexibility so that the client can spend whatever time is needed for preparation or for the last goodbye. Moreover, scheduling during a calm period will avoid placing the client in the potentially awkward situation of grief expression in a crowded waiting room. When such scheduling cannot be achieved, it is necessary to allow the elderly client whatever time may be necessary for emotional expression and to use the clinician's extrance to leave the clinic.

Recovery Strategies

At and immediately subsequent to deathwatch is not the time to gather information regarding potential resources for long-term adjustment. After the acute experience of grief has run its course, acceptance and resolution can be facilitated by encouraging the elderly's active involvement in decisions regarding burial. Such participation usually signifies closure (Link 1984) and should not be misinterpreted as a desire to replace the pet (Rosenberg 1984).

For all pet owners, but especially in the case of the elderly, the advisability of pet replacement is an important issue and deserves further comment. We have already spoken of the people-pet bond and the significant role that this attachment plays in the affectional system of the elderly. The disenfranchisement of the bereavement process combines with the restricted nature of alternative opportunities to display nurturance and to receive support to produce a severely traumatic situation at pet death. It is only logical to conclude that the stressful nature of pet death can be somewhat moderated by replacing the lost pet.

As sensible as replacement sounds, there are certain precautions that need to be considered. As we have continually urged, the personal importance of completing the process of grief and mourning cannot be overestimated. It would be certainly inappropriate, if not emotionally destructive, to suggest pet replacement prior to the completion of bereavement (Katcher 1980). Any such suggestion at this time may be interpreted by the elderly pet owner as a denial of the individualized significance of the dead pet as a value attachment object. Under these conditions, suggesting replacement may activate defenses that can prolong bereavement by enabling the elderly to interpret replacement as disloyalty to the memory of the dead pet. Consequently, we suggest that questions regarding replacement should originate with and be clearly verbalized by the pet owner.

Even when replacement is of interest, many elderly owners will not avail themselves of this opportunity. In our survey of elderly respondents in

Michigan and Florida, both owners and nonowners expressed substantial disagreement with the statement "upon the occasion of pet death, elderly pet owners will choose to replace the lost pet" (Stewart et al. 1985). Given the importance of the people-pet bond, the disinclination toward pet replacement is somewhat curious. The finding that pet ownership tends to be inversely associated with age suggests that the belief that a replacement pet will outlive its owner and have no one to care for it may be an important element in the decision of elderly owners not to replace their lost companions. In order to avoid this fear, it can be suggested that elderly pet owners might look into the advisability of selecting an elderly companion animal or one that is scheduled to be euthanized by a local humane society as a means of population control. Other possibilities might include making prior arrangements with family and friends for the care of a replacement animal if its elderly owner predeceases it. Although many moral and ethical questions are raised by these alternatives, we believe they are worthy of serious consideration.

Perhaps the most important strategy during recovery is to identify and enhance the availability of significant-other support systems (Sullivan and Fudin 1984, Link 1984). Although human contact and reassurance will not substitute for the absence of a pet, the veterinarian is advised to offer further assistance through personal contact and to make whatever referrals to medical or mental health professionals as deemed appropriate (Quackenbush 1984). To the extent that compassion has been present throughout the death process, the rapport between veterinarian and client will be sufficient for the clinician to inquire about family and other significant others in the client's environment who can be recruited for socioemotional support. If such support is not present, the establishment of an accepting group could be facilitated through the development of a central registry at county veterinary associations. This may be particularly critical in situations of extensive isolation of the elderly from family and friends. All professionals who have contact with the elderly, especially those who are severely isolated, should be particularly sensitive to the warning signs of depression, complicated bereavement, anxiety or panic states, suicidal thoughts and other affective disorders that can be generated by the loss of a companion animal. If society is to recognize human grief reactions to the loss of a pet animal as legitimate and nonpathological phenomena, illustrative of the fact that human-pet bonds reflect more than property management, the enfranchisement of grief in caring communities becomes increasingly necessary.

Notes

1. All but 4 percent were sixty years of age or older, with 41 percent aged seventy or older. Sixty percent of the sample was currently married and 92 owned their homes. Weekly contact with friends were reported by 65 percent of the sample, with 84 per-

cent describing such contacts as being important. In general, the sample maintains a relational network and exhibits only limited social or emotional isolation.

2. Questionnaires were mailed to 375 practicing veterinarians in locations containing significant concentrations of elderly clients. After a follow-up, a usable sample of 209 respondents was selected. This sample was equitably distributed through the time in practice spectrum, with more than 80 percent defining their practice as small animal treatment and 25 percent reporting that clients sixty-five years of age or older constitute 40 percent of their practice.

References

Antelyes, J. 1984. "When Pet Animals Die." In *Pet Loss and Human Bereavement,* edited by W.J. Kay et al. Ames: University of Iowa Press.

Archov, P. 1977. *Pet Therapy: A Study of the Use of Companion Animals in Selected Therapies.* Denver: American Humane Association.

Averill, J.R. 1968. "Grief: Its Nature and Significance." *Psychological Bulletin* 70, 721–48.

Bustad, L.K. 1980. *Animals, Aging and the Aged.* Minneapolis: University of Minnesota Press.

Corson, S.A., E.O. Corson, P.H. Gwynne, and L.E. Arnold. 1977. "Pet Dogs as Non-verbal Communication Links in Hospital Psychiatry." *Comprehensive Psychiatry* 18, 61–72.

Doka, K.J. 1986. "Disenfranchised Grief." Paper presented to the Forum for Death Education, Atlanta, Ga.

———. 1987. "Silent Sorrow: Grief and the Loss of Significant Others." *Death Studies* 11, 455–69.

Elwell, F., and A.D. Maltbie-Crannel. 1981. "The Impact of Role Loss upon Coping Resources and Life Satisfaction of the Elderly." *Journal of Gerontology* 36, 223–32.

Fox, M.W. 1984. "Pet Animals and Human Well-Being." In *Pet Loss and Human Bereavement,* edited by W.J. Kay et al. Ames: University of Iowa Press.

Friedman, E., et al. 1984. "Health Consequences of Pet Ownership." In *Pet Loss and Human Bereavement,* edited by W.J. Kay et al. Ames: University of Iowa Press.

Harris, J.M. 1984. "Nonconventional Human/Companion Animal Bonds." In *Pet Loss and Human Bereavement,* edited by W.J. Kay, H.A. Nieburg, A.H. Kutscher, R.M. Grey, and C.E. Fudin. Ames: University of Iowa Press.

Katcher, A.H. 1980. "Euthanasia and the Management of a Client's Grief." *Comparative Continuing Education in Small Animal Practice* 11(2): 115–20.

Katcher, A.H., and M.A. Rosenberg. 1978. "Euthanasia and the Management of the Client's Grief." *Compendium on Continuing Education for the Practicing Veterinarian* 12, 888–97.

Keddie, K. 1977. "Pathological Mourning After the Death of a Domestic Pet." *British Journal of Psychiatry* 131, 21–35.

Levinson, B. 1972. *Pets and Human Development*. Springfield, Ill.: Thomas.

———. 1984. "Grief at the Loss of a Pet." In *Pet Loss and Human Bereavement,* edited by W.J. Kay et al. Ames: University of Iowa Press.

Link, M. 1984. "Helping Emotionally Disturbed Children Cope with Loss of a Pet." In *Pet Loss and Human Bereavement,* edited by W.J. Kay, H.A. Nieburg, A.H. Kutscher, R.M. Grey, and C.E. Fudin. Ames: University of Iowa Press.

Lynch, J.L. 1979. *The Broken Heart: The Medical Consequences of Loneliness*. New York: Basic Books.

Paulus, E., et al. 1984. "Death of Pets Owned by the Elderly: Implications for Veterinary Medical Practice." In *Pet Loss and Human Bereavement,* edited by W.J. Kay, H.A. Nieburg, A.H. Kutscher, R.M. Grey, and C.E. Fudin. Ames: Univeristy of Iowa Press.

Quackenbush, J. 1984. "Social Work in a Veterinarian Hospital: Response to Owners' Grief Reactions." In *Pet Loss and Human Bereavement,* edited by W.J. Kay, H.A. Nieburg, A.H. Kutscher, R.M. Grey, and C.E. Fudin. Ames: University of Iowa Press.

Rosenberg, M.A. 1984. "Clinical Aspects of Grief Associated with Loss of a Pet." In *Pet Loss and Human Bereavement,* edited by W.J. Kay, H.A. Nieburg, A.H. Kutscher, R.M. Grey, and C.E. Fudin. Ames: University of Iowa Press.

Ryder, E.L. 1984. "Development of a Social Work Service to Deal with Grief after Loss of a Pet." In *Pet Loss and Human Bereavement,* edited by W.J. Kay, H.A. Nieburg, A.H. Kutscher, R.M. Grey, and C.E. Fudin. Ames: University of Iowa Press.

Rynearson, E.K. 1978. "Humans and Pets and Attachment." *British Journal of Psychiatry* 133, 550–55.

Stewart, C.S., et al. 1985. "The Elderly's Adjustment to the Loss of a Companion Animal: People-Pet Dependency." *Death Studies* 9, 383–93.

Sullivan, W.H., and C.E. Fudin. 1984. "Psychosocial Model of Veterinary Practice." In *Pet Loss and Human Bereavement,* edited by W.J. Kay et al. Ames: University of Iowa Press.

Thomas, G.P. 1982. "When a Pet Dies." *Modern Veterinary Medicine* 63, 273–77.

Voith, V.C. 1984. "Owner/Pet Attachment Despite Behavior Problems." In *Pet Loss and Human Bereavement,* edited by W.J. Kay et al. Ames: University of Iowa Press.

Walshaw, S.O. 1984. "Role of the Animal Health Technician in Consoling Bereaved Clients." In *Pet Loss and Human Bereavement,* edited by W.J. Kay et al. Ames: University of Iowa Press.

15

Disenfranchised: Divorce and Grief

Terry L. Martin

T he dissolution of a marital relationship is a form of disenfranchised grief. Marital separation is a particularly serious form of personal loss, but societal disenfranchisement of divorce grief prolongs and exacerbates the distress of divorce.

Introduction

A number of authors have noted the existence of special populations (such as ex-spouses, homosexuals, and others) that are unusually vulnerable to the effects of grief (for example, Doka 1988, Kimmel 1978). Certain experiences not usually seen as significant losses have been identified (Goodyear 1981, Hayes 1981, Hendrick 1981, Herman 1974). It remained, however, for Doka to synthesize and identify the concept of disenfranchised grief as "grief that persons experience when they incur a loss that is not or cannot be openly acknowledged, publicly mourned and/or socially supported" (1987, p. 3). Disenfranchised grief is seen as a consequence of *(a)* societal refusal to sanction the relationship as significant; *(b)* community failure to recognize the loss as significant; and *(c)* societal failure to recognize the griever, or widespread indifference to the griever's feelings.

Doka's most significant contribution has been to highlight the paradox of disenfranchised grief: "The very nature of disenfranchised grief exacerbates the problems of grief, but the usual sources of solace and social support may not be available or helpful" (1987, p. 8). One special form of disenfranchised grief is the experience accompanying the dissolution of a marriage.

The Nature of Divorce Grief

Grief as a Consequence of Divorce

Those involved in the breakup of a marriage gain a new partner even as they lose the old one: grief becomes a constant companion. In an interview with the author, one young woman recalled the agony of her separation:

I was lost. I kept looking for his car to pull up. I wanted to call him but couldn't face the rejection again. I kept staring at that stupid phone hoping it would ring, that it was all a mistake. . . . I was hysterical. I'd go for long walks and cry. I'd go to the grocery store and cry. I remember telling myself, "This is it, you've finally lost it." The strangest thing was how painful the emptiness can be. I kept looking into myself and seeing nothing. It's like looking in a mirror and not seeing yourself. . . . I'd get these migraine headaches. I remember lying on the bathroom floor with a towel on my head and looking up at the toilet and saying, "There goes your life."

A number of studies have pointed to the pain of divorce as a form of grief (Bohannan 1970, Crosby, Lybarger, and Mason 1987, Crosby, Gage, and Raymond 1983, Freund 1974, Hagemeyer 1986, Herman 1974, Weiss 1975, Wiseman 1975). Several factors have been identified as mediating variables to explain the disproportionality of grief among the participants of a divorce. These include the individual variables of age and gender, as well as situational variables such as *(a)* degree of social support, *(b)* presence or absence of children, *(c)* remarriage, and *(d)* the roles played by the divorcing partners. Chief among the mediating variables is whether the participant was an active or passive agent in the partitioning process (Crosby, Gage, and Raymond 1983, Goode 1956, Kessler 1975, Spanier and Casto 1979). Kressel (1980) has suggested that the noninitiator may take as long as three years to recover fully. In a similar vein, O'Conner (1976) proposed readiness as the key variable in divorce adjustment. She hypothesized that the opportunity to grieve in anticipation of a divorce would enhance the griever's postdivorce recovery. Her results were mixed, with possibly some derived advantage in terms of self-acceptance. Hence, there is some indication that when one spouse favors and initiates the divorce, the postdivorce adjustment period is less traumatic. An alternative conclusion is that the initiator begins his grief work sooner, suffers in lonely silence during the preinitiation period, and finishes first.

Although the search for significant mediating variables continues, Crosby, Lybarger, and Mason (1987) suggested that the key variable in divorce adjustment "may well yet prove to be the grief work itself, i.e., the process of mourning and actively dealing with one's own sense of loss" (p. 20).

Divorce versus Death

Although both death and divorce create similar stressors and comparable responses, the thoughtful reader will question whether divorce is equivalent in this sense to death. What differences exist between divorce and death, or, more accurately, between divorcing and dying? Divorcing and dying are both active, ongoing processes involving action, interaction, responding, decision making—active and, to a greater or lesser degree, goal-directed behavior. However, as the curtain closes on each process, the concluding acts differ drastically. Death is universal, inevitable, final, and irreversible. Divorce is not. Moreover, subsequent interactions with the environment are substantially dissimilar as well.

It is proposed that grief occurring as a function of divorce is more complicated than grief engendered as a consequence of death. Divorce intensifies grief at two levels: (1) the individual's response to the divorce process itself; and (2) the environment's response to the divorcing individual. This latter case represents the disenfranchisement of divorce grief.

Neither the individual's responses nor the environment's reactions to the individual are singular operations. There is a constant interplay among the cognitive, behavioral, and affective aspects of the individual and societal and familial scripts, designs, and social norms. Attitudes toward death as well as divorce have not remained static. Death, however, represents a given. Divorce remains a potentiality—an increasingly likely possibility—not a certainty. The disenfranchisement of divorce grief is seen in the pattern of interactions between the array of fluid responses of the individual and evolving societal notions regarding divorce.

The Problem of Grief in Divorce

The Individual's Response to Divorce

At the response level, two major factors intensify divorce grief relative to death grief: (1) the more pervasive presence of decision-making behavior in divorce grief; and (2) differences in the individual's attribution choice of perceived control over divorce, versus control over death.

The decision to divorce is a sobering one, but it is not the final one. Decisions are made about disposition of property and possessions; about status and rights of parenting; about temporary and permanent living arrangements and financial obligations. Assignment of fault is proposed, asserted, negotiated, and rejected.

The majority of decision making often falls to the active agent. Ambivalence is natural, with a strong desire to exit a difficult relationship coexisting with the anxiety and fear that is associated with an uncertain, uncharted future. Aldrich (1974) pointed to the special impact of ambivalence on anticipatory grief during the dying process. Decisions regarding curative versus palliative care, surgical versus chemical or radiological intervention, and active and passive euthanasia can exacerbate the active, surviving agent's guilt about omissions or commissions in the care of the dying. By contrast, the finality of death encourages the griever to confront feelings of ambivalence and guilt: "This may be in marked contrast to the pre-divorce period of dissatisfaction on the part of the active agent in divorce which may extend over a period of months and years" (Crosby, Gage, and Raymond 1983). The role of the initiator of the divorce process is a dynamic one. It carries the potential for significant ambivalence and guilt. As Crosby, Lybarger, and Mason (1987) have stated, "In short, responsibility for one's actions plays a much greater role in the resolution of grief resulting from divorce than it does in the resolution of grief resulting from death" (p. 25).

Although the bulk of decision making resides with the active agent, it remains the lot of the noninitiator to face the inevitable aftermath of many of those decisions. The passive agent must actively confront the rejection inherent in the disunion process. Deep emotional pain is often masked by anger and hostility. The presence of deeply painful feelings, as well as mental confusion and disorganization, impel the individual to wrestle with the meaning of his or her experiences. Frankel (1963) suggested that the search for meaning represents a powerful human motivation. Glick, Weiss, and Parkes (1974) reported that a substantial number of their sample or widows sought to establish meaning out of their husbands' premature deaths. Unfortunately, most of literature on grief fails to address the role of personal meaning in adjustment to loss. Martin (1987) challenged future researchers with the following:

> Future efforts in the area of adjustment to loss must accord the individual a creative, active role in ascribing meaning to the loss experience. Viewing adjustment to loss as a function of threat suggests a framework for synthesizing the complexity of the loss experience with the importance of individual meanings. (p. 84)

The efforts of Abramson, Seligman, and Teasdale (1978) in reformulating Martin Seligman's (1975) model of learned helplessness provide a framework for understanding the role of personal meaning in the grief responses to death and divorce. Learned helplessness refers to a generalized expectancy that events are independent of one's own responses. Consequently, individuals characterized by learned helplessness believe that their coping behaviors are futile. Abramson, Seligman, and Teasdale (1978) suggested that there are two types of helplessness: personal and universal. In both types the person believes the outcome is not contingent on his or her behavior. However, personal helplessness results in the individual's perception that other people would be capable of achieving the desired goal or escaping the undesirable event, while he himself (or she herself) cannot. This results in apathy, problems with persistence, and loss of self-esteem. In universal helplessness, the individual perceives that no person could avoid the undesirable event. People experiencing universal helplessness share most of the same undesirable consequences as those experiencing personal helplessness with one critical exception: they do not suffer loss of self-esteem.

The awesome finality of death evokes a sense of helplessness in the survivor. The universality of death encourages the griever to view his or her plight as a form of cosmic impotence, the shared cost of living.

Being rejected also evokes a certain sense of helplessness. Divorce, however, lacks death's finality and universality. For the noninitiating participant in a divorce, there exists ample opportunity to witness the apparently successful attempts of others to preserve their marital relationships. Equally available are opportunities for contemplating one's personal inadequacies. Data on the physical and mental health status of the widowed and divorced point to the presence of greater physical and mental health disturbances among the divorced than among the widowed (Spanier and Thompson 1983). This suggests a certain devaluation of the self among the divorced.

Unlike widowhood, divorce is an event tailormade for feeling bad about oneself. Unlike death, marital loss does not summon forth social support and understanding.

The Disenfranchisement of Divorce Grief

Our society promotes success by striving to give every individual some chance for success. It does not tolerate failure. Since divorce represents a preventable failure, divorcing persons are subject to societal repudiation and punishment. Much of the punishment is indirect. It is seen in changes in the divorced individual's social network of interpersonal relationships. Punishment is meted out as existing institutional supports erode. It is also evident in the lack of approved rituals marking the transition from couple to partnerless persons.

Social Network Disenfranchisement. Included in an individual's social network are relationships with the family of origin, the family of the former spouse, the former spouse, and friends and acquaintances. Not included in the current discussion are relationships with children.

Generally, members of the family of origin are somewhat supportive of the divorced person and often provide significant services (Spanier and Casto 1979), but emotional support appears hindered by a reluctance of separated and divorced individuals to tell their families of their marital problems (Weiss 1975). Although interactions with family of origin members seem to remain constant or increase after divorce, many people believe their standing in the family has suffered as a consequence of their divorce (Weiss 1975).

Kin relationships often weaken following divorce. It should be noted that children often play a pivotal role in the quality and frequency of postseparation contacts with in-laws. Still, many individuals report less satisfaction with in-law interactions (Weiss 1975).

Many researchers have discussed the volatile postmarital relationship between ex-spouses. Weiss (1975) has stated that divorce does not end a relationship but merely changes it. The attachment bond characterizing the marital relationship persists for months, sometimes years after the relationship has formally ended. Initially, contacts between ex-spouses tend to remain somewhat antagonistic. The conflict decreases over time, but women nourish a degree of anger and resentment toward their ex-spouses longer than do men (Hetherington, Cox, and Cox 1978), although a study in help-seeking behavior among divorced persons revealed that, next to close friends, ex-spouses represent the most sought-out category of social support (Chiriboga et al. 1979).

Close friends remain the single most sought-out group for advice and support (Chiriboga et al. 1979), yet divorce causes change in friendship networks. Consistent agreement exists among researchers regarding the decline in both interaction and importance of predivorce friendships for the divorced, with married friends suffering the highest casualty rates (Spanier and Casto 1979, Weiss 1975). Hetherington, Cox, and Cox (1978) observed increased contact with other divorced persons.

Marital separation has an often negative impact on the individual's social network. Freund (1974) noted the stark differences between losing a husband to death and losing one through divorce. Whereas friends and relatives generally rush to the side of the widow, the situation for the divorced woman is "startlingly different" (p. 41). Freund continued:

> Instead of being met with an understanding of the type of struggle the divorcée must face, and of the support she needs, she is often met with hostility, rejection or fear. Many of her friends disapprove of what she has done or what has happened to her. . . . People do not consider it a failure or the wife's fault if her husband dies. But if there is a divorce, silent suspicions are often present, whether they be with or without foundation. . . . The grief suffered by a divorced person thus goes unrecognized and the working through process is not supported. In many subtle ways it is also aggravated by the rejection and suspicion of those who would be in a good position to help. (p. 41)

Unique in divorce literature is the work of Kitson et al. (1980) comparing the reactions of widows and divorcées to the loss of a spouse. Their data suggested that divorcées feel much more restricted and isolated from others than do widows. The divorcées were more likely to report that their friends were more jealous of them when the friends' spouses were around. Most significantly, the women in the Kitson et al. (1980) sample believed that divorcées were more likely than widows to lose status and respect as a result of their change in marital status. Collectively, these results support the hypothesis that widows have less restricted attitudes about social relationships than do divorcées. Berman and Turk (1981) found that of all the major areas of concern and of problems which affect divorced individuals, "difficulties with peer and social relations are most highly related to both greater mood disturbance and lower life satisfaction" (p. 187).

Institutional Disenfranchisement. In the United States marriages are being dissolved at the rate of one every twenty-seven seconds, or more than 1 million each year (Glick 1984). What is remarkable is the inadequacy of institutional response to a family crisis of this magnitude. Even among the helping professions, psychiatry, psychology, social work, ministry, counseling, and medicine pay only scant attention to divorce. Few professionals wish to become involved in the postdivorce world, which is often viewed as destructive (Fisher 1968).

Religious institutions have not been particularly forthcoming with succor and support. Freund (1974) found many of the separated and divorced neglected, even shunned by their faith communities. Hagemeyer commented on the loss of community experienced by the divorced: "A change in attitude by the faith community is often unintentional, but nevertheless experienced as ostracism and disapproval. For many, the divorce from community may make it seem that nothing in the world is stable" (1986, p. 243).

The Absence of Ritual. Ritual has been defined as "the symbolic affirmation of values by means of culturally standardized utterances and actions" (Taylor 1980, p. 198). People in all cultures are inclined to use ritual behavior as an effective means of expressing and reinforcing important sentiments.

Functions of rituals include validation and reinforcement of values, reinforcement of group loyalties, relief from psychological tensions, and restabilizing of patterns of interaction disrupted by a crisis (Taylor 1980). Rituals differ from other behaviors in that they are formal—repetitive and stereotyped. They often occur at set times and in sacred places (Rappaport 1974).

Given the high incidence of divorce, the absence of ritual is remarkable. One of the most important functions of a ritual is socialization into a new role. There is nearly unanimous agreement among researchers that the absence of an approved social role presents a unique problem for the divorced. Kitson et al. (1980) found the status of the widow to be more clearly defined, with norms for mourning a death; nothing comparable exists for mourning a divorce. Mourning rituals provide a means for disposing of the body, and they provide general guidelines for social gatherings and acts of support and sympathy. The societal customs of marking gravesites or building monuments for the deceased are complemented by symbolic memorialization of the lost relationship through memorial grants and endowments.

By contrast, the only relatively consistent custom the divorced can anticipate is a legal document and an attorney's fee. However, I have recently noted the appearance of "Happy Divorce" cards in local shops, as well as a surge in divorce "parties." Unfortunately, most of those in attendance are usually "celebrating" their own recent pain.

In addition to providing an active model for socialization into a new role, ritual also restricts behaviors. Widows, for example, are expected to conform to existing norms regarding the establishment of new romantic relationships. This can be difficult for many, especially those completing their grief work sooner than is socially ordained. For the divorced, the opposite is often true. Levy and Joffe (1978) have suggested that termination of the marital relationship is characterized by three major phases: separation, individuation, and reconnection. Individuation is seen as a time of transition from one life-style to another. Individuation is, in fact, a recapitulation of the adolescence, with all of its attendant confusion, experiments, and failures (Levy and Joffe 1978). Among the divorced, relationship experimentation is often conducted without regard to internal or socially prescribed limits and can result in rejection, further self-deprecation, and guilt. Without the benefit of socially sanctioned limits, the divorced often accumulate new scars before old wounds have healed.

Implications for Intervention

Marriages fail. Adjusting to marital failure is a formidable task. Divorce grief is largely unsanctioned suffering—it is a disenfranchised loss experience. Bohannan (1971) has acknowledged the unique character of divorce grief and indicted existing public and private support systems:

> Emotional divorce results in the loss of a loved object just as fully—but by a quite different route of experience—as does the death of a spouse. Divorce is difficult because it involves a purposeful and active rejection by another person, who, merely by living, is a daily symbol of the rejection. It is also made difficult because the community helps even less in divorce than it does in bereavement. . . . Divorce is even more threatening than death to some people, because they have thought about it more, perhaps wished for it more consciously. But most importantly—there is no recognized way to mourn a divorce. The grief has to be worked out alone and without the benefit of traditional rites, because few people recognize it for what it is. (p. 42)

Effective interveners are those who recognize the uniqueness of divorce grief and view it as a type of disenfranchised loss. Counseling efforts should focus on facilitating grief work (see, for instance, Worden 1982). There are two general areas of concern in treating divorce grief: (1) the response of the individual to the divorce, and (2) the disenfranchisement of the divorced griever.

Loss of Relationship

Divorce grief is not about the mourning of the death of an individual. It is a response to the death of the marital relationship. Relationship loss presents the griever with several challenges:

Relinquishing the dream

Accepting new roles

Adjusting to the change in finances

Reestablishing physical and emotional intimacy

Preserving the self

Marital dreams are often the products of a cherished childhood fantasy of meeting the beautiful prince or princess, falling in love, being awakened sexually by the lover's kiss, and riding off into the sunset to "live happily ever after." The alternative dream is a function of a need to escape an unfortunate, unhappy childhood household, and a craving to establish the "perfect relationship" and to become the "perfect parent." The self-destructive bitterness displayed by some of those divorced can be alleviated only when they learn to accept the reality of a less than perfect world. In addition, failure to relinquish the dream can condemn the individual to repeated attempts at fulfillment of the wished-for-relationship—as well as repeated failures.

Role change is a by-product of divorce. Being single again presents the individual with many of the challenges already discussed. The presence of children, however, poses an immediate loss to both parents. For the non-custodial parent, the sense of loss is especially acute. The variety of daily shared activities must now be compacted into weekend visits. The custodial parent is faced with the sense of loss that accompanies relinquishing the children to the former spouse for visitations. This is particularly difficult if unresolved, seething anger is the hallmark of the postmarital relationship. Counseling efforts should include *(a)* clarifying ambiguous feelings between ex-spouses; *(b)* resolving lingering animosities; and *(c)* educating the spouses about the child's need for a continuing loving, accepting relationship with both parents.

Divorce often results in loss of property and income. Many divorced persons face the reality of restructuring existing budgets and learning to live within their means, while others must learn financially related skills. Still others may wish to find a job for the first time, change jobs, or start a new career. Counselors may assist individuals with financial planning as well as provide career counseling.

The challenge in meeting physical and intimacy needs overwhelms many of the newly divorced. Fears of being hurt again interact with uncertainties about how to find a new partner. Initial efforts at intimacy may be hampered by uncertainties regarding existing moral standards and one's own system of values. Therapy can help divorced clients understand their ambivalent feelings. Individuals may be encouraged to explore opportunities for social interactions. Of special concern to the person reentering the world of single adults is the presence of sexually transmitted diseases. Counselors should not assume that previously married individuals are aware of the threat of AIDS and other STDs.

Threats to self-esteem are roadblocks to recovery among the divorced. Active agents in the divorce process frequently experience a sense of guilt, while passive participants are burdened with feelings of helplessness and failure. Divorce may also effect a loss of identity. The marital relationship often serves as a primary source of self-definition, with marital partners forming "the basis for the development of a highly integrated 'couple reality'—that is, an intimate, dyadic world view" (Stephen 1984, p. 4). Divorced individuals may feel frightened and confused, as though they have lost their identity. A supportive counseling alliance is needed to aid individuals in reestablishing a sense of self and in repairing damage to self-esteem. Counselors not afraid to challenge cognitive distortions regarding culpability, failure, and powerlessness may reap substantial therapeutic gains.

The Disenfranchised Griever

Doka (1987) has examined the impact of grief when death interrupts a nontraditional relationship. Many of the same circumstances surrounding the loss of a nontraditional relationship are present in divorce, including the lack of formal and informal support systems and the absence of socially sanctioned rituals. As a consequence, Doka suggested the possibility of atypical manifestations of grief among some survivors of nontraditional relationships. Clinicians should acknowledge the potential for pathological grieving patterns among the divorced population. Anger is frequently unresolved and is often displaced onto what remains of the griever's fragile support system. Of particular concern is the lack of ritual, which encourages expression of repressed feelings of anger, guilt, and shame. The burden of providing social acknowledgment of the loss as well as sanctioning the pain of the experience often falls to the counseling relationship. In order to meet this challenge, therapists should *(a)* stimulate a search for meaning in the divorce experience, and *(b)* legitimize appropriate grief-related responses.

The search for meaning in divorce may be assisted by the creative therapist. Arranging for "mock ceremonies" or symbolic funerals may encourage catharsis and reassure the griever of the significance of his or her loss. Clients can be encouraged to publish a formal announcement of the marital dissolution in local newspapers. Counselors may draw upon their own value systems to stimulate the search for meaning. Sympathetic clergy may be an excellent resource for certain clients, as well as existing support groups.

Counselors may elect to use letter writing, tape recording, or talking to an empty chair to stimulate expression of feelings and to provide an opportunity for closure. Ultimately, it is the security of an accepting, nonjudgmental therapeutic relationship that legitimizes feelings, begins the search for meaning, and promotes healing.

References

Abramson, L.Y., M.E.P. Seligman, and J. Teasdale. 1978. "Learned Helplessness in Humans: Critique and Reformulation." *Journal of Abnormal Psychology* 87, 49–74.

Aldrich, C.K. 1974. "Some Dynamics of Anticipatory Grief." In *Anticipatory Grief,* edited by B. Schoenberg, A. Carr, A. Kutscher, D. Perez, and I. Goldberg. New York: Columbia University Press.

Berman, W.H., and D.C. Turk. 1981. "Adaptation to Divorce: Problems and Coping Strategies." *Journal of Marriage and the Family* 43:1, 179–89.

Bohannan, P. 1971. "The Six Stations of Divorce." In *Divorce and After,* edited by P. Bohannan. Garden City, N.Y.: Doubleday.

Chiriboga, D.A., A. Coho, J.A. Stein, and J. Roberts. 1979. "Divorce, Stress and Social Supports: A Study in Helpseeking Behavior. *Journal of Divorce* 3:2, 121–35.

Crosby, J.F., B.A. Gage, and M.C. Raymond. 1983. "The Grief Resolution Process in Divorce." *Journal of Divorce* 7:1, 3–18.

Crosby, J.F., S.K. Lybarger, and R.L. Mason. 1987. "The Grief Resolution Process in Divorce: Phase II. *Journal of Divorce* 11:2, 17–39.

Doka, K. 1987. "Silent Sorrow: Grief and the Loss of Significant Others." *Death Studies* 11, 455–69.

———. 1989. *Disenfranchised Grief.* Lexington, MA: Lexington Books.

Fisher, E.O. 1968. *Help for Today's Troubled Marriages.* New York: Hawthorne Books.

Frankel, V. 1962. *Man's Search for Meaning.* New York: Washington Square Press.

Freund, J. 1974. "Divorce and Grief." *Journal of Family Counseling* 2:2, 40–43.

Glick, I.O., R.S. Weiss, and C.M. Parkes. 1974. *The First Year of Bereavement.* New York: Wiley.

Glick, P.C. 1984. "How American Families Are Changing." *American Demographics* 6, 21–25.

Goode, W. 1956. *Women in Divorce.* New York: Free Press.

Goodyear, R.K. 1981. "Termination as a Loss Experience for the Counselor." *The Personnel and Guidance Journal* 59, 347–49.

Hagemeyer, S. 1986. "Making Sense of Divorce Grief." *Pastoral Psychology* 34:4, 237–50.

Hayes, R.L. 1981. "High School Graduation: The Case for Identity Loss." *The Personnel and Guidance Journal* 59, 369–72.

Hendrick, S.S. 1981. "Spinal Cord Injury: A Special Kind of Loss." *The Personnel and Guidance Journal* 59, 355–58.

Herman, S.J. 1974. "Divorce: A Grief Process." *Perspectives in Psychiatric Care* 12, 108–12.

Hetherington, E.M., M. Cox, and R. Cox. 1978. "The Aftermath of Divorce." In *Mother-Child, Father-Child Relations,* edited by J.H. Stevens, Jr., and M. Mathews. Washington, D.C.: National Association for the Education of Young People.

Kessler, S. 1975. *The American Way of Divorce: Prescription for Change.* Chicago: Nelson Hall.

Kimmel, D. 1978. "Adult Development and Aging: A Gay Perspective." *International Journal of Aging and Human Development* 10, 237–48.

Kitson, G., H. Lopata, W. Holmes, and S. Meyering. 1980. "Divorcées and Widows: Similarities and Differences." *American Journal of Orthopsychiatry* 50, 291–301.

Kressel, K. 1980. "Patterns of Coping in Divorce and Some Implications for Clinical Practice." *Family Relations* 29:2, 234–40.

Levy, T.M., and W. Joffe. 1978. "Counseling Couples through Separation: A Developmental Approach." *Family Therapy* 3, 267–76.

Martin, T.L. 1987. "The Effect of Death Education on Adjustment to Loss. Ph.D. diss., University of Maryland, College Park.

O'Conner, N.D. 1977. "An Exploration of the Effects of Anticipatory Grief versus Acute Grief on Recovery After Loss of Spouse among Divorced and Separated Women." *Dissertation Abstracts International* 37(9-A), 5708.

Rappaport, R.A. 1974. "Obvious Aspects of Ritual." *Cambridge Anthropology* 2, 2–60.

Seligman, M.E.P. 1975. *Helplessness: On Depression, Development and Death*. San Francisco: Freeman.

Spanier, G.B., and R.F. Casto. 1979. "Adjustment to Separation and Divorce: An Analysis of 50 Case Studies." *Journal of Divorce* 2:3, 241–53.

Spanier, G.B., and L. Thompson. 1983. "Relief and Distress After Marital Separation." *Journal of Divorce* 7:1, 31–49.

Stephen, T.D. 1984. "Symbolic Interdependence and Post-Breakup Distress: A Reformulation of the Attachment Construct." *Journal of Divorce* 8:1, 1–16.

Taylor, R.B. 1980. *Cultural Ways*. 3d ed. Boston: Allyn and Bacon.

Weiss, R.S. 1975. *Marital Separation*. New York: Basic Books.

Wiseman, R.S. 1975. "Crisis Theory and the Process of Divorce." *Social Casework* 54:4, 202–12.

Worden, J.W. 1982. *Grief Counseling and Grief Therapy: A Handbook for the Mental Health Practitioner*. New York: Springer.

16
Youth and the Disenfranchised Breakup

Louis E. LaGrand

The breakup of a love relationship is a frequent major loss in the lives of the adolescent and young adult.[1] As with all loss experiences there is a wide variety of responses from the young, depending on their self-esteem, the degree of emotional investment in their relationships, and how dependent they were on the relationship to meet personal needs. Consequently, the breakup of a love relationship may result in a high-intensity grief response that lasts for months or years, or a low-intensity response in which adaptation to life without the other is a matter of several days at best. This chapter addresses the high-intensity response, which is exacerbated by a support network that minimizes the importance of the loss to the griever and unwittingly increases the individual's grief work.

The Young Adult Study

Ten years ago I initiated the Young Adult Study with a small grant from Potsdam College. The purpose of this descriptive research was to identify the types of major loss experiences encountered by the seventeen to twenty-four-year-old, the subsequent physical and emotional reactions experienced, and how one coped with loss. It began as an attempt to assess the impact of death on college students and developed into a large-scale analysis of various losses when it became apparent that death was but one of a number of massive changes that this age group must deal with.

Data was collected from young people in diverse educational settings: private liberal arts colleges, engineering schools, public liberal arts colleges, and two-year technical and community colleges. Presently, data has been obtained from more than four thousand students in fifteen institutions of higher education in two states. It has resulted in more than sixty thousand observations on loss and grief from young adults as they have experienced loss.

Each subject in the study was asked, "What do you consider to be your most recent major loss?" Next, the survey instrument asked for responses on emotions experienced, physical reactions, and coping techniques employed. More than sixty different losses were identified. Significantly, more than one thousand respondents (27 percent) indicated that the breakup of a love relationship was their most recent major loss. Not infrequently these breakups were followed by intense grief responses. In some instances these responses were as devastating to the griever as if he or she had been mourning the death of a loved one.[2]

Why Young Adults and Adolescents Are at Risk

In order to appreciate the impact that a breakup has on the seventeen- to twenty-four-year-old age group, a brief review of their developmental tasks will provide the background for assessing responses.

It has been suggested that there are five psychosocial issues of adolescence and early adulthood: identity, autonomy, intimacy, sexuality, and achievement.[3] Because in late adolescence and early adulthood the central developmental task of establishing one's personal identity is the overriding concern, loss experiences are given but cursory attention until one suffers such a life change. Included in this search for identity are career choices, questions of emotional autonomy, changes in social roles, and key questions such as "Who am I?" and "How will I fit into my community and peer group?" Self-consciousness also tend to pervade the development of cognitive and social abilities.

The crisis of identity versus identity diffusion (lack of a sense of self) is one that Erikson tells us is the basis for adolescence being a period of uprootedness: "Like a trapeze artist, the young person in the middle of vigorous emotion must let go of his safe hold on childhood and reach out for a firm grasp on adulthood."[4] Success in this endeavor is directly dependent on the nature of one's interpersonal transactions. Because of the ongoing nature of the process of identity formation, the loss of significant peers or family members through death, divorce, breakups, or severed friendships can be especially traumatic: "The social context in which the adolescent attempts to establish a sense of identity exerts a tremendous impact on the nature and outcome of the process"[3] (p. 255). Therefore, the social support system takes on special significance at a time when growth and development are dominant themes.

Specifically, there are seven developmental tasks that adolescents and young adults must complete to reach successful maturation:

1. Acquire new social skills
2. Achieve a masculine or feminine sex role

3. Accept changes in one's body
4. Achieve emotional independence from parents and other adults
5. Make an occupational commitment
6. Develop a personal ideology
7. Achieve a membership in the larger community[5]

These adaptational demands in themselves are the basis for much stress and tension. They also underlie the onset of anxiety reactions and mild depression, the latter considered the most common psychological disturbance of this age group.[6] Further, as Erikson states, "A sense of identity is never gained or maintained once and for all . . . it is constantly lost and regained, although more lasting and more economical methods of maintenance and restoration are evolved and fortified in late adolescence."[7] Many theorists believe that identity development tends to carry on well into adulthood.

Young people also define themselves in relation to three general goals: demonstrating competence, demonstrating mastery, and winning social approval.[8] Social approval includes self-control, being strong, and possessing a sense of independence. Appearance is a formidable concern. All of these goals are seriously threatened and heavily influenced by major loss experiences. Also, in late adolescence (age eighteen to twenty-one), when one leaves home and establishes greater independence, support systems needed in times of major loss are not as firmly rooted and available as they were in earlier years. This transition period often finds one hesitant to break down the image of invulnerability. Therefore, when confronting major loss experiences, many adolescents and young adults face problems of self-image:

> The ongoing tasks of adolescence, the pressures of school, the sanctions against emotional expression, and the difficulties others have in perceiving his needs and supporting them, may all mean that the process of mourning is a rather private one for many adolescents; or that it occurs in bursts, intermittently, when circumstances are favorable and the ego allows this regression.[9]

Given this demanding time of life as a background for confronting losses of various kinds, it is important that we stress four additional factors that impinge upon the coping abilities of many adolescents and young adults, causing additional hardships:

1. Grief is not considered to be a positive, expected response to loss.
2. Realistic attitudes toward breakups and other major loss experiences are virtually nonexistent.
3. Pressure to conform exclusively to parental value systems often causes communication problems.

4. Support systems, consisting of family members and sometimes friends, react to the breakup as merely a part of growing up, thereby minimizing the meaning of the loss to the griever. The result is disenfranchised grief.

The discovery that breakups and other major losses are real is a threatening experience especially when there is little help available to guide one through the maze of emotions and behavior that follow. Psychologist Therese Rando characterizes the youthful response to loss through a death as follows:

> Many adult responses to the death will be seen, but they will be complicated by typical adolescent problems: resistance to communicating with adults, overconcern about the acceptability of their responses to others; alienation from adults and sometimes peers; lack of knowledge of the social expectations; and other development issues that may compromise the task of mourning, such as emotionality and sexual conflict.[10]

Quite similar responses to a breakup prevail. These factors may delay the grieving process or become salient forces in the suppression of specific feelings surrounding any significant loss event.

An additional complicating factor is the assumption by young people that loss and grief are associated exclusively with death, which during the early years of life seems to be irrelevant and foreign to the frantic pace of work or study. Gradually, however, separation from loved ones in a variety of forms begin to occur to the extent that grief is often experienced, though still not recognized as the result of loss. The young are not alone in this regard. Young and old alike seem to fail to recognize the results of separations other than death as grief responses. But grief is present in *all* separation experiences. It is manifested in shock, numbness, disbelief, anger, guilt, and a host of other emotions. Most young people are surprised but relieved to discover that their reactions to loss are truly grief experiences. In this way their behavior becomes explainable.

The Intensity of Response

The nature of physical and emotional responses to a breakup is varied. In many instances these responses parallel the grief response to the death of a loved one. A number of counselors have suggested that divorce triggers grief that is as devastating for some individuals as the death of a relative or friend.[11] My data suggest that an equally intense grief period, similar to that in relation to the death experience, does occur in response to a breakup when the individual has been totally dependent on the ex-boyfriend/girlfriend.[2]

Depression, loneliness, and feelings of emptiness are among the most common emotions reported. Anger, feelings of rejection, and guilt are also frequently listed. Interestingly, denial tends to be experienced in a number of breakups, as suggested by Brenda, who said: "At first I denied it, thinking, he doesn't really want this to end (I still think that from time to time), but then I stop myself and say, it doesn't matter if he really wanted to or not; the fact is he did—accept it." Jim said, "*Do not* deny the inevitable when you see it coming. Do not try to fool yourself into thinking you can change an unchangeable situation." Others feel "there is something wrong with me" or question their values and beliefs. Maria said, "I was in disbelief when my relationship ended because I felt confident and safe and left myself vulnerable." Shelly wrote, "I basically withdrew and shut off my emotions until I could cope with them. My family to this day does not know. I didn't really let anyone know about the hurt because I was ashamed." Many young people experience a loss of self-confidence and self-esteem because of their feelings of rejection.

The most frequent physical reactions include crying, insomnia, and digestive disturbances. Twenty-eight subjects reported that they had vomited as a result of their breakup, indicating the severity of their reactions. One respondent reported "jaw displacement due to tension." Another reported "shaking when I see him." Numerous physical complaints were cited: headaches, numbness, chills, weakness, nausea, exhaustion, backaches, labored breathing, weight loss or weight gain. Alcohol and other drug use was engaged in by some in an attempt to deal with emotional pain.

The following excerpts from anecdotal data provide additional insight into the turmoil experienced by some subjects:

Because I felt I had cut myself off from other people I renewed old friendships and created new ones. In addition, I made a decision to enter therapy, as much for my own growth as for coping with the loss.

He explained to me why we broke up and asked me my feelings. First, I told him that I hated him and as we have talked (over the past two months) I am gradually starting to get rid of some of the hatred and anger that I have towards him.

There was a brook sitting at the bottom of a hill in the wood behind my house where I went to be alone so I could cry, think, and not have anyone around to bother me. I just wanted to be alone. After about six months or a year a female friend and I got to talk about the situation and she helped me overcome my loss. We became good friends and I finally realized that life has to go on and that there's more to my life than just one girl who didn't love me anymore.

The most helpful thing was that he was far away from me, so I got it into my head to think of him as dead. This way I wouldn't try to fight to save a relationship that had to end. I didn't dwell on it either. The most helpful advice I got was to talk about it but try not to burden all my friends with it. This encouraged me to seek counseling, which was a more neutral way of dealing with it than listening to my friends tell me over and over what a jerk he was. After counseling I made a resolution not to speak his name, which really helped me to keep him out of my mind. The more I mentioned him the more I thought about him. By not mentioning him I was able to let the memory of him just slip away.

Minimizing the Breakup

What leads to additional pain and complicated grief for the young person coping with the breakup is minimizing the loss. This occurs in several ways. The most obvious is for older adults to insist, "You will get over this; it's a part of growing up." That is quite true. However, this is not the time or place to make such a statement to one who is deeply hurt. The perception of the griever's support system becomes: "They do not understand what this means to me or what I am feeling." It often causes the griever to withdraw and limit the sharing of feelings with those individuals.

The root cause of disenfranchised grief following the breakup of a love relationship lies in the differences in perceptions of the event between support persons and the griever. Since perceptions are the personal meanings we give to experience, older support persons often view the loss less seriously. This is reflected in the nature of their supportive behavior. Such a shallow view is further reinforced when support persons believe that the griever is better off without the person he or she broke up with. Early in one's grief this observation may initially be unacceptable, while later in grief work one begins to understand that perhaps "I am better off without him [or her]."

Sometimes close friends tend to minimize the nature of the loss and the degree of emotional investment in the ex-boyfriend/girlfriend when they try to influence the griever to date again too soon after the breakup. Although going out again with a new friend is often a source of reestablishing self-confidence and importance, many young people need time to deal with their feelings and sort out their thoughts about trust, commitment, and the causes of their breakup. Once again, the lack of understanding by friends of the needs of the griever tend to reduce the influence of the support system in helping the individual make an adjustment to what is considered a major life change. The griever who believes that no one understands his or her plight feels isolated and alone at a time when human contact is essential in the coping process.

The Role of Overdependency

In many male-female relationships at all ages there is a tendency for one partner to forfeit his or her individuality to the extent that the other is expected to provide for most personal needs, make decisions, and give nurturance. When this one-sided condition grows, the receiving partner establishes an identity primarily through the other. This is a potentially dangerous relationship because the individual fails to recognize his or her own strengths and to develop latent abilities. In particular, one's self-esteem is regulated by the other rather than by one's own internal resources.

Another devastating result of the overdependent relationship, in addition to the loss of personal identity, is that the increased time and focus of energies by the dependent person on the other minimizes the number of healthy relationships with friends. Then at the time of the breakup there is frequently a weak support system to turn to during the grief process. Adaptation is often complicated at a time when understanding and nurturance from others is essential. The dependent relationship has restricted emotional growth and development. What was thought to be love was simply infatuation with the other. Truly loving relationships are never dominated by one partner; there is a mutual commitment to the other's well-being.

Twenty-one-year-old Jennifer put it this way:

> I would have been better prepared if I had not devoted so much time to the relationship, causing it to be almost exclusive of other relationships. Now I realize that I need to expand my base of friends (and support people), and not "put all of my eggs into one basket." Had I done this before, I believe that the breakup of that relationship would not have caused me to feel as though the rug was being pulled out from under me or my entire world was falling apart.

Jackie said, "In the situation I was in I would have been better prepared to cope if I had not been so dependent on one person to the point that I lost sight of who I was. Having a life of your own is extremely important, so that you can have an identity of your own." What Jackie is saying is that you can love one person more than others and still develop your interests, cultivate those interests, and your personality. This is a powerful belief to develop to replace the common conviction that "I am never going to find another like him [or her]."

The dependent person is highly influenced not to think for him- or herself. Accordingly, overdependent people develop a belief system that reduces their assessment and decision-making skills markedly. This is commonly observed in the irrational beliefs about the self and one's breakup after the loss occurs. The individual blames the self, is convinced there will never be another love in life, and is unable to rely on the self to recover and go on with life. As Maria observes:

> I think that it is important *not* to let your whole life revolve around one person. If I had known what a completely different person I would become during our relationship, I probably never would have entered it in the first place. It is important to rely on *yourself* first because you are the only person who can ultimately be strong. *Never* place your entire future in another person's hands because if that person is ever taken from you in any way, you will be lost. My loss has helped me grow so much as a person.

Maria learned a very important lesson from her breakup: one must be able to rely on oneself first, to use one's inner resources to cope with the many changing circumstances of life. Her "love" was limiting, not freeing her to grow as a person.

Janet explained her ability to cope this way: "What helped me cope with my breakup was the realization that I am not less of a person because of the loss, but actually more than I was before. I have grown because of my acceptance of the challenge to grow."

Implications for Counselors and Educators

Normalize the Emotions Associated with the Breakup

As was mentioned earlier, the emotions that accompany a breakup are frequently overwhelming. In many instances, the breakup of a love relationship is the first major change in one's life. Consequently, the depth of emotional response is alarming. Shock, panic, guilt, or anger may surface in ways never previously experienced. Not infrequently, this results in thoughts that one is losing one's sanity and going out of control. The sense of rejection spawns feelings of helplessness and hopelessness, that there is no future.

Given the nature of the relationship, built on overdependency or irrational beliefs about what constitutes love and commitment or both, intense emotions should be considered normal. It is critical to point out that it's "okay to feel what you're feeling," that the person is not different or unusual for what he or she is experiencing. This can be accomplished verbally or nonverbally by the accepting manner of the teacher or counselor. It also implies that crying is perfectly acceptable and should be encouraged. In essence, the counselor is giving the individual permission to grieve.

Encourage the Expression of Thoughts and Emotions

The breakup must be treated as a *genuine* loss experience in which the individual is allowed to talk and ventilate feelings as desired. It initially implies permitting the repetition of description of the breakup, how it might have been prevented, or who was at fault. This review of the relationship is very similar to the review that must take place after the death of a loved one. It is especially important when the breakup has been minimized by friends. The abandonment by "friends" after a few weeks not only isolates the griever but ends the process of repetition and review that is helpful in eventually letting go. This verbalized review is often needed because of the reminders of relationship losses that are constantly featured in the songs and television shows that youth are bombarded with. Letting others know what is happening inside is not a sign of weakness. Rather, this sharing process is an intelligent approach to healing.

Furthermore, the denial of certain feelings occurs not only with the death of a loved one but also with major loss experiences. Providing an atmosphere where feelings can surface without embarrassment is important. Young people need safe places and safe people. Twenty-three-year-old Doreen put it this way:

> My biggest help in dealing with the end of my relationship was my friends. They were all so great. My closest friends were far away. All I would have to do is call them. They didn't say much. They just listened to me babble on and on and on. While I was babbling on the tears just rolled down my face. Just to have someone there to listen, whether or not they have gone through a similar experience, is the best medicine for a broken heart.

Educate About the Grief Process

Young people need to understand that the chaos they are dealing with is a process that accompanies *any* meaningful loss. All too frequently grief is only associated with the death of a loved one, in their views. To understand that grief is the natural result of the degree of emotional investment in the person or object of loss brings a new perspective to their assessments. This will not lessen the pain of traumatic change, but it can provide a base for evaluating themselves and realizing that love and grief go hand in hand. As Schneidman has suggested, grief is the ransom we pay for loving.[12]

Equally significant is the awareness that grief is uniquely individual. Just as loss is in the eye of the beholder, so too is one's response to loss. This implies that young people are not unusual or strange because of the way they choose to grieve. Nor should they grieve according to someone else's agenda.

The freedom of sadness as they experience it is a gift in the process of adaptation. To grieve is a normal human expression when expected continuity in a relationship ends. This is an important belief to embrace;[13] beliefs are critical grieving tools. However, they must understand that the searing pain has to be endured before it subsides; it cannot be circumvented, it must be faced. That is a condition of having invested emotionally in another.

Help Fashion a Support Network

Time and time again the presence of others who are trying to understand and who are willing to listen endlessly and permissively is a common denominator for progress in one's grief work. The counselor may evaluate the number of support persons available and suggest that the griever use these individuals. Obviously, support persons are not always aware of the needs of those grieving a breakup; in some instances they can cause additional hardships. Therefore, it may be necessary for the griever to express his or her needs to trusted friends. As awkward as this may appear, there are few trusted friends who would not provide the time and energy to perform specific tasks. To be asked for help by a friend is an honor. We must break through the ethic that "one must be strong" and go it alone, and replace that with the concept of interdependence: we need each other at various times when we are vulnerable. The same applies to asking parents and relatives for assistance. There is nothing wrong with asking for help.

One of the most influential relationships that can assist in the transitional period is one in which the support person has experienced a breakup and survived. Being able to discuss feelings with another who has had to deal with similar circumstances is often a blessing in disguise. Since the support person has some insight into the depth of feelings accompanying such a loss, he or she can often provide the comfort and understanding so sorely needed. Barbara express this viewpoint when she wrote:

> The most helpful people were people who had gone through the experience. No one else understood the pain. Other people would just brush it off and say, "Forget about him." But you can't forget about a person you loved so deeply and planned to spend your future with. You can't brush off two years of your life. One of the most helpful people I went to was a counselor in the city of Rochester. He told me it was okay to feel bad and to hurt—and not to let anyone tell me that I shouldn't grieve. Before this I had been led to believe that I shouldn't cry. I felt very guilty because my grief lasted for several months. Sometimes I still grieve, although not as often. [This was written one and a half years after the breakup.]

Suggest Limiting Reminders of the Relationship

In beginning the key task of accepting the breakup, it will be helpful to suggest to the griever to minimize or eliminate, insofar as possible, the common reminders of the relationship. This means taking letters, mementos, inexpensive gifts, and other shared objects and putting them in a trunk or box to be stored away for the present. Such an approach will help reduce unnecessary reminders of the ex and the flood of emotions that usually accompanies the experience. This is in no way an attempt to curtail the normal expression of emotion, but rather begins the process of letting go and reducing false hope that the relationship can resume as before. It may mean taking a picture off the nightstand or refusing to wear a certain piece of jewelry. In any event, these gestures symbolically show that one is actively participating in the recovery process.

In some instances it may also be appropriate to suggest that the griever stay away from specific social settings where the ex may be encountered with someone new. Such an encounter can be especially difficult early in one's grief work. The same suggestion may be appropriate when it comes to visiting a place that was mutually considered "our favorite."

Help Restore Self-confidence and Self-esteem

Many disenfranchised breakups call into question one's beliefs, perceptions, and feelings toward the self. The force of emotions can greatly affect levels of self-esteem. In addition, the fact that young people have not fully developed their coping skills is a complicating factor in completing grief work.

As with most major loss experiences, consistency in the support network plays a strong role in self-acceptance. Realizing that parents and friends do care and are trying to understand and comfort is reassuring. This is illustrated by Carrie, who said,

> Knowing that my mother was there and would understand was a great help to me. She said that things would work themselves out for the best in the end and suggested I try to get involved in new relationships. She also gave me some needed self-confidence and reassurance that I would have little trouble meeting new guys and making new friends.

Establishing friendships is an important step in replacing feelings of being devalued with thoughts of importance and positive regard. As Jill observed,

> Meeting new and different people helped me feel more confident and develop a better attitude toward myself. This confidence helped me start believing that this wasn't the end of the world, that there are lots of other people and maybe I'll find the "right" one for me. Overall I feel the loss strengthened me as a person.

This same confidence and growth evolves through professional counseling. Sheila tells us,

I started to see a counselor at the college counseling center and he helped me gain perspective. The loss of my boyfriend through a breakup came right after my parents' separation and the death of my grandmother. Between my aunt and uncle, the counselor, my friends, and just finding new things to motivate me I learned to accept the loss.

The teacher or counselor can provide consistency in support by being available when the young person needs to talk, encouragement in strengthening existing relationships and developing new ones, and insight for reestablishing belief in the self. Suggest reading and rereading appropriate materials on grief, love, and self-worth. Prescribe exercise. Knowing that someone truly cares is a lifeline during the turbulent weeks of establishing a new identity.

Despite a busy schedule, the teacher or counselor who takes the time to establish rapport, who shows continuing interest (even an occasional phone call), and who relates to the disenfranchised breakup as an authentic source of grief will provide a nurturing atmosphere conducive to acceptance and healing.

Notes

1. L. LaGrand, *Coping with Separation and Loss as a Young Adult* (Springfield, Ill.: Thomas, 1986).

2. L. LaGrand, "The Breakup of a Love Relationship as a "Death Reaction," in *Creavity in Death Education and Counseling,* ed. C. Corr, J. Stillion, and M. Ribar (Lakewood, Ohio: Forum for Death Education and Counseling, 1983).

3. L. Steinberg, *Adolescence* (New York: Knopf, 1985).

4. E. Erikson, "Identity and Uprootedness in our Time," in *Varieties of Modern Social Theory,* ed. H. Ruitenbeek (New York: Dutton, 1963), pp. 55–68.

5. J. Stevens-Long and M. Cobb, *Adolescence and Early Adulthood* (Palo Alto, Calif.: Mayfield, 1983).

6. J. Weiner, "Psychopathology in Adolescence," In *Handbook of Adolescent Psychology,* ed. J. Adelson (New York: Wiley, 1980).

7. E. Erikson, Identity and the life cycle. *Psychological Issues,* 1959, 1, 118.

8. M. Maehr and D. Kleiber, "The Graying of Achievement Motivation," *American Psychologist* (1981), 36.

9. B. Raphael, *The Anatomy of Bereavement* (New York: Basic Books, 1983), pp. 155–56.

10. T. Rando, *Grief, Dying, and Death* (Champaign, Ill.: Research Press, 1984), p. 162.

11. W. Hafer, *Coping with Bereavement from Death or Divorce* (Englewood Cliffs, N.J.: Prentice-Hall, 1981); and I. Tanner, *The Gift of Grief* (New York: Hawthorne Books, 1976).

12. E. Schneidman, "Reflections on Contemporary Death." In *Creativity in Death Education and Counseling,* ed. C. Corr, J. Stillon and M. Ribar (Lakewood, Ohio: Forum for Death Education and Counseling, 1983).

13. L. LaGrand, *Changing Patterns of Human Existence: Assumptions, Beliefs, and Coping with the Stress of Change* (Springfield, Ill.: Thomas, 1988).

17
Psychosocial Loss and Grief

Kenneth J. Doka
Rita Aber

Introduction

One of the most memorable horror movies is *The Invasion of the Body Snatchers*. The premise is chilling. Unknown entities for unknown reasons seize the bodies of unsuspecting victims. These victims continue to lead seemingly normal lives. The parasitic consciousness now inhabiting the bodies gives only subtle clues to this new existence, which are perceived by those closest. The viewer is relieved when the film ends. The invasion is, afterall, only a celluloid fantasy.

But a similar premise is played out daily in the real lives of real people. Persons whom they love have changed. Of course, change is natural and inevitable as people grow and develop. Even in a minor event, such as writing or reading this chapter, both author and reader may, even should, experience minute change. When one person experiences a change, that change may very well affect others in his or her relational web. Since most of the changes are both slow and minor, they often have minimal impact on significant others. Over time, however, these incremental changes, as well as dramatic ones, can be quite significant, causing adjustments in relationships.

Not all of these changes are fraught with problems. In some cases, like that of a couple who both gradually become more mature and sophisticated, both parties in the relationship may change in similar ways, each adjusting to the modifications of the other. In other cases, changes in one may be complemented by changes in the other, as, for example, when a wife becomes more assertive and independent as her husband becomes debilitated and dependent. And then, in other situations, the changes in one party or dissimilar changes in both may lead to the dissolution of the relationship. "We've grown apart," "Our interests changed"—these are often explanations for divorces and other separations.

However, when change is dramatic, and particularly when it is not perceived as intentional, the situation can be especially difficult. Mental illness, chronic brain disorders such as Alzheimer's disease, substance abuse, and other difficulties can have a significant impact on the personality of an individual and can radically affect the lives of others around him or her. But because this change is perceived as beyond the control of the person, options like divorce or separation may be effectively precluded. Lezak says this well:

> Any noticeable change is apt to leave family members feeling a little cheated, or annoyed, or impatient, and a little guilty about those feelings. . . . The spouse cannot divorce with dignity or in good conscience. Gratitude, fond memories, feelings of responsibility, guilt, and fear of social condemnation contribute to the reluctance of a once happily married spouse to divorce his hopeless mate. (1978, p. 593)

In these cases, then, the premise of the "body snatchers" is played out. The bodies of victims are invaded by what seem to be mind snatchers, and as a result family and significant others suffer a profound sense of loss. But since the person is still physically alive, grief may not be recognized or considered appropriate. This chapter explores the dimensions of grief in those who must cope with the significant personality changes of relatives or friends.

Definitions of Death

In the very early years of thanatological research, writers indicated the many ways in which death could be perceived. Two are particularly useful in understanding the bereavement patterns related to significant personal change. Sudnow (1967) defined social death as those cases in which a person, though physically alive, is treated like a corpse. By this definition, a person is socially dead when "relevant attributes of the person begin permanently to cease to be operative as conditions for treating him" (1967, p. 74). A person who is comatose or a highly disoriented and institutionalized Alzheimer's patient might be perceived as socially dead by families and significant others. Kalish adds that perceptions of social death occur on a continuum: "A given person may be socially dead to one individual, to many individuals, or to virtually everyone" (1966, p. 73).

Psychological death refers to those cases in which the person ceases to be aware of self—not only does he not know who he is—he does not know that he is" (Kalish 1968). In psychological death the consciousness is perceived as dead.

Both of these definitions of types of death are relevant to the varied conditions that can create significant personal change, particularly those conditions characterized by profound disorientations, which is the type of death often perceived by relatives and friends. For here, the person remains a part of the family's immediate environment and the person's consciousness is recognized as existing, although in an altered state.

We can refer to psychosocial death in those cases in which the psychological essence, individual personality, or self is perceived as dead, though the person physically remains alive.[1] Psychosocial death can occur under many different conditions and in many different circumstances. It has long been recognized that relatives of those victimized by chronic brain syndromes such as Alzheimer's often experience deep feelings of loss. In discussing reactions of families of Alzheimer's patients, Cole, Griffin, and Ruiz note: "Family members may also feel a profound sense of loss, as a loved one who was once a vital person gradually loses mental, physical and social abilities" (1986, p. 28). Other conditions, such as mental illness or substance abuse, can also create a sense of psychosocial death. Conditions creating psychosocial death do not always have to involve mental illness, or physical, social, and psychological deterioration. Religious conversion or membership in a cult may also cause sudden and significant personality change (Addis, Schulman-Miller, and Lightman 1984). Even recovery from mental illness or substance abuse can lead to abrupt personality changes that might adversely affect relationships with others.[2] Satel and Southwick describe such a case:

> In attention deficit disorder, residual type, the irritability, impulsivity, restlessness, and inattentiveness are longstanding and may well serve as a core around which personality traits, cognitive style and social behavior crystalize. With a rapid change in these "core" symptoms, which have been incorporated into the individual's personality, his or her sense of self and characteristic ways of responding to events and other people are likely to be challenged. (1987, p. 1362)

In each of these cases there is a significant change from the person who he or she once was. Those who related to and were committed to that person's earlier self will notice this change, for though that person is still physically alive, his or her personality is markedly altered. The qualities of the person to whom one was attached are no longer present. As one spouse of an Alzheimer's victim once said, "All you have is a shell mocking what once was." The person is psychologically dead. There is loss, there is grief.

Dealing with Unresolvable Grief

There has been considerable documentation showing that those who experience dramatic change in a significant other or the psychosocial death of a loved one also experience grief reactions. Researchers have found that relatives experience depression and stress, which will often be manifested physically (Wasow 1986, Liptzin, Grob, and Eisen 1988, Quayhagen and Quayhagen 1988).

Guilt is often one of the most pervasive reactions, and it can be multifaceted. As with physical conditions, relatives may often believe they misdiagnosed or misunderstood earlier behaviors of the victim which could have been indicative of changes to occur. They may think that had they acted on these earlier signs they might have been able to mitigate, delay, or even forestall subsequent difficulties. In many of these situations, particularly those involving substance abuse, mental illness, or adherence to cults, they may experience a relational guilt, believing that their own inability to be an effective parent or good spouse contributed to the problem.

In addition to guilt feelings related to the causation of the condition, there may be considerable guilt related to the ways in which these relatives are coping with that condition. Because of heightened levels of stress, significant others may respond in intemperate though understandable ways to the aberrant behavior of the victim. And since that behavior is perceived as beyond the control of the victim, the significant other may feel that such responses are inappropriate. Significant others may also feel guilty over their own negative feelings toward the victim (Lezak 1978). Such guilt may be especially prevalent in conditions in which the significant changes result from perceived recovery. In these conditions, significant others may find it difficult to verbalize or even comprehend their own feelings of loss. They may feel considerable guilt about even harboring any feelings of longing for that unrecovered state. And their feelings of loss may not be validated by others. There may be guilt too over varied coping strategies. For example, although respite care may be extremely important in coping with the daily demands of those experiencing dementia or mental illness, there may also be guilt over leaving care to others (Quayhagen and Quayhagen 1988). A decision to institutionalize is also likely to be fraught with guilt.

While guilt, stress, and depression are common grief reactions to psychosocial loss, all other responses to grief may be evident as well. There may be considerable anger: at caregivers and relatives whom the family consider unsympathetic, unhelpful, or unrealistic; at the victim; at an unresponsive society; or even at God or the powers that be. People experiencing psychosocial loss may still feel that the victim can control behavior. They may feel a deep sense of abandonment. They may resent the victim for not meeting companionship or sexual needs, or feel that the victim's social and sexual demands are dehumanizing. There may be cognitive symptoms such as depersonalization, confusion, and an inability to concentrate. They may experience physical manifestations of stress and grief.

Although the intensity and nature of grief reactions to psychosocial losses are affected by all the same variables that affect any response to loss (such as the nature of the relationship, family and social support, and circumstances surrounding loss), two critical variables are unique to this form of loss.

In psychosocial death, the loss may be experienced by one person, many persons, or even a community. The degree to which the loss is experienced by others will depend on factors such as the level of disability or change in the person, the degree to which the knowledge of the change is shared and/or perceived by others, and the initial connectedness of the victim in the lives of others. For example, an Alzheimer's victim's condition can be known throughout the community or jealously guarded by the family. The severity of the condition can be acknowledged by all family members, all or whom then experience loss, or vigorously denied by some, particularly those whose life does not include the necessity of interaction with the victim. Keeping the condition secret may cause additional stress and burden, depriving significant others of available support. However, in certain circumstances, open acknowledgment of the change may lead to additional stressors with the community and a sense of censure. For example, parents of a teenager who is mentally ill may be reluctant to acknowledge the fact since they perceive that others may blame them for the condition and ostracize their child even if he or she should recover.

Another variable related to psychosocial loss is that the underlying condition causing psychosocial death can be viewed along a continuum of reversibility to irreversibility. Each point of that continuum can create different difficulties in grieving. With irreversible conditions, the loss is certain, and though that knowledge may be resisted by defense mechanisms such as denial, there will often be a sense of hopelessness. The irreversibility of that loss may create high levels of ambivalence and subsequent guilt as one copes with the daily tasks of life. There may be a sense that therapies are useless and time spent on the person is wasted and unappreciated. There may be deep, guilt-provoking desires for the victim's institutionalization or even death.

In situations that are perceived as reversible, there may be sustaining hope of eventual recovery, reconciliation, and resolution. But there may also be increased impatience with the slow pace of recovery and intensified feelings of anger toward a victim who is perceived still to have some sense of control. And caregiving others may have a heightened sense of responsibility that adds to the perceived burden. Recent research, for example, by Liptzin, Grob, and Eisen (1988) found that over time relatives of depressed patients felt more burden than did relatives of dementia patients, since the latter often grew to accept the fact that the relative's decline was inevitable, irreversible, and thus beyond their control. As Bennett and Bennett (1984) note, hopelessness sometimes can help families experience less blame and measure accomplishments in terms of endurance and adaptation rather than cure.

Though significant others experience grief in psychosocial loss, they may find it difficult to resolve such grief. Worden (1982) suggests that four tasks are necessary before grief can be resolved: accepting the reality of death; experiencing the pain of grief; adjusting to a life without the deceased; and withdrawing emotional energy from the deceased and reinvesting it in others. Yet the very nature of psychosocial death can make grief unresolvable.

It is difficult to accept the reality of death, even psychological death, when the person continues to be part of daily existence. The physical appearance, continuation of mannerisms, mysterious onset of disease—all contribute to a situation in which the bereaved may continue to deny the reality of loss.

The very nature or psychosocial loss also complicates resolving the pain of grief. Grief therapists have recognized that dealing with the affective responses to grief involves an emotional decathexis whereby one gradually reviews the relationship and resolves the emergent feelings inherent in such a review (Rando 1984). It is a time-consuming and painful process as one slowly explores the many layers of relationship built over time.

Such decathexis is often effectively impossible in psychosocial loss. For one thing, there simply isn't time. This interrelates with another difficulty: psychosocial loss does not create space for emotional detachment. Rather, the demands on time spent caring for the person are likely to increase. And new, often painful layers of the relationship are likely to be built as significant others deal with both the insatiable demands of care, and the changed and often bizarre behavior of the person, causing new stress, shame, guilt, anger, and helplessness.

The behavioral modifications that accompany the resolution of grief are also often precluded. The changed behavior of the person, particularly if it is deviant, may cause considerable modification in their interactional network, perhaps even isolating the family and others from social support. These persons may find it difficult to withdraw energy from the victim. In fact, their investment in that person may be increased. And simultaneously they have to adjust to a life that does not include the person as they knew him or her, and adjust to a new, often complicated, life with the new, emergent identity of the changed person. In the more common contexts of this type of loss, such as dementia and mental illness, they may have to adjust to a new, harsher existence without the companionship, role, and support previously provided by the victim.

This may be particularly difficult for the spouse. In situations of psychosocial loss, particularly dementia or mental illness, the spouse often finds his or her role ambiguous or confused. He or she may not be able to define the new status. Many speak of confusion in social roles: "Are they still married, or widowed, or at some unnamed position in between?" (Fabisewski and Howell 1986, p. 115). They may find a lack of recognition and social support: "The spouse cannot mourn decently. Although he has lost his mate as surely and permanently as if by death, since the familiar body remains, society neither recognizes the spouse's grief nor provides support and comfort that surrounds the bereaved by death" (Lezak 1978, p. 593).

The spouse becomes what Grossman and Grossman (1983) called a pseudowidow, or, perhaps more aptly, a cryptowidow; he or she remains legally albeit not behaviorally married. This ambiguous role continues and even intensifies if the spouse is institutionalized and is no longer part of daily activity and the day-to-day environment, for the remaining spouse is limited in ability to rebuild his or her life. In one case, a wife had cared for her husband for eight years prior to institutionalization. He had been institutionalized for two years and was highly disoriented. She was sixty-three and had developed a relationship with a sixty-five-year-old widower, who wanted them to live together, preferably married. She felt uncomfortable with the idea of either cohabitation or divorce, but she felt that this was a natural and desirable step in the relationship. She feared that if the relationship failed to evolve in this way, she might eventually lose him. In this case her children and family were supportive of the relationship and of any steps that she might take. Other spouses in similar cases may have less support.

In summary, then, psychosocial death complicates grief. The grieving person experiences deep personal loss, but the very nature of the syndrome complicates emotional responses, creating ambivalence, anger, and guilt. The condition can isolate the primary caregiver from critical sources of support. Yet when grief is convoluted, it is essentially unresolvable. Because the afflicted person is physically alive, and may even be part of the immediate environment, the emancipation from ties, which is the essence of grief work, is precluded. In fact, early resolution of grief can be detrimental. It can lead to a total withdrawal from the victim which can further complicate grief at the time of death. At best, significant others may achieve a partial resolution—a temporary resolution of feelings that allows those others to maintain emotional equilibrium, recognizing the losses experienced while continuing to give care. Grieving is, in effect, held in a state of partial suspension.

Interventions

In counseling individuals who are experiencing psychosocial loss, there are several interventions that will ameliorate client's grief.

Provide Education about the Underlying Condition

It is important to assess a client's knowledge and perception of the victim's underlying condition. Often clients' understanding of that condition can be faulty. In asking a client to describe the underlying cause, a counselor can determine whether the client's theory of causation sustains false hopes or unrealistic beliefs (for example, that the victim can control behavior). Such perceptions can subsequently be challenged. Counselors also need to be sensitive in this assessment to both the client's level of sophistication and his or her beliefs about causation and treatment which might underlie such responses as guilt, blame, or anger, or inhibit cooperation with treatment protocols.

Exploring the client's beliefs gives counselors the opportunity to provide education about the underlying syndrome at the client's level. Counselors should be aware of, and should suggest to clients, resources that might facilitate this process. Associations, self-help groups, experts, and nonprint and print media, particularly books by people who have experienced such loss, can all be useful sources of information in the education process. Such education not only provides realistic information about the nature and course of the condition, but it also enhances a sense of coping and control by allowing clients a meaningful sense of activity and providing opportunities for them to anticipate and plan for future contingencies.

Assist Clients in Dealing with the Emotional Issues Related to Loss

Often clients can feel constrained in recognizing and expressing their emotions. Since the victim is alive, living in the same environment, and defined as not responsible for his or her state, clients may lack the opportunity for emotional expression, feel personally inhibited from expressing negative emotions, or even face social sanction from friends and relatives who consider such expression disloyal or unfeeling. Specifically, counselors may *(a)* allow, encourage, and validate emotional expression; and *(b)* assist clients in exploring the many manifestations of guilt.

Guilt, as was discussed earlier, is a common reaction to psychosocial loss and may relate to factors preceding the change, incidences occurring during course of treatment, or situations expected in the future. Some guilt may be explored and defused as clients are educated about the condition. But counselors may need to discuss further and resolve such feelings. Useful interventions in resolving such guilt may include:

Offering assurances that such feelings are normal

Suggesting writing letters to the victim, addressing an empty chair, speaking a sense of personal apology

Exploring alternative coping strategies that allow the clients to recognize the legitimacy of their response and the lack of viable alternative actions, or to treat the guilt-provoking incident as a learning experience from which they now better understand their behavior and the conditions that contributed to it and have grown through it, developing alternative strategies for future incidents.

Reaffirming that a sense of burden is subjectively and individually defined

Clients may add unnecessary guilt by comparing their reactions to the victim's condition with varied role models and others in their lives. They need to be reminded that the burden posed by another's condition is highly subjective and affected by many variables such as their own coping skills, support system, prior relationship, resources, and so forth. Thus it is often unhelpful to engage in extensive comparison of response to the condition without considering the many variables that can affect the perceived burden.

Although guilt may be a prevalent emotion, it is not the only one. As was stated earlier, clients may experience considerable fear and anxiety related to the state and future of the victim, the client's own condition and future, and the impact and implication of the condition on the other members of the family. These latter fears can include such concerns as worries over the emotional reactions of other family members, faulty genetic legacy, or even possible similarities between the victim and others close to the client. Anger and crises in faith and belief structures are just some examples of other common reactions that may be evident. Probing for such responses allows the client to verbalize such feelings, assess those responses, and develop strategies for more effective coping.

Assist Clients in Recognizing and Responding to Changes in Their Own Lives, Changes in the Life of a Significant Other

When people experience significant loss in their lives, they are likely to find that their lives subsequently change. Thus, in psychosocial loss, people will often experience many modifications in the daily course of their lives. They may lack the prior companionship, cease previously enjoyable activities, take on new responsibilities, lose contact with friends or relatives, and have unmet psychological, social, sexual, and financial needs. These secondary losses can occur with such rapidity that the client may not realize just how profoundly his or her own life has been altered or develop effective coping strategies. In response, counselors may wish to try several approaches.

First, they may want to review with clients the ways in which their lives have changed. Often the sample question, "In what ways has your life changed since _____," can release a flood of responses. Counselors and clients can then explore which of these secondary losses are most significant, what losses can be regained (perhaps in a modified way), and responses and strategies for dealing with such loss.

Next, counselors may want to discuss the nature of the client's support system. Here clients and counselors can consider such issues as assessing the extent and nature of the support system (which may provide strategies for respite and resumption of missed activity), the clients' use of that support system (which may allow further discussion of coping styles and problem solving abilities), and "surprises" in the support system (for example, people clients were surprised to find were there for them, as well as people clients felt were not supportive). The latter issue is particularly significant because it may provide further opportunity for the counselor both to discuss emotional responses such as anger and resentment, and to help clients develop their problem-solving skills and coping strategies. Upon assessment, clients may recognize that they did not adequately communicate their needs or feelings to others in their support system or that they used those others in inappropriate ways. For example, in one case a woman was very angry that her daughter seemed unable to listen to her complaints about the demands placed upon her by her spouse's dementia. Upon reflection, the woman realized that her daughter's strengths were always in active "doing" rather than listening. Once she realized that, she modified her expectations of her daughter and found that she was extremely supportive as long as the mother confined her requests to asking for help in active tasks such as providing rides for her father or doing chores.

Counselors can also assist clients in finding additional sources of support such as self-help groups, day care and respite programs, and, if necessary, institutional care. Often this approach has additional value for it allows clients to reduce stress and to take directive actions that may diminish guilt and reaffirm control. But counselors must do more here than simply have the client identify needs and sources of support. In some cases, counselors may need to explore client resistance and ambivalence toward such support. As Quayhagen and Quayhagen (1988) note, some caregivers may experience considerable guilt over leaving the care of the victim to others, and accepting help from formal agencies may no longer allow the defense of denial.

With the client, a counselor can explore role problems, dilemmas, and ambiguities. One of the most significant problems of psychosocial loss, especially for spouses, is that it creates considerable role strain and additional burdens. For example, the spouse may remain legally married but effectively be widowed because the companionship and sexuality which were part of the prior relationship no longer exist. Often in these situations it is helpful for client and counselor to explore the tensions, ambiguities, burdens, and difficulties that accompany the state of cryptowidowhood. It is also helpful to explore all possible options, because even if an option is precluded for moral or practical reasons, the very consideration of that option reaffirms a client's sense of control and reduces the feeling that the future is totally constrained. For example, in a case mentioned earlier, a woman whose husband was institutionalized with Alzheimer's disease became involved in a relationship with another man, but she decided she would not at this time either divorce her demented spouse or cohabit with her new love. Exploring those options, however, allowed her to affirm that she did have some control over events and that decisions made now were not necessarily final.

Counselors may wish to discuss the ways in which clients generally cope with change and the ways they are coping with it now, assessing which of their strategies are effective (reaffirming and reinforcing such skills) and which are not (providing opportunity to assess and develop better strategies). They may also want to explore current ways in which clients deal with stress, and, when necessary, teach clients effective stress-reduction techniques. They can explore the clients' caregiving role. Clients are often very willing to take on caregiving responsibilities, but they may make decisions that do not adequately take into account their own or the other's role. For example, a client's decision to quit work to take care of a spouse with Alzheimer's disease may remove him or her from a support system, eliminate necessary respite, and create financial problems. One might try to find other ways to resolve the issue. Thus, counselors need to assist clients periodically in assessing their caregiving plans and roles and in reviewing alternative plans. And finally, counselors can legitimize the needs of clients to help them recognize and balance their own needs with the demands of care.

Help Clients Realistically Plan for the Future

The nature of psychosocial loss often encourages an attitude of "one day at a time." In many ways such a perspective is functional. With reversible conditions, future contingencies can be endless. With irreversible syndromes, the future can be dismal. Nevertheless, it is important for the clients, at times, to plan for the future. Such planning can allow a sense of control, rehearse problem-solving skills, anticipate future issues, and provide necessary research and lead time. In such sessions, it is important that counselors reaffirm both confidence in the client's ability and coping skills, and realistic hopes.

When Necessary, Allow Clients to Develop Their Own Rituals for Saying Goodbye

One of the most difficult problems of psychosocial loss is that there are no ways, no rituals, to recognize the changed status and to say farewell. If clients express such a need, they may be able to develop small ritual acts (such as perhaps burying or removing old love letters) that allow a sense of closure.

Supportive counseling, then, may not necessarily resolve the grief evident in psychosocial loss. But it can provide clients with essential assistance in coping with daily demands and in facilitating later grief adjustment. And it can ease the pain evident in the dilemma of psychosocial loss, so curiously captured in Gottfried von Strassburg's poem *Tristan and Isolde* (c. 1210): "They live as living, they live as dead/Thus still they live and yet are dead."

Notes

1. This use of the term varies from an earlier use by Weisman (1972), who referred to psychosocial death as the set of psychological and social factors that interact with physiological factors in determining death.

2. In discussing people who are physically ill, Sudnow (1967) notes a similar phenomenon: he describes the "Lazarus syndrome" in which comatose or near comatose patients revive and recover. Often families have a difficult time coping with such change.

References

Addis, M., J. Schulman-Miller, and M. Lightman. 1984. "The Cult Clinic Helps Families in Crisis." *Social Casework* 65, 515–22.

Bennett, M.I., and M.B. Bennett. 1984. "The Uses of Hopelessness." *American Journal of Psychiatry* 141, 559–62.

Cole, L., K. Griffin, and B. Ruiz. 1986. "A Comprehensive Approach to Working with Families of Alzheimer's Patients." *Journal of Gerontological Social Work* 9, 27–39.

Fabisewski, K.J., and M.C. Howell. 1986. "A Model for Family Meetings in the Long Term Care of Alzheimer's Disease." *Journal of Gerontological Social Work* 9, 113–17.

Grossman, S., and C.A. Grossman. 1983. "And Then There Was One." Paper presented to the Northeastern Gerontological Society, Newport, R.I., May 6.

Kalish, R.A. 1966. "A Continuation of Subjectively Perceived Death." *The Gerontologist* 6, 73–76.

———. 1968. "Life and Death: Dividing the Indivisible." *Social Science and Medicine* 2, 249–59.

Lezak, M. 1978. "Living with the Characterologically Altered Brain Injured Patient." *The Journal of Clinical Psychiatry* 34, 592–98.

Liptzin, B., M.C. Grob, and S.V. Eisen. 1988. "Family Burden of Demented and Depressed Elderly Psychiatric In-Patients." *The Gerontologist* 28, 397–401.

Quayhagen, M.P., and M. Quayhagen. 1988. "Alzheimer's Stress: Coping with the Caregiving Role." *The Gerontologist* 28, 391–96.

Rando, T.A. 1984. "Grief, Dying and Death: Clinical Interventions for Caregivers." Champaign, Ill.: Research Press.

Satel, S., and S. Southwick. 1987. "Consequences of Abrupt Reduction of Chronic Symptoms." *American Journal of Psychiatry* 144, 1362.

Sudnow, D. 1967. *Passing on: The Social Organization of Dying.* Englewood Cliffs, N.J.: Prentice-Hall.

Wasow, M. 1986. "Support Groups for Family Caregivers and Patients with Alzheimer's Disease." *Social Work* 31, 93–97.

Worden, J.W. 1982. *Grief Counseling and Grief Therapy,* New York: Springer.

Part IV
Disenfranchised Grievers

T his section considers those in our society who are (wrongly) considered incapable of grief: the very young, the very old, and the developmentally disabled. As widespread as such myths are, they deny the ability of people to attach, to love, to recognize loss in their environment, and to mourn.

Ellis begins this section by considering the mourning of young children. His conclusion, well supported in the literature, is that young children do indeed grieve and that adults need to assist them in developing a supporting context that will facilitate their mourning. Perhaps Ellis's chapter and the research that supports it will lead to new social recognition that the critical question is not the simplistic "Do children mourn and at what age?" but rather "In what ways do children, at varying ages, understand death and deal with loss?"

Moss and Moss consider the other end of the age continuum—the very old—and point to a double disenfranchisement. Typically the very old are perceived as being too frail and fragile to cope with loss and are disenfranchised as mourners; at the same time, others, such as adult children, are often disenfranchised when they experience the death of someone very old, because in our society, where the old may be devalued and their death expected, such loss is often discounted.

Lavin breaks new ground in considering the mourning of developmentally disabled persons. Until recently, the bereavement of the developmentally disabled was rarely a concern. Quite simply, most developmentally disabled persons did not survive to an age at which they would be likely to experience the loss of significant others. And those who did were often hidden in institutions, only marginally connected to families. In recent years, however, this situation has changed radically. Developmentally disabled persons (with the notable exception of those with Down's syndrome) now have life spans equivalent to those in the general population, and they are likely to live within communities, maintaining long-term relationships with both biological families and chosen families consisting of roommates, housemates, and fellow workers. In this new context, then, there is a greater likelihood that they will experience loss. And there may be something in common with the situation that Moss and Moss point to in the very old: perhaps here too the general devaluation of the retarded may disenfranchise not only their losses, but also the losses of family and friends who mourn the death of a retarded child, sibling, or friend.

Taken together, these chapters provide a powerful reaffirmation of the common human capacity to love, and with it the capacity to mourn the loss of that love. Hence the question asked earlier can be applied to any population—both those considered here and others, such as the mentally ill or the confused. The question is not "Do they mourn?" But "In what ways does any group understand and experience loss?"

18

Young Children: Disenfranchised Grievers

Richard R. Ellis

Young children in the United States today seem to be among the disenfranchised grievers of our society. The reported observations of parents, teachers, mental health professionals, members of the health professions, funeral directors, and writers clearly indicate that the significant adults in the lives of young children tend to exclude them from participation in the rituals of family burial and grieving. Certainly this is not true for all children, but the numbers of children known to have been excluded is sufficient to raise our concern. Our concern is twofold. One is for the children who are denied opportunity to benefit from the family community in grief or are discouraged from grieving privately as individuals. The other is for the well-meaning, caring, perhaps loving adults who promote the exclusion of children out of a lack of information or understanding, misinformation, or their own death anxieties.

On the basis of research reports and reports of clinical observations, one may begin to speculate about the roots of the disenfranchisement of young children from grieving. However, from several perspectives an individual's grief is itself complex: in its origins, its meanings to the griever, its overt and covert manifestations, its effects upon the griever over time, and its possible outcomes. So too are the intentions and motivations of the disenfranchising adults complex. Thus the bases for even tentative conclusions about causes and effects here are at best tenuous. Some speculation can lead to either research questions or hypotheses that warrant investigation or testing.

A sizable literature describes the ability of children to react to separation from the mother, separation from other caregivers, to object loss, to death of loved ones and others. These descriptions, however, clearly indicate a lack of agreement regarding the age at which children are able to manifest these reactions. These are differences of opinion about what constitutes grief reactions, grief, and mourning in childhood. Major arguments come from proponents of psychoanalytic, developmental, and cognitive views.

From those who have psychotherapeutic contact with children there is more certainty about the negative effects separation and loss by death can have upon children, particularly when the child is disenfranchised from griev-ing. Similarly, and perhaps with more potential for even greater damage, there are negative consequences for those who carry unresolved childhood grief into adulthood.

By some definitions of grief, grieving, and mourning, young children are capable of experiencing grief, and they do grieve and mourn, perhaps when they are as young as six months of age.

Numerous examples of how adults have disenfranchised children from the grieving process have been reported. Their range in creativity, fabrication, and sometimes unwitting insensitivity is considerable. Rather than protecting the child from some supposed trauma, this approach in each case leaves the child unprotected from potentially negative consequences of delayed, restrained, or unresolved grief; the child is also left vulnerable to negative con-ditions that can appear later in adulthood and are associated with unresolved grief.

Schaefer and Lyons (1986) relate several incidents in which families disen-franchised the young children from their grief and mourning. Two examples will suffice. Michael and his grandfather had been the best of friends, pals really, since Michael was born. Grandpa lived upstairs, Michael and his parents downstairs. When Michael was about seven years old, he and his parents moved several miles away, assuring Grandpa they would see him on Thanksgiving Day. That day, then Christmas, came; but Grandpa didn't come, call, or send a card. Michael's parents explained that Grandpa was away. Michael was filled with torturing questions: What had he done to Grandpa? Didn't Grandpa love him? What was the matter? Two years later Michael's parents told him Grandpa had died soon after they moved. Another example is that of Jerry, now twenty, who recalls that his grandmother died when he was a young child. Right away his parents sent him across the street to stay with a neighbor and kept him there until after the funeral. He could not understand why he was exiled, and not allowed to be with his family or see his grandmother. He thought then that she must look horrible. No one talked with him about anything. Michael and Jerry were disenfranchised from their grieving and mourning by probably caring but misguided parents.

Infant Imagery

Until this century most young children witnessed dying, death, grieving, mourning, and funerals, usually within their own homes. As late as the Vic-torian era adults encouraged children to think about their own deaths and the deaths of others; funerals were ostentatious, cemeteries were prominent in most towns, and children were in attendance at deathbed scenes (Gorer 1965). Nineteenth-century mortality rates were high around the world. Thus it was quite likely that the lives of most children naturally included firsthand observations of dying persons, dead bodies, and the grief of those bereaved.

But something happened early in the twentieth century—particularly in the United States. We were changing from an agrarian society to an industrialized nation. More and more people were living in the cities and towns rather than in rural areas. Advances in transportation enabled more people to be much more mobile. The extended family was no longer in proximity; members lived at great distances from each other. People began doing less for themselves and began using varieties of emerging services. Better medical and health care became centered in the cities and larger towns. No doubt these and other factors contributed to fundamental changes in the ways American adults viewed themselves and others. Perhaps those same factors influenced the change that occurred in American attitudes toward dying, death, grieving, and mourning.

Thanatologists[1] know today's Americans as a death-denying people (Becker 1973, Lifton 1979). Of course not all Americans necessarily deny or fear death, but the available evidence indicates that the majority of us qualify as death deniers. Adults transmit this denial, usually accompanied by assorted fears and anxieties related to dying and death, verbally and nonverbally to the children. Because young children are particularly dependent upon the adults in their lives, they rely upon those adults for cues and clues about how to interpret events. Although it is true that our ancestors in earlier centuries possessed far less information from research and observations about child development than we now have, they probably would be baffled by our attitudes toward death and by the ways in which so many of us try to shield our children from knowledge of death.

We often act as if we believe our not being straightforward with children about death will surely protect their natural innocence, ensure them an untroubled childhood, or we believe that even our discussions with children about a death or a death-related topic will terrify, perhaps traumatize, them irreparably (Stillion and Wass 1979). This thinking, however well intentioned it might be, is almost childlike in its naiveté.

Adults sometimes ask what a very young child could know about death. We do not know for certain. However, it is arguable that the formation of something very like images of death begins at birth (Lifton 1979). These are image-feelings of separation, disintegration, and stasis which Lifton characterizes as "death equivalents," precursors of later feelings about actual death. We carry our early images throughout our lives. For each death equivalent there is its counterpart. Of the three, separation-connection is most fundamental; with disintegration-integrity and stasis-movement, it significantly affects development of the infant's "inner life."

Within the first four to six months of life, attachment behavior is evolving in the infant. Also within this time frame the infant learns to recognize his or her mother (Bowlby 1969). Lifton (1979) concludes that either preceding or accompanying the infant's active attachment is something resembling a discriminating image; the imagery of separation is the precursor of the idea of death. Otto Rank (1952) believed birth to be a trauma for the infant, a negative experience. He associated this "birth fear" with separation, "loss of mother." Freud (1936) wrote that young children were capable of having anxieties, all of which reduced to one feeling: loss of a loved one.

Overlapping with separation-connection is disintegration-integrity. Feelings of separation are often associated with an inner sense of disintegration. To this point Mahler, Pine, and Bergman (1975) speak of the fear of annihilation through abandonment. It was Melanie Klein (1952), though, who understood that an active death instinct, a Freudian idea, caused the fear of annihilation.

Although statis-movement has not been a large contributor to psychological theory, Mahler, Pine, and Bergman (1975) observed that, as in later life, the infant offers clues to her or his inner state via statis-movement. For developing children, however, that state of sleep is one of the earliest models they use in trying to understand the state of death. The idea of death becomes associated with imagery of total statis (Lifton 1979). There is evidence that infants do react to separation and the threat of separation and to connection and the anticipation of connection. Infants strive to maintain integrity. The newborn arrives with the capacity to cry, to signal discomfort, to signal the mother to come closer.

Ideas of Young Children

There is reason to believe that the young child does harbor fears in his or her inner world. They are not innate, however, but are the products of the child's perception of the world (Becker 1973). Of course the child is completely dependent upon the mother or some other significant person for survival. Each of the child's cries of hunger, pain, or discomfort is usually met with food, love, or soothing touches. The child comes to believe that she or he has unlimited powers: sound the signal, needs are met—all by the child's own magic. Thus the child develops an inaccurate, confused idea about cause-effect relationships. Confusion arises when the child's socializers frustrate some of his or her wants—the child's magic does not always work. Processes of socialization are frustrating, at time painful, and all children at some time wish their socializers dead (Wahl 1965). The child senses that she or he possesses magical powers but also comes to sense that she or he does not have complete control over those powers. Becker (1973) describes this part of the child's inner world as one of confusion, chaos, even terror. In the real world one pays a price for holding a belief in personal magical power.

It is also arguable that even infants have some awareness of being and nonbeing. Adah Mauer (1966) aptly describes the experiments of the healthy baby, six months old, with changes of being occurring through activities such as the peek-a-boo game. As another example, place a cloth lightly over the baby's face and observe how he or she forcibly removes the covering and searches for your face for reassuring smiles, and wants to do it again and again. Granted, the baby is not necessarily thinking about being/nonbeing, or about death, but the dynamics of separation/reunion are present. These and other emotional components will become part of their later ideas about living, life, and death.

Evidence of early cognitive development in young children comes to us via Robert Kastenbaum's (1974) delightful anecdote about a sixteen-month-old boy. The incident, now a classic story, hits the point so tellingly. Out walking with his father, a well-known scientist, the boy began to observe a fuzzy, creeping caterpillar. It was not long before he also observed an unseeing adult foot step squarely on this caterpillar: squish. The boy looked at what was left of the caterpillar and finally, in a tone of thoughtful certainty, said, "No more." This very young child had considered a set of data, arrived at a conclusion (which happened to be correct), and expressed it with a parsimony of language typical of his age range but upon which adults would be hard put to improve. Other children of about this age have been heard to summarize parallell situations with "All gone." Similar observations of young children's behavior have led a number of researchers to study the development of children's thinking, notably the Swiss psychologist Jean Piaget (1973).

From the work of Sylvia Anthony (1940) we learn that young children do indeed think about the topic of death. Anthony studied children in England, ages three to thirteen, via parent's descriptions of their children's interest in death, children's responses to a story-completion task, and data from intelligence tests that included death topics. Although death did not appear in the story-completion stem, about half of the responding children referred to death in their story completions. Anthony found the children's responses falling into five developmental stages. The youngest children expressed ideas about death that were inaccurate and not always clear; some children seemed ignorant of the word. The five- and six-year-olds expressed meanings that did not match reality. At age eight or nine almost all the children offered realistic explanations.

Maria Nagy (1948) studied the development of children's ideas about the meaning of death. She interviewed 378 boys (51 percent) and girls (49 percent), living in the greater Budapest, Hungary, area. Her research participants came from different social levels, schools, and religions; intelligence levels ranged from dull normal to superior, with most children in the "normal" range. She characterized her sample as falling within three major developmental stages:

Stage 1 (ages three to five): Death is departure, often like sleep, a changed existence. Death is temporary; there are degrees of death. Elements of fantasy are here. This view is expressive of the child's egocentric view of the world.

Stage 2 (ages five to nine): Death is a creature, a person (Nagy found this personification of death in all ages of her sample, but it seemed most characteristic of ages five to nine); some children used *death* and *dead* interchangeably. Death may be an eventuality, but it is not universal. This view is egocentric or anthropocentric. Fantasy is present, but to a lesser degree than in stage 1.

Stage 3 (ages nine to ten): Death is inevitable. Death is universal and irreversible. This view is realistic, reflective of the child's general view of the world.

Later studies of American children have not always supported Nagy's ideas about developmental levels. Certainly American children expressed different emphasis. For example, a study (McIntyre, Angle, and Struempler 1972) of children in the Midwest found three- to five-year-olds tending to emphasize organic decomposition of the body and little or no use of fantasy. While the Hungarian five to nine-year-olds emphasized personifications of death, their American cohorts rarely did.

There is controversy about how children come to hold views of death, about the roles of a variety of factors deemed to affect arrival of those views. For purposes of our discussion here the issue is not *how* but *whether* very young and young children do in fact have views of death. Kastenbaum and Aisenberg (1972) not only support the idea that young children have ideas about death, about nonbeing, but they argue that these ideas begin forming not long after birth. Myra Bluebond-Langner (1975, 1978) studied forty terminally ill children in a Midwest hospital; they ranged in age from eighteen months to fourteen years, and most were three to nine years old. She reported that all eventually knew that they were dying, that they were engaged inescapably in an irreversible process. We contend that the answer to whether young children have ideas about death is in the affirmative.

Ability of Young Children to Grieve and to Mourn

Are young children capable of grief? If so, to what extent? Death is a loss. For the young child separation from a significant other, especially the mother, is a loss. Bowlby (1969) finds that infants separated from their mothers proceed through protest, despair, and apathy. Indeed, many young children express anger because they believe the death of a parent or sibling is deliberate abandonment (Krupnich and Solomon 1987). In adults this protest often is expressed as denial and anger. Both children and adults engage in their despair similarly (feeling acute pain, unhappiness, and decreasing hope). Unlike most adults, young children often regress in their behavior. Bowlby (1961) reported that institutionalized children in their apathy seemed to give up trying to cope; many became sick. The very young child's need for the mother is practically equated with the need for survival (Stillion and Wass 1984).

In general the sense of loss one feels relates to the strength and quality of the attachment to the person or thing lost (Bowlby 1969). More specifically, certain factors also may affect the griever. For example, there is evidence that children not yet five years old are more vulnerable to personal loss than are older children (Bowlby 1980). Also, both children and adults seem to tolerate expected death somewhat better than sudden death (Furman 1974). Bereaved children typically ponder some frightening questions: Is it my fault? Did I do (cause) it? Who will take care of me now? Will I die? (Krupnich and Solomon 1987).

Whether adults believe it or not, whether adults like it or not, children come into contact with death. Children can experience the death of others as a threat to their own safety or being. Children living with the prospect of their own dying are as frightened by it as are others, who may be more mature: "Of course children are concerned about death. Children have a basic need to make sense of the world and of themselves in it" (Wass and Corr 1984, p. 1). Death-related objects and events are all around, each a potential object of curiosity and a learning opportunity for the child: a dead pet, a dead animal on the road, a funeral procession on the street, wilted plants, the buds of spring and leaves of fall, the talk of adults about death, certain television shows, and more. Furman (1974) points to all of these as opportunities for adults to engage the child in dialogue, helping the child to explore, to ask questions, to learn. When death is a personal loss to the child, it is hardly the optimal time for the child's initial experience in talking about the death of a loved one. Indeed, Furman's (1974) study of childhood bereavement found bereaved children who were experienced in talking about death before a parent died were more able to handle the death than were children who had not had the opportunity.

The ways in which some young children respond to news of a death and behave while engaged with their grief and mourning can confuse those who are older and developmentally more mature. Feelings, emotions, and beliefs are all aboil within the child. For example, a child may sob or wail and a few minutes later begin playing as if nothing were wrong. A child may sob uncontrollably only while sleeping and be able to cry openly only at a later time. A child may appear to be uninterested, and may or may not be able to discharge the pent-up grief at a later or much more distant time. At times the child appears to have lost interest in the death, or seems indifferent, or seems to have forgotten all that was said. Actually the child may be striving to achieve some moment of respite or a brief distance from the heat of the pain.

Needs of Bereaved Young Children

Adults render a distinct disservice to young children when they, however well intentioned they are, disenfranchise the children as grievers and mourners. Humans are never more vulnerable than during their infancy and early childhood. Young children require constant, consistent, accurate, truthful, loving support and attention. They need to know they are included, not excluded. They need to know they are loved, lovable, safe. They need to know they will continue to be loved, cared for, and safe, and will remain members of the family, enjoying its protection.

Family protection comes in the form of a unified family group, the place called home, the food on the table, clothes to wear, friendship, and guidance. Not allowing children to ask their death-related questions, to receive thoughtful and understandable responses, to know why people are sad and crying, to participate in family funeral activities, and to express their emotions is intolerable folly. One demonstrates neither love nor understanding of children by "protecting" them through attempts to cloak them in ignorance either with lies and deceit or by isolating them at a time when they desperately need to be with and to interact with those upon whom they must depend for their very survival. One cannot really protect children from knowledge about death, from some of the pain of loss, from a natural curiosity about the world and what goes on in it. Further, children may in the absence of knowledge invent facts and stories more terrifying than reality. Not helping children develop ways of interpreting death is to leave them unarmed when a death occurs. Recall Dan Schaefer's (Schaefer and Lyons 1986) example of Michael, who now says, recalling that his parents waited two years to tell him that his best friend–grandfather had died, "It was a terrible time for me. They certainly didn't spare me any pain . . . I still had to deal with the feelings of losing Grandpa" (p. 2). And now what about his feelings toward his parents?

A young child disenfranchised from his or her grieving and mourning is a diminished child: isolated from love when it is most needed, stifled in curiosity when it is pointing to ways of exploring and learning about the environment, thwarted in intellectual and emotional development. Though a number of researchers and clinicians have suggested that early childhood bereavement (that is, loss of a parent) is linked to adult depression, Birtchnell (1980) offers a caution: The quality of the bereaved child's relationship with whoever assumes parenting of the child can be more influential than the bereavement on the risk of adult depression.

During grief and mourning the young child needs at least one adult available to him or her, one whom he or she knows, cares for, and trusts. This person probably will be most effective in helping the child if he or she is not given to strong, emotional outbursts of grief but can be with the child for periods of time to offer emotional support, to answer questions, and, very importantly, to elicit from the child what he or she is thinking. Family members would do well to remember that when a child loses one parent, the child loses the other parent too. The surviving parent gets lost in his or her own grief and may not be psychologically available to the child, at least for a while.

In talking with young children, effective adults find out the levels of thinking and expressing of which the child is capable, and set the level of explanation to the child's developed powers of understanding. The adult proceeds slowly and periodically checks with the child to find out what he or she has heard. Further, the child does not benefit from being given an explanation that is based in deceit or fantasy when later the child will have to relearn an accurate explanation. For example, the mother dies and the father explains to their young child, "Mommy got very tired and her body got so tired she went to sleep and she won't wake up anymore." From then on when the father came home from work tired and weary, the child would become very upset. She was terrified that she or anyone could become so tired as to fall asleep and not ever awaken. The child refused to do anything she thought might make her tired. Eventually the father had to replace the first explanation with an accurate one and to work with the child to help her unlearn the first one.

Granted, it takes some courage and some willingness to grapple with very personal and demanding issues in order to deal with a bereaved child in meaningful ways. Granted, most adults are not particularly prepared for the task. But there is no defensible reason for leaving a young child alone to work his or her way through the incomprehensible tangles and thoughts, feelings, emotions, and contradictions known to adults as bereavement, grief, and mourning.

More children can be enfranchised to grieve. Adults can become better informed about the nature of grief, how different factors can impinge upon the grief reaction and process, how adults can experience it, how children of different ages and phases of development can experience it. Adults can become better prepared to assist children with their grief. It is true that approximately one hundred years ago adults generally viewed children as miniature adults. Since then we have learned more about children, and we have developed better ways of disseminating information. Continuing neglect, even when benign, of our children is hardly justifiable and is not what most of us want.

Note

1. Thanalogy—from the ancient Greek, Thanatos, god of death. A thanatologist may engage in study, research, teaching, and writing about matters relating to dying, death, grief, mourning, and bereavement; a thanatologist also may render a profes-

sional service to persons concerned about or experiencing dying, death, grief, mourning, or bereavement.

References

Anthony, S. 1940. *The Child's Discovery of Death.* New York: Harcourt, Brace.

Becker, E. 1973. *The Denial of Death.* New York: Free Press.

Birtchnell, J. 1980. "Women Whose Mother Died in Childhood: An Outcome Study." *Psychological Medicine* 10, 699–713.

Bluebond-Langner, M. 1975. "Awareness and Communication in Terminally Ill Children: Pattern, Process, and Pretense." Ph.D. diss., University of Illinois.

———. 1977. "Meaning of Death to Children." In *New Meanings of Death.* edited by H. Feifel. New York: McGraw-Hill.

———. 1978. *The Private Worlds of Dying Children.* Princeton: Princeton University Press.

Bowlby, J. 1961. "Childhood Mourning and Its Implications for Psychiatry." *American Journal of Psychiatry* 118, 481–98.

———. 1969. *Attachment and Loss.* Vol. 1, *Attachment.* New York: Basic Books.

———. 1980. *Attachment and Loss.* Vol. 3, *Loss: Sadness and Depression.* New York: Basic Books.

Freud, S. 1936. *The problem of anxiety.* New York: Norton.

Furman, E. 1974. *A Child's Parent Dies: Studies in Childhood Bereavement.* New Haven: Yale University Press.

Gorer, G. 1965. *Death, Grief, and Mourning.* London: Doubleday.

Kastenbaum, R. 1974. "Childhood: The Kingdom Where Creatures Die." *Journal of Clinical Child Psychology* 3:2, 11–14.

Kastenbaum, R. and R. Aisenberg. 1972. *The Psychology of Death.* New York: Springer.

Klein, M. 1952. "On the Theory of Anxiety and Guilt." In *Developments in Psychoanalysis,* edited by M. Klein, P. Heimann, S. Issacs, and G. Riviere. London: Hogarth Press.

Krupnich, J., and F. Solomon. 1987. "Death of a Parent or Sibling during Childhood." In *The Psychology of Separation and Loss,* edited by J. Bloom-Feshbach and S. Bloom-Feshbach. San Francisco: Jossey-Bass.

Lifton, R. 1979. *The Broken Connection.* New York: Basic Books.

Mahler, M., F. Pine, and A. Bergman. 1975. *The Psychological Birth of the Human Infant.* New York: Basic Books.

Mauer, A. 1966. "Maturation of Concepts of Death." *British Journal of Medicine and Psychology,* 39, 35–4.

McIntyre, M., C. Angle, and L. Struempler. 1972. "The Concept of Death in Midwestern Children and Youth." *American Journal of Diseases of Children* 123, 527–32.

Nagy, M. 1948. "The Child's View of Death." *Journal of Genetic Psychology* 73, 3–27. Also reprinted with some editorial changes in H. Feifel (1959), *The Meaning of Death* (New York: McGraw-Hill).

Piaget, J. 1973. *The Child and Reality—Problems of Genetic Psychology.* New York: Grossman.

Rank, Otto. 1952. *The Trauma of Birth.* New York: Brunner.

Schaefer, D., and C. Lyons. 1986. *How Do We Tell the Children? A Parent's Guide to Helping Children Understand and Cope When Someone Dies.* New York: Newmarket Press.

Stillion, J., and H. Wass. 1979. "Children and Death." In *Dying: Facing the Facts,* edited by H. Wass. Washington, D.C.: Hemisphere.

————. 1984. "Children and Death." In *Death: Current Perspectives,* 3d ed., edited by E. Schneidman. Palo Alto, Calif.: Mayfield.

Wahl, C. 1965. "The Fear of Death." In *The Meaning of Death,* edited by H. Feifel. New York: McGraw-Hill.

Wass, H., and C. Corr, eds. 1984. *Childhood and Death.* Washington, D.C. Hemisphere.

19
Death of the Very Old

Miriam S. Moss
Sidney Z. Moss

Introduction

This chapter discusses normative deaths—deaths of elderly persons in the United States. With the relative decline of infant mortality and better control of infectious diseases, the time of death is becoming more predictable: more and more persons die in their old age. Over two-thirds of all deaths are of persons sixty-five and over (Brody 1984). Although persons eighty years and over represented only 2 percent of the population in 1980, they constituted 31 percent of all deaths (Brody 1984).

Demographers do not agree on whether the length of the human life span is increasing or whether there is a compression of mortality within the later years of the current life span (Hayflick 1987). It is expected, nevertheless, that in the next half century there will be a rapid increase in the number and proportion of deaths in the population age sixty-five and over (Brody 1984).

The following discussion focuses primarily on persons who are very old—age eighty or over. We would argue, however, that the impact of the deaths of persons who are in their later sixties or seventies is in many ways similar to that discussed here.

In this chapter we examine bereavement in response to the death of very old persons. Although many factors tend to devalue the bereavement process and disenfranchise the griever, the impact of the death may be of considerable significance, particularly if the bereaved survivor is very old. We suggest that when the survivor and the deceased are both very old, the grief is doubly disenfranchised. We explore these questions: What are some of the factors associated with disenfranchisement of a survivor's response to the death of an old person? What are the personally and socially significant themes in bereavement for the old person?

As long ago as 1951, Stern, Williams, and Prados emphasized that there has been a paucity of literature about death of the elderly. Subsequently

---

This chapter is dedicated to the memory of Richard Kalish, our mentor and friend, who died in middle age and was a pioneer in thinking and writing about death for all ages.

Herriott and Kiyak (1981), Kastenbaum (1969), Osterweis, Solomon, and Green (1984), Raphael (1983), and Riley (1983) have noted the lack of conceptualization about death and bereavement over the life span. But, old age and death, not strangers to each other, are often inextricably tied. Feifel (1959) suggests that one of the reasons why we tend to reject the aged is that they remind us of death. Aging has been termed "anticipatory death" (Pollak 1980). There is some evidence that older people, even when active and competent, tend to be involved in "rehearsal for death" (Kalish 1985). The fields of gerontology (the study of the lives of older persons) and thanatology (the study of dying and death), however, have found little common ground. Neither has fully integrated the literature of the other into its own. This is an exploratory and speculative chapter, based on a review of some literature in these two fields.

Death is generally viewed as uncontrollable and undesirable, but in some ways it may be preferable to loss of mind, feelings of uselessness and of being a burden, pain, and suffering (Marshall 1980). Although an old person is increasingly proximate to death, the specific time of death is not predictable. Few die at the expected and right time; in some sense, nearly all deaths seem premature.

The specter of death may pervade the last year of life; there may be times when a family expects that the person will die, only to have him or her recover. A recent study of the final year in the life of two hundred older persons (Moss 1984) found that 24 percent of the closest survivors said that there was a time before the final week when they thought the person was "about to die" but did not.

Myerhoff (1978) describes what is perhaps a rare example of an appropriate death (Weisman 1972), that which one would choose for oneself if one were in the position of the dying. She reports in detail on the final celebratory hours of the life of ninety-five-year-old Jacob:

> Jacob's death revived the idea, or at least the hope, that sometimes people die meaningfully, properly, and purposively. Death is often felt as the final manifestation of helplessness, accident, and disorder but here it seemed apt and fulfilling. Too often, death flies in the face of human conception, reminding us of our ignorance and impotence. It finds the wrong people at the wrong time, it mocks our sense of justice. But here it did the very opposite and made such obvious sense that it appeared as a manifestation of a higher order and morality. (p. 227)

Societal Devaluation of the Very Old

First, we will examine some aspects of the way in which old people are devalued, and then some themes in older persons' attitudes toward death. This analysis will help in understanding some of the sociocultural attitudes toward death of older persons and older persons' responses to the deaths of others.

Persons in their advanced years are not a homogenous group. Twenty-three percent of those age eighty-five and over live in institutions, and 20 percent while living at home need help in tasks of everyday living (Taeuber and Rosenwaite, in press). Thus, about half of the persons in this age group are relatively independent in their daily lives.

Older persons have lived in a world in which their social-cultural value tends to diminish with advancing years. Ageism systematically stereotypes and stigmatizes the elderly because they are old, seeing them as senile, rigid, disengaged, and sexless (Butler 1969). Older people themselves tend to take on the stereotypes, and thus ageism becomes a self-fulfilling prophesy. For younger persons, ageism prevents positive identification with the elderly.

Many older persons suffer a sequence of incremental impairments—partial deaths (Berezin 1977)—in themselves and others. They may die after months or years of decline, with multiple chronic conditions or illnesses, not infrequently dependent on others for home care or institutional care. Most older persons die of long-term chronic illnesses; 70 percent of deaths are caused by heart attack, cancer, and stroke (Brody 1984). Illness may carry with it a theme of potential demise. Pills and medications taken regularly may be reminders of one's vulnerability (Pollak 1980). Thus, the death of an older person may be less likely to be unexpected than that of a younger person (Owen, Fulton, and Markusen 1982–83).

Often the older person has lived a long and fulfilling life. There is a tendency to lose roles in later years: of worker when one retires, of spouse when one's husband or wife dies, of sibling with the loss of one's last sibling. A significant group of very old persons may have fewer resources than younger persons: less money and smaller social networks. Often one has few responsibilities for others, less functional roles in daily life. When the elderly die they may have fewer unfulfilled tasks (Kalish and Reynolds 1976). Thus, the very old may be devalued.

Older Persons' Attitudes toward Death

A basic developmental task of the elderly is coming to terms with death (Erikson 1963, Lieberman and Tobin 1983). There is, however, little generalizable information from research that tells us about aged persons and their psychosocial experiences before death (Schulz and Schlarb 1987–88). We can only conjecture about some of the ways in which death plays a meaningful role in their lives. Pattison (1977) has discussed the multiple ways in which people at younger ages cope with the "living-dying interval," the period of time after being informed of their limited life expectancy. In reviewing the social-psychological process of dying—the psychological autopsy—Weisman and Kastenbaum (1968) found that awareness of impending death could lead to withdrawal or to active engagement. It is likely that very old persons, being part of a heterogeneous group, would also use a range of styles in coping with finitude.

Old persons have more experience with death. They probably have known more people who have died, have been to more funerals, have visited more cemeteries than have younger persons (Kalish and Reynolds 1976). They may have become somewhat more able to imagine a world without themselves in it, as they experience the deaths of others, as they make a will or consider what they will leave behind them.

Many older persons have, therefore, in some ways come to terms with their own finitude (Kowalski 1986b, Marshall 1986, Swenson 1976). Using ever changing reference groups of significant others, they experience an ongoing process of calculating their life expectancy (Marshall 1980). In a sense there is a developmental determinism taking place. As a person gets older both the person and others who are close to him or her independently modify the calculus of life expectancy. Many have felt that they have had bonus years beyond those of their parents.

If old persons are faced with frailty and dependency, it is not unusual for them to express a wish to die. This wish is acted out in the high suicide rate among elderly men. An old person's recurrent wish to die may represent a foreshortening of their calculus of time left to live, and reflect the complex dialectic between a wish for survival and acceptance of death.

Freud (1917), however, suggests that it is not part of human nature to imagine the world without one's self in it. Cognitive awareness of the increasing closeness of death may or may not lead to resignation or emotional acceptance of one's personal death. An elderly woman's monologue in Samuel Beckett's play *Rockabye* portrays this ambivalence powerfully. With a strong urge to live as she rocks in her chair, she delays death by repeatedly saying "not yet," until she becomes mute at the final curtain. Most old persons may not wish to go gentle into that good night (Thomas 1946).

Not only do old persons have complex attitudes toward their own deaths, but their perceptions of the longevity of peers are also multifaceted. They may have an expectation that their family and friends will continue to live as long as they do. Perhaps this is an example of the principle of conservation (Marris 1974), which projects continuity of one's social network and sees the threat of discontinuity as loss.

Social Context of the Death of an Older Person

An older person who is dying may be treated as if socially dead (Glaser 1966). It is not unusual for other people to say that they would not want to live with the degree of impairment of the dying person (Kastenbaum 1972). Surely if the lives of older persons are of less value to a society, their deaths will have less impact, and the ensuing bereavement and grief will be less socially supported.

When one hears about a person's death, often the first question asked is, "How old was he [or she]?" The intent of this simple query is complex: It may be to compare one's own age or the age of significant others to that of the deceased. It immediately evokes concern about one's own calculus of finitude, offering reassurance or threat. Awareness of the age may also help one to judge the fairness or inequity of the death. It places the deceased person and his or her life within an understandable social and developmental context. It brings to mind life tasks of the deceased that have been completed or left undone. If the person was very old it may imply that the mourner needs less comforting.

If the person was young, general rules of equity seem to be violated. He or she was deprived of a fair share of life. The death upsets the normal order of things. The "pecking order of death" is observed when the oldest and sickest die first (Kastenbaum 1969). Thus, death of the young is "off time" (Neugarten 1970). When a very old person dies, there is a sense of timeliness (Kastenbaum 1969). The death may be much less devastating than that of a younger person; it may represent a smaller social loss (Blauner 1966).

Callahan (1987) takes the idea of "on time" deaths to what he sees as a logical, ethical conclusion. He is a leading spokesperson arguing against life extension and life supports for the old. His highly controversial position suggests that their deaths are timely after they have completed a "natural biography," which occurs about when they have reached their eighties.

There is a tendency not to mark the death of the very old with a wide range of customary funeral rituals (Owen, Fulton, and Markusen 1982–83). Often the funerals for older persons are relatively small. Many friends have died, as have family members in the same generation. Those who do survive may not attend because of limitations on their health or mobility. At the end of a long life the network of social support that has accompanied one over a lifetime has few surviving members; one's "social convoy" (Kahn and Antonucci 1980) has diminished.

Many old people die alone, without family present (Owen, Fulton, and Markusen 1982–83). This too marks the decreased social value of the person's life and death (Kastenbaum 1969). To the extent that older persons live in communities with other elderly, or have daily lives that are partially segregated from those of younger persons, their death may in some ways take on the mantle of a routine event and appear to make less impact.

Since the lives and the deaths of older people tend to decrease in social value, it is likely that the expression of grief is less socially meaningful when the deceased (and/or the survivor) is very old (Volkart and Michael 1957).

Impact of the Death of the Elderly

Thus far we have explored many factors that may play a role in the devaluation of the lives and deaths of older persons. Nevertheless, as we will argue in the remainder of this chapter, the impact of bereavement is potentially intense and highly significant when a very old person dies, regardless of health and competency.

Responses to death may differ, depending on the type of relationship between the survivor and the deceased (Osterweis, Solomon, and Green 1984). Spousal deaths (Gallagher, Thompson, and Peterson 1981–82, Lopata 1979), parent deaths (Kowalski 1986a, Moss and Moss 1983–84), and sibling deaths (Moss and Moss 1986) may each evoke a different dynamic of bereavement. This chapter is very limited, in that it does not explore these differences.

Next, we examine four aspects of the impact of the death of an older person:

1. The survivor's view of personal finitude and death
2. The survivor's sense of self and personal identity
3. The social context of the survivor's daily life
4. The survivor's experience of grief

1. Impact on the Survivor's View of Death and Personal Finitude

The process of bereavement leads to a shift in one's sense of finitude. As Kalish (1986) suggests, the survivor tends to examine the existential meaning of life and death. Often an elderly person's death (such as that of a parent or older sibling) means the loss of a natural buffer against death. The survivor may feel closer to the head of the line, closer to his or her own death (Moss and Moss 1983–84). The loss of a grandparent or great-grandparent may also evoke a shift in the personal meaning of death.

When a very old person dies there tends to be an affirmation of the rightness of the death, that it is on time. The survivor wants to make a good, coherent biography of the life of the deceased and its ending. This may help the survivor to affirm that he or she too may die after a long, full life (Marshall 1986). The death of an old person may engender a shift in the calculus of one's own distance from death. One's personal life expectation may increase, inching up from seventy to eighty and beyond.

When the survivor is also very old, additional factors come into play. With the death of a peer, an older person may experience yet another promise of the imminence of his or her own mortality. There is some socialization to death for the very old. Death is more salient; they think and talk more about it (Kastenbaum and Aisenberg 1972), but it is less frightening (Kalish and Reynolds 1976). Research on death anxiety has done little to help us understand the meaning of death for the very old (Kastenbaum 1987–88).

Considering the length of family ties and the frequency of long-term friendships, the survivors may well have known the deceased person at the height of physical and mental powers and noted the decline over months and years. When an age peer dies, one is faced with the impact of the passage of time and a shortened distance from death.

2. Impact on the Survivor's Personal Identity

The central issue of later life is the preservation and maintenance of self-integrity, self-continuity, self-identity (Erikson 1963, Lieberman and Tobin 1983). The death of a significant person is a threat to the survivor's sense of self. Marris (1974) suggests that the fundamental crisis of bereavement is not the loss of the other but the loss of self.

Death of an older person may initiate a review of shared associations and experiences, thus helping to legitimate one's own biography (Marshall 1986). Each person has multiple life themes that "identify the personal, idiosyncratic ways of experiencing and communicating meaning" in his or her life (Kaufman 1986, p. 115). The survivor's life themes and values help to integrate the meaning of the death and preserve the continuity of the self.

While affirming life, the survivor also is faced once again with the end of the life cycle. Experiencing the loss of a significant person, one sees the playing out of the passage from Ecclesiastes: "To everything there is a season, and time to every purpose under the heaven: A time to be born, and a time to die; . . . a time to mourn, and a time to dance" (3:1–4). Some may accept the inevitability of the death of a person who has lived a full, long life. Death is clearly in its place. It may be seen as the gateway to an afterlife, to heaven.

A death, though a reminder of one's own vulnerability and finitude, may also involve a sense of triumph. One may be glad to have survived and not to be the one who died (Kalish 1985, Raphael 1983). The rightness of the death of the other may affirm the rightness of the continuity of the self. Regardless of the age of the survivor, it may be comforting to survive. As the death reaffirms the continuing existence of the survivor, there may be a surge of efforts to preserve and care for the self. These efforts are basically ego enhancing: an affirmation of self in the now, and a sense of continuity into the future.

On the other hand, the loss of a significant person also diminishes the sense of self (Kaplan 1983). For an old person the death may reinforce his or her sense of decline and evoke partial grief for the self. This may increase his or her vulnerability to other losses and subsequent deaths (Thoits 1983).

3. The Impact on the Social Context of the Survivor's Life

To understand the impact of a death, it is important to see the loss within the social context of the life of the survivor, as well as to place it within the web of other losses (Simos 1979, Viorst 1986). For older persons, the loss of another may occur within a limited and shrinking network. New relationships may create threats of new losses and may be avoided. Often the survivor has previously lost other persons with whom to share memories of the deceased. There is an adaptive value of shared grieving, which may facilitate social cohesiveness, particularly in the bonds with other survivors.

Since friends are a major source of support for the bereaved, and older persons tend to have a diminishing circle of friends, such losses for the old person may be particularly difficult. Most old women are widows and have lost close relationships with men (Raphael 1983). As mourners they lack the resources and supports of men.

The daily life of the survivors may be affected by the death. If they were actively involved in caregiving for the old person, the death may mean the sudden cessation of the satisfactions and burdens of daily care, of constant concern, of visits to the hospital or nursing home. There is no replacement, however, for the loss of the unique person (Freud 1960) or the care-eliciting behavior evoked by that person.

Death of an old person represents a break in continuity with the past. Who now can be the reservoir of family history, events, and traditions? The deceased old relative may represent "family." Although a sense of the person's presence may persist, a reorganization of the family may occur in patterns of intimacy, caring, commitment, sense of family feeling, reciprocal identity and support (Moss and Moss 1986). For example, inheritance may bring about shifts in family alignments as members reapportion the resources of the deceased. Thus, the bonds in the family as well as in other membership groups may be affected by an old person's death (Kaplan 1983).

For a surviving older person, the death may occur in a sequence of other deaths or losses. The impact of multiple or sequential losses is great and may lead to "bereavement overload" (Kastenbaum 1969). Unless there is the opportunity to work through a previous loss, bereavement overload in old age may generate many behavioral and somatic problems (Gramlich 1968, Kastenbaum 1969, Thoits 1983). These may include preoccupation with bodily functions and a deep sense of loneliness. Threats of other losses, such as serious illness in any generation of the family, may also intensify the impact of the death.

Past losses constitute a pool of grief experienced over the lifetime. A death leads one to recall other losses in the recent as well as distant past. It may evoke despair and helplessness. On the other hand, successful mastery of past losses may lead to an affirmation of one's coping capacity. Perhaps, having moved ahead after the death of one parent, the survivor will find his or her ability to cope with the death of the second parent to be enhanced. Alternately it may leave one doubly bereft as an adult orphan (Moss and Moss 1983–84). Adaptation levels as well as expectations change over time, and thus similar events may evoke different emotional responses (Schulz 1985).

4. The Experience of Grief and Bereavement

The survivor's attitudes toward death, the sense of personal identity, and the social context are reflected in the experience of grief. Grief is tempered by cultural prescriptions and proscriptions in regard to mourning. In general our society frowns on the expression of emotion during grief and encourages denial. This may be particularly the case for the death of the older person or for the older survivor.

There is, to our knowledge, no systematic research that examines the range and characteristics of grief in response to the death of a very old person. The spectrum of grief responses is probably broad. It may include denial and the avoidance of any emotional expression, no tears or sadness. There may be, however, an intense and prolonged response, perhaps including preoccupation with the deceased, anxiety, hostility, guilt, loss of interest in daily routines, and social withdrawal from other persons. These responses may underlie somatic problems or profound psychological disturbances such as depression (Clayton and Darvish 1979). Reactions to the loss of a significant other may have similar basic themes across the life span (Bowlby 1980).

There is much uncertainty about how one should express grief, with what intensity, and to whom (Rosenblatt, Walsh, and Jackson 1976, Herriott and Kiyak 1981). There is also no precise end point for grieving. Pain and loss can remain or recur over a lifetime (Osterweis, Solomon, and Green 1984).

Since most of the deaths of older persons are not fully unanticipated but follow multiple chronic illnesses or conditions, there is usually time for some psychic preparation by the survivor. There is no consistent evidence, however, that anticipatory grief reduces grief after the death (Rando 1984). If the deceased person had experienced much pain and suffering toward the end of life, the survivor may have anticipated relief after the death. How anticipatory grief or a pending sense of relief may affect the quality of the grief is unknown.

There are various ways in which guilt may enter into grief for a very old person. There may have been guilt arousing omissions and commissions in the past. If there was a lingering process of dying, the survivor may have wished for death, and the wish may elicit guilt. The survivor may question whether his or her grief is sufficient in quality, intensity, and duration. There may be guilt in surviving, particularly with the loss of a spouse.

Although there is no clear distinction between pathological grief and normal grief (Osterweis, Solomon, and Green 1984), preventive psychiatry has as its basic premise that unexpressed grief can subsequently be associated with mental illness. Raphael (1983), Parkes (1986), and Volkan (1975) suggest that it is important to give sorrow words, to express deep feelings of grief and loss. Parkes and Weiss (1983) assert that grief is complicated when it is suppressed, interrupted, delayed, or concomitant with other losses.

There may be a tendency to use denial as a defense against loss. The survivor may attempt to rationalize the death and withdraw feeling toward the event. Denial has its benefits and its costs (Simos 1979).

Grief, although an individual experience, generally occurs within a family context. Other than examples of the patterns of family sharing of grief within younger clinical populations (Paul and Grosser 1965), little is known about the ways in which grief is shared among family members suffering the loss of an old person.

The availability of other persons with whom to share one's grief may be helpful. Younger persons are more likely to have a spouse or significant other in their household, hence someone to grieve with them. The impact of the death may be greater for old persons who live alone if they have no one to provide continuing support and solace.

There is evidence that the emotional experience of older persons are at least as intense and enduring as those of younger persons (Schulz 1985). Thus, the experience of grief in the elderly may well evoke responses as varied and significant as those of younger persons.

Implications

We have suggested that the process of bereavement over the death of a very old person is multifaceted and that its impact is often not socially recognized. The bereaved person may lack the opportunity to acknowledge and express the loss, and thus feel disenfranchised. Many survivors mourning the death of an elderly person are denied an opportunity to participate fully in the bereavement process.

The death of a significant old person can be a threat to the survivor's sense of self. If the survivor can recognize the depth of the loss, he or she may be better able to deal with expressed and latent affect (Worden 1982). Coming to terms with one's feelings can be ego supportive, can facilitate uncomplicated grief, and can reduce the likelihood of depression. Normal grief does not involve the consistently strong negative self-image that is found in clinical depression (Gallagher et al. 1981).

Counselors and other professionals should try to develop creative primary prevention approaches by reaching out to the bereaved through churches, community housing for the elderly, hospitals, and funeral homes. Help could be provided to families from the time they begin to struggle with partial grief and the anticipation of death, through the time of actual bereavement.

What are some of the implications of our discussion for the families of nursing home residents, and for the residents themselves?

Should one inform a very old person that a relative has died? Although each death may be seen as a threat to self, and a series of losses may be particularly hard to bear, it is generally appropriate to share the news of the death with the very old. Often the older person does "know." There is also the possibility that the death may become known through other channels—for example, from other people who read obituaries. Generally, it is respectful of the dignity of the person to tell about the death, and dehumanizing not to tell. Death should be acknowledged as a part of life.

The nursing home is often recognized as a terminal placement. Deaths of roommates, tablemates, and acquaintances are everyday occurrences. Residents often expect deaths of others as well as their own. They may have a good feeling if a peer dies quickly and without suffering. Yet they not infrequently say, "Why did God take him when I'm waiting to die?"

In an institution, there is a constant tension between the wish to deny death and its impact, and the reality of its frequent occurrence. Both staff and residents feel uncomfortable with the successive losses. It may be helpful to develop a ritual reflecting a life-affirming attitude. This could highlight the achievements of the deceased, emphasizing a full and meaningful life, with death as its natural ending. It may also help to legitimize the survivor's own biography.

An administrator in one Catholic nursing home described low attendance at wakes in funeral homes. After she arranged for all wakes to be held in the nursing home, nearly all the residents attended and enjoyed the experience. This prompted a teenage volunteer to comment, "These people talk about going to a wake like we think of going to the movies."

Though families of deceased nursing home residents are bereft, they may find social supports for their grief. We recommend that staff make every effort to acknowledge the depths of grief that may be experienced by the family and to develop programs to help families cope with their loss.

Staff, however, may be limited in their capacity to provide empathy and support. They may have built up defenses against the pain of continuous loss. If the institution makes an effort to provide a forum for staff to express and receive support for their feelings, this may enable them to be more of a resource for bereaved families.

A major implication of this discussion is that it highlights the need for research on the interaction between old age and bereavement. The following are only a few areas that need systematic study:

1. To what extent does the death of a very old person lead to shifts in the survivor's attitude toward death, in the sense of self, or in the social world of the survivor?

2.   Do people change in their expression of grief as they get older? Do the very old experience degrees of intensity, duration, and psychological distress different from what they experienced when they were younger? Is there a shift over the life span in the degree to which the expression of grief is a solitary rather than a family or group experience? Is the very old person more detached or numbed as a result of frequent losses? Is there more or less somatization accompanying bereavement? Are there differences reflective of shifts in the way subsequent cohorts are socialized to express emotions? Are there gender differences?

3.   To what extent do ethnic, cultural, and religious groups share or differ in their attitudes toward the death of the elderly? Do they vary in how they legitimize or disenfranchise a full expression of grief?

4.   How does the quality of the relationship between the deceased and the survivor affect the process of bereavement? Specifically, what is the impact of the patterns of interaction, the qualities of positive affect and negative affect, the instrumental and emotional supports, the intensity of the bonds of family unity?

5.   How do we disentangle the impact of old age and of disability on bereavement? Is there a different process of bereavement when the deceased old person had been active and independent versus dependent and impaired? To what extent are the characteristics and duration of the terminal illness determinants of the course of bereavement? To what extent is old age itself a legitimization of death?

6.   What are the similarities and differences in patterns and expectations of grief when the very old person is a spouse, or a parent, or a sibling, or other family relation?

7.   If the very old person is the survivor, and if he or she is suffering from physical or cognitive impairment, is grief disenfranchised?

8.   What is the impact upon a very old person's attitude toward death and expression of grief when he or she lives in housing for elderly or in a nursing home? Does death in an age-segregated setting serve to disenfranchise grief?

9.   What is the impact upon a very old person of the death of a child (Moss, Lesher, and Moss 1986–87), or another person in a younger generation? What is the impact of the death of a friend in late life?

In summary, we suggest that it is necessary to recognize the complexity of the process of bereavement and the potential disenfranchisement of the grief in response to the death of very old persons. This process is mirrored in older persons themselves when they survive the deaths of significant others. Systematic exploration of the interface between very old age and death is long overdue.

References

Beckett, S. n.d. *Rockabye and Other Short Pieces*. New York: Samuel French.

Berezin, M.A. 1977. "Partial Grief for the Aged and Their Families." In *The Experience of Dying,* edited by E.M. Pattison. Englewood Cliffs, N.J.: Prentice-Hall.

Blauner, R. 1966. "Death and Social Structure." *Psychiatry* 29, 378–94.

Bowlby, J. 1980. *Attachment and Loss*. Vol. 3. New York: Basic Books.

Brody, J.A. 1984. "Facts, Projections, and Gaps Concerning Data on Aging." *Public Health Reports* 99, 468–75.

Butler, R.N. 1969. "Ageism: Another Form of Bigotry." *The Gerontologist* 9, 243–46.

Callahan, D. 1987. "Terminating Treatment: Age as a Standard." *Hastings Center Report* 17, 21–25.

Clayton, P.J., and H.S. Darvish. 1979. "Course of Depressive Symptoms Following the Stress of Bereavement." In *Stress and Mental Disorder,* edited by J.E. Barrett. New York: Raven Press.

Erikson, E. 1963. *Childhood and Society*. New York: Norton.

Feifel, H. 1959. "Attitudes toward Death in Some Normal and Mentally Ill Populations." In *The Meaning of Death,* edited by H. Feifel. New York: McGraw-Hill.

Freud, S. 1917. "Mourning and Melancholia." In *Complete Psychological Works,* Standard Ed., vol. 14, edited by J. Strachey. London: Hogarth Press, 1987.

———. 1929. Letter 239 to Binswanger. In *Letters of Sigmund Freud,* edited by E.L. Freud. Translated by T. and J. Stern, 1960. New York: Basic Books.

Gallagher, D., C. Dessonville, J.N. Breckenridge, L.W. Thompson, and P. Amaral. 1981. "Similarities and Differences between Normal Grief and Depression in Older Adults." *Essence* 5.

Gallagher, D.E., L.W. Thompson, and J.A. Peterson. 1981–82. "Psychological Factors Affecting Adaptation to Bereavement in the Elderly." *International Journal of Aging and Human Development* 14, 79–95.

Glaser, B.A. 1966. "The Social Loss of Aged Dying Patients." *The Gerontologist* 6, 77–80.

Gramlich, E.P. 1968. "Recognition and Management of Grief in Elderly Patients." *Geriatrics* 123, 87–92.

Hayflick, L. 1987. "The Human Life Span." In *Realistic Expectations for Long Life,* edited by. G. Lesnoff-Caravaglia. New York: Human Sciences Press.

Herriott, M., and H.A. Kiyak. 1981. "Bereavement in Old Age: Implications for Therapy and Research." *Journal of Gerontological Social Work* 3, 15–43.

The Holy Scriptures. 1944. Philadelphia: Jewish Publication Society of America.

Kahn, R.L., and T.C. Antonucci. 1980. "Convoys over the Life Course: Attachment, Roles, and Social Support." In *Life Span Development and Behavior* 3, 253–86.

Kalish, R.A. 1985. "The Social Context of Death and Dying." In *Handbook of Aging and the Social Sciences,* 2d ed., edited by R.H. Binstock and E. Shanas. New York: Van Nostrand Reinhold.

———. 1986. "Death." In *Encyclopedia of Aging,* edited by G.L. Maddox. New York: Springer.

Kalish, R.A., and D.K. Reynolds. 1976. *Death and Ethnicity: A Psychocultural Study*. Los Angeles: University of Southern California Press.

Kaplan, H.B. 1983. "Psychological Distress in Sociological Context." In *Psychological Stress: Trends in Theory and Research,* edited by H.B. Kaplan. New York: Academic Press.

Kastenbaum, R. 1969. "Death and Bereavement in Later Life." In *Death and Bereavement in Later Life,* edited by A.H. Kutscher. Springfield, Ill.: Thomas.

————. 1972. "While the Old Man Dies." In *Psychosocial Aspects of Terminal Care,* edited by A.H. Kutscher. New York: Columbia University Press.

————. 1987–88. "Theory, Research and Application: Some Critical Issues for Thanatology." *Omega* 18, 397–410.

Kastenbaum, R., and R.B. Aisenberg. 1972. *The Psychology of Death.* New York: Springer.

Kaufman, S. 1986. *The Ageless Self.* Madison: University of Wisconsin Press.

Kowalski, N.C. 1986a. "Anticipating the Death of an Elderly Parent." In *Loss and Anticipatory Grief,* edited by T.A. Rando. Lexington, Mass.: Lexington Books.

————. 1986b. "The Older Person's Anticipation of Her Own Death." in *Loss and Anticipatory Grief,* edited by T.A. Rando. Lexington, Mass.: Lexington Books.

Lieberman, M.A., and S.S. Tobin. 1983. *The Experience of Old Age: Stress, Coping, and Survival.* New York: Basic Books.

Lopata, H.Z. 1979. *Women as Widows.* New York: Elsevier North Holland.

Marris, P. 1974. *Loss and Change.* New York: Pantheon.

Marshall, V.W. 1980. *Last Chapters: The Sociology of Aging and Dying.* Monterey, Calif.: Brooks/Cole.

————. 1986. "A Sociological Perspective on Aging and Dying." In *Later Life: The Social Psychology of Aging,* edited by V.W. Marshall. Beverly Hills, Calif.: Sage.

Moss, M.S. 1984. "The Last Year of Life." Unpublished manuscript.

Moss, M.S., E. Lesher, and S.Z. Moss. 1986–87. "The Impact of the Death of an Adult Child on Elderly Parents." *Omega* 17, 209–18.

Moss, M.S., and S.Z. Moss. 1983–84. "The Impact of Parental Death on Middle-Aged Children." *Omega* 14, 65–75.

————. 1986. "Death of the Adult Sibling." *International Journal of Family Psychiatry* 7, 397–418.

Myerhoff, B. 1978. *Number Our Days.* New York: Dutton.

Neugarten, B.L. 1970. "Adaptation and the Life Cycle." *Journal of Geriatric Psychiatry* 4, 71–87.

Osterweis, M., F. Solomon, and M. Green. eds. 1984. *Bereavement: Reactions, Consequences and Care.* Washington, D.C.: National Academy Press.

Owen, G., R. Fulton, and E. Markusen. 1982–83. "Death at a Distance: A Study of Family Survivors." *Omega* 13, 191–225.

Parkes, C.M. 1986. *Bereavement.* Madison, Conn.: International Universities Press.

Parkes, C.M., and R.S. Weiss. 1983. *Recovery from Bereavement.* New York: Basic Books.

Pattison, E.M. 1977. "The Experience of Dying." In *The Experience of Dying,* edited by E.M. Pattison. Englewood Cliffs, N.J.: Prentice-Hall.

Paul, N.L., and G.H. Grosser. 1965. "Operational Mourning and Its Role in Family Therapy." *Community Mental Health Journal* 1, 339–45.

Pollak, O. 1980. "The Shadow of Death over Aging." *Annals of the American Academy of Political Science* 447, 71–77.

Rando, T.A. 1984. *Grief, Dying, and Death.* Champaign, Ill.: Research Press.

Raphael, B. 1983. *The Anatomy of Bereavement.* New York: Basic Books.

Riley, J.W., Jr. 1983. "Dying and the Meanings of Death." *Annual Review of Sociology* 9, 191–216.

Rosenblatt, P.C., R.P. Walsh, and D.A. Jackson. 1976. *Grief and Mourning in Cross-Cultural Perspective,* New Haven: HRAFP Press.

Schulz, R. 1985. "Emotion and Affect." In *Handbook of the Psychology of Aging,* edited by J.E. Birren and K.W. Schaie. New York: Van Nostrand Reinhold.

Schulz, R., and J. Schlarb. 1987–88. "Two Decades of Research on Dying: What Do We Know about the Patient?" *Omega* 18, 299–317.

Simos, B.G. 1979. *A Time to Grieve: Loss as a Universal Human Experience.* New York: Family Service Association.

Stern, K., G.M. Williams, and M. Prados. 1951. "Grief Reactions in Later Life." *American Journal of Psychiatry* 108, 289–94.

Swenson, W.M. 1976. "Attitudes toward Death among the Aged." In *Death and Identity,* edited by R. Fulton. Bowie, Md.: Charles Press.

Taeuber, C.M., and I. Rosenwaite. In press. "A Demographic Portrait of America's Oldest Old." In *The Oldest Old,* edited by R. Suzman and D. Willis. New York: Oxford University Press.

Thoits, P.A. 1983. "Dimensions of Life Events That Influence Psychological Distress: An Evaluation and Synthesis of the Literature." In *Psychosocial Stress,* edited by H.B. Kaplan. New York: Academic Press.

Thomas, D. 1946. *The Collected Poems of Dylan Thomas.* New York: New Directions.

Viorst, J. 1986. *Necessary Losses.* New York: Simon and Schuster.

Volkan, V.D. 1975. " 'Re-Grief' Therapy." In *Bereavement: Its Psychological Aspects,* edited by B. Schoenberg, I. Gerber, A. Wiener, A.H. Kutscher, D. Peretz, and A.C. Carr. New York: Columbia University Press.

Volkart, E., and S. Michael. 1957. "Bereavement and Mental Health." In *Explorations in Social Psychiatry,* edited by A. Leighton. New York: Basic Books.

Weisman, A.D. 1972. *On Dying and Denying: A Psychiatric Study of Terminality.* New York: Behavioral Publications.

Weisman, A.D. and R. Kastenbaum 1968. *The Psychological Autopsy: A Study of the Terminal Phase of Life.* New York: Community Mental Health Monographs, no. 4.

Worden, J.W. 1982. *Grief Counseling and Grief Therapy.* New York: Springer.

20
Disenfranchised Grief and the Developmentally Disabled

Claire Lavin

Developmentally disabled people are like all the rest of us in most respects. We all share the need for love, approval, achievement, and relationships with others in our lives. We all laugh, cry, love, and hate. We all live and we all will die, and those close to us also live and die. Our reactions to these events will be shaped by many factors. Our emotional stability, previous experiences, and our intellectual endowment will all affect the way we react to significant experiences in our lives. Thus, those among us who are developmentally disabled will react in ways that differ, to some extent, from the way the rest of us react because of their specific characteristics or differences.

It is often easy to stereotype the developmentally disabled and consider all people with that label as having the same characteristics. However, developmentally disabled people vary as much as do normal people across an array of qualities. In discussing those behavioral characteristics of the developmentally disabled that affect their reactions to death, it is important to reemphasize the fact that they have the same basic physiological, social, and emotional needs that we all have. Additionally, they vary among themselves as widely as do those in the so-called normal population. Keeping these caveats in mind, then, we can discuss the ways in which the developmentally disabled are most likely to differ from the norm, and the implications of these differences for the grieving process.

Characteristics of Developmentally Disabled

The mentally retarded developmentally disabled demonstrate impaired mental abilities. They perform below their chronological age in academic areas and in social areas as well. They use more inappropriate and less chronologically appropriate social behaviors. They function below the level one would expect on the basis of their chronological ages. Their reactions to the loss of significant others in their lives may also be on a level lower than that of their normal age mates. For example, they may not understand the idea that death is irreversible and think that the dead person will return. In addition to these cognitive deficits, there are other characteristics that will shape their reactions to death.

Most of the developmentally disabled can be described as "other directed." They do not have confidence in their own ability to solve problems, so they rely on other people to solve their problems for them. Traditionally, they have experienced caretaking at school, at home, or in institutional or group living situations. Consequently, they have not developed a sense of independence and the ability to test response to events in their environment. They expect to be guided and to be told what to do. In helping them deal with death, therefore, direct instruction and guidance will be needed to help them cope with grief.

The developmentally disabled have also been described as having an external locus of control. They see fate, chance, or forces beyond their control as responsible for what happens to them. Caregivers need to help them understand that death is not the result of a capricious fate but rather the end of a natural cycle of life and death that governs all living things.

In general, the disabled have difficulty with interpersonal relationships. Their poor self-concepts and limited social skills provide a double handicap when it comes to forming meaningful relationships with others. The awkwardness that many people feel in meeting and conversing with new friends is exacerbated in this population. They do not have the smooth social skills that normal people can draw upon to offer, say, words of comfort. They may feel sorrow and want to express it but may lack both the words and the socially appropriate tools to do so.

In terms of learning characteristics, the developmentally disabled have a number of learning differences related to poor short-term memory. They have poor selective attention and do not focus on a learning task and attend to all of its relevant dimensions. They also organize information poorly and then have difficulty recalling it later. They do not group details, organize facts sequentially, or use inner speech strategies. They have difficulty with generalizing information learned in one situation to a different situation. They do not transfer what they have learned. Finally, abstract thinking is difficult for the disabled. They are far more adept at dealing with concrete material.

These learning patterns indicate that in terms of teaching the disabled how to cope with death, the material should be made as concrete as possible and tied to their actual experiences. The caregivers must focus the individuals' attention on the skills to be mastered, since they may not focus appropriately on their own. Since the disabled have poor memory skills, caregivers must provide for repetition of the learning task. For example, one demonstration of the way to approach the bereaved family will not be sufficient. Several explanations plus modeling and role playing may be needed before the individual is able to approach a mourner, extend his hand, and say, "I'm very sorry." Since the disabled have trouble generalizing to other situations, caregivers must clearly draw the parallels between the death of a pet, a previous funeral, and so on, and the present experience. Finally, caregivers should not assume that the individual has developed the basic understandings, remembers the things to do, or will automatically say or do the appropriate thing. Each assumption must be checked and reinforcement provided where necessary.

Reactions to Death

In light of these characteristics, then, how do the developmentally disabled react to death?

If they have been sheltered all their lives, they may face the death of a loved one unprepared. Often parents shield their normal children from death and are reluctant to include them in the rites of mourning, keeping them away from wakes and funerals. There is a greater tendency for the parents of the developmentally disabled to continue the shielding process longer. Thus the disabled, although chronologically at an age to participate in mourning rituals, may be denied access to them. They therefore are not exposed to role models who show them how to cope effectively with death. The value of participating in wakes and funerals lies in learning how to deal with loss by watching significant others in their lives do so effectively. The rehearsals, it is hoped, will include the funerals of older and presumably more distant relatives, such as grandparents, uncles, aunts, and others. When faced with a closer loss, such as that of a parent, the developmentally disabled will be better prepared to deal with the loss because of these previous encounters with death.

For those disabled people living in institutions, participation in death rituals may have been similarly restricted. When long-term companions or caregivers die, the disabled may not have participated in the final rites of passage. Without the opportunity to enter fully into the grieving process, they are denied closure and the opportunity to work through their reactions to the end of the relationships.

The social skills of the developmentally disabled are, in general, not equivalent to those of the normal population. For the retarded, social skills may be far below the level expected according to their chronological age. For the mildly impaired, such as the learning disabled, poor social skills go hand in hand with the disability. The proper tone of voice, comforting phrases, and modulated behaviors all appropriate in grief situations may not come naturally to the disabled. In fact, their inappropriate choice of behaviors and blunt statements may seem particularly inappropriate at a time of loss and may cause a negative reaction on the part of those also involved in the grief process. During a time of loss the disabled do not need negative feedback, which may exacerbate an already negative situation.

Normal people learn many important things in life in an incidental manner, just by living. They learn how to act at a funeral or wake by observing others. The disabled are not as apt to learn things incidentally. They need to be taught specifically how to act at a funeral since it is unlikely that they will simply pick up information. Caregivers of the disabled must provide direct instruction on all of these topics to augment meager incidental learning.

The developmentally disabled have stronger intellectual skills for dealing with the concrete than they do for the abstract. They understand best when they can actually see and handle materials, not when they are asked to deal with abstract concepts. Since death, the hereafter, God, and so forth, are highly abstract concepts, the developmentally disabled in general will have difficulty in dealing with them. Explanations must be made as concrete as possible since abstract theological explanations will be meaningless. For example, in describing God as a loving father, citing the example of the individual's father will be understood better than will an explanation that God is the creator of the universe.

One of the primary intellectual characteristics of the developmentally disabled is limited ability to transfer information gained in one situation to another. With normal children and adults, this transfer occurs easily. For the disabled, elaboration is needed to have skills transfer. For the disabled, therefore, caregivers and family members need to draw clear parallels between the present death and previous death experiences so that the individual sees the relationship between them.

Teaching Coping Skills

The point was made earlier that, in many ways, the handicapped are like the nonhandicapped. Far too few in the normal population have been adequately prepared to deal with emotional crises in life, and with death and dying. Familiarity with both of these topics is crucial to the adjustment of both the handicapped and the nonhandicapped in adult life. Since the disabled are not as apt to take the initiative in learning about these topics, it is crucial that the schools and caregivers assume this role. The disabled are generally externally controlled—that is, someone in authority tells them what to do and how to do it. When they perform incorrectly, that authority figure tells them how to fix their error. In dealing with death, also, specific instruction is necessary, although caregivers may not always be aware of this fact.

Prior to teaching specific skills to the developmentally disabled, it is necessary first to conduct a task analysis of what skills are required. The task analysis must identify specific behaviors that can be modeled or taught in a stepwise sequential fashion. For example, when a family member has died, the developmentally disabled person must be prepared for the mourning rituals. He should be able to greet those who come to express condolences and shake their hands. He should also be able to make an appropriate verbal response. If participation in the funeral requires knowledge of prayers, sitting next to the casket, or tossing flowers, the disabled individual must be taught to perform these actions in a socially acceptable manner.

How is this to be accomplished? A four-stage approach involving preparation, direct instruction, modeling, and emotional support is advisable.

Preparation

In helping the developmentally disabled cope with death, the first step is to prepare them to be exposed to death experiences. The period of preparation is important for everyone, but particularly for the developmentally disabled, who need a longer time span and concrete experiences to develop concepts. There are a number of books that are written simply for the young child which can be used with the disabled.

A second vicarious preparation can incorporate television shows and, if a VCR is available, the use of videotapes. Many films depict death in a callous manner without exploring the implications of its finality. These would not be appropriate as preparation materials. There are some films that do depict death and dying in a sensitive manner. In viewing a film or show, the following guidelines may be helpful:

1. Prepare the individual for the film and direct his attention to the key events. For example: "This film is about a man who knows he is dying and wants to help his family get ready for it."

2. Clarify the initial concepts of death, the funeral , and so on. For example: "Do you know what a funeral, death, a wake is?"

3. Give concrete examples of the above concepts and relate them to the individual's personal experiences. For example: "Do you remember when we found that dead robin on the driveway? It could not move, sing, or fly anymore. It was dead."

4. View the film with the individual and answer questions as they arise. Also, comment on concepts you wish to stress. For example: "Many people are crying. People feel sad when someone dies."

5. At the end of the film, share your feelings and reactions to the film. For example, "I felt sad that he died, but I think he was happy that his pain was over. How did that film make you feel?"

6. Review the major concepts at the end of the film as well. For example:

"When someone dies, all of his friends and relatives come together to make one another feel better. It is nice to go and tell them you are sorry."

The third type of preparation should include living things that will die: plants, fish, pets. The experience of losing a plant or pet you are fond of parallels less painfully the loss of a human being. For most people, plants are a good starting point because less intense emotions are attached to them than to animals—although in some instances this may not be the case.

Caring for plants in the garden provides a note of warmth while they are alive and a valuable lesson when they die. The care of the plants should be viewed from the beginning in terms of their life cycle. When planting the seeds or young seedlings, comment on their life cycle. For example: "These geraniums are beautiful. They will give the yard a happy look until the cold weather. When the cold weather comes, they will die. All living things die." As the weather becomes cold and the end of their life cycle approaches, reinforce this concept. After the frost, involve the individual in composting the plants, if possible, so that they can enrich the earth in the future. Comment fondly on the pleasure the plants provided. For example: "Even though it is winter now, I still remember those beautiful red flowers."

The progression to animals involves stronger feelings of attachment, particularly when pets are involved. Starting with a tank of tropical fish will probably provide a death experience fairly soon. Again, emphasize the concept, when starting the tank, that you will care for the fish until they die and that all living things die. When a fish dies, speak about the sad feelings when something you love is not around anymore. For example: "I am sorry the fish died. It is always sad to lose something you love even though you know that all living things die." The disposal of the fish or a larger animal can also provide the opportunity for going through a funeral or burial-type experience. Include the individual in deciding where and how the fish or pet will be placed. For example: "We can put him in a box and place it near this bush. If we put a stone over it, we will remember where he is."

Direct Instruction

The death of older friends and relatives of the disabled provide opportunities to practice skills developed by direct instruction. The caregiver must analyze the skills that need to be taught and teach them one by one, providing repetition and reinforcement. The authority figure or guardian should describe what will occur at the wake or funeral, one aspect at a time. For example, to teach the individual how to offer condolences, this person should (1) demonstrate the way one approaches a family member and waits to be noticed; (2) next, hold out his hand and shake firmly; (3) next, say, "I'm very sorry." These skills should be practiced one at a time in sequence until they have been mastered. The responsibility for identifying and teaching the key behaviors falls on the caregiver, since, as has been noted previously, the restricted experience of the disabled individual and his limited incidental learning skills may not have provided him with these appropriate behaviors. The disabled person should be prepared to find people crying and know that people express their sadness this way.

Since the disabled have limited ability to transfer skills, they may not use the practiced skills in the appropriate setting. When brought to the funeral home, the disabled person should be instructed to watch the caretaker, and then to do as he had practiced previously. Appropriate reinforcement should be given for the correct behavior.

As painful as death experiences with animals are, those involving people are many times more difficult. One hopes that the first death experience will not involve a particularly close relative, for intense emotions will interfere with the learning process you are trying to develop. In preparing the individual to cope with the death of an individual, the previous experiences with films, books, plants, and animals should be recalled. The emotions, mourning process, and burial should be referred to in order to give concrete examples of what the death of a person is like. Role playing of the skills should be helpful.

In addition to skill instruction, the individual must be prepared for the setting he will find. The intense emotions may upset him unless he anticipates them. Recall the emotions that friends and relatives will be experiencing. Ask what things you could say to make them feel better. Have the individual practice with you. For example, "cry" and have him come up to you, shake your hand, and say "I'm sorry." Practice until you both feel confident with this behavior. Provide details of what the individual will encounter. If there will be an open coffin, flowers, a religious service, and so forth, explain the details and the meaning of them. If the individual must participate, explain how.

Modeling

Once you have prepared the individual as best you can, you are ready for the first mourning experience. Enlist the aid of a friend or relative. (1) Review with the individual the condolence words and procedures: "You remember how you shake hands; then what do you say?" (2) Instruct him to watch what you do at the wake or funeral. (3) The second person who is helping you will shadow the individual and provide support and reinforcement should your attention be snagged by someone else you can't ignore. Instruct the disabled person always to stay next to you or this friend.

Your primary role at this first event is to model the correct behavior so that the individual can copy it. As he does so appropriately, reinforce the behavior. For example, say, "You looked at him and shook hands very well" or "You said 'I'm sorry' very well." Interpret events that might be confusing as they occur. For example: "People are placing flowers there to show their love." Limit your stay. You do not want to overdo the first experience. After the condolence visit, review the event and answer quetions. This experience may trigger questions about your death. Answer honestly and provide information about the provisions you have made. For example, says, "All living things die and some day I will die. I hope it's not for a long while. When I die you will live with _____."

Gradually, expand the length of your stay and the types of death rituals to which you expose the individual. After wakes or shivas, move to part or all of the funeral or memorial service, and then to the actual burial. Be guided by the reactions of the individual. Provide plenty of time for discussion of feelings and reactions and clarification of concepts.

As it can for most people, religion can provide support to the developmentally disabled in dealing with death. Share your faith and religious beliefs regarding the purpose of life and the hereafter. Discuss the meanings of the religious services and even help plan your own service. The goal of this preparation is to enable the disabled to cope with the loss of the most significant people in their lives: their primary caregivers and close friends. In helping them you help yourself deal with this momentous and inevitable event.

Emotional Support

In addition to the mourning rituals, the developmentally disabled have to be prepared for the adjustment period that comes thereafter. Emotional support in the form of open discussion and outward display of emotions should be encouraged. For example, if you cry, explain, "I'm crying because I feel sad. People cry when a friend dies." If the person also cries, say, "You are feeling sad because you lost your friend." A comforting touch and being there can help the individual cope.

Recall with the individual the happy times you had with the dead person. Keep a picture of him if it is not upsetting. Refer to your feelings openly. Your goal here is to encourage the disabled person to express his emotions by being open about your own. You also model an appropriate way of dealing with the emotions. As you cope, he learns that he too can cope and how to do so.

Grief for all people has both physical and psychological manifestations. The physical reactions of loss of appetite and sleeplessness accompany psychological distress in feelings of emptiness and exhaustion. A sense of guilt over things left unsaid or undone may also linger. When any of these reactions are overly exaggerated, professional help may be needed.

The death of a significant person in our lives affects all of us. When this person is the primary caregiver for a disabled individual, a very real concern may arise in terms of future placement. Every effort should be made to deal with this issue long before it occurs. Estate planning, guardianship, and life change decisions should all involve professionals and the disabled individual who should clearly know what provisions have been made for him.

Summary

This chapter has discussed the characteristics of the developmentally disabled that affect their ability to express and cope with grief over the loss of significant figures in their lives. A four-stage model of preparation, direct instruction, modeling, and emotional support has been presented as a framework within which to help the developmentally disabled deal with death, and to deal with the loss and significant life changes that may accompany it.

Part V
Professional Perspectives

Throughout this book, the contributing authors have attempted to provide a perspective on the unique aspects of many particular types and circumstances of disenfranchised grief. In this section, the perspective changes. Here, the authors apply the concept to their own profession, indicating the ways that other professions can use the perspective in their practices.

Each professional who cares for the bereaved has had to deal with the disenfranchised griever. And for each profession, the phenomenon of disenfranchised grief raises its own distinct issues, problems, and concerns.

It is certainly an issue for the clergy. The problems of the disenfranchised griever can be very troubling for this group. On the one hand, many clergy define their role as that of agents of reconciliation, seeking to extend God's love and peace to those hurt, troubled, and alienated. However, many of the conditions and circumstances that give rise to disenfranchised grief pose troubling moral and theological issues. Factors often contributory to HIV infection such as homosexual behavior or IV drug addiction are condemned by many churches. Cohabitation, premarital relationships, extramarital affairs, divorce, and abortion may face different degrees of disapproval in different churches. And clearly many disenfranchised grievers are alienated from the support and solace that religion can provide, complicating grief reactions.

Clergy have responded to the disenfranchised grievers in different ways. Some have strongly condemned many of the behaviors that lead to disenfranchised grief, offering comfort only to those defined as truly repentant. Others have defined their ministries differently, seeking to succor all, regardless of situation. Still others have tried to draw a distinction between the theological and pastoral, maintaining a theological perspective that may not condone the morality of certain actions but separating that position from a pastoral ministry that serves the suffering. In this approach it may be appropriate to condemn smoking but needlessly insensitive to remind the lung cancer victim of his or her at-risk behaviors. In such situations the victim, already feeling the "law" of his or her actions, needs to hear the good news of God's perpetual peace.

John Abraham and Dale Kuhn write from the latter two perspectives. Abraham, writing as a parish pastor, defines his ministry in terms of reconciliation and builds on the special relationship that clergy can have with the disenfranchised griever. Kuhn, a pastoral counselor, discusses how clergy can break the prevailing silence of disenfranchised grief and reintegrate the griever into a faith community.

If clergy minister on the battlefields of bereavement, funeral directors are often on the front lines. Hocker's chapter addresses the dilemma that many funeral directors face. On one hand, they are businessmen bound by contract and ethics to provide a specific set of services for which they are contracted. On the other hand, they are compassionate and caring individuals who recognize the many forms of grief and pain. As Hocker points out, in many cases of disenfranchised grief these dual demands conflict. His chapter offers sensitive guidelines for professional and compassionate service.

Nathan Kollar's chapter can have applications for both professions. Dr. Kollar, a college professor, has a long interest and expertise in ritual. As many of the authors have asserted, ritual is a powerful therapeutic tool for resolving grief. The disenfranchised, however, are often denied rituals. Kollar explores the power of rituals, suggesting that the disenfranchised be incorporated and involved.

Other professions have their own perspectives on disenfranchised grief. Elise Lev, an associate professor of nursing, discusses such grief from the perspective of her profession. In a chapter that is consistent with Lois Dick's perspective, Lev notes that not only do nurses deal with the disenfranchised griever, but they are often victims of disenfranchised grief. Elliott Rosen's concern is with the hospice, now increasingly serving disenfranchised survivors of AIDS-related deaths. His guidelines for hospice workers can be applied to other circumstances of disenfranchised grief and to other health care facilities. Finally, David Meagher's chapter, from the perspective of the counselor, provides a valued summation. Meagher reaffirms that the needs of the disenfranchised griever remain the same as those of any griever. But although the goals of counseling are the same, the lack of social support places the counselor in a unique "surrogate" role, with special responsibilities.

In any section like this, there is always a sense of incompleteness. Certainly but for space other perspectives could be included. For example, a lawyer might wish to address the legal issues of disenfranchised grief, reviewing law on related issues such as cohabitation and affirming the needs of the terminally ill to protect their rights and the rights of those they love. Doctors and ethicists could address issues of disclosure and treatment. The list could continue. Nevertheless, overall, the section clearly affirms that each profession that cares for the dying and bereaved must grapple with the issue of disenfranchised grief.

21

A Pastoral Counselor Looks at Silence as a Factor in Disenfranchised Grief

Dale Kuhn

Twenty years after his retarded sister died, a forty-year-old man reflected, "I was a college student home on spring break when she died. We buried her and I returned to school and did not say a word to anyone about her death. She was retarded, and I think because of that I never felt like I had a sister and so I never really knew how to grieve her."

When a loss is unusual, or a person who has been lost has been excluded from the normal activities of family or group because he or she is different from or unknown to the family or group members, those who are grieving the lost one often feel awkward about expressing their feelings for fear that others will not understand. This hesitancy to express grief can lead to silence. Others simply do not know and therefore cannot understand what has happened and how it has affected the one who is grieving. This lack of expression and under-standing, and the continued silence all lead to the experience of a disenfran-chised grief, as described by Doka and others.[1]

The pastoral counselor—usually a clergy person who has specialized in counseling, sometimes a theologically and psychologically trained layperson—sees many people who have been silenced by others in their faith group or who have silenced themselves. These are often people who have remained silent for years, only to have a personal or relational crisis surface the unresolved loss. These are often people who feel abandoned by God and struggle with shame.

The man who lost his retarded sister was very religious. His sister had never been involved in the activities and rituals of his local congregation; she had even been baptized in a private ceremony after religious services one Sun-day. Individuals in the congregation knew of her only vaguely. He had not told his friends at school about her at all. His faith group, the group of reli-gious leaders and people like himself he joined with to worship God, to develop deeper relationships, and to find meaning in life's events and circum-stances, had been cut out of this part of his family's life. Those in his social group, who could have talked with him about his loss, were silenced by his failure to tell them about his sister and, subsequently, about her death.

The religious congregation or faith group is often the first place a person turns for support and comfort at the time of a loss. If not seeking it openly, an individual will turn to the ceremony of the religious service or to the words of a Scripture reading or sermon for solace as well as an explanation for a loss. When the loss is openly acknowledged, special services can be arranged, as in the case of a death. Prayers are offered during regular worship services, and not only focus the concerns of the congregation on the loss but also announce the event.

When the congregation or the faith group is aware of the loss, there are often groups of people who are ready to respond with a meal either in the home of the griever or at the place of worship. In some congregations, individuals are assigned to those who are grieving in order to make follow-up visits. Often, the loss is recognized years later by the placing of flowers in a worship service at the anniversary of the loss. At times something is dedicated to the memory of one who has died, which serves to honor the dead one as well as remind all of the reality of the loss.

Obviously, losses most likely to be responded to in this manner involve deaths in the family. Losses that may not be recognized, understood, or sanctioned by faith groups include divorce, suicide, the breakup of a homosexual relationship by death or separation, the death of a pet, the birth or death of a retarded child who was institutionalized or "hidden," loss due to alcoholism, death due to AIDS, or a loss due to illegal or immoral activity. The lack of recognition can lead to disenfranchised grief.

When the local congregation or faith group does not or cannot respond, people often end up searching out pastoral counseling. The pastoral counselor may be in a unique position to help these people untangle their grief because she or he, in addition to being trained to use psychotherapy, is usually sensitive to the religious issues that arise with disenfranchised grief.

Noting the importance of religion in the grief process, Erich Lindemann[2] supported this point of view in 1944 at a meeting of the American Psychiatric Association:

> Religious agencies have led in dealing with the bereaved. They have provided comfort by giving the backing of dogma to the patient's wish for continued interaction with the deceased, have developed rituals which maintain the patient's interactions with others and have counteracted the marked guilt feelings of the patient by Divine Grace and by promising an opportunity for "making up" to the deceased at the time of a later reunion. (p. 65)

The local congregation is in a unique position both to assist and to silence grievers. Through its use of assurance of an afterlife, its community of support and rituals, it offers the grieving individual a chance to express grief, understand and cope with the loss, and turn to others for understanding and company. At its best, the congregation and its representatives will provide a safe enough place for the griever to turn. This is especially true if the loss is a death in the family.

Other, more unusual losses are often more difficult for the congregation and for individuals close to the griever to respond to. This may be because of a faith group's tendency to tune in to the news of a death or an anticipated death rather than to a loss. Many of the metaphors that faith groups use have to do with "life" or "death" or "life after death" or "resurrection from the dead." In an effort to correct this, Mitchell and Anderson[3] insist that "loss, not death, is the normative metaphor for understanding those experiences in human life that produce grief" (p. 19). They suggest that the religious community and others would be able to respond much more sensitively with this understanding, and to assist more effectively in helping people cope with a variety of losses that are not always due to death.

Losses as a result of a chosen activity are especially difficult to respond to. Divorce, death due to AIDS, death due to alcoholism, loss of freedom because of a crime, or loss of love because of an affair—these are examples of what many see as losses due to choice. The temptation, perhaps because of the unavoidable human desire to fix blame, is to be unsympathetic. Consequently, if the loss is perceived to be a result of a life-style that the church or society disapproves of, the grief will be not recognized or responded to. A silence ensues.

Religious groups understand family. It is a concept often used to understand the relationships in a particular congregation. Ironically, if the loss cannot be understood in that family context, it is much more difficult for the religious group to respond. Even if the loss is a death in the family, but a death of a retarded child, for example, both the family and the faith group may have more difficulty recognizing and addressing the grief issues, since there will probably be ambivalent feelings about the role of the deceased in the family and about this person's death. Friends and family may be relieved at the death of the child but feel guilty with this reaction. This is often another occasion for silence to prevail.

These and other unusual losses can lead to a silence that inhibits the working through of grief. This silence is most often self-imposed and is a result of an awareness of the inability of people in the congregation—including the minister—to deal with the impact of the pain of bereavement and the resulting need to adjust to that pain.

> Mike [not his real name] was twenty-five years old and depressed and concerned about his fifty-year-old dying father who had been diagnosed with AIDS. Mike, the oldest in the family, felt the responsibility to care for him. There were several complicating factors: Mike lived nine hundred miles from

him. His father was gay and also a cross dresser. Few of Mike's friends were aware of his father's condition. He felt unable to ask his father to live with him. Mike feared his friends' rejection.

He had considered turning to his minister for guidance, but feared judgment from him as he had openly condemned homosexuality from the pulpit and declared AIDS as God's punishment for that behavior. He had attempted to confide in a few select friends, but was aware of their pulling away from him and their lack of interest—which he experienced as disapproval.

William F. May[4] suggests that people commonly avoid talking about death because they see in it an "immensity that towers above every resource for handling it" (p. 50). With this he offers the idea that to be silent about death is a sign that it is so overwhelming that words are unable to define it or to bring relief. He continues, "Silence has its origin in the awesomeness of death itself. Just as the Jew out of respect for the awesomeness of God would not pronounce the name Jahweh so we find it impossible to bring the word death to our lips in the presence of its power" (p. 49). Psychologically, silence has its roots in the defenses of denial, repression, or suppression. These are mechanisms that used to protect the psyche from pain and anxiety. Consequently, the grieving individual will check both internally his or her own psychological readiness to express grief and externally the environment to see if the expression of such grief is safe enough. Mike, just mentioned, found it especially clear that the environment was not safe and so made the decision to be quiet about his grief.

The more unusual the loss, the less safety the grieving person is likely to feel.

> Once he began his counseling, Mike not only discussed his feelings about losing his father to AIDS, but also the loss of his father when he was a child and his father decided to move out of the family to pursue his own life-style. His father's request that he have a funeral service both as a man and as a woman made the desire to keep silent stronger, as it was not really clear to Mike just who he was getting ready to bury—and just who he was getting ready to mourn. He had come to know his father as both man and woman, for his father would periodically present himself at family functions as a male or as a female. He could hardly imagine asking his minister to do one funeral, let alone two.

There is a cycle of silence that gets established when there is an unusual loss. If the loss does not fit the common experience of the religious community, the individual griever often imposes a silence on self to hide his or her discomfort with the object that was lost or with the way the object was lost. This silence is then reenforced by a communal silence—in this case by the silence of the congregation—because the community does not find out about the loss or feels just as uncomfortable about it as the individual does. The communal silence sparks shame or guilt in the individual for the strangeness or messiness of the loss. At times, the griever or the one who has died is blamed for making bad choices. This gives the individual all the more reason not to grieve openly and reenforces the desire to keep everything quiet.

The result is that the individual never ends up dealing with the loss because he or she deals instead with the shame or embarrassment of being different rather than with the loss of a loved one. At this point the psychological defense of denial is often used to keep the grieving individual's self-esteem intact.

The forty-year-old man mentioned earlier was a young boy too embarrassed about his sister's and his family's differentness to deal completely with his loss or his wish for a normal sister. Because he had not mourned that original loss, he could not mourn his sister's death until a number of years had passed and a crisis in his marriage drove him to seek help. In Bowlby's[5] terminology, he had detached himself from this early experience and had become emotionally unresponsive to it (p. 7).

Obviously, breaking the cycle of silence is an important factor in helping those who have experienced unusual loss. Often this means giving the individual someone with whom to talk. An experience of loss will precipitate a selfish preoccupation with the self that will resemble an infantile self-centeredness. This is necessary for survival. It calls attention to the need for care and protection at this moment of loss. Mitchell and Anderson[3] suggest that "the abnormality of grief is frequently a consequence of the refusal to grieve or the inability of the grieving person to find those willing to care" (p. 18).

A pastoral counselor can offer someone who is grieving much the same as what other counselors are able to offer: someone who cares and is trained to listen; someone who can be objective and is able to intervene in sound clinical ways; someone who has time to work through some of the more complicated reactions in unusual grief or disenfranchised grief.

The pastoral counselor may be at an advantage in other ways. He or she may be more familiar with the faith issues that people who are grieving are dealing with. Silent, disenfranchised grief will, like other emotions not dealt with, lead to depression and other mental disorders. Jackson[6] suggests that "acute mental illness involves a breakdown of faith at one or more of these levels: in things, through a disorientation of reality; in people, through fear and suspicion; and in the cosmic structure, through apprehension and a dread of meaninglessness" (p. 112). May[4] states, "In the presence of death our philosophies and moralities desert us" (p. 49).

At the same time, the pastoral counselor may bring a clearer understanding of the reactions of the faith group and can help the griever sort out helpful from not-so-helpful responses.

Mary [not her real name] was a high school graduate who gave birth to a child before she was married. Initially she chose to keep the child and raise it while she continued to live with her parents. Shortly after the child was born, she decided to give the baby up for adoption. She married the child's father but divorced him after two months. When she sought counseling, she was full of disenfranchised grief.

She made it clear that she had initially decided to keep the child because she thought that it would hold together her relationship with the young man and make amends to her religiously conservative parents. She stated that she never talked with them about her decisions because she felt that she had a responsibility to work out her own problems. She sought help from her minister but was told that she should keep coming to church and stay active in the youth group.

She did continue attending church but was met with silence (which she perceived as disapproval). The silence convinced her that her old friends were ashamed of her. This reinforced the shame that she already felt.

Loss may mean separation not only from the lost object but also from the community that is affected by the loss. In this case, the minister and the congregation were probably affected by this young woman's loss of innocence. They may have seen it as a rejection of their own values. They may have feared that to embrace her in her loss and grief would have been to sanction her premarital sexual activity. Mary felt the separation, stopped attending church, and thereby reinforced the separation.

The cycle of silence in this case was broken when Mary was able to speak of her loss to someone who was less attached to her local congregation and to the dogma it fostered. A pastoral counselor is often in a better position to understand since he or she is farther away from congregational life and is less preoccupied with the question, how is this going to affect or reflect on the life of the congregation—or my life?

The cycle was also broken when Mary met a man who was willing to understand and accept her, found another church to attend, and began speaking to other single women who had given up their newborns.

Religious groups are beginning to struggle with the need to recognize unusual losses. Pastoral counselors Mitchell and Anderson make a brief call for this in their book *All Our Losses, All Our Griefs*.[3] The Episcopal bishop of Newark, John Shelby Spong, also recognizes this need in his book *Living In Sin: A Bishop Rethinks Human Sexuality*, specifically in the area of divorce.[7] He suggests a liturgical service to mark the end of a marriage. His thought is that marking the loss of a marital relationship with a ceremony invoking God's blessing on the parties involved will enable people to experience forgiveness rather than shame. This also gives the community an opportunity to respond with more than silence and provides a way for it to stay connected with the divorcing parties—despite the unusual or awkward loss. It can serve the same function as the visitation at the funeral home: to provide a structure loose enough to bring people together with those most affected by the loss without forcing anyone to make statements they are not ready to make or to do something they are not ready to do.

The faith group, historically one of the most common sources of comfort for the griever, can be the most troublesome. Is this because, as some might argue, people have trouble bearing the responsibility for their actions? There seems to be clinical evidence to the contrary. Many people will punish themselves for their unusual losses by withdrawing and as a result will "act out" their unfinished business by getting into trouble. This suggests that disenfranchised grief begets disenfranchised grief.

> An example is a middle-aged woman who never expressed any feeling about her husband's physical disability due to cancer. She responded with stoicism, resolutely claiming that this was not his fault. Nevertheless, in the four years that followed his diagnosis she had two affairs that destroyed her marriage and alienated her children.
>
> Later she concluded that she simply could not admit her anger with her husband for ruining their lives and with herself for not taking better care of him in the first place. She felt she could have prevented the loss of a normal husband. She ran away from her reaction and in the process punished both her husband and herself—all of it unconsciously. Disenfranchised grief begets disenfranchised grief.

This suggests to all who work with grieving people the importance of exploring behaviors that do not make sense or that cannot be explained by the griever. It also suggests that religious people need to be open to understanding their own unclear or unconscious motives for hesitating to respond to unusual loss. To fail to do this might make them participants in arranging for more loss and more grief that is disenfranchised.

Despite their disappointing experiences with faith groups, many people continue to search for God or a Higher Power. The attempt seems to be to find a way to provide some order out of the chaos that loss often brings—especially loss that seems atypical and is connected with guilt. The pastoral counselor can be the steady presence who understands that loss comes in many different forms, and once the loss is understood and experienced openly, it can lead to a greater awareness of the importance of the lost object, the place that the object had in the life of the griever, and of how the individual's God or Higher Power can be experienced in the persons who are able to be present and to share grief in the middle of what feels like chaos.

References

1. K. Doka, "Disenfranchised Grief," paper presented to the Annual Meeting of the Forum for Death Education and Counseling, Atlanta, Ga., April 1986.

2. E. Lindemann, "Symptomatology and Management of Acute Grief," in *American Journal of Psychiatry* 101, 141–49.

3. K. Mitchell and H. Anderson, *All Our Losses, All Our Griefs* (Philadelphia: Westminster Press, 1983).

4. W.F. May, "The Conspiracy of Silence," in *Pastoral Care of the Dying and Bereaved,* edited by Reeves et al. (New York: Health Sciences Publishing, 1973).

5. J. Bowlby, *Attachment and Loss: Loss, Sadness and Depression,* vol. 3 (New York: Basic Books, 1980).

6. E. Jackson, *Understanding Grief* (Nashville, Tenn.: Abingdon Press, 1957).

7. J.S. Spong, *Living in Sin: A Bishop Rethinks Human Sexuality* (New York: Harper and Row, 1988).

22

The Clergy and the Disenfranchised

John Abraham

During my first year as a professional priest, I served in a parish whose custom it was to greet the clergy at the door on the way out after worship. After some months of hearing such nebulous comments as "lovely sermon," I concluded that time so spent was not very constructive and, moreover, was oppressive to those who may simply want to leave without being "trapped" at the door by the clergy. I thought that folk had just as much a right not to shake my hand and that practically barricading the door with my presence was forcing them into an unsolicited encounter. So I discontinued the practice—but not for long.

About three weeks thereafter a parishioner came to inquire quietly about my no longer greeting folks and to let me know that she missed this custom. I of course explained at some length my reasons and rationale, stating that it simply did not seem very worthwhile when I could spend the time better having a longer chat with those who might seek me out during fellowship time instead of at the door, and that I felt it a bit manipulative to plant myself at the door. Then I asked, "Other than having 'always done it this way,' what is so important to you"? After a moment of sincere reflection, the woman answered, "Often, that is the only time I touch someone else that week."

I was surprised and shocked. And I have since revised my decision to the extent that I now do greet folks at the door more often than not. Touch is important to any healthy being, and I ceased withholding that touch altogether at the church door. Part of the pain of disenfranchised grief is the loss of touch. Not everyone can reach out, touch, ease that pain. This is one strength that clergy have. Clergy can touch everyone. And the church has the license to foster an atmosphere wherein all may not only shake hands but hug as well. How many institutions promote hugging? I and my present congregation now do. Yes, we're still free not to hug or to expect a hug, but we are also free to hug.

Touching is a small example indicative of the special prerogatives of the clergy which can be helpful in serving disenfranchised grievers. Among those prerogatives are uninvited intervention and the perspective of innocent ignorance.

Clergy not only may but are called to intervene. Physicians no longer make house calls; I do. Two days ago, I got the secondhand information that a parishioner's sister's home had burned to the ground. As a priest, I was perfectly free (if not even expected) to call, to express concern, and to "stick my nose into" the family's terrific loss. Grief was facilitated by my intervention. And such interventions are all the more poignant when the situation is one of unsanctioned loss. Because the griever is unlikely to raise the subject, clergy initiative can serve to open the floodgates of grief. This is often true in the event of any death or loss (which remain unpopular topics of conversation) but is especially true when the nature of the bereavement is disenfranchised.

The perspective of innocent ignorance affords clergy the opportunity to inquire about a loss. When someone says, "I've lost a friend," my innocent ignorance asks to be informed. By asking about the nature of the relationship the clergy not only learn more personally and professionally themselves, but they may also facilitate the grieving process.

It is also often the privilege of the clergy to know about circumstances that others do not. I know, fairly well, who is gay in my congregation. I know less, but some, about the affairs. I know who is devastated after being fired. I know whose parrot, gerbil, or dog died. I know who died alone at the age of ninety-six in a nursing home. I know whose neighbor was murdered. I know who had a miscarriage. I know who was living with a lover. The point is that many friends, neighbors, colleagues, fellow church members do not even know these things. The clergy are privileged to know, and they are even more privileged to enter into the lives of others on a meaningful level. It is incumbent upon us to use that privilege well by respecting that confidence.

Another advantage typical of my profession is the ability to network. My counsel is certainly not always the best, but I'm often able to make the appropriate professional referral. Clergy can tell the person whose beagle died which veterinarian may be more sensitive to the needs and wishes of the bereaved; or which psychologist, psychiatrist, or chaplain has experience in and is open to different aspects of loss; which support groups exist and what they're like; and, on a purely personal level, who else may have undergone a similar experience. I'm in the position to know of others and can offer assistance like, "Did you know that the Smiths' dog died last week? Maybe you'd find it helpful to talk together," or "I know of two others who've lost gay lovers this year. May I mention your situation to them with the possibility of fostering some mutual support?"

Clergy too have the advantage of being able to involve themselves with, and assist, disenfranchised grievers as they struggle to find meaning and sense in their losses and in their lives. For after all the job of religion is to interpret life—to interpret the world. My experience is largely limited to the Episcopal Church, and more limited to the four congregations in which I have served as the ordained leader. Our (Christian, Episcopal) "interpretation" is not the same as that of others, but it may offer some general applications. My personal disposition is and has been rather liberal and open-minded. And I value the right question more than the right answer. It seems to me that part of the task of clergy is to assist people in asking the right questions along their life's spiritual pilgrimage. To wrestle with doubts, uncertainties, fears, hopes, and longings has, in my experience, proved more fruitful than getting answers from others. That is, only I can answer my basic religious questions authentically. The quest may involve more pain, more struggle, and more time, but the yield more closely fits who I am, what I experience, and with whom I interact. We are all theologians when engaged in this task of seeking meaning—meaning beyond ourselves in relation to the world we know. One role of the clergy is to foster that role of theologian, to be clear ourselves and to ask others about making sense of life.

The conclusions we reach may not always be absolute and certain. Life holds ambiguity, inconsistency, and mixed feelings. Take the hidden grief of abortion, for example. Seldom do men or women who speak with me about the loss of an abortion (freely elected) have cut-and-dried feelings. The issue is not clearly black or white. People often feel both the relief of having terminated the pregnancy and the grief for a life that might have been. It is my conviction that God gives us the capacity to feel both (relief and grief) together. And God gives us the freedom and the responsibility to make difficult choices. Best to make informed choices, but eventually such choices are made and who better to decide than the individual(s) involved? I am also convinced that most major decisions are made on the basis of insufficient information. Whether it be abortion, moving, ending an affair, or other decisions that will have the consequence of disenfranchised grief, it would be nice to know more than we can know. We're called to make the best decision possible and to trust in the future, to trust in God.

Loss is not always brought about by a decision on our part: it befalls us. But we can decide how to respond. And whether the response is finally bitter or accepting depends on one's theological disposition. It seems to me that we can choose a God who controls every little thing, or a God who is loving and kind. We can't have it both ways. When tragedy strikes, we cannot always know why, or always find good therein. Sometimes life deals misery without compensation and without understanding other than that such things happen and are part of the sometimes unfair world in which we live. To claim otherwise and to offer easy and benign answers is, perhaps, to thwart the grief process by obscuring the acceptance of the reality of the loss. When others ask, "Why?" I ask, "Why not"? What makes us think that such losses cannot or will not happen to us? It is important to recognize that God is still God. God is a loving God who does not orchestrate pain and loss, but who sustains us throughout. Life goes on. And, although it is difficult or impossible to perceive at the time, life will most likely hold better times. I don't mean here the Polyannaish "everything will be okay," but rather a simple trust in the fundamental worth of living. Life is good, God is good, and God's creation is primarily good. As clergy, we offer hope.

Particular religious concepts can be of help in addressing disenfranchised grief. To the gay lover who is angry at the deceased for an AIDS death brought on by previous infidelity, where is forgiveness? To the spouse whose paramour has died, where is reconciliation? To the former spouse whose now divorced mate has died, where is the gratitude for the love once there? Were there no blessings to be counted? To the parents whose infant has died, was there no love? God gives us the capacity to love, and that capacity continues.

This struggle may, in fact, be complicated by religious issues. Often, for example, disenfranchised grief may be complicated by guilt that may have religious overtones. Perhaps the guilt is inappropriate based not on behavior but on the responses of others. Would that we could be more gentle—on ourselves and on others.

Clergy may need to be careful of adding to that difficulty. Clergy may often experience conflict between their own responses and the official position of the church. As Bishop John Spong states:

> Many times clergy have shared with me the fact that the standards they reflect in their pastoral ministries differ sharply from the official positions of the church. The church has stated with regularity that genital sexual activity is neither appropriate nor moral except inside the bond of marriage. Yet many, if not most, of the couples coming to our clergy to receive the church's blessing in holy matrimony are in fact actively engaged sexually with each other and, in numerous cases, already living together. (1988, p. 1)

This dichotomy applies to many situations regarding the disenfranchised. My solution is to draw a line between the pastoral and the theological.

The church, like any human institution, is a flawed, frail, fallible entity. And like most mainline (established) institutions, the church is slow to change. I believe the church sometimes to be wrong or to be inadequate in its formal position, and it has a higher calling to be right. A careful study of Holy Scripture would surely affirm the perception of our Lord as embracing *all people*, especially the widowed, the leper (or today's persons with AIDS), the orphaned, the poor, children, prostitutes, criminals, and those otherwise marginalized in our society.

In those situations in which the guilt is appropriate, where one has indeed transgressed in thought, word, or deed by acts done or left undone, the church may serve to absolve one of the guilt. Our Episcopal Rite of Reconciliation does so. After hearing one's confession, the priest proclaims:

May Almight God in mercy receive your confession of sorrow and of faith, strengthen you in all goodness, and by the power of the Holy Spirit keep you in eternal life. Amen.

The priest then lays a hand upon the penitent's head (or extends a hand over the penitent), saying one of the following:

Our Lord Jesus Christ, who offered himself to be sacrificed for us to the Father, and who conferred power to his Church to forgive sins, absolve you through my ministry by the grace of the Holy Spirit, and restore you in the perfect peace of the Church. Amen.

Or this:

Our Lord Jesus Christ, who has left power to his Church to absolve all sinners who truly repent and believe in him, of his great mercy forgives you all your offenses; and by his authority committed to me, I absolve you from all your sins: In the Name of the Father, and of the Son, and of the Holy Spirit. Amen.

The priest concludes:

Now there is rejoicing in heaven; for you were lost, and are found; you were dead, and are now alive in Christ Jesus our Lord. Go (or abide) in peace. The Lord has put away all your sins.

The penitent responds:

Thanks be to God. (*Book of Common Prayer*, 1976: p. 451)

This forgiveness is available for all who desire it and is in no way restricted, and confessions may be heard anytime and anywhere.

The church may help further with the reminder that the best remedy for (appropriate) guilt is noble and virtuous action in the future. And bad acts do not make for a bad person. We all fall short of perfection from time to time. This reminds me of the line, "The trouble with being a perfectionist is you never get there!" It may be helpful to differentiate between the person and what the person does. We may not like a particular behavior, yet still like or love the person doing the behaving. We may do regrettable things, but we are not regrettable human beings. Indeed, we are "human beings" and not "human doings"! All people are sacred and are loved by God.

The act of confession is but one example of how the church's ritual role can enfranchise the disenfranchised. Perhaps here too the church will need to broaden its concept of ritual. I recall my first year out of seminary, when I was assistant to the rector of a large parish. An old woman's dog (her primary companion) had died, and she wanted to know if I would do the funeral. Upon consulting with the rector, I was informed that we neither bury nor have worship events for deceased dogs. "Where's a dog's soul?" he asked me. "Where's yours!" I wish I'd responded. Now, I'm more than willing to construct liturgies for pet burials.

And perhaps the church will need to broaden its focus and programs as well. It seems to me that the church can only best address those who are disenfranchised when it makes a deliberate, intentional, specific effort to do so. Without such special efforts (programs, emphases) it becomes all to easy to refer to church as "family" and to foster "family" programs. What does the repeated description of church as "family" say to those beyond the conventional, stereotyped nuclear family?

There are other ways in which the clergy or the institutional church get in the way of helping those bereaved through disenfranchised loss. One such problem seems to me to be in the manifestation of a general spirit of joyousness. I think of churches adorned with banners that proclaim messages as such JOY, REJOICE, CELEBRATE, and so forth. These positive words and their attendant symbols are, of course, important and are part of a reflection of the mosaic of life. But somehow the church universal seems to err in the expression of only part of life's mosaic. Where are the banners that proclaim FRUSTRATION, SADNESS, TROUBLE, GRIEF, and the like? It was Proust who said, "We are healed of suffering only by experiencing it to the full." And good grief means working through painful feelings. Does the church do us a disservice by, in some ways, ignoring this side of life? I'd love to see a banner exclaiming, GOD DAMMIT! embodying the hurt and outrage we sometimes feel. Surely God's big enough to take it!

Some parishes have the lovely custom of having children adorn a cross with flowers on Easter. The flowers, along with pious platitudes, can mask the reality of the cross: a sign of alienation (disenfranchisement) and death. Two pieces of art in my office speak to this aspect. One is a woodcut by Robert Hodgell, titled . . . BUT DELIVER US FROM UNPLEASANTNESS. It depicts the crucified Christ hanging behind a large sheet of flowers and largely blocked from view by the flowers. In front of these stands a devoutly pious preacher, smiling skyward, with a solemn, heads-bowed congregation seated before him. The only one of the congregation looking up at the cross is a small child. Ah, the wisdom of children! This kid seems to be saying, "Hey, wait a minute, there's a dead man there!" At the risk of entering into the reality of "unpleasantness," the church can better fulfill our need for life beyond death: by first recognizing the loss and the feelings and the process involved in moving beyond. Also on my office wall is a painting incorporating the words of the philosopher and spiritualist Yevgeny Yevtushenko: "Telling lies to the young is wrong! Proving to them that lies are true is wrong! Telling them that God's in his heaven and all is right with the world is wrong!"

Too often unsanctioned grief is met with church responses such as "It was God's will," "It must have been for a good reason," and the like, referring to the death. I'm reminded of the joke wherein the child is consoled upon his cat's death by being told that God took the cat because God loved the cat. To which the boy asks, "What does God want with a dead cat?" Moreover, the question might well be: "Doesn't God love me enough to leave me the cat [the lover, the infant, the job]?" Sometimes we even go so far as to imply or to explain that someone who died deserved to die because of immoral behavior. This is nonsense, and guilt inducing as well.

One role of the clergy is to affirm life in all of its scope, to embrace suffering as well as joy, and to remind others of their worth and self-esteem whatever the circumstances. Doing so is complicated by the institution of the church if it refuses to accept the very real effects of disenfranchised grief. And churches are rather conservative institutions, which are slow to enter into such realities of cohabitation, abortion, or other circumstances of disenfranchisement in an affirming and supportive way. Sometimes this kind of conspiracy is kindly intentioned, as can be seen in the constant reference to our congregation as "family." Meant in a friendly way to convey closeness and intimacy, what does this label say to the single person? To the widowed or divorced? To those in nontraditional relationships? I would suggest that these kinds of generalizations work against respecting the integrity of those faced with disenfranchised loss. Clergy need be sensitive to this, and may need be reminded to treat each individual in his or her own right.

The clergy have the advantage of, usually, the trust and respect of those with whom they are dealing. We are afforded the opportunity to exercise sensitivity and understanding. We are usually welcomed as being compassionate and caring. Yes, there is the detriment of difference, the special status of clergy, but that difference opens more doors than it closes. True, we don't have all the answers and cannot take others' pain away, but we can enter into their suffering and guide them through life's vicissitudes and misfortunes. Thereby we can lighten the load of grief by sharing it.

As advocates of love, hope, and peace, we have much to offer others and to enable within others. It strikes me that we may be especially effective (or damaging) when approached with those situations involving disenfranchised grief. The one seeking counsel is usually open, vulnerable, and ready for some kind of change. We may shape that change for better or for worse. And sometimes the challenge is only to listen.

I remember about six years ago when, during coffee hour after worship, I was engaged in conversation with a woman whose voice was quite hoarse. With the hubbub of many (and some practically simultaneous) conversations during coffee hour, I didn't inquire and didn't think much of her raspy voice. Since she was frail and elderly, I phoned later in the week to see how she was doing, at which point she offered her theory about having lost her voice. Said she, "My parakeet died last week, and he was the only one I had to talk to." Surely I can listen as well as a parakeet!

In concluding this chapter, I return to the touching. That which informs me most is my tradition: Christian. As a Christian I'm informed foremost by Holy Scripture. Jesus Christ exercised a ministry of healing and of touching. And who did he touch most often and most readily? The disenfranchised.

References

Book of Common Prayer. 1976. New York: Harper and Row.

Spong, J.S. 1988. *Living in Sin? A Bishop Rethinks Human Sexuality*. New York: Harper and Row.

23

Unsanctioned and Unrecognized Grief: A Funeral Director's Perspective

William V. Hocker

Introduction

"Charlie and I had a special relationship," said the voice on the other end of the funeral home phone, "and I am telling you this in confidence because of the request I am about to make." "Charlie" was a middle-aged widower who had been killed in an automobile accident. "Janet," who made the phone call, was a middle-aged divorcée who had been "seeing" Charlie for some time, and there had been thoughts of marriage; however, since Charlie's children lived out of town they were unaware of his relationship with Janet, and she did not want to cause any problems when they found out about her. Consequently, her request was to come to the funeral home after scheduled viewing hours and be allowed to spend some time privately with her deceased boyfriend. There was no difficulty in staying a bit late to accommodate her request.

This scenario is repeated many times each day across the United States. People who are experiencing grief feel the normal impulse to mourn, but when their grief is either unrecognized or unsanctioned, the mourning process can be frustrated and disrupted. This example is simple; many others are much more complex.

The study of grief and its effects does not have a long history, compared with many other areas of study. It is only in recent years that the body of knowledge about grief has dramatically increased and become more sophisticated. Still, the emphasis has been on the loss of a family member. The implication has been that the only time people grieve is when family members or close platonic friends die; however, as the changes in all areas of our society rapidly accelerate, new relationships have emerged with inceasing prevalence. These relationships transcend the traditional relationships of the nuclear family, the multigenerational family, and the extended family. Many of these relationships have indeed existed for years but have heretofore not been as prevalent nor have they had such an impact on society. This is exactly what one would expect as patterns of love and marriage change.

As the futurist Alvin Toffler says in his book *The Third Wave,* "A powerful new tide is surging across the world today, creating a new, often bizarre, environment in which to work, play, marry, raise children, or retire."[1] And, we might well add, in which *to grieve and mourn.* Toffler goes on to say, "Many of today's changes are not independent of one another."[2] Changes in one area of society affect or are the result of changes in other areas of society. For instance, one in seven children is raised by a single parent, and "about one-third of the 63 million U.S. children under 18 do not live with their natural parents."[3] It is not surprising that in many cases this is the result of nontraditional relationships; it is not surprising that new words such as *palimony* are coined to express new relational considerations. It is also expected that patterns of grief and mourning change because of these circumstances.

We can conclude that there is a scarcity of information specifically in the areas of unsanctioned and unrecognized grief for two reasons. First, the full blossoming of knowledge in the area of grief in general is fairly recent, and second, new types of relationships have increased in prevalence as a result of societal changes. Because of this recent phenomenon, our knowledge is still in the developmental stages.

This chapter will explore the unique aspects of specific types of unsanctioned and unrecognized grief from various perspectives, attempt to develop more of an understanding of this type of grief, and suggest how caregivers from various disciplines may better position themselves to serve those involved. Obviously, there are things in common in all types of grief, but attention will be paid to the differences that can complicate the grief experienced by those whose grief is either unsanctioned or unrecognized. Special attention will also be given to the funeral director and his unusual role.

Specifically, in many cases of the death of a person involved in an unsanctioned and/or unrecognized relationship, the mourning process is distorted for the survivor. Most behavioral scientists accept a general grief cycle, although there can be significant overlapping and deviation. The stages proceed somewhat as follows:

1. Denial
2. Alarm/fear/numbness
3. Despair/confusion
4. Pining/searching
5. Anger/guilt
6. Identification/hypochondria
7. Depression
8. Acceptance and a gradual return to society

Dr. Rita McDonald argues that "every person's reaction to death is as individual as a thumbprint. There are some commonalities, but you can't generalize as to what's normative."[4] Nevertheless, a chapter like this must generalize to reach general conclusions.

Grief is loss and deprivation that lead to a process called mourning. Mourning is a consequence of true grief, is a psychological necessity, and the prognosis in a "normal" cycle is an ultimate healthy resolution that enables a person to return to a functional role in society. When the grief cycle is distorted, disrupted, or frustrated, the survivor is thrust into an even more complex and difficult cycle of mourning that can (1) delay resolution, (2) make the process more severe, (3) result in pathological responses, or (4) all of the above.

Sources of information will be based on existing literature, limited first-hand and third-party interviews, observations from my years as a funeral director, and case studies.

Unsanctioned and unrecognized grief take a wide variety of forms, with consequent broad implications. This chapter will be restricted to unsanctioned male/female relationships and the major implications. Unsanctioned relationships of this type can include cohabitation without benefit of marriage, extramarital affairs, and trial marriages; however, many of the dynamics also apply to other stigmatized relationships.

To sanction is to confirm, validate, justify, or give approval to. Therefore, we can further broadly define *unsanctioned* in terms of grief as (1) having no legal basis for existence, and (2) not being accepted by society as a whole. The legal aspect is significant. First, a legal relationship is said to exist when there is a legal contract—that is, a marriage license. Second, a blood relationship is also a legal relationship and includes family members such as children, parents, brothers, sisters, grandparents, grandchildren, and cousins. The primary legal consideration at death is inheritance: who is the legal heir? When a death occurs, an immediate concern of the funeral director is to determine who has the authority to direct postdeath activities, including final disposition of the body. In almost all cases, the next of kin has this right. This can lead to difficulties: "Disagreements among family members over final arrangements sometimes occur. The funeral director's determination as to whose instructions must be followed is easy when a surviving spouse is among the contending parties. It is not as easy to resolve conflicting instructions from family members, such as brothers and sisters, who share the same degree of kinship with the decedent."[5] It is even more difficult and awkward when a person who has no "legal" relationship but *was* living with the deceased determines to take charge. There can be a conflict between a genuine and personal but unsanctioned relationship and a biological/legal relationship.

In addition to the inheritance of an estate, there are further considerations that depend on legal relationships, such as who is entitled to Social Security benefits, veteran's benefits, and various types of pensions. It suffices to say that people outside of legal relationships have few legal rights, although there may be some in the case of surviving children. Although society generally fails to recognize and sanction some relationships, the law by its very nature is largely indifferent.

Before discussing case studies, it is important to explore the nature of human relationships. This is a key element in any type of grief since human relationships are so essential to human existence and since they are somewhat mysterious and unquantifiable. "Blessed are those who mourn, for they shall be comforted," says the Scripture verse (Matt. 5:4); however, the lines between who mourns and who does not mourn are difficult to delineate. What qualifies a person to mourn? Who has the right to mourn? Obviously, the person who has a relationship to the deceased is the one who suffers the loss of that relationship and to the degree to which that relationship was intense is the degree to which the survivors feel the loss. As one scholar put it, "I believe that there are many contributing factors and that the personality of the bereaved person and his or her *relationship* with the dead person are probably the main determinants.[6]

Relationships are a primary value in human existence; this has been well documented by psychotherapists not only from a behavioral point of view but also from the developmental: "It goes without saying that this research into the very beginning of psychic life is not a study of conditioned reflexes, but of the emotional dynamics of the infant's growth in experiencing himself as 'becoming a person' in meaningful relationships;[7] "One very influential school of thought viewed personality development as the result of past interpersonal relationships."[8] There is much support for the thesis that personality development takes place internally as a result of human relationships.

Furthermore, in classic depth psychology, relationships are to the soul what food is to the body: "The good life, in Freud's view, is one that is full of meaning through the lasting, sustaining, mutually gratifying relations we are able to establish with those we love."[9] The imponderable reality is that human living *is* personal relationship, for when these relationships are lacking, the human is incomplete: "Total separation, absolute complete separate individuality, seems impossible to human beings for it renders existence meaningless."[10] In addition, lack of relationship interferes with performance: "The individual human being may have tremendous intelligence and in combination with others can achieve wondrous things, yet if he is emotionally alone he is helpless in the face of reality.[11]

Along with relationship in personality formation, loss of relationship has an equal effect on the individual:

Relationships that evolve over the years cannot suddenly be disrupted or destroyed without leaving the person physically changed. The reality is that all relationships inevitably will be dissolved and broken. The ultimate price exacted for commitment to other human beings rests in the inescapable fact that loss and pain will be experienced when they are gone, even to the point of jeopardizing one's physical health. The same companionship that keeps people healthy can also seriously threaten their health when it is taken away.[12]

Case Studies

Given the primacy of human relationships, we can further conclude that grief results when a relationship is terminated by death and that the grief does not depend on whether the relationship was sanctioned or recognized. People involved in unsanctioned or unrecognized relationships can and do grieve as much as anybody, and sometimes more. Case studies are helpful in relating to the foundation that has been established. Of course the names used here are all fictitious.

In the opening example concerning Janet and Charlie, Janet felt like an outsider, cheated at another chance for happiness since marriage had been contemplated. She was not accepted by or approved of by Charlie's children, who were greatly concerned with having a smooth funeral service and a problem-free estate settlement once they became aware of the relationship. She did attend the funeral but sat alone in the rear of the chapel and was also alone at the cemetery, holding back her grief for propriety's sake. Further, friends and relatives who knew about the relationship felt awkward in expressing their sympathy to her—after all, she and Charlie hadn't been married. These circumstances led to simultaneous anger and guilt and a very difficult grief experience for Janet. It would have been much easier had their relationship been sanctioned and accepted by society. On the positive side, the fact that the funeral director understood, listened to her, and permitted her private viewing seemed to help in the short term.

The next case history involves a young man who was killed in a mining accident. A young woman named Sarah arrived at the funeral home a few hours after the accident and was obviously very upset when she inquired about funeral arrangements. During the course of the conversation she simply said, "We were married." "Oh," said the funeral director apologetically, "then you are the wife?" "Well," she said, "we weren't really married." The couple had been living together. The parents of the young man were from out of state, and they subsequently contacted their local funeral director to have the body transferred to their hometown. They knew nothing about Sarah, and since they were the legal next of kin they had the authority to direct what was to be done with the body. Sarah, who was embarrassed by the type of relationship she had had with the deceased, chose to remain silent and was left alone in her grief. She was consequently denied any part in the funeral ritual, including viewing the body, which could have been helpful to her. Concerning viewing of the body, Whitaker states:

> Two separate studies have demonstrated that the survivors generally do not approve of closed casket funerals and they are uncomfortable when the body of the deceased is not available for any of several reasons; undoubtedly this accounts for the great efforts expended in trying to recover the bodies of people after unusual accidents.[13]

In addition, Sarah's choice not to intrude on the parents' grief was a result of consideration for the parents, the social stigma attached to the relationship, and the lack of legal rights. Once again, the grief process was delayed and frustrated as her life took on the characteristics of loneliness, alienation, and hopelessness. Unfortunately, there was little the funeral director could do in this case, except listen.

Case history number three is more complicated. John was married to Joan, and they were subsequently divorced after having a child. John was living with Ann, with whom he had a child, when he was killed in an automobile accident. Again, the question of legality arose. Joan's marriage had been terminated; Ann was never married to John. However, each had a child by John, and a legal blood relationship existed between the deceased and both children, although neither child was of the legal age of majority. Joan felt she had more authority to direct arrangements because she had been married to John. Ann felt she had more authority because she was living with John. Fortunately, John's mother was still living and was the next of kin. She was pulled in opposing directions, and the funeral director was thrust into a delicate and difficult situation because he inevitably was the mediator. In this case the principals were able to agree and compromise on initial funeral arrangements, and the services proceeded on a strained but functional basis. The initial awkwardness and restraint of emotions did neither woman any good. Joan was frustrated further in her grief because she had not wanted the divorce and she now had a child to raise with no alimony and no insurance money. Ann was frustrated because she lost the man with whom she was living and had a child that she had to raise alone. She kept repeating that she was only concerned about her daughter's interests; however, there was virtually no estate. The grief of both women was partially unsanctioned and partially unrecognized. Neither could properly grieve because of the strained circumstances. Neither could receive unconditional support from friends and community. Both had legal and financial problems arising from the death, and, once again, grief was exacerbated and the grief response was distorted. In this case, the funeral director was able to help by talking with both women privately. He was able to listen and understand while they both "unloaded." Not favoring either party, he was able to handle important details such as who rode in the family car and who sat where at the church and at the cemetery. These were all potentially explosive issues.

During conversations with both women and the mother, it is clear that none of the three has resolved her grief to this date. It can only be hoped that a normal and healthy grief resolution will eventually be achieved; however, the circumstances have delayed resolution and made the grief more severe.

The last case history is even more unusual. A woman named Shirley was estranged from her husband, Sam. She was seeing a man named Bob who was also estranged from his wife. Neither married couple was divorced; however,

Shirley and Bob planned to marry when legal details were resolved. They had met members of each other's families, and a trip was planned within a week to meet those they had not yet met. While Shirley was preparing dinner for an evening with Bob, her estranged husband, Sam, came to her home and killed her and then shot himself to death with a pistol. There was outrage in the community, and Sam's very large and emotional family blamed Bob for the double tragedy, even though it was Sam who did the shooting. The funeral arrangements proceeded with great media attention, difficulty, and tension. Bob had to leave town for a time and could not participate in any way in post-death activities. He experienced many of the difficulties previously mentioned, along with intense guilt. Subsequently, his unresolved grief led to alcoholism, sexual promiscuity, and general dysfunction in his personal life. This was clearly a case of pathological responses, since "behavior detrimental to one's own social and economic existence" is characteristic of pathological grief.[14]

Characteristics of Unsanctioned Grief

We can now summarize some of the main characteristics of this type of grief to support the basic thesis that the grief process of persons involved in an unsanctioned and/or unrecognized relationship often is distorted. Since these characteristics are all interrelated, there is admittedly a great degree of overlapping; however, we can identify several major categories.

1. *Social stigma.* A lack of social approval has many ramifications. The survivor is often embarrassed because the relationship is unsanctioned: "A loss that is viewed as real and valid can be more readily mourned than a loss that is shrouded in secrecy and shame."[15] As much as a person may think he or she is intellectually and philosophically independent, we are all affected by what society thinks. This results in an awkwardness and a reluctance to be assertive, because there is no sanction. The result is a sense of loneliness and alienation. An important corollary of social stigma is lack of community support:

> Within all cultures throughout history there has been a support system for persons in grief. This support system contains four basic elements: a close-knit family unit; a caring community of friends and neighbors providing a social fabric of reinforcement and support; a deep-rooted philosophical or religious attitude toward death; and the continuity and stability provided by known and repeated ceremonial forms and rituals.[16]

Most of the elements of this support system are only partially available or not available at all when a relationship is clouded by social stigma.

2. *Absence of mourning rituals.* The value of ritual in all areas of life is easily documented:

> Rock concerts, family reunions, beauty pagents, wedding receptions, Thanksgiving dinners, parades, little league baseball contests and board games such as 'Monopoly' and 'Candyland,' though diverse and seemingly unrelated, are actually quite similar in one important aspect—all these activities are popular rituals. Each provides participants and spectators with means to express significant, though sometimes obscured, cultural beliefs and values. Popular rituals are enactments in which people participate in communal celebration of highly valued ideals and myths. They are regularly repeated, patterned, social events which help us to shape our relationship to other people and to our culture as a whole.[17]

The funeral is another important ritual or rite of passage. All major life changes are observed by ritual. Some of the major life changes are birth, graduation, marriage, death, and many, many others. Our attendance at a funeral expresses how meaningful our relationship with the deceased was and gives strength to the survivors. The funeral ritual is based on our profound ideological belief in the importance of the individual. Further, "the absence today of social expectations and rituals facilitating mourning is likely to contribute to the occurrence of pathological reactions to bereavement, although I would not go so far . . . in suggesting that this may be the chief cause of maladaptive behavior."[18] This is further confirmed by Whitaker when he states, "If we combine the psychological aspects of grief and the sociological familiarities it is found that the funeral ritual resolves a portion of guilt of the survivors. This is for the individual and for the community."[19] When survivors are denied participation in mourning rituals, an important aspect of the recovery cycle is missing.

3. *Grief may not be expressed at the proper time.* Again, because of circumstances surrounding this type of grief, emotions are restrained, stifled, and frustrated. Grieving is also delayed because of hostile relationships at the time of death, embarrassment because of social stigma, and what one may consider an attempt at propriety on the part of the unsanctioned survivor. As Jackson states, "The grieving period can be delayed but it cannot be postponed indefinitely, for it will be carried on directly or indirectly. If it is not carried on directly at the time of loss it will be done later at a much greater cost to the total personality."[20]

4. *Economic and legal problems.* A surviving partner, as well as surviving children, may have been financially dependent on the deceased in this type of relationship. This would add to the burden of the loss. A number of other difficulties are possible, as in the case of a man whose ex-wife was named as beneficiary on his insurance policies. He wanted to change the designation and name the woman he was living with as beneficiary to provide for the child he had had with her. His untimely death prevented this.

Legal problems of inheritance can arise. Another man was living with a woman who was not his wife during divorce proceedings. When he died unexpectedly, a legal battle over the home he was living in ensued because it was jointly held and the divorce was not final. Economic and legal difficulties can complicate grief and make recovery difficult for all concerned in this type of relationship.

5. *Emotional problems.* As was stated before, there are commonalities in all grief; however, these commonalities can differ in an unsanctioned relationship by being more exaggerated. These can include intense guilt, unresolved anger, frustration because of shattered dreams, repression of emotions, and physical difficulties, as well as other possible pathological reactions to grief.

Suggestions for Caregivers

With these major characteristics and differences as a background, we can next discuss suggestions for caregivers.

1. *Recognize the grief.* We must first recognize that the grief is unsanctioned but also that it is valid. We can then proceed to identify the particular dynamics that are involved, which may include the following:

Are there surviving children, and are they adult or adolescent?

Is there a surviving husband or wife?

Are there difficulties with other survivors?

Are there any support systems available?

Are there economic or legal complications?

Are there pathological reactions to this grief?

Is grief being delayed by restrained emotions?

Is there embarrassment because of social stigma?

When we recognize which individual characteristics are the most prominent in a particular case, we can proceed to be of help.

2. *Listen.* The therapeutic value of being able to express oneself when bereaved cannot be denied. A major complaint of people who suffer bereavement is that nobody really wants to talk about their loss. This was repeatedly expressed several years ago when I interviewed parents of deceased adult children. They indicated that family and friends avoided talking about their loss mainly because they thought it would surface painful memories. However, the interviews, some of them years after the death, proved to be thera-

peutic and cleansing because for some it was their first real opportunity to talk about it. To be a good listener is a particularly strong asset for a caregiver.

It is also important to point out that confidences are often shared with the funeral director and other caregivers during the listening process. Most people instinctively have confidence in the professional integrity of caregivers, and these professional confidences must be strictly observed by the caregiver. If confidences are not kept, the consequences for the bereaved and for the caregiver can sometimes be disastrous. The therapeutic value of "opening up" to someone who is willing to listen is enhanced when the bereaved are assured that confidences will be kept.

3. *Be understanding.* There is no substitute for being genuinely understanding in our relationship with survivors. I would like to expand on this point by means of a personal example. My father died suddenly and unexpectedly years ago, one day about noon. The balance of the day was spent in notifying relatives and making initial decisions. The following day was filled with funeral details, tending to my mother, tending to my five children, who were all very close to my father and who were all under ten years of age, and trying to greet relatives who were arriving for the funeral. There was very little time for personal considerations or personal grief, not to mention time to think about the many complex problems that his sudden death had brought about. Although I thought I was doing well, it is only in retrospect that I realize that my emotions were very much on the surface. People continued to come into the funeral home as usual with their postdeath problems that demanded my attention—papers to sign, death certificates to deliver, and advice on cemetery property. At one point I became completely frustrated because I could not attend to the details of my own father's funeral; it was almost as if a funeral director didn't have the right to grieve. These people all knew that my father had died, and I felt that they were being intrusive by not permitting me at least a little time. This greatly upset me in my subjective emotional state. The next morning, as we prepared to leave the funeral home for the services in church, however, a friend of my father's came in to talk to me. He offered his sympathy and said, "Well, you have some difficult challenges ahead of you, raising the young kids, taking care of your mom, and continuing to operate this firm." His simple words had an instant healing and tranquilizing effect on me. My inner thoughts were: What do you know— somebody really does understand. The simple comment validated and confirmed the grief that I felt and indicated that somebody really understood the difficulties I was facing. The feeling that somebody understood was extremely helpful and meaningful to me at the time, and the experience has helped me in my professional life. People who are experiencing grief *need* understanding. People whose grief is unsanctioned may be even more needful, since they may have no one to talk to. Just a little understanding can be immensely helpful. Understanding, empathy, and sensitivity are essential traits for an effective caregiver.

4. *Faciliate.* Sometimes the little things are exceptionally important for survivors at this particular time. "Do you need a ride to or from the hospital? Shall I gather the personal effects for you? Are there any telephone calls you would like me to make?" These details are opportunities for any caregiver, and the funeral home can attend to numerous functional details, going above and beyond the call of duty. When disputes arise because of unsanctioned grief, a primary function of the funeral director is to be the mediator by using his unique talents to bring people together and reach harmonious decisions. Although the "next of kin" have legal authority, the funeral director can smooth the way and attempt to recognize and also provide for the needs of the survivor of an unsanctioned relationship. This is why recognition, listening, and understanding are initially so important.

5. *Take personal inventory.* This final suggestion for caregivers focuses not so much on the bereaved as on the caregiver. Specifically, we should all take a personal inventory on how we feel about circumstances that lead to all types of grief. I would like to use an unusual but true story to begin to illustrate how we can examine ourselves. A funeral director friend of mine received a phone call from a bachelor antique dealer. The man told my friend that he had taken his pet pigeon to the veterinarian and was told that the pigeon was dying. He wanted to know if my friend's rather large firm could do anything to help him dispose of the remains. Although this firm had no provision or procedure for handling this type of request, my friend told the caller that he would try to help him in any way that he could, because the man sounded so sincere. Three days later the man arrived at the funeral home with the dead pigeon carefully placed on a piece of velvet in a wicker basket. During the course of conversation, the man told my friend that he had found the pigeon injured on the highway one day, had taken it home and nursed it back to health, and daily took it with him to his antique shop, where the bird fluttered around and had kept him company for a number of years. He was clearly very upset, since the pigeon was his only companion, and he sat in a chair holding the wicker basket and rocking it. Subsequently, my friend engaged a plumber to make a metal container for the pigeon to accommodate the man's wishes, and the antique dealer took the pigeon in the container and buried it on his property. About a week later, my friend received a glowing letter from this man thanking him for his kindness, consideration, and sensitivity in what he realized was an unusual situation. He particularly thanked him for not *ridiculing* him or his request.

By using this example, I am not trying to focus on the death of a pet, but rather on the various ways that grief can be experienced by another human being.

Let me cite one further example. A female psychologist fulfilled a tour of duty during the war in Vietnam. She was greatly affected by the tragic loss of so many young men while there. When she arrived back in the United States and began working in and around hospitals, she thought that people who grieved over the loss of a ninety-year-old parent were being silly. She felt that an old person had already lived his or her life and that the survivors should not grieve because there was no comparison between an old person's death and that of a young man. She is now a specialist in grief therapy and relates that as she gradually grew in her professional life, she came to the conclusion that all genuine grief is valid, no matter who experiences it and no matter what the circumstances are. In her words, she came to realize that *"pain is pain."*

The point I am trying to emphasize with these two examples is that grief is a subjective experience and it is easy for us to diminish or demean another's grief when we consider the loss not to be significant or when we personally disapprove of the circumstances that existed before the loss. It is easy to trivialize or discount the grief of another, especially in an unsanctioned relationship, and this is why a personal inventory of our attitudes can be so important to us as caregivers.

It is admirable that all of us have moral standards or value systems. But this is not the issue. The issue is that our personal beliefs or prejudices can impair our ability to be of help by making it difficult for us to be objective. Concerned caregivers do not have the right to make judgments. To be effective we must be able to tolerate views and circumstances that are different from our own.

Conclusion

To sum up, the emotional relationship that existed between persons involved in an unsanctioned relationship must not be demeaned or overlooked. It must be viewed as valid, and the rupture of that relationship because of the death, as well as the need to mourn, must be recognized. Untold and unlimited opportunities exist for the conscientious caregiver to be of help to a fellow human being, and a pleasant spin-off is that the caregiver also benefits. In Klein's words, "Understanding of other people, compassion, sympathy and tolerance, enrich our experience of the world, and make us feel more secure in ourselves and less lonely.[21]

Notes

1. Alvin Toffler, *The Third Wave* (New York: Bantam, 1981), p. 1.
2. Ibid., p. 2.
3. *Facts from the Foundation,* 2:1, 1987, National Foundation of Funeral Service, Evanston, Ill.
4. James Breig, quoting Dr. Rita McDonald, in "How to Talk to Your Kids about Death," *U.S. Catholic* (Jan. 1987).

5. Peter Ellsworth, "The Right to Make Funeral Arrangements," *Michigan Funeral Director's Association Journal* (Feb. 1987), p. 6.

6. Colin Murray Parkes, *Bereavement: Studies of Grief in Adult Life* (New York: International Universities Press, 1972), p. 142.

7. Harry Guntrip, Schizoid Phenomena: Object Relations and the Self (New York: International Universities Press, 1969), p. 243.

8. Paul DeBlassie, *Inner Calm: A Christian Answer to Modern Stress* (Liguori, Mo.: Liquori Publications, 1985), p. 42.

9. Bruno Bettelheim, *Freud and Man's Soul* (New York: Knopf), p. 220.

10. Guntrip, *Schizoid Phenomena*, p. 267.

11. Ibid., p. 417.

12. James L. Lynch, *The Broken Heart* (New York: Basic Books, 1977).

13. Walter W. Whitaker, "The Contemporary American Funeral Ritual," in *The Popular Culture Reader*, 3d ed., edited by Christopher D. Geist and Jack Nachbar (Bowling Green, Ohio: Bowling Green University Popular Press, 1983), p. 278.

14. Edgar N. Jackson, *Understanding Grief* (Nashville, Tenn.: Abingdon Press, 1957), p. 168.

15. Samuel Roll, Leverett Millen, and Barbara Backlund, "Solomon's Mothers: Mourning in Mothers Who Relinquish Their Children for Adoption." In *Parental Loss of a Child*, edited by T.A. Rando (Champaign, Ill.: Research Press, 1986).

16. Royal Keith, "Advice to Funeral Directors on Assisting Bereaved Parents," in *Parental Loss of a Child*, edited by Therese A. Rando (Champaign, Ill.: Research Press, 1986), p. 475.

17. Whitaker, "Contemporary American Funeral," p. 263.

18. Parkes, *Bereavement*, p. 142.

19. Whitaker, "Contemporary American Funeral," p. 282.

20. Jackson, *Understanding Grief*, p. 143.

21. Melanie Klein, *Envy and Gratitude* (New York: Dell, 1975), p. 269.

24

Rituals and the Disenfranchised Griever

Nathan R. Kollar

H ave you ever looked out the window of an airplane, car, or bus and felt you were moving when you didn't expect to? Then, as moments sped by, you suddenly realized that it was not you that was moving but the vehicle next to you? You experienced movement even though you were not moving. Sometimes what we expect to experience determines what we do experience.

In this chapter we deal with what happens when our normal ritual expectations regarding grief cannot be met—our grief is disenfranchised. We also describe ways to change the griever's environment so that, although socially disenfranchised, one's grief may be ritually expressed. We first look at ordinary ritual patterns and their role in grieving. We then see how the public presence of the disenfranchised griever may challenge these normal bereavement patterns. We end with a review of some ways in which the experience of postdeath rituals may remain the same while the constitutive elements that go to "provide" it change.

The Nature of Postdeath Ritual

Rituals are patterns of activity. They are both social and personal habits. They are socially approved and transmitted patterns of living that manifest and affect our deepest concerns. Kissing, eating, handshakes, marriage celebrations, and worship services are examples of rituals. So too are war games, wrestling matches, and funerals.

Rituals are part of living and of life. They pattern our daily life and our entire life cycle. We need ritual to live. Without rituals we would be forced to begin anew every day and with every relationship since there would be no pattern for beginning.

Knowing how to celebrate a birthday party or graduation; how to recognize the pattern of good grammer or the nonverbal dynamics of conversation; how to write a sympathy card or a business letter—all these are examples of life made easy and more full through ritual. Although some rituals may at times be oppressive to some of us, life without ritual would be chaotic and destructive to all of us.

The reason life would be chaotic and destructive is that rituals provide the patterns that hold life together. Rituals enter into every aspect of our life for they are, by nature, holistic.

Their holistic nature is evident in the way they affect our minds, will, and heart. Rituals stir up passions. Rituals affect our conscious as well as our subconscious selves. People involved in a ritual might suddenly find themselves crying, ill at ease, or content and satisfied. They may have no conscious reason for such feelings, but the ritual has affected them at another level of existence.

Ritual is communal. Rituals are primarily agents of unity and convergence among those celebrating the ritual. The symbols that constitute a ritual bind those in the ritual together. The term *symbol* is derived from the Greek, *symbolon, symballein.* The verb literally means "to throw together." The noun form of the word refers to a mark or tally used for identification. An object was broken and at a later date joined by the respective holders to form a unity and authenticate their identities. The verb form *sym* in Greek suggests a bringing together; *symballein,* therefore, implies assembling or making one that was fractured or divided. Through symbols those engaged in ritual express and enforce togetherness. A cohesive social group is recognized by common symbols and rituals; a weak one has difficulties in agreeing on rituals and their place in communal life. Good ritual builds community; weak ritual destroys it. Our life in community enculturates us to both the performance of ritual and its affects.

Rituals point beyond the here and now. Ritual engages the senses with those realities beyond immediate sensible apprehension. Patriotism, hope, security, power, importance, social and individual identity are all examples of realities beyond immediate sensible apprehension. One might even suggest that one's personhood is also, beyond immediate sensible apprehension and thus in need of our bodies' symbolic expression to put us in the presence of another. Ritual is always involved with more than we can sense, yet it needs the sense to enable us to experience the presence of that which is beyond sensation.

A ritual both hides and reveals what it makes present. Sometimes it covers one aspect of the interfacing presences while uncovering another aspect. This is why the same ritual may be the source of a deep experience at one time of our lives and boredom at another time. The presence of realities beyond the senses is always subject to the ebb and flow of changing contexts.

We must realize too that rituals always have many meanings. Rituals are a dynamic intersecting of things, persons, and people that are capable of being interpreted in many different ways. The birthday party from the perspective of the mother, the daughter, the daughter's boyfriend, and another male friend are at least four different ways of engaging the same event. These meanings depend on the context of the ritual for further specification. When the context is changed, usually the meaning of the event changes for those involved. A funeral ritual celebrated when my parent dies is one event; another funeral celebrated when the president of my school dies is another. The context is significant for determining the meaning of each event.

Although good ritual always allows room for the spontaneous and individual, repetition and pattern are constitutive to its existence. This makes ritual a conservative element in any society because it functions as a way of bringing the entire community together: the living and the dead; the present and the absent. Rituals come and go, but their coming and going are linked to the community and/or the culture itself. Good ritual can join an individual to a vital community and the basic realities of life; bad ritual can alienate an individual and destroy his or her relationship to others and life in general.

This relationship of people we call community is essential to understanding ritual. Ritual builds community as well as presupposes community. Consequently ritual has the ability to reinvoke past emotion, to bind the individual to his or her own past experience, and to bring the members of the group together in a shared experience. A ritual, though essentially repetitious, is able to express and constructively channel the reactions of the celebrants. The individual, in a funeral ritual, for example, should be able to find his or her emotions, thoughts, doubts, and convictions resonating within the ritual. The community, on the other hand, should find its deeply felt grief and desire to help engrained in the ritual action. A ritual does not destroy the person. Nor does it take away freedom. Rather, it provides a context within which the personal feeling of all the mourners can be expressed, and it offers each individual the occasion to support freely every other individual in this celebration.

Not all rituals are equal; my eating breakfast with a spoon is not as significant as a person's taking the presidential oath. Some Roman Catholic communities, for instance, see some rituals, sacraments, as so different from others that they change reality. The central symbols of the ritual—people, bread, wine, oil—become sacred symbols of God's presence. In other words, certain rituals, within the tradition of a community, are seen to be central to the existence of the community and to those members of the community. All communities have such rituals. In particular they have rituals that mark our passage from one status in the community to another. These "rites of passage" mark birth, adulthood, marriage, and death. They are essential to a community's life and to an individual's life in the community. Postdeath rituals, with the funeral as their pivot, are part of a rite of passage wherein the bereaved acknowledge the reality of death and their hope for life.

Naturally, any postdeath ritual, to be effective, will necessarily reflect the characteristics of ritual we have reviewed, as well as those characteristics that are unique to its nature as a rite of passage. These characteristics will affect the nature of the grief of the disenfranchised as well as the enfranchised. Let us look first at the goals of a typical postdeath ritual, the funeral, and then review the basic structure and expectations of the entire funeral. We do this in order to establish the ritual expectations of the bereaved. Once knowing the expectations, goals, we can investigate the possible insertion of the disenfranchised into the achievement of these goals.

The Goals of the Funeral Ritual

The *physical goal* of the ritual is to cope with the biological needs of all concerned. At the very least this demands the removal of the body and the diminishment of the possible harmful physical suffering of the mourners.

The *social goal* is to cope with death and its effects upon the deceased, mourners, and society in general—to provide group support for the mourners and express the changing relationship brought about by death. Thus, the funeral should provide an opportunity for the ritual manifestation of shared loss and the ritual means by which the support of the community of mourners is conveyed to the bereaved. It should also demonstrate the community's understanding of the relationship of the living to those who have died. It should, in addition, begin the process of strengthening relational patterns among the living.

The *psychological goals* are to sanction emotional reorientation of the mourners by helping them accept the reality of the death and the feelings toward the reality. Thus, the funeral should accomplish these goals: (1) it should assist in the reinforcement of reality for the bereaved; (2) it should aid in remembering the deceased and begin the recapitulation of the relationship; (3) it should eventuate in the freedom of developing new relational patterns without violating the integrity of previous relationships with the deceased; (4) it should offer an opportunity for the release of authentic feelings.

The *religious goal* is to offer a unified vision of life and death while providing a ritualistic way of enacting that vision. Thus: (1) it should enable mourners to be more meaningfully related to religious resources for coping with suffering; (2) it should offer perspectives on the meaning of life and death in the light of the present loss; (3) it should assist the mourners intellectually and emotionally to comprehend more fully human nature as a unity of body and spirit.

These goals are essential to any good postdeath ritual. Together with the general characteristics of ritual they make up the ritual expectations of postdeath ritual. The rituals associated with disenfranchised grief must at a minimum attend to these characteristics and their expectations. This minimum can be seen in the following suggestions.

A Summary Description of Postdeath Ritual

Postdeath rituals are at best imitative of those already in existence.[1] When we examine good postdeath rituals we see that they include people, symbolic objects, and recognized structure.

The recognized structure would include the following steps:

1. Entry into the time, place, or relationship. The mood here is to indicate a separation from ordinary living and an affirmation of the relationship of the individual(s) gathered to the deceased.

2. A core symbolic act. The act can be as simple as reaching out and touching a tombstone, or it can be an intricate, imaginative exercise involving a reliving of a significant moment in life with the deceased.

3. Time to absorb what is occurring. This may be provided through silence, song, or further action. Its purpose is to build on the core symbolic act.

4. Leave taking. As we must enter into ritual to touch realities beyond the momentary self, we must leave it to live our ordinary lives. This is always a delicate moment, for if the two preceding steps achieve their goal, the participants may not want to leave, yet they must. Sometimes it is appropriate to have the participants carry something tangible away with them; at other times it is more appropriate to leave the scene gradually.

This structure will succeed if we keep in mind that it should provide an opportunity for the following:[2]

Regeneration, in which the deceased lives again in the memory of all present and an opportunity is provided for all present to face up to their past, present, and future relationship to the deceased.

Identification, in which the survivors recognize their share in the life of the deceased and their responsibility for guarding the values for which he or she lived. It is here too that people are given the opportunity to see that it is by their identification with these values that they will immortalize the deceased. The ritual should provide us with the opportunity to identify with the values of that person.

Communal awareness comes in a recognition that by the death of the deceased the bereaved have become a new community. When one of our friends dies, we are not the same. This change must be recognized. Whenever a prime minister or president dies in office, the nation recognizes that it is not the same. A husband's or wife's death immediately affects the entire family. But what holds for nation or family also holds for the less formal communities of sport, work, and religion. The survivors are not quite the same people as they once were. Each must reestablish his or her relationship with the others. The rite should provide the opportunity for all to come and do this.

Confirmation of communal values that form the foundation of the reason for living. Death cannot be seen as the victor among the living or there is no reason to keep on living without the significant other.

Finding a suitable outlet for identification, substitution, and guilt. All of these will have a suitable outlet if the rate provides for the three just mentioned elements. The purpose of the rite is to provide everyone an opportunity for emotional release and communal awareness. The rite does this through remembering the deceased both as a valuable person and as an important member of the community.

The participants in the funeral ritual have a sense of what an ordinary funeral experience is when they participate in the funeral. As in our initial description of the movement of the airplane, there is in the funeral ritual an expectation, because of the ritual pattern, of what should occur in a funeral celebration. When it occurs, the goals of the ritual are achieved; when it does not, they are not achieved. When the disenfranchised griever is present, the goals may not be achieved because he or she is not accepted into the bereaved community. However, it may be possible to modify the ritual environment in such a way that the expected experiences will occur even though the ordinary public ritual is not the same. This is equivalent to moving everything around the plane so that one has an experience of moving while standing still.

We have reviewed the structure and goals of the postdeath ritual; let us now examine the relationship between disenfranchised grief and the postdeath ritual to see what we can "move around" in order to deal with the grief of the disenfranchised.

Disenfranchised Grief and Postdeath Rituals

The disenfranchised griever is alienated. The sense of alienation may be self-originating or based in actual social rejection of the individual. In either case the griever feels that he or she is not wanted within a certain group of people. It is as if a sign were poste: DON'T CRY HERE.

Neither an individual nor a society can live without such boundary signs. They are a fact of life. Our patterns of life and society are reflections of this all-important reality—identity is determined by boundaries[3] The physical boundary of our body determines our physiological identity; the "limit" of what we will and will not do determines the boundary of our morals. The examples can go on forever. But the principle remains. Boundaries are present. They shape and form us. There are signs posted at these boundaries warning us to beware of crossing them.

The disenfranchised griever, while recognizing life's boundaries, also recognizes that the death of this significant other must be acknowledged through ritual—after all, rituals are essential to living. But while they are essential for life, they are also essentially communal. The disenfranchised griever represents an individual from another community of values who wants to violate this community's boundaries and thus its perceived identity. The public presence of the disenfranchised griever challenges the ordinary rituals of life that reflect the celebration of these boundaries and the values they establish.

There are many types of postdeath rituals, with their respective purposes and constituencies. To ignore the complexity of the issues involved is to neglect the reality of these rituals. We cannot, however, deal with all the goals, rituals, or constituencies. We will focus only on the disenfranchised griever in relation to the funeral. In doing so we acknowledge the significant ethical, social, and psychological concerns for everyone involved. To highlight some of these concerns, let us begin with four scenarios.

Four Funerals

Wendell was fifty-seven when he died. His three grown children and wife of thirty years decided to hold a memorial service for him a week after his accident. Everone in the small town knew of the service, and his friends prepared to attend it.

Anna was doubtful whether she should attend. Anna had been Wendell's mistress for fifteen years. She annually went on a two-month vacation with him, and they spent many weekends together at her country home. Only Wendell's wife knew about Anna. Wendell was Anna's only friend and lover. His death was devastating. How does she ritualize her grief?

Mary and Bill went through the motions of preparing for the funeral. Just the day before they had been informed that their daughter had been murdered. Julie was, unknown to them, four months pregnant. She had been going to college. Her boyfriend was despondent and could not function. Mary and Bill went about the funeral preparations. They were Roman Catholic and thus made arrangements for a funeral mass as well as a brief wake.

Andrew had killed Julie. He knew it. The authorities knew it. He wanted the money for drugs. She had it but wouldn't give it to him. "Why did she have to hit me? I wanted her money, not her anger," he said. He wanted the money. So he killed her.

He was sorry for killing her. He was sorry. If he could attend the funeral and share in everyone's sorrow maybe the haunting memory of her scream would go away. Should he be encouraged to go to the funeral? Shoud he be accepted for a public role in the funeral ritual?

There were seven survivors. Seven who had worked the camps. No one understood their pride, their sense of accomplishment at being able to dispose of so many with such efficiency. If people like them had not done their duty with such a high sense of professionalism the country would never have survived. Now there were six. The lieutenant had died. They were all old now. No one appreciated what they had done. But together they had done their duty, together they would solemnly mark each of their deaths so that what they had done for their country would not be forgotten.

Diana read about the death of her former captor. Her nights were still haunted by dreams of those men doing their will with her, her mother, and sisters. Only she remained. Only they remained. Each haunted by memories of Auschwitz. She knew the time, the place, and the people who were to gather. As if drawn by an eternal destiny she packed her bags and left to celebrate the death of one she hated. Should she participate in the ritual? How?

Sally's friend and lover died after an extended illness. She and Sally had been intimate for seventeen years. Everyone in town knew them and their relationship. Everyone came to accept them as they were, even though they could not publicly honor such a life-style. But the obvious shared love, nonconfrontational to others yet affirming of each other, gained the respect of everyone. The town wished to celebrate the death of Marylyn. How do they affirm their grief for Marylyn without advocating the homosexual life-style of others?

In each of these scenarios there are many who grieve. But their grieving is not the same. In each of these scenarios there is a funeral. Those who grieve will each play a different role in the ritual, and the ritual will affirm and affect something different for each of them as a consequence of the ritual and the role they play in it.

We have already clarified what we mean by ritual. We must reflect briefly on what is meant by grief. "Grief is the emotional response to the loss of a significant other." This definition of grief allows room for positive and negative emotions. The emotions associated with grief may range from elation at the person's death to deep agony over life without him or her. Grief also deals with the loss of a significant other. One may be significant because it is pivotal to our hate or our love. Grief may occur as a consequence of either love or hate. Our understanding of grief determines the range and complexity of the disenfranchisement of grief. I have discussed the above definition in other places.[4] But it is essential for understanding what follows. Such grief is to be distinguished from bereavement, which may be seen as the role one is expected to play in response to the loss of a loved one. Notice that bereavement emphasizes what others expect us to do when we have lost someone we are expected to love. Social expectations are central to bereavement. Personal, emotional response is central to grief. We may be bereaved without grieving and we may be grieving without an opportunity to be bereaved. Both situations are difficult ones for the individual to experience. We are concerned here with grief without bereavement. In our first scenario, Anna and Wendell's wife may both be grieving for quite different reasons; only his wife is expected to be in a state of bereavement. In actual fact Anna may be deprived of any form of externalized, recognized grieving for Wendell.

Surely the reader senses that we are reviewing the core of disenfranchised grief theory. We are reviewing it because I am convinced that the current models of grief are insufficient for carrying on a clear discussion. They claim too much for their interpretive ability. Yet we must speak about grief even though we are severely limited. We go on because beyond the words and the theories are real people hurting more than they have to because of our possible insensitivity to their situation. I go forward, however, with the understanding that a discussion of disenfranchised grief includes recognition that one grieves for someone he or she hates or loves (a significant other) and the range of feelings encompasses all the human feelings. A discussion of grief excludes no human feeling as necessarily inappropriate in the face of death.

What then of the disenfranchised griever vis-à-vis ritual? Ritual presupposes some sort of community, with all its values and boundaries. Thus there will be a tension between the community and its enfranchised grieving and the individual who, for one reason or another, does not fit the normal, or enfranchised, pattern of grieving. We are faced with a conflict of individual rights[5] and communal rights: to grieve, to grieve publicly, to be affirmed in one's grief by a community, to expect a bereavement role in postdeath rituals.

This listing of possible rights is a brief outline of the ethical issues involved in what follows. But over it all hangs the stark reality that ritual manifests and affects social value. Public ritual celebrates and reinforces public, communal values. A community celebrates what it holds in common in order to deepen and pass on these commonly held values. A funeral, or any other postdeath ritual, does the same. A disenfranchised griever, if he or she desires to sustain his or her values and life-style, is by definition over and against the set of social values celebrated by the community. A celebration presupposes commonly held agreement on fundamental communal values.[6] The presence of the disenfranchised challenges the communality of value— what can be done in this situation, on the side of the community, on the side of the disenfranchised?

Significant Questions

The answers to the following questions can help make the decision whether to include the disenfranchised in the public ritual.

1.   What is the nature of the life-style of those present? A life-style that takes a public stand against commonly held values means that the person's recognized presence will challenge the nature of the community gathered to

celebrate the person's death. How valuable is it to honor the many and their grieving, as contrasted with the one and his or her grieving? Is this a conflict of rights? Who is to resolve the conflict? With what consequences?

2. Is the life-style in agreement with the group's stated or presumed values? Most communities reflect the dominant religious and/or cultural values. Unless there is some reason to expect otherwise, ritual is celebrated in accord with those norms. Only when someone's values and life-style are significantly different would we need to look to some of the suggestions offered in the next section.

3. Do those gathered know and understand the ritual? It is not unusual that people would not understand the ritual. Anyone who has taught death education realizes the vast ignorance people have of their own and others' traditions surrounding death. Not understanding the ritual, people usually react only to the most obvious language and ritual action. Contemporary ritual usually supports two extremes: uniformity and diversity. The symbols used in the ritual leave room for diverse interpretation, yet the context of the symbols lead to a narrow or pluralistic interpretation. The Nazi captors in the earlier example, for instance, narrow the community of celebrants as they increase the use of Nazi symbols; they broaden the community as they use religious symbols without any allusion to their former lives.

4. Does the person affirm the entire ritual or only certain parts of it? It would not be unusual for the disenfranchised to have a significantly different meaning of the deceased's life and death. How this is affirmed or not affirmed in the ritual will determine the participation of the disenfranchised.

5. What role does the person wish to play—does he or she accept the community's interpretation of that role? If the person accepts the communal interpretation of the role, he or she can participate without too much difficulty.

6. Does the individual's presence bring the community together or destroy it? Sometimes the disenfranchised would wish to destroy the enfranchised community because they oppose those values. If one includes the possibility of deep anger consequent to the death of a person, it is possible that the disenfranchised may want to use the ritual not so much to express grief but as a means of expressing deeply felt anger resulting from past rejections. Even if one is not angry going into the ritual, it is probable that the ritual itself would touch off such a reaction.

7. Does the person's presence improve his or her ability or that of the community to live creatively with ambiguity, uncertainty, even chaos? Does it help or hinder maturation? How necessary is the public, community-affirmed bereavement for one's grieving process?

8. Will his or her presence really achieve the grief-goal for the individual and/or the group? This is a very important question. Certainly we have been describing the relationship between grief and public ritual in an ideal way.

Although grief must be ritually expressed, it may not be in such a public forum as the funeral. Most grief literature attests to the fact that grief really begins when the funeral is over. Thus both public and private postdeath ritual plays a role as important, if not more so in the grieving process as the funeral ritual.

The answers to these questions will indicate what will happen if the disenfranchised griever takes a public role in the funeral. It may easily happen that the griever's acceptance of this bereavement role will destroy many of the funeral's goals. It may be a question of whose rights should prevail: the individual's or the community's. One should not be too quick to move toward public modes of expression in order to achieve grief goals. There may be other ways of achieving the same objective.

There is always the choice of grieving in private. Many times this is the only choice the disenfranchised have. In many instances the disenfranchised are such because they are alienated from society. On the edge of social existence they may create subcommunities of like kind, yet they are still "different." Their grief will reflect that difference. Death is part of life and grieving is also part of life: this life, now, as we live it. Our grieving will, therefore, reflect that difference that is unique to each of us.

Suggestions for Involving the Disenfranchised in Postdeath Rituals

There are many ways, however, that the rituals we have grown up with still play an important part in our lives, even though we may have drifted away from those values that lie at their base. The following are suggestions dependent upon the normal grief process and the rituals associated with that process. In other words, we are describing ways to change the environment in such a way that one will experience many of the same things one would in the normal environment—as when I felt the plane moving when it wasn't really.

Individual Rituals Imitative of the Public Ritual

Some have found the writing of a letter to a dead person a profound experience. An ordinary ritual, letter writing, incorporated into the grief process becomes an expression and transformation of one's grieving. Grievers can also imitate the public rituals of their religious, ethnic, or work community in private or with a small group of friends. A memorial service held within the gay community of friends for one of their members who is being buried by a nongay community would still be acknowledged as functionally effective according to most current models of grief. A private act imitative of public ritual would be, for example, if Wendell's mistress chose a significant item of Wendell's and, with great solemnity, took it to the gravesite for burial—or burned it if he was cremated. The public ritual of body disposition, becoming private, offers an avenue for the ritualized expression of the loss of a significant other.

I would suggest, however, that whenever possible these rituals never be done without anyone knowing about them or someone being present. I cannot emphasize enough that rituals affect the whole person. Sometimes they stimulate dimensions of the personality we are not aware of. Especially in death-related rituals, profound depths of the person are stirred up. We must always provide for the unexpected by letting our friends know what we are doing and/or by asking them to assist us in the ritual itself.

Ritualization by and with Significant Others

Contemporary life in North America is, for the most part, pluralistic. We live in many communities. We have friends and enemies in many communities. Many times these communities and the individuals who participate in them do not intersect. With the death of a significant other it is possible to enlist the aid, through ritual, of one community to share the grief that burdens us. The one who grieves touches all communities by the death that affects him or her. It is possible that while one may more properly be bereaved in one community, one may more properly be grieved in another. In a more general way communities may provide anonymous mourning rituals where the specificity of grief does not necessarily have to be articulated, yet the bereaved may gather together in the common cause of remembering.

Anonymous Mourning Rituals: Religious and Secular

Many religions have special times set aside for remembering the dead. These ritual moments in a service or during the year should be taken advantage of to offer the disenfranchised an opportunity to grieve. The same may be said of secular services. Memorial Day can be the occasion of remembering the dead. If certain communities would set aside time during these national days of remembering actually to remember all the dead, many of the disenfranchised would have an opportunity to participate in a meaningful postdeath ritual. Anonymous rituals are those in which people gather for the sole purpose of remembering the dead. The rituals themselves never specify the circumstances surrounding the death or anything else that would call attention to the reasons for one's disenfranchisement.

Anniversary Rituals

Anniversary reactions are generally acknowledged as a significant part of the grieving process. The anonymous mourning rituals often parallel opportunities for anniversary rituals. But beyond such gatherings it may be appropriate and even necessary for the disenfranchised griever to perform a special ritual on the person's birthday or on some other holiday. Usually there are special persons, places, things, songs, and actions that become part of any intimate relationship. With a little imagination it is an easy step to integrating one of these special symbols into a short rite of memory.

Public Ritual Acted Out by Public Authorities
in Private Situations

Civil, religious, and professionals associated with death rituals bring with them an aura of the public they serve, even in private situations. Thus a priest saying a mass in remembrance of the dead person, with the disenfranchised griever present, is a way of acknowledging the "rights" of all concerned. A funeral director can certainly be enlisted to engage in an imitation ritual of a wake and/or body disposal. The public person, even when not acting in public, brings with him or her into the ritual situation an invisible public to a private situation. When that airplane outside my window begins to move, I feel I am moving. My senses give me the wrong impression because I am expecting something else. When a public figure is doing something he or she usually does, we sense that it is official and public even though it may not be.

Reconciliatory Rituals

People change. Communities change. The death of someone significant to many people sometimes helps everyone realize the consequences of their action. Sometimes it takes a death for people to realize how they have been excluding someone. People do become reconciled with one another. Room must be left in our ordinary rituals to achieve such reconciliation. There are many traditional signs of reconciliation in our culture: the handshake, forming a circle around a significant object, sharing a common task . . . these are just a few of those signs. The offer for reconcilation should be made whether it is accepted or not. One does find, however, that the offer, though rejected during a ritual early in the mourning process, may encourage reconciliation later in the process—perhaps at some later anniversary celebration.

Ritual Places

There are public ritual places where private things may be done in a private way. Cemetaries, tombs, and monuments are just a few such places. A pilgrimage to one of these may be a significant way of marking one's grief.

Authentic and Inauthentic Rituals

All the suggestions up to this point have skirted the issue of disenfranchised grief publicly expressed within a ritual composed of "enfranchised" grievers. Are we not lying to ourselves—being inauthentic—by pretending we are doing something in public when we are not? Not to forthrightly speak out about one's relationship to another through taking on the bereavement role is to deny reality, to suggest that the disenfranchised griever is no griever at all.

Such claims of inauthenticity for the postdeath rituals find their base in those theories of grief that model grief as bottled energy that must be let out, or use a "let it all hang out" model of authenticity. It is well recognized, for instance, that one can grieve in private. Many people express their grief through minimal public ritual. Many religions and ethnic groups severely limit both in place and time public displays of grief. Certainly those limits imposed by the friction of interfacing cultural values do not necessarily produce harmful effects in the personality. The pressure of daily life as well as a pervasive cultural inability to deal with grief beyond the first few weeks of death result in a type of disenfranchisement for every griever. The suggestions for grieving provided here can be of benefit to all, not only to the disenfranchised. The authenticity of grieving is often in the personhood of the griever. None of us ever fully expresses his or her grief for the other—that is why grieving takes so long and occurs in so many ways. We learn quite early in life that there are acceptable and unacceptable ways of expressing our feelings. Feelings of anger, sex, hunger, laughter become ritualized or communally patterned to enable us to express our feelings without harm to others (society). Grief is a feeling that also needs ritual. This chapter has suggested how everyone, enfranchised or disenfranchised, may learn from knowing communal rituals. Knowing our rituals is knowing ourselves—and that is always the beginning of wisdom.

Notes

1. The best example of the necessity of imitating rather then creating a new ritual can be found in Mona Ozouf, *Festivals and the French Revolution,* trans. (Cambridge: Harvard University Press, 1988.

2. For an elaboration of this description see my book *Death and Other Living Things* (Dayton, Ohio: Pflaum/Standard, 1973), pp. 59–67.

3. Hans Mol, *Identity and the Sacred* New York: Free Press, 1976).

4. See especially my "Models of Grief: Limits of Theory," to be published by the Foundation of Thanatology, and also Camille Wortman and Roxane Silver, "Coping with Irrevocable Loss," in *Cataclysms, Crises, and Catastrophes: Psychology in Action,* edited by G.R. VandenBos and B.K. Bryant (Washington, D.C.: American Psychological Association, 1987).

5. We must be sensitive to the fact that often the theoretical discussion of and the political agitation for "just rights" is an ideological mask for power relations. For further distinctions and discussion, see my article "People's Rights and Provincial Duties," *Religious Education* 67 (1973), 690–709.

6. A detailed analysis of the relationship between communal values and membership in community is found in my article "Church Membership: Some Dynamics of Belonging and Reconciliation," *Explorations: Journal for Adventurous Thought* 2 (July 1984), 5–20.

25
A Nurse's Perspective on Disenfranchised Grief

Elise Lev

Health care professionals who care for dying patients are the survivors of many losses during the course of their work. Although they experience sense of loss, they do not have the socially recognized right or role of the grieving person. Thus the usual sources of support given to a grieving person, such as the increased attention of family and friends, are frequently not available to caregivers. As a result the grief of the health care professional may be disenfranchised. Focusing on the caregiver as a survivor is one framework for examining disenfranchised grief.

Nurses and Dying Patients

Although all the living are the survivors of the deaths of others, professionals who work with dying patients perform services needed by dying patients and may perceive themselves as survivors. Some health care professionals spend a great deal of time dealing with dying patients or patients facing life-threatening illnesses. Kalish (1985) notes that nurses find themselves interacting with both the dying and survivors of the dying more than any other professional group. Nurses also focus on care-related tasks, while doctors frequently focus on cure-related tasks. According to Kalish, discouragement is inevitable for people in the health care professions who have a "cure" orientation when patients fail to improve or worsen despite the efforts expended.

Benoliel (1975) notes that our society rewards lifesaving activities and technical achievement rather than achievement of job satisfaction from work with patients whose main needs involve human care-oriented concerns. Care-oriented behaviors are devalued because of the historical association with "woman's work." Nursing has paid considerably more attention to understanding and dealing with patients' need for emotionally supportive behavior than has medicine. Care-oriented behaviors are nurturing, supportive, or "motherlike" behaviors and are contrasted with the orientation of medicine, which is designed to cure patients through such approaches as medical examination, diagnosis, and treatment. Nurses seem to have accepted care-oriented behaviors as part of their professional work, despite the grieving that this care may elicit (Kalish 1985).

It has been suggested that the outcome of encounters with death inevitably becomes associated with grief, as caregivers grieve for those who died as well as for themselves and the losses they will suffer. Raphael (1982) suggests there are differences in the reactions of male and female health care workers. She asserts that males acknowledge their emotions less frequently than females, because of societal expectations. Although females are more likely to acknowledge their emotions, the consequence of this acknowledgment may be that females are perceived as being weaker than males.

Determinants of Grief

Concerned with the effects of grieving, Parkes (1974) identifies specific determinants of grief such as personal experiences, mode of death of the deceased, relationship with the deceased, social, economic, cultural and religious factors, social support, and other life stressors and opportunities. These determinants of the grief reaction may predict the outcome of bereavement as well as the differences among individuals in their responses to the death of a patient. Other determinants of the grief reaction involve the closeness of the mourner and the deceased, as well as the extent to which the mourner believes the death might have been prevented (Bugen 1977). Specific research has not been conducted to assess whether these determinants of the grief reaction apply to caregivers as well as to others who experience losses. However, recent literature suggests that the response of professional caregivers may be similar to that of survivors (Sheard 1984).

It has been noted that grief is commonly seen in nurses (Kalish 1985, Lerea and LiMauro 1982, Shanfield 1981, Sheard 1984, Stowers 1983). Parkes (1974) asserts that grief in survivors occurs shortly after bereavement and fades as time passes. It is not known whether caregivers who experience frequent losses also experience grief that fades in intensity or whether professionals experiencing grief behave differently from other grieving populations. Do caregivers whose grief may be disenfranchised experience a gradual mitigation in the pain of grieving and a restructuring of their world as time passes?

Psychic Numbing

Raphael (1982) describes the survivor syndrome as "psychic numbing," or a "shutting-out-process," which may be an adaptive function to protect the survivor from the death of others. Raphael (1982) suggests that health care professionals may have experienced higher than average levels of perceived deprivation in their childhoods, which may heighten their reactions to the dying and may make caregivers more likely to use defense mechanisms such as psychic numbing.

A number of studies suggest that both physicians and nurses may cope with dying patients by avoidance, withdrawal, isolation of the patient, or other behaviors that serve to restrict personal involvement with the dying. The avoidance of dying patients by nurses has been shown to be a very real occurrence (Lev 1986). It appears that personal contact or interaction with the dying person is the most feared. The person suffering from pain appears even more likely to be avoided, which may be due to the fact that such patients elicit feelings of helplessness on the part of the health care professional. Perhaps patients who are unwelcome reminders of the limitations of professional's care are avoided. Medicine and nursing can neither totally cure all patients nor completely alleviate their pain. Patients facing life-threatening illness or patients experiencing pain are a reminder that control over one's fate may be an illusion, and this may be so unbearable for some that avoidance of these patients is the result.

It may also be that empathy with unfortunate people is lacking in contemporary society. Perhaps people are unable to comprehend experiences of which they are ignorant. Dying in modern society generally takes place in an institution, away from home and family, as opposed to the experience of dying in earlier times. In addition, Americans today are constantly bombarded graphically with bad news from the media and may defend themselves by becoming desensitized to the pain of other people because of the sheer volume of reported disasters to which they are exposed on a daily basis. It may be that health care professionals restrict personal involvement with the dying in order to protect themselves from disenfranchised grief. Such reactions may be similar to psychic numbing.

Grief and the Caregiver's Perception of Care

There has been little research focusing on identifying grief in health care professionals. Although much literature focuses on burnout and stress among nurses, few studies attempt to link these reactions to the effects of grief. Dolan (1988) suggests that providing care perceived to be meaningless leads to anger, stress, and burnout among ICU nurses. According to Dolan (1988), nurses in ICUs are conflicted by a lack of consistent guidelines associated with resuscitating patients. She identifies inappropriate resuscitation as that which takes place with patients suffering from diseases or conditions that have destroyed all hope for the quality of life.

A system that prolongs the life of people who cannot recover has been called into question by ethicists and health care providers. Lester (1988) notes that suicide occurs in patients who feel hopeless regarding their future quality of life, such as patients suffering from chronic renal disease.

Brody (1988) describes a twenty-five-year-old patient who suffered extensive head injuries and demonstrated no evidence of higher brain function. The patient has been kept alive for two and a half years by nursing care and the administration of medications to fight infection. The family visits daily, begging their child to respond, although the futility of the situation has been explained by the health care providers. Caregivers perceive the patient's care to be a "waste of their time and a misuse of their abilities," as well as an unacceptable financial burden to society. Staff believe provision of care to other patients is impeded by the allocation of time and resources given to this patient.

Giving care that is perceived as inappropriately prolonging biological life raises questions for caregivers. Dolan (1988) asks whether useless treatment is ever ethical. Brody (1988) uses a model of conflicting values to analyze the situation and recommends the need for protocols that provide for processes by which providers can discontinue care deemed to be inappropriate.

Freud (1930) discusses the significance the role of work plays for people who find meaning in their professional activities. He states, "One gains the most if one can sufficiently heighten the yield of pleasure from the sources of psychical and intellectual work." One wonders at the conflicts that may be caused when work takes on the characteristics of meaningless activity. What are the effects of giving care perceived to be meaningsless? Is the grief of the caregiver heightened when patients who are perceived to be without hope are being cared for? Does the nurse feel guilty for reactions that may serve to restrict interaction with patients and families who face hopeless treatments? Do stress and burnout of nurses increase when care is perceived to be meaningless?

Identifying Grief in Caregivers

Kalish (1985) notes that nurses develop symptoms common to all grieving people; they cry, feel depressed, have difficulty concentrating, express anger, anxiety, and experience symptoms such as fatigue, headaches, insomnia, and appetite loss. It has been noted that professionals tend to have a more narrow view of the symptoms of grief perceived to be within normal limits than do members of a group of newly bereaved people (Klaus and Shinners 1982–83). The training of health care professionals emphasizes pathologic processes to a greater extent than normal or growth-related processes. It may be that when grief appears in the caregiver, it is identified as such only when it is expressed in a way perceived to be pathological, or when it appears to interfere with a person's usual functions. Studies of health care professionals who learn to resolve their grief reactions or where growth is the outcome of their grief appear to be nonexistent. Perhaps because of the training of caregivers, the pathological end result of grief may be the first reaction that is noted. One study of nursing managers linked loss and grief reactions to behaviors that impair professional practice (Clark 1984). Perhaps tracing pathological grief reactions backward might reveal disenfranchised grief.

Grief in caregivers may develop in response to various situations, such as previous unresolved loss, the actual or anticipated death of a patient, or feelings of guilt. Raphael (1982) suggests that both doctors and nurses may be motivated by perceived deprivation in childhood to enter a helping profession. Shanfield (1981) notes that discussions of unresolved previous losses were common in an educational seminar for health care professionals which focused on death and loss. Reactions to the actual or anticipated death of patients may include reactions that are not therapeutic for the patient. Denial may be employed by the caregiver in response to his or her own fears (Cassileth 1979, Kalish 1985, Schoenberg et al. 1972). Although a balance of identification with the patient and detachment from the patient is necessary for the well-being of both patients and caregivers, this balance may be elusive in its achievement.

Needs of Caregivers

Feifel (1965) notes that many demands are made on those who deal with the dying, such as being confronted with anxieties about dying, antipathy toward overidentifying with patients, a sense of triumph in outliving patients, and an inability to help other patients. A preoccupation with feelings of guilt on the part of the survivor has been noted in bereaved populations (Shanfield 1981, Feifel 1965), and this guilt has been traced to various roots, such as the perceived inability to provide care, to meet family needs, and to be present at the time of death. Guilt may also be related to previous unresolved losses, as in the case of a nurse whose patient's death elicited her own memories of a painful loss of a loved one (Stowers 1983).

Vachon (1978) identifies a number of reasons why hospice workers choose to work with dying patients. The reasons include resolving past losses, relieving one's own feelings of guilt, perceiving oneself to have a special calling, proving that one can care for the dying better than others may have cared for their own dying loved ones, having a hidden agenda, wanting to make this work one's entire life, and having unrealistic expectations of the tasks required by the role. The reasons that brought caregivers to work with the dying may simultaneously render them more susceptible to grief and the stresses of working with dying patients.

Studies of people who are themselves survivors of cancer or other life-threatening illnesses reveal certain predictable outcome behaviors in terms of their further development and transformations. Such changes are frequently associated with a refocusing of life's priorities, as in the case of a nurse who became a clinical specialist in oncology after surviving Hodgkin's disease (Shanfield 1981).

When the personal needs of the caregivers are not met, one outcome may be burnout. The term is used to describe a person once fired up by his or her motives for working with the dying but currently feeling extinguished by the work. Kalish (1985) points out the need for caregivers to be aware of their own motives for working with the dying in order to prevent themselves from becoming ineffective in their work and possibly doing harm to themselves and their patients.

Coping with the Caregiver's Grief

Coping with the grief of the health care professional has recently received increased attention. It has been suggested that the support the caregiver receives from others may be a critical element in preventing burnout. Perhaps in order to prevent self-destruction or overload, support is needed to sustain the multiple expectations of working with the dying. Maintaining distance from others is the opposite of relatedness in Buberian terms, and distance may be employed as a defense mechanism to prevent burnout. The support a caregiver receives from others may be the additional ingredient necessary to enable him or her to enter into a therapeutic relationship with dying patients without risk to the self (Buber 1965, Lev 1986).

Feifel (1977) suggests that nurses may be discouraged from entering into a therapeutic relationship with patients whose doctor or family decides that the truth about the diagnosis is to be withheld. Contacts with such patients may be in an atmosphere of depersonalized care, as the nurse maintains distance because of the unrealistic constraints that have been imposed. After the death of such patients, grief on the part of the nurse may be exacerbated because of the nurse's feelings of guilt for not providing humane enough care.

Various interventions have been suggested as ways of coping with grief in the caregivers. Sharing feelings with other professionals or receiving social support from others is one frequently suggested intervention (Clark 1984, Sheard 1984, Stowers 1983, Raphael, Singh, and Bradbury 1980). Although the psychological processes of denial and repression protect people from emotional pain and appear useful in allowing the person to grieve in manageable doses, when feelings of grief are not permitted expression, they appear to return at a later date. Parkes (1974) notes that anything that continually allows a person to avoid or suppress the pain of grief, such as the continuous use of tranquilizers, can be expected to prolong mourning and the resolution of the grief process. Lindemann (1944) notes that the essential task in grieving is for the individual to review the relationship with the deceased and to express sorrow and the sense of loss. Not until an individual has accepted the loss can his or her social readjustment be completed.

The importance of allowing nurses to express their feelings after the loss of a patient is asserted by Stowers (1983), who describes a conference after the loss of a patient: "No one laughed and no one ridiculed her thoughts and feelings or those of others." The importance of allowing people to express their feelings in a nonjudgmental environment is stressed. Raphael, Singh, and Bradbury (1980) refer to a debriefing session where the experience of the loss of a patient is shared with others and talked through. This mechanism was found to be helpful in the subsequent adjustment of the caregivers. Sheard (1984) also notes the critical importance of having a conference after a patient's death where caregivers can review their involvement with a patient and share their memories of the patient.

Cassileth (1979) notes that as staff become better able to handle their own uncertainties, they become more effective with patients. In the absence of formal case conferences, frequent informal discussions may facilitate the practice of collegial support. The experiences of a staff nurse in a hematology clinic of a city hospital seem to demonstrate that when attention is given to staff problems, caregivers can become more effective with patients. A situation is described in which a nurse did not know how to respond to a patient. That patient, diagnosed with Hodgkin's disease, had been attending the clinic on the same day as another patient with the same diagnosis. Both were treated with chemotherapy. When one patient suddenly stopped coming to the clinic, the other patient asked the nurse why. Later the nurse said to a colleague that she had told the patient she did not remember his friend because she did not know how to respond, since the patient's friend had died. The colleague responded that this is a really difficult situation and one in which there is no clear-cut "right" answer. After discussing the situation it was decided that the fear of the unknown may be more frightening to the patient than the reality. One way of responding to the patient might be to explain that his friend had not responded to the treatments as he is responding. The nurse could discuss the fact that the ability to attain a complete remission is 100 percent greater in patients with no systemic symptoms of the disease, as was the case in this patient's situation. His friend had lost more than 10 percent of his body weight prior to coming for treatment (Lev 1981).

Caregivers may consider the possibility of organizing collegial support where none exists. Collegial support does not have to involve all staff, nor large amounts of time. The above discussion took place over a shared lunch. All that is needed is a small group of staff willing to meet regularly and willing to look to each other for support. The ability to share feelings and experiences and not be judged by colleagues is the critical element. It is also important to let others know they are welcome to attend.

Other suggestions to aid caregivers in coping with grief include attending a patient's funeral, posting a photograph of the patient on a bulletin board, and visiting or calling a family member (Sheard 1984). Getting away for a few days may be helpful. Some units have "mental health days" that caregivers may use to take time off after a patient dies in order to attend to their own needs. It is suggested that caregivers find ways of having fun and developing leisure interests away from the job. Following good health practicies, such as getting exercise, proper nutrition, and rest, are also encouraged (Kalish 1985).

For some caregivers, having expertise in an area of health care may be equated with achieving mastery and control over that area. Equating the role of a physician with that of an omnipotent healer may be practiced by society, as well as by physicians and students. Feifel (1965) suggests that physicians as a group demonstrate *more* fear of death than others and may have entered medicine as a way of dealing with their above-average fears of death. Continuing the myth of the physician as a powerful healer may interfere not only with the ability of physicians to give care, but also with their self-awareness (Cassileth 1979, Spikes and Holland 1975). Garfield (1978) notes that physicians rarely discuss their personal feelings regarding specific patients and there are few or no structured mechanisms that allow such discussions to take place. The result is that the medical community participates in perpetuating the myth that physicians do not need to deal with their feelings, and this belief may have severe emotional consequences for some.

Garfield (1977) describes defense mechanisms physicians may employ, such as saying, "I can't get emotionally involved." "How long has this horrid affliction persisted?" is Garfield's response, for he maintains that emotional difficulties related to confronting life-threatening disease are normal rather than the exception. Denying this normal human behavior may force health care professionals to resort to extreme psychological defense mechanisms.

Denial on the part of the health professional has received considerable attention. Garfield (1978) describes an oncologist who stated that he had never had a patient who died. Further investigation revealed that when a patient seemed near death, the oncologist transferred the patient to avoid being the physician of record on the death certificate. When treatment toward cure was no longer a possibility, the physician denied that he had any responsibility to continue the relationship. Thus he perceived that maintaining emotional and physical comfort and managing pain were not part of his perception of medical practice. While this example may seem extreme, Weisman (1977) notes that no one should underestimate the tendency to deny and that sharing concerns with others can be instructive and beneficial, and can provide insight into one's professional practice.

It has been shown that nurses who conceal job-related stress exhibit reactions such as physical and emotional distancing from patients, families, and staff and feelings of inadequacy, anger, frustration, and impatience; they may also express a desire to leave their current job and/or the nursing field. Such concealment results in stress-related illness and/or burnout (Larson 1987). Extreme psychological defense mechanisms such as anger, denial, depression, resignation, somatic symptoms, exhaustion, burnout, and disturbed interpersonal relationships may be exhibited by health care professionals (Garfield 1978, Larson 1987, Spikes and Holland 1975, Raphael 1982). Such reactions may indicate the need for the health care professional to seek support in coping.

Depending on the nature of the defensive behaviors, support in coping may range from collegial support, clinical supervision, and counseling to hospitalization. It is critical for professionals to maintain a nonjudgmental attitude toward the health professional who is in need of psychological help, despite the fact that such patients appear to be even more threatening than patients who are not involved in health care. Literature on health care providers who are in need of medical and/or psychiatric intervention has been mainly anecdotal. The author observed the staff of an in-patient psychiatric unit repeatedly ignore and avoid a psychotic patient who was also a qualified surgeon, although the staff continued to respond to other patients in the unit. Student nurses expressed the erroneous belief that a health care professional "should not" be in need of psychological help, as if having knowledge of an illness could inoculate one against that illness.

It appears that health care professionals who become patients may have feelings of conflict regarding their assumption of the patient role and relinquishment of the provider role. Feelings of low self-esteem, feelings of guilt and shame, and feelings of denial of the need for psychological help may be common to those who perceive themselves to be all-powerful caregivers (Caroselli-Karinja and Zboray 1986, Piner and Miler 1952). The inability to accept help may lead to a continuance and/or worsening of inappropriate psychological defense mechanisms.

Interventions for health care professionals who care for dying patients involve education regarding the needs of the patient and families, as well as helping professionals identify and deal with their own attitudes. Health care professionals are encouraged to ventilate their feelings regarding patients. Feelings of inadequacy, guilt, and anger may be elicited and revealed to be related to unresolved feelings of omnipotence. Reality testing is used to demonstrate that feelings of worthlessness and despair are irrational and thus to enable the caregiver to function more effectively. Encouraging open expression of grief is emphasized. Each health care professional is assisted in finding a tolerable level of feelings evoked by patients and to view this level of tolerance as a human limit rather than as a personal inadequacy. Viewing the acceptance of professional help as support for one's human tolerance may help professional caregivers accept help without feeling guilty about the need for it (Raphael 1982, Spikes and Holland 1975).

Educating Caregivers

Literature on nurses' attitudes toward death and dying patients seemed to indicate that when death was encountered early in the nurse's career as a student, it was experienced as stressful. Lack of preparation for experiences with death and dying patients left nurses ill-prepared to cope. Quint (who currently publishes under the name J.Q. Benoliel) notes (1967) that students' attitudes, aquired through acculturation, affect their behaviors as practitioners and interfere with their ability to provide care to dying patients. Following Quint's research, the study of attitudes of nurses toward death and dying patients increased. Educators compiled materials to teach nursing students about death and dying, and courses were designed to teach skills to facilitate coping with death and dying patients. Altering attitudes is perceived to be a long-range process, and difficulties continue to be reported relating to the measurement of attitudes and behaviors, the length of the educational program, and whether or not the program contains an experiential component (Lev 1986).

One study found that courses for health care professionals that focus on death and dying can be effective in changing attitudes and behaviors toward dying patients. There was less fear of dying patients and fewer avoidance behaviors associated with nurses' dealing with the dying after such a course (Lev 1986). The course was fourteen weeks in length and had an experiential as well as a didactic component. A key premise was the belief that a long-term, guided experience of involvement with dying patients and their families facilitates for the student those tasks involved *in dealing with* grief and the grieving process. A common outcome of the mourning process in students is a greater sensitivity to the needs of patients and families which results in more humane care. McCorkle (1982) notes that the result of programs in death education for health care professionals may be that students develop a support network that provides appropriate feedback, encourages further development of collegial support, and provides a buffer to prevent grief.

Stephens (Werner and Korsch 1976) identified critical issues in educating medical students and stated that students' feelings of vulnerability were heightened after encounters with death and dying patients. To prevent students from protecting themselves by dehumanizing patients, Stephens advocated providing support systems for medical students. Believing support could be provided most effectively in small groups, he proposed year-long groups that met several hours each week. The group leaders were practicing physicians, rather than psychiatrists or behavioral scientists, in order to provide students with role models. One of the teaching strategies used was videotaping patient interviews in order to critique the interviews in the group. Allowing the student to express emotions without fear of being seen as weak or unsuitable for professional advancement was stressed. The objective of the group was to allow students to be aware of their feelings and to develop adaptive defenses that would not interfere with relating sensitively to patients and providing comprehensive care.

Conclusions

Further research appears to be needed to determine whether caregivers who experience the frequent death of patients experience more disenfranchised grief than do those whose patients die less frequently. It has not yet been determined whether there is a relationship between the caregiver's perception of the appropriateness of care and disenfranchised grief. Whether disenfranchised grief has long-term effects in caregivers has also not been determined. No doubt the reader can formulate other questions relating to the effects of disenfranchised grief on caregivers.

Identifying the grief reaction, accepting the wide range of behaviors associated with grief, examining one's motives for working with dying patients, and accepting one's human tolerance all appear to be important in preventing disenfranchised grief. One hospice professional announced she was leaving the hospice setting and used the analogy of a relay runner when she said, "I ran with the baton for as long as I could, but now it's time for me to pass it to you."

Distancing from patients may lead to nonhumane care for the patients, as well as to disenfranchised grief for the health care professional. Open communication seems to be invaluble in preventing both nonhumane care for patients and disenfranchised grief for caregivers. Perhaps by assisting people to develop patterns of open communication when they are students, educators can prevent maladaptive reactions in both patients and caregivers.

References

Benoliel, J.Q. 1975. "The Realities of Work." In *Humanizing Health Care*, edited by J. Howard and A. Strauss. New York: Wiley.

Brody, B.A. 1988. "Ethical Questions Raised by the Persistent Vegetative Patient." *Hastings Center Report* 18:1, 33–37.

Buber, M. 1965. *The Knowledge of Man*. New York: Harper and Row.

Bugen, L.A. 1977. "Human Grief: A Model for Prediction and Intervention." *American Journal of Orthopsychiatry* 47:2, 196–206.

Caroselli-Karinja, M.F., and S.D. Zboray. 1986. "The Impaired Nurse." *Journal of Psychosocial Nursing* 24:6, 14–19.

Cassileth, B.R. 1979. *The Cancer Patient: Social and Medical Aspects of Care*. Philadelphia: Lea and Febinger.

Clark, M.D. 1984. "Loss and Grief Behaviors: Application to Nursing Managerial Practice. *Nursing Administration Quarterly* (Spring), 53–60.

Dolan, M.B. 1988. "The Coding Question: Noncancer Patients." *Archives of the Foundation of Thanatology* 14:3.

Feifel, H. 1965. "The Function of Attitudes toward Death." *Death and Dying: Attitudes of Patient and Doctor* 5:11, 632–41.

———. 1977. *New Meanings of Death.* New York: McGraw-Hill.

Freud, S. 1930. *Civilization and Its Discontents.* 3d ed., trans. by Jo Riviere, 1946. London: Holgar Press.

Garfield, C.A. 1977. "The Impact of Death on the Health-Care Professional. In *New Meanings of Death.* edited by Herman Feifel. New York: McGraw-Hill.

———. 1978. *Psychosocial Care of the Dying Patient.* New York: McGraw-Hill.

Kalish, R.A. 1985. *Death, Grief, and Caring Relationships.* Monterey, Calif.: Brooks/Cole.

Klaus, D., and B. Shinners. 1982–83. "Professional Roles in a Self-Help Group for the Bereaved." *Omega* 13:4, 361–75.

Larson, D.G. 1987. "Helper Secrets." *Journal of Psychosocial Nursing* 25:4, 20–27.

Lerea, L.E., and B.F. LiMauro. 1982. "Grief among Healthcare Workers: A Comparative Study." *Journal of Gerontology* 37:5, 604–08.

Lester, D. 1988. "Suicide and Disease." *Archives of the Foundation of Thanatology* 14:3.

Lev, E.L. 1981. "Developing a Model for Teaching Chemotherapy of Hematologic Disorders." *National Intravenous Therapy Association* 4:5, 337–46.

———. 1986. "Effects of Course in Hospice Nursing on Attitudes and Behaviors of BSN Students and Graduates toward Death and Dying Patients." Ph.D. diss., Teachers College, Columbia University.

Lindemann, E. 1944. "Symptomatology and Management of Acute Grief." *American Journal of Psychiatry* 101, 141–48.

McCorkle, R. 1982. "Death Education for Advanced Nursing Practice." In *Death Education for the Health Professional,* edited by J.Q. Benoliel. New York: Hemisphere.

Parkes, C.M. 1974. *Bereavement: Studies of Grief in Adult Life.* New York: International Universities Press.

Piner, M., and B. Miler. 1952. *When Doctors Are Patients.* New York: Norton.

Quint, J.C. 1967. *The Nurse and the Dying Patient.* New York: Macmillan.

Raphael, B. 1982. *The Anatomy of Bereavement.* New York: Basic Books.

Raphael, B., B. Singh, and L. Bradbury. 1980. "Disaster: The Helper's Perspective." *Medical Journal of Australia* 1, 445–47.

Schoenberg, B., A.C. Carr, D. Peretz, and A.H. Kutscher. 1972. *Psychosocial Aspects of Terminal Care.* New York: Columbia University Press.

Shanfield, S.B. 1981. "The Mourning of the Health Care Professional: An Important Element in Education about Death and Loss." *Death Education* 4, 385–95.

Sheard, T. 1984. "Dealing with the Nurse's Grief." *Nursing Forum* 21:1, 43–45.

Spikes, J., and J. Holland. 1975. "The Physician's Response to the Dying Patient." In *Psychological Care of the Medically Ill,* edited by James J. Strain and Stanley Grossman. New York: Appleton-Century Crofts.

Stowers, S.J. 1983. "Nurses Cry, Too." *Nursing Management* 14:4, 63–64.

Vachon, M.L.S. 1978. "Motivation and Stress Experienced by Staff Working with the Terminally Ill." *Death Education* 2, 113–22.

Weisman, A.D. 1977. "The Psychiatrist and the Inexorable." In *New Meanings of Death,* edited by Herman Feifel. New York: McGraw-Hill.

Werner, E.R., and B.M. Korsch. 1976. "The Vulnerability of the Medical Student: Posthumous Presentation of L.L. Stephens' Ideas." *Pediatrics* 57:3, 321–28.

26
Hospice Work with AIDS-related Disenfranchised Grief

Elliott J. Rosen

T his chapter will address various dimensions of hospice work with AIDS patients and their families, particularly as it relates to the phenomenon of disenfranchised grief. We will examine some aspects of hospice and its philosophy of health care delivery, proceed to explore the relationship between AIDS and disenfranchised grief, look at specific bereavement patterns in AIDS survivors, and propose some general guidelines for hospice workers in their work with these patients and their loved ones.

An Overview of the Hospice Movement

If the publication of Elizabeth Kübler-Ross's *On Death and Dying* (1969) can be credited with increasing the attention paid to the phenomena of illness, death, and grieving, we must look to the hospice movement as having begun the process of institutionalizing our concern in these areas. As recently as 1974 there was one hospice program in the United States, treating a handful of patients and virtually unknown even to the medical community, let alone the lay public. By 1987 there were 1,683 recognized hospice programs serving more than 170,000 patients and their families (Parker 1988). These numbers grow significantly each year as hospice becomes the norm in palliative care throughout the country. Hospice programs, of course, take a variety of forms, and the predominant mode is now home care, rather than a hospital- or nursing home–based model. Hospice programs clearly represent a dramatic change in social policy and a revolution in the health care sector which has led to a significant shift in the way we look at the terminally ill. This has fostered a concomitant concern with patients' families, both during the period of illness and after death (Rosen 1987).

The present-day hospice also represents a reaction to the depersonalization of hospitals and to the technological developments in medicine that create deficiencies in humane care of dying patients. Although the roots of the hospice concept are centuries old, credit for the modern hospice movement belongs to Dr. Cicely Saunders, whose London hospice, founded in 1961, broke the ground. It is important to note that the British hospice movement, although representing a revolution of sorts in the medical community, nevertheless was rooted in strong, traditional Christian values. This is reflected in the names of many of the English hospices: Saint Joseph's, Saint Ann's, Saint Margaret's, Saint Luke's, and, of course, Dr. Saunders's own Saint Christopher's. The North American hospice movement is decidedly more secular and claims nondenominational, nonchurch–related institutional and community support (Stoddard 1978). It is, however, similarly rooted in traditional Judeo-Christian values, and its personnel, who are drawn to the care of the ill and dying, often identify themselves as church/synagogue affiliated and credit their religious/spiritual values as strong components of their motivation for their work in hospice (Vachon 1987). Along with the care of the dying patient, hospice is committed to serving the family, and many, if not most, hospice programs incorporate bereavement follow-ups (and often ambitious bereavement programs) as part of their work.

This brief overview of the hospice movement is presented here because of its relevance to our consideration of hospice care for AIDS patients, whose loved ones have special needs as they struggle with their grief and loss. The nature of the AIDS patient and the ways in which his or her "family" is defined may vary in many respects from traditional community standards. Although most hospice personnel are deeply committed to the care of patients, it should be noted that such personnel, both professionals and volunteers (the latter group representing a significant sector of the hospice effort), come from backgrounds that make it difficult for them to accept the dramatically divergent nature of the survivors with whom they must deal. AIDS continues to assail in particular the homosexual and IV-drug-using communities, and terms such as *family* and *loved one* perforce take on new meaning. Geis, Fuller, and Rush (1986) confirmed in their study of lovers of AIDS victims that religion and the religious community have added enormously to the burden borne by AIDS survivors. The idea that death and damnation are punishment for bad behavior, particularly sexual, was felt strongly by the respondents in their study. Thus, planning for bereavement support for AIDS survivors will require new ways of thinking and planning for hospice personnel that will, indeed, demand flexibility.

In 1986 there were approximately nine thousand deaths from AIDS, and of these patients more than two thousand were served by a hospice (Parker 1988). In each succeeding year, the numbers of AIDS-related deaths have grown, as have the number of such patients served by hospice programs. In fact, there are now hospice programs exclusively dedicated to working with AIDS patients. The bereavement follow-up in these programs is obviously more naturally in tune with the special needs of survivors and reflects an accumulated experience base in treating the disease and in counseling patients' loved ones (Beresford 1986). However, outside large urban areas, few hospice programs are likely to be dedicated to AIDS patients exclusively, and it is necessary for workers who will be working with cases such as these to be attuned to the special needs of this group.

AIDS and Disenfranchised Grief

In few other areas of care for the dying and their loved ones is the concept of disenfranchised grief likely to be more powerfully demonstrated than with AIDS. Doka (1986, 1987) and others (Gyulay 1975, Folta and Deck 1986) have pointed out that when survivors are denied the opportunity to acknowledge openly or publicly mourn a death, a phenomenon is likely to develop which alienates and disenfranchises the mourner from the opportunity for public support and grief resolution. Needless to say, this disenfranchisement can be actively fostered by others. However, there are cases where it is likely a function of the mourner's own experience, quite apart from any external reality. The nature of AIDS and its psychosocial meaning relegate both the patient and his or her survivors to a marginal place in society. Disenfranchisement of the mourner is fostered by the dreadfulness of the illness and its perceived communicability, its social stigma, and the general attitude of fault or blame assigned by society to AIDS sufferers, as well as to their loved ones. While clearly no longer a disease that touches only one sector of society, AIDS remains a malady that is viewed as reflecting aberrant sexual/social behavior. The homosexual and IV-drug-abusing segments of society are perceived as both responsible for their own fate, as well as dangerous to the population at large. Nongay, nondrug-abusing AIDS sufferers are frequently referred to as "innocent victims," as opposed to those who somehow are not "innocent."

Hospice professionals are acutely aware that all grief work neither begins nor ends at the time of death. Hospice bereavement programs attempt to address the issues related to anticipatory grief as well as carefully plan appropriate follow-up for survivors. While this is true for all patients' families, the AIDS patient's survivors present certain issues in bereavement care that are qualitatively different, the most important of which is that the terms *family, loved ones,* and *survivors* take on significantly new meaning. Disenfranchisement from the entitlement to grieve the death of the AIDS-deceased may, in fact, be considered a typical rather than unique circumstance. It is instructive to note that the grief observed in AIDS survivors may, as a rule, more close approximate what is typically described as pathological grief reaction, incorporating rage, fear, and shame far out of proportion to the "normal" parameters of mourning. AIDS survivors appear likely to struggle more with grief that remains unresolved, and parents of AIDS victims would be at greater risk for developing the symptoms attendant to interminable grieving (Rosen 1988b). Thus, AIDS presents a particular challenge to a hospice bereavement program: to develop a strategy for grief resolution which accepts both atypical patterns of grief and disenfranchisement as the norm.

It has been noted that the need for survivors to look to socially accepted "rules" for grieving is a common phenomenon (Worden 1982). Our society accepts, unambiguously, the entitlement of parents, spouses, siblings, and, to a somewhat lesser degree, other relatives and close friends to mourn a death. Additionally, there are consensually agreed-upon temporal limits that dictate our responses to the death of a loved one. It is not unusual for others to criticize the mourner's reactions if they are characterized by too uncommon an emotional intensity or too protracted as time limit. While these limits may vary, depending upon the ethnic or cultural values of families (Rosen 1988a), as well as on other factors, they are generally accepted by others. The inherent nature of disenfranchised grief is the refusal of others to validate or sanction grief that defies accepted standards, and thus many who grieve the death of a loved one from AIDS may be automatically disenfranchised.

Bereavement Patterns in AIDS Survivors

Although there is as yet a lack of empirical research that addressed the unique grief of AIDS survivors, many anecdotal reports, and my own observations in working with this population, suggest some common characteristics that should contribute to our understanding of the issues with which AIDS survivors struggle. The following is in no way intended to be a complete description of the unique aspects of AIDS grief, but rather is an attempt to highlight four of the more likely issues that have been observed as powerful and not uncommon manifestations of this grief. For each issue a short description of a case will be presented.

1. The foremost factor in coping with an AIDS-related death would appear to be the *powerful social stigma* that surrounds the disease. The isolation and rejection that accompany AIDS do not cease at the point of death but continue for the survivor long after.

> Jim a successful attorney, had lived quietly and unobtrusively with his lover, Pat, a stockbroker, for ten years. Neither had "gone public" regarding their homosexuality, and when Pat was diagnosed with AIDS, the couple determined that they would maintain the status quo as long as possible. Pat's condition deteriorated and Jim cared for him at home, finally calling upon the local community hospice for help. The response was positive, and two hospice volunteers provided enormous help for the couple during the last few months of Pat's life. Following Pat's death, however, Jim reported that

neighbors in his apartment house ignored him and seemed to go out of their way to avoid contact. He feared that he was "simply being paranoid," but some five weeks after the death the co-op board received a petition requesting that they review the "acceptability of certain elements" who were living in the complex. For his entire life Jim had been private and circumspect about his homosexuality and never acknowledged his sexual preference publicly, or, more recently, the nature of his relationship with Pat. The reaction of his neighbors and others prompted Jim to change in ways that had heretofore been unquestioned in his life. He instituted a lawsuit against his co-op board, called upon a local gay activist organization for help, and began a long-overdue process of finding a way to "be himself."

2. The *lack of social santions,* particularly for homosexual relationships, may automatically disenfranchise the mourner, not only invalidating his grief but creating a situation where otherwise commonly accepted rights of survivorship are denied.

When Martin, thirty-four, saw that his condition was deteriorating and that he would need more intense care, he decided to leave the large city in which he was living with his lover, Sean, and return to his family's home in the suburbs where his parents and sister had agreed to care for him. Sean came for visits frequently, often staying overnight for the weekends. His relationship with his lover's family was strained, and although they tolerated his presence they remained unaccepting of the men's homosexual relationship. A local hospice program was involved with his family in the last few weeks of Martin's life, and the social worker made some efforts to facilitate communication between Sean and Martin's parents and sister. This was basically unsuccessful, and some months later, when Martin died, his family summarily refused to allow Sean in the house and would not allow him to attend the wake or funeral. Sean was rebuffed when he requested that he be given certain of Martin's possessions that were in the family home. He soon thereafter suffered a severe grief reaction, which resulted in clinical depression accompanied by serious thoughts of suicide. Psychotherapy with Sean addressed, in particular, his need to have his loss and grief validated, and this was ultimately accomplished by his joining a bereavement group for AIDS survivors.

3. A great concern for many AIDS survivors is the *fear regarding their own health status.* This may be quite a legitimate concern, particularly for survivors who have had sexual contact with the deceased. In such cases it is vital that the survivor be tested and, in fact, retested for some reasonable period, to determine whether he or she is HIV-positive. However, this fear of contamination has also been observed in other survivors who have no rational justification for assuming that they are ill. In this latter case what may be operating is a variation on the theme of disenfranchement.

Marion, a fifty-nine-year-old widow, had recently lost her daughter, Louise, to AIDS after having been marginally involved with her physical care during the last year of the illness. When she explained her request for seeking psychotherapy this otherwise rational, well-functioning woman contended that she was certainly HIB-positive and wanted to prepare for her own death. Upon questioning there seemed little reason to assume that Marion was ill or had contracted the disease. Her conviction was firm, however, and it became increasingly clear that although on one level her obsession with her own health was related to an overidentification with her dead child, in a more complex way it allowed her to cope with her grief. Marion felt cut off from family and friends who had, she felt, spurned her since her daughter's death. People close to her commiserated with her to the extent of generally sympathizing with her loss, but their sympathy was often accompanied by veiled suggestions that her drug-abusing daughter was not truly worthy of being mourned. What emerged was Marion's deeper belief that she was somehow responsible for the fact that Lousie had "turned out bad" and that she was thus not entitled to mourn her child. Work with Marion focused upon accepting her daughter's having made choices for herself as an adult, understanding her own guilt and looking at her child-rearing more objectively, and helping her to accept her entitlement to mourn and to reach out actively to others for help. It was this latter factor that proved most helpful; when Marion became convinced of her entitlement to grieve, and in a sense enfranchised herself, she was able to turn to others and find ways to have her grief validated.

4. The *need for secrecy and the shame and guilt* that families experience in relation to their children's life-style and/or sexual preference is a common difficulty in coping with the illness. Survivors are likely to create a position for themselves with friends and extended family which leaves them alienated and disenfranchised in their grief. Such a condition is not likely to occur only after death but will be present during the illness, creating problems in patient care and major obstacles to the process of anticipatory grieving.

When Donald left home at twenty-one, he and his older sister, Louise, remained in close contact by letter, telephone, and occasional visits over the years. While his family "knew" that Donald was gay, the subject had never been discussed with him or among family members. Louise never discussed it with her husband or her three grown children (although they also "knew"), and she and her mother never spoke about it. Donald lived a productive life in a distant city for twenty-five years. When he called hs sister and asked her to come and see him because he needed to speak with her about a problem, she took the next plane to be at his side. She was shocked to find him quite ill and debilitated, in what were to be the last six months of his life. He was being cared for at home by his lover and an excellent hospice team, and Louise shuttled back and forth to see him over the next several months. Their widowed mother, Marie, made two short trips to see her son, becoming quite ill herself on both occasions. She barely spoke to her son's partner and refused to accept offers of conversation with hospice team members. The hospice social worker offered many suggestions to Louise for opening up the subject of Donald's homosexuality and imminent death with their mother but soon realized that the secrecy with which they had always dealt with the subject could not be violated. Louise was able to talk to her brother about his secret life for the first time and was encouraged to open up the subject with her own family, which she did. While she was recovering from her loss a year later she appeared with her mother in a bereavement group for AIDS survivors (she lied to her mother about where they were going!), and after a number of weeks, during which Marie refused to talk, she finally began to open up. She had not felt entitled to grieve openly (despite her profound depression) because "these things are not okay for us Italians." The group was helpful in enfranchising her as a legitimate mourner, despite the shame she felt about how her son died.

These four categories of bereavement patterns only serve to suggest some general parameters for understanding the experience of AIDS survivors. Other issues that are fairly common and may result in the disenfranchisement of the mourner are homophobia, both on the part of others and internalized, the survivor's own positive diagnosis of AIDS or ARC, a positive HIV positive diagnosis, the utter fatigue that accompanies caring for someone with such a complicated and debilitating disease, the sense of guilt or sin that may be already present internally or that is fostered by society, and the severe impact of multiple losses, which are often present for many AIDS survivors.

Guidelines for Hospice Workers

There are a number of guidelines that may prove helpful to hospice team members who work with the bereavement issues of AIDS survivors. Each of these has a special relationship to issues of disenfranchisement that are central to an understanding of grief reactions in this population.

1. It is a general rule, of course, that the facilitation of grief does not begin with the patient's death. It begins long before that time in the process of helping loved ones to commence anticipatory grieving. There is an ironic aspect of anticipatory grief in response to AIDS: death is undeniable, and there seldom exists any margin for hope, particularly in end stages of the disease. Hope for miracles is seldom expressed in the face of AIDS. It thus becomes necessary to support patients and their loved ones in preparing for death and discussing possibilities for healing in the future. The AIDS patient should be actively included in this process to the fullest extent possible. The actual physical care of any patient is a powerful component of anticipatory grief, but a further difficulty encountered with AIDS patients' loved ones is

an occasional aversion to involving themselves in active physical care of the patient. The anxiety that accompanies fear of contagion cannot be ignored and is not limited to family members but often includes medical care personnel as well. Hospice team members must be attuned to this phenomenon and create alternatives to direct physical care. The goal is to enable families to participate in care of the patient in such a way as to avoid their disenfranchisement from the process of anticipatory grieving, and this may be accomplished in ways other than direct physical caretaking.

2. A point the author has found intriguing in his work is that an unusually large percentage of AIDS patients and their families express powerful feelings of spirituality and closeness to the Divine. While it may be argued that this is not unusual for people in terminal stages of any illness, my observation is that it is far more intense and more typical with AIDS than with other conditions. It is also interesting to note that this is not necessarily a turn toward *organized* religion, but rather to a more universal spirituality that easily includes disparate elements of a variety of religious faiths. In a recent group therapy session of persons with AIDS, a conversation took place among a few members (one a fundamentalist Christian, one raised as a Catholic but estranged from the church, and one Jewish) regarding their closeness to God, his unquestioning love for them, and the certainty of a kinder afterlife which would surely have sounded foreign to theologians of any one of these religions. What they were expounding was a kind of syncretism of the warmest and most loving dimensions of all religion, with little concern for the particular moral or ethical teachings of any one.

The meaning of this phenomenon is unclear, and I do not have any evidence beyond my own experience and the anecdotal reports of others to substantiate it. However, it is an observation worth noting and should be considered seriously by those who work with AIDS patients and their loved ones. One possible explanation is that the terminal stages of an illness often trigger a process of "life review," which may include a consideration of one's past moral behavior. Many AIDS victims have led lives as society's disenfranchised and in the final stages of life may experience spirituality as a way to find the love and acceptance denied them in their lives. Another aspect of this life review is the harsh reality that most AIDS patients are quite young and have only begun to live their lives before becoming ill. Thus, a turn to the spiritual may be an attempt to find meaning in a foreshortened life. Whatever its significance this spiritual turning can create an opportunity for hospice workers to move even closer to patients and families and to create an atmosphere condusive to good grief resolution in the future.

3. Hospice personnel must demonstrate flexibility in the way they think about family. The whole concept of "family" may be greatly complicated in cases of AIDS, and it is important for workers to attune themselves to the needs and desires of the patient. As was discussed earlier, there are frequently

cases in which competing demands are made by loved ones who see themselves as legitimate and others as less so. Herein lies the roots for disenfranchised grief, and it is a prodigious task to find methods for including all those persons who deserve entitlement. The key to success in this endeavor is an understanding that the inclusion of any one person as an entitled mourner does not automatically disenfranchise another. It is helpful to consider that the patient should be actively included in identifying significant others whenever possible. This can be a difficult task, involving careful mediation and attending to the desires of the patient and the sensitivities of family members. In later stages of AIDS, as with other illnesses, patients may become incapable of lucid communication, and thus workers should make every effort to determine from the patient, before the onset of dementia, coma, or mental incapacitation, who is to be considered as part of the "family." This will often require the worker's interpretation of the patient's wishes to loved ones and includes a responsibility to enfranchise significant others to be part of the grieving family.

4. A corollary to this previous point is the awareness that survivors of AIDS are frequently plagued by feelings of ambivalence related to the stigma and shame that accompany the disease. Some survivors may not wish to have the cause of death revealed, while others may have motives for doing the opposite. (The author recently treated a family who had published an obituary in the local paper which announced the cause of their son's death as cancer; the same day a death notice appeared in another paper—placed by their son's lover—which acknowledged his death from AIDS.) It is helpful for some communication between these two "factions" *and* the patient to take place before death, rather than allowing the two to vie later for legitimacy, each undoubtedly claiming (and believing) that his or her wishes reflect those of the deceased. In some situations this failed communication has existed for years and will directly result in the disenfranchisement of someone. It may be possible for the trusted hospice worker to effectuate necessary acceptance and make peace, although such a situation can raise the difficult issue of confidentiality. The paradox created here is that the worker wishes to mediate between the two factions and may feel the necessity of revealing confidential information given to him or her by others (or even the patient) in order to achieve the goal of enfranchisement. As a family therapist the author frequently finds it necessary to explain to all involved parties that it may become important to reveal information when it will aid in the goal of better communication and ultimate family peace. The issue of confidentiality should not be ignored, but at the same time we must be aware of our commitment to the well-being of the survivors, particularly those who might, without our help, find themselves disenfranchised from their entitlement to grieve.

5. Workers must be attuned to the possibility that mourners may be disenfranchised by their own religious beliefs and/or by the faith community.

As noted earlier, this is not an unusual experience for persons with AIDS and their families. It is possible to intervene here, however, by identifying sympathetic clergy who can play an important role in demonstrating the loving and accepting dimensions of religion and the faith community. It is also worthwhile to provide values clarification sessions for personnel so that they can be even better attuned to the "moral baggage" that they bring to their work. Coupled with the strong feelings of spirituality discussed earlier, a sympathetic member of the clergy and a hospice worker with a deeper understanding of his or her own spiritual self can be enormously helpful to patients and their families. It is also possible to encourage the development of special rituals to ease the pain of loss, as well as to enfranchise the survivors as part of a larger grieving community. A contemporary and poignant example of this is the enormous memorial quilts created throughout the United States. In a recent bereavement group one member shared her weekly progress in designing and executing her quite beautiful contribution to the giant quilt. Group members gave advice and suggestions and vicariously participated in this nationwide effort of enfranchisement.

6. Along with the many psychological dimensions of AIDS there is the very real fear of contamination by the disease. Survivors may fear that they are infected with AIDS, may know that they are, or may be diagnosed HIV-positive. This will contribute to their disenfranchisement in many ways and can result in depression and suicidal risk. It is important to help survivors realistically assess these risks and suggest ways in which they can find appropriate medical care as well as psychosocial supports.

7. Finally, it is the author's strong conviction that more than any other method, groups for AIDS survivors are the most effective way to facilitate grief work. As has been shown here, disenfranchisement is likely to be inherent in the grief process for AIDS. Ultimately there can be no better way to alleviate this condition and invite people to rejoin the mainstream than by helping them to connect in a sympathetic and supportive way with other sufferers. Groups for AIDS survivors are available in many places, as are groups of HIV-positive persons and persons with AIDS. In some places workers have begun a process of helping to create networks for AIDS survivors, and recent developments in public health policy may make funding for outreach even more available. In a letter recently received from a participant in an AIDS bereavement group, the value of finding this kinship with others was powerfully expressed:

> The hardest part was feeling that no one could ever understand and that no one would ever want to be with me again. Sitting with these people for all those weeks made me realize that we are all part of something bigger and

that I'm not alone. I know now that I don't have to feel dirty and ashamed because I had a son with AIDS. I wish there were some way to tell our stories to everyone so that the world would understand that there is nothing wrong with us and that we never have to feel ashamed or alone again.

References

Beresford, L. 1986. "AIDS and Bereavement." *NHO Hospice News* (Oct.), 4–7.

Doka, K.J. 1986. "Loss upon Loss: The Impact of Death after Divorce." *Death Studies* 10, 441–49.

———. 1987. "Silent Sorrow: Grief and the Loss of Significant Others." *Death Studies* 11, 455–69.

Folta, J., and E. Deck. 1986. "Grief, the Funeral, and the Friend." In *Acute Grief and the Funeral,* edited by V. Pine, A.H. Kutschner, D. Peretz, R.C. Slater, R. DeBell, R.J. Volk, and D.J. Cherico. Springfield, Ill.: Thomas.

Geis, S.B., R.L. Fuller, and J. Rush. 1986. "Lovers of AIDS Victims: Psychosocial Stresses and Counseling Needs." *Death Studies* 10, 43–53.

Gyulay, J. 1975. "The Forgotten Grievers." *American Journal of Nursing* 75:9, 1476–79.

Kübler-Ross, E. 1969. *On Death and Dying.* New York: Macmillan.

Parker, A.T. 1988. "A Report on Hospice in America." *Thanatos* 13:1, 4–5.

Rosen, E.J. 1987. "Teaching Family Therapy Concepts to the Hospice Team." *American Journal of Hospice Care* 4:4, 39–44.

———. 1988a. "The Ethnic and Cultural Dimensions of Work with Hospice Families." *American Journal of Hospice Care* 5:4, 16–21.

———. 1988b. "Family Therapy in Cases of Interminable Grief for the Death of a Child." *Omega: Journal of Death and Dying.* 19:3, 187–202.

Stoddard, S. 1978 . *The Hospice Movement.* New York: Vintage.

Vachon, M.L.S. 1987. *Occupational Stress in the Care of the Critically Ill, the Dying, and the Bereaved.* Washington, D.C.: Hemisphere.

Worden, W. 1982. *Grief Counseling and Grief Therapy.* New York: Springer.

27

The Counselor and the Disenfranchised Griever

David K. Meagher

The Grief Process

Of all the stresses one confronts in life, the death of a loved one appears to be the most difficult with which to cope. Left alone by the event of the death, calling upon personal resources that never seem quite adequate, even in the best of times, one seeks solace and support. It is in this time of sorrow that the plaintive individual, seeking understanding and support, turns to those significant others with whom he or she has meaningful relationships. Social and familial support are essential contributing factors in a successful process of grief resolution.

Grief is a process of physiological, social, and somatic reaction to the perception of a loss (Rando 1984). It is a holistic process that is necessary, normal, and universal. Grief is a response inherent in being a human (Barton 1979). In a loss of a loved one through death, it must occur. All humans grieve. After suffering the loss of a loved one in death there is a period of time during which the affected person is distressed and unable to function as she did prior to the loss. She becomes the object of sympathetic and/or empathic care. Recovery occurs when this grieved person replans her life and achieves a new and independent level of functioning (Parkes and Weiss 1983). Grief that is absent, masked, or suppressed is abnormal and becomes pathological.

Grief should be a healing process. As such, it generally includes a succession of rituals involving social support designed to help initiate recovery. The grief process relies strongly on the presence of established forms of socially approved belief systems and mourning rituals. It is an important part of the usual means of dealing with loss (Schoenberg et al. 1970). In the disruption and confusion of grief, the rituals provide direction and meaning to the griever.

Schneider (1984) suggests that while all attempts to cope and resolve grief involve difficulty, the most difficult loss to support occurs when the assumption is made that people who make anomalous life choices or have deviant lifestyles do not deserve support. The social response is one of rejection, shunning and an attitude that "they're getting what they deserve." The result of this attitude is that a person in grief is deprived of the recognition and support necessary for successful grief resolution. This person may be said to be in disenfranchised grief.

This chapter will describe those aspects of grief that are accentuated by disenfranchisement and will discuss the special tasks and coping skills necessitated by the absence of social recognition and support. Last, with the basics of disenfranchised grief in place, principles and techniques of counseling the disenfranchised griever will be presented.

Anita, a thirty-two-year-old immigrant, was a mother of a five-year-old daughter and was receiving welfare assistance when she decided to enroll in a local public college to seek the better life a degree is supposed to bring. During Anita's first year in college, her daughter was removed from her care and placed in foster care by the local social service agency. Child neglect was the reason given for the mother-daughter separation, although Anita professes innocence of any wrongdoing. Subsequent to this, Anita became pregnant and decided to carry the fetus to term. In her second year of college Anita gave birth to a boy. She informed all her instructors of the pregnancy and birth and indicated that she would return to her classes the week following the birth.

Anita did not return for three weeks. When she did return she said nothing about the birth or the additional absences. It was very obvious that she wanted to become inconspicuous in her classes: she would sit in the back of the room and hide behind other students. When questioned about the additional time away from her classes, Anita quietly stated that she had had to be in court on some "minor" legal matter. It was much later in the semester, when advised that she would be able to request a medical withdrawal from her classes if she were able to provide proof of a medical problem associated with the birth, when she described the nature of her current conflict. The day after the birth of her son, social services removed the infant from her care since she had a record of child neglect and was accused of being an abusive parent.

When asked if she had received any help from any person or social service agency after each of the losses, Anita responded in the negative. Her reply to inquiries concerning how she spent her time after the baby was removed from her care was that she cried a great deal. No one seemed to recognize these experiences as legitimate grief; therefore, no one attempted to support Anita in her grief. The prevalent response was: "Everyone is better off with the children in foster care."

Disenfranchised Grief

To disenfranchise is to deprive an individual of a right or a privilege. In the case of grief, the individual is deprived not so much of a right or privilege but of the opportunity to perform a necessary task: grief work. Doka (1986) defines disenfranchised grief as grief that a person experiences when he incurs a loss that is not or cannot be openly acknowledged, publicly mourned, and/or socially supported. Disenfranchised grief is a complicated grief, not simply because it is unrecognized and unsupported, but because it must not be revealed. Revelation may result in a more intense negative social response. This may be particularly the case in an AIDS death, where a homosexual survivor may be perceived as a carrier of the HIV virus. Other disenfranchised loss experiences may include pet loss; death of a lover in an extramarital relationship; fetal loss (through miscarriage and abortion); the excommunicated (including the objects of a social death attitude); the abusive (sometimes alleged) parent(s) who have children taken away from them by local social services; parents who voluntarily give up their children for adoption; and individuals who give up home, family, and community in the "name of love."

As was previously stated, there is strong agreement in the thanatological literature that a major factor influencing the resolution of grief is the presence of social support. Osterweis, Solomon, and Green (1984) describe the need for the availability of supportive others who will permit or elicit an emotional release in the bereaved. Doyle (1980) states it very succinctly when she writes that emergence through all phases of bereavement is, at the very least, dependent upon the individual's expression of feelings to others who are understanding, supportive, and concerned. The grief process relies on the presence of established forms of societally approved belief systems and rituals.

Worden (1982) identified three social factors that seem to play an important role in the development of a complicated grief reaction:

1. A loss that is socially unspeakable (the disenfranchisement caused by AIDS and illicit sexual relationships)
2. A loss that is socially negated, as if it had never occurred (miscarriage and abortion often do not bring on a social recognition of a loss experience)
3. An absence of a social support network for the individual in grief (the outcasting of those who engage in illicit or illegal behaviors)

It is the absence of these social supports that creates a disenfranchised grief response. Particularly it is the absence of a supportive sharing other that contributes to the uniqueness of disenfranchised grief. Schneider (1984) posits that the completion of grief involves an active public phase, involving caring others, which frees and restores the individual from feeling besieged by grief.

Barton (1979) offers a number of possible complicating factors that may lead to disenfranchised grief and difficulties in the expression of feelings related to a loss, and thus difficulties in the grief process:

1. Isolation from the occurrences surrounding the death, resulting in inadequate sensory perceptions necessary for the acknowledgment of its reality

2. Inability of other family members to legitimize the feelings related to grief

3. Lack of access to usual ritual or belief systems employed in the management of loss and the grief process, resulting in an inability to participate in the grief process during the established grief period

4. Dislocation from the usual sociocultural and religious context for the expression of grief

5. Religious conflict, which leads to suppression of feelings

6. Personal isolation, with an inability to establish other supportive relationships after the death of a significant person

Two unique aspects of grief for the person who has been disenfranchised are:

1. The absence of other affected individuals with whom one may share the feelings of loss and pain, thus giving validity to the felt grief

2. An absence of a social environment that will allow for public manifestation of grief and provide for societal permission to grieve

Initially, grief is a time of emptiness, pain, rejection, uncertainty, and fear. The griever is like the child who is not feeling well. He reaches out for the understanding and comforting arms of someone who seems to know what is wrong and how to erase the pain. In death we, the survivors, come together to support each other. We need not speak, for we know what the other is feeling; we are, after all, feeling it ourselves. Our cries are accepted and shared, our loneliness and sense of rejection is lessened. We are among loved ones. Our life, though disrupted, remains somewhat safe and secure. It is from this foundation that we will eventually rebuild our life. The absence of sharing with similarly affected individuals may cause the griever to feel intense anger and jealousy. The anger may be directed at society and its mores, which may be the cause of the lack of recognition and acceptance of the individual as a legitimate griever. Jealousy may be felt, as the disenfranchised observes that "other grievers have each other." The comfort and sharing that the disenfranchised sees taking place in the others is something he severely needs.

Because of the nature of the relationship prior to the death, the disenfranchised griever may not be able to reveal publicly the impact the death has had on him. All emotional responses to the death may have to be made in private. If the relationship between the deceased and the disenfranchised griever was one that could not be publicly revealed, the survivor may have to resort to camouflaging his feelings and thoughts when in public, lest others learn of the relationship. This concern may cause the grieved person to feel fear and frustration. The fear may present itself when one suspects that one's behavior or words will reveal a relationship that society considered illicit. Frustration is the result of the many feelings seeking realization, yet these feelings must be hidden. The griever finds it most difficult to vent the feelings and to cope with the consequences of them on his life. Although most of the functions of grief work can be performed in social isolation, social support from relatives, friends, and other affected individuals may facilitate the process and ameliorate the distress.

Grief Work

Grief is work. It requires active participation on the part of the person in grief. She must perform certain tasks that, upon completion, allow for grief to end and living to continue. A compilation of these tasks, as identified in the literature (Worden 1982, Stroebe and Stroebe 1987, Parkes and Weiss 1983), would be:

> To accept the reality of the loss, search for meaning in the experience, and to arrive at an intellectual recognition and explanation of the loss
>
> To achieve an emotional acceptance of the loss and experience the pain of grief
>
> To adjust to an environment in which the deceased is missing, regaining mastery over one's life
>
> To withdraw emotional energy, reinvesting it in new relationships, thus creating a new identity

Accepting the Reality of the Loss. A person in grief needs to confront and acknowledge that a loss has occurred in order for the adaptive coping process necessary for successful resolution of grief to begin. The griever cannot deny the fact of the loss. He needs to arrive at answers to the following questions: "Why did it happen?" "What will the impact of this death be on the rest of my life?" The person may attempt to protect himself by denying or minimizing the meaning of the loss. This may be accomplished by rationalizing the loss as less significant than it actually is, a conclusion easily reached when there is no evidence to the contrary, as in a socially unrecognized loss. The "illicit" lover may conclude that if the deceased had truly loved him, she would have initiated proceedings to give the relationship social validity. Thus, the griever may say, "If she truly loved me, she would have left her husband and married me."

The survivor of an AIDS-related death may lessen the significance of the loss by focusing on the possibility of contagion caused by the deceased's disease. The statement "If he really cared for me he would not have put me at risk" might be an indication of a denial or reduction of the meaning of the relationship.

The true nature of the relationship may also be denied. The statement "I did not want to have a baby anyway" after a stillbirth, or "The whole relationship was only a physical thing" after the breakup of a love relationship, may be examples of denial. In some disenfranchised grief experiences, denial may manifest itself as a denial that the deceased actually existed; therefore, there is no need to grieve.

Achieving Emotional Acceptance. Pain is a necessary response to the loss of a loved one. The intensity of the pain experienced is directly related to the investment in the relationship. The pain, therefore, must be acknowledged and confronted. In the absence of acknowledgment and confrontation now, the pain will eventually manifest itself. This manifestation may be subtle or it may be obvious, but it will surface. The survivor will have to deal with the pain at the time of the loss, or he will confront it many years later; but he will have to deal with it! A problem lies in the fact that the later manifestation may be in the form of a pathological response. When society does not admit or recognize the sufferer of the pain, it permits the griever to conclude that grieving is unnecessary, especially if he is engaged in denial.

Emotional acceptance occurs when the survivor no longer needs to avoid reminders of the loss for fear of experiencing intense pain and remorse. For this state to be reached, there must be repeated confrontration with every element of the loss until the intensity of distress is diminished to the point where it becomes tolerable: to where the pleasure of recollection outweighs the pain of loss (Parkes and Weiss 1983).

Adjusting to a Changed Environment. Our lives are a compilation of each and every relationship we have had. Each influences us and each is influenced, in turn, by all of our other relationships. All of our relationships fit together to form a whole, similar to a completed puzzle. The loss of one or more parts leaves a gap, the nature (the roles and the person) of which is irreplaceable. The person experiencing this loss must work toward adapting to the missing piece. In a disenfranchised grief experience the griever may not be completely aware of all the missing pieces. He may not be aware of all the ways in which the deceased has affected his life. The result may be a nagging sense of incompleteness even after the griever believes he has come to terms with the loss. He needs to develop new skills for coping. This involves, in part, learning to take on some of the roles that were filled by the deceased, to create a new identity, and to regain mastery over one's life.

Withdrawing Energy and Reinvesting It. Resolution of grief entails a process of divestment. Divestment is a procedure by which one removes his initial investment from one object and reinvests it in another. It consists of two components: introjection and decathexis. Introjection is a process by which the griever creates within her mind a representation or mental image of the deceased (Rando 1984). Decathexis is a process in which all the feelings, thoughts, memories, and expectations that bound the griever to the deceased are gradually worked through by being revived, reviewed, felt, and lessened (Rando 1984). The conclusion of the divestment is the completion of the grief work. Grief ends when the griever is able to say, "I loved [emphasis on the past tense] him when he was alive but I cannot continue to love him, no matter how hard I try. I have learned an important thing about myself. I can and will love again."

In addition to the difficulties all bereaved persons experience in completing this task, the disenfranchised griever has to confront the possibility of becoming involved in a similar experience again. If the grief is disenfranchised because the nature of the relationship was socially outlawed or because it was a relationship that threatened the life of the two principal partners or others, the survivor must examine ways to reinvest that do not recreate a similar threat or harm to himself or others, though he may wonder if he is capable of anything else.

Coping Skills

Grief work requires active participation on the part of the affected survivors. It might also be considered a labor of love, taking care of the self because of the love that was present prior to the death. Escape, avoidance, and suppression are not possible, therefore not constructive, coping responses. No one can remove grief from another. Drugs and alcohol are not successful in eliminating thoughts and feelings; at best they delay the inevitable. Sleep allows for a momentary escape, but one must eventually awaken to the cause of the stress. It is best to confront and work to resolve, to adapt successfully to the consequences of, the loss. To complete these tasks, the disenfranchised griever needs to:

Vent his feelings, to talk about the relationship and the feelings of loss

Validate the relationship for himself

Resolve guilt that may arise because of the nature of the relationship and perhaps the manner in which the death occurred

Find a way to internalize the memory of the deceased and carry it with him for the rest of his life while actively reinvesting his feelings

Venting. Grief has been described as a process of emotional response to real, perceived, or threatened loss. The feelings associated with loss are innate, necessary, and universal. It is their manifestation that is socially specific. Since the feelings are innate, it is best to bring them out, to share them, to ventilate. The denial of these feelings or the suppression of them does not cause them to disappear. On the contrary, they will remain, growing in intensity, forever seeking actualization (Maslow 1969). The griever must learn how to communicate his feelings to himself and to others. This communication should allow for the identification of the feelings, an examination of their source, and the development of coping strategies to reduce their intensity.

For a survivor to vent requires the willingness of others to listen, as one would in a sanctioned loss experience. The prerequisite to listening is the recognition and acceptance of the validity of the loss and the need to grieve.

Validating the Relationship. The relationship between the survivor and the deceased existed. It was real. As such it facilitated the realization or fulfillment of perceived needs. The effect of the relationship resulted in some changes in the personhood of the parties to the relationship. The survivor needs to recognize the nature of the relationship. He must admit to its existence. There may be a tendency, especially in a disenfranchised grief experience, to recreate in one's mind the nature of the relationship and the reasons for the involvement of each person. This may result in assigning blame where no blame existed or constructing a picture of the self as a manipulated and abused victim.

Resolving Guilt. Death-related guilt is an emotional response composed of self-blame and self-accusation about events leading up to the death. Death-related guilt may be legitimate or illegitimate (Rando 1984), or it may be a guilt felt because one is a survivor. The guilt experienced may be exaggerated or it may simply be dismissed. A guilt experience appears to be a universal response to a loss of a loved person. There is a strong probability that the intensity of guilt increases in a disenfranchised grief. Society contributes to this disenfranchisement in the form of its religious and legal systems. It has ritualized the forms of dealing with guilt that are absolute (Raphael 1983) but not appropriate for resolving guilt in disenfranchised grief.

It is imperative that guilt be examined, eliminated, or accommodated. Unresolved guilt in grief may provoke an attempt at self-punishment on the part of the distressed survivor.

> Sherry, an eighteen-year-old college freshman, had become pregnant during a spring break trip to Florida with her boyfriend. Sherry's parents were Catholic and were staunch advocates of the church's position on abortion. Although she had no strong feelings about abortion, Sherry was not able to reveal the pregnancy to her parents.
> Sherry received abortion counseling through her college counseling services. She also described receiving what might be called "supportive coercion"

in favor of a decision for abortion from her boyfriend. Sherry decided to terminate the pregnancy. After the abortion, Sherry's boyfriend expressed his relief, told Sherry it was the right decision, and said she should forget the whole experience. Sherry could not. Images of what her "baby" looked like began to appear in her mind. Her family and religious opposition to abortion began to fill her thoughts. Sherry began to feel a sense of loss. Part of her, she felt, had died, and the death was her fault. She felt trapped. She needed to confide in someone. But who? She feared hurting her parents, and she feared their ostracism. She "knew for sure" she had been excommunicated by the church. Her boyfriend did not seem to understand her feelings. He was too relieved. Sherry also felt some relief, but in addition to the relief, she felt intense guilt and a need to grieve her loss. In her confusion and aloneness, Sherry attempted, unsuccessfully, to end her own life.

The potential for guilt after an abortion is often unrecognized. The unwanted pregnancy is perceived as the problem; the choice of termination is seen as the solution. In addition, there may be a sense of wrongdoing in one or both of the parents. Family moral values and religious tenets learned throughout one's life may reinforce feelings of transgression and culpability. The guilt may seem to be unpardonable.

The griever needs to engage in some reality testing to determine the nature and source of the guilt. She needs to discuss her feelings with a nonjudgmental, sensitive listener. She needs to examine all the acts of commission and omission, thoughts, and feelings that seem to be the basis for the felt guilt (Rando 1984).

Resolution of guilt in grief requires an internal process of self-forgiveness, restitution, and a letting go of the hold on the guilt (Schneider 1984, Weizman and Kamm 1985). Rando (1984) suggests that in the case of legitimate guilt the griever might do something altruistic for others, equivalent to the option of performing some community service in lieu of a jail sentence, as a way of atoning for the transgression.

Internalizing the Memory. For many grieved individuals the most difficult skill to learn and use is one that has the semblance of a contradiction. The individual has to learn how to create and internalize a realistic image of the lost loved one, decathect by developing a new relationship with the deceased, and actively invest emotionally in other new relationships.

Memories and objects that assist in the maintenance of memories must be retained and cherished. A new relationship with the deceased must be developed. It must be a relationship of the past and, in the case of a belief in an afterlife, of an otherworld future. It can never be a relationship of the present or of a future in this world. The void created by the loss and felt in the present must be filled with new relationships involving known or newly encountered persons.

In summary, successful coping in grief necessitates a great deal of hard work. It is a process requiring active participation on the part of the survivor. There are coping skills one must learn to use in order to complete the requisite tasks of adaptation.

The skills are difficult to learn and the tasks arduous, even in a supported grief reaction. In disenfranchised grief the process may be perceived as Herculean; the resolution, unachievable. The disenfranchised griever is a prime candidate for grief counseling. The definition of disenfranchisement offered earlier infers that, if anyone is in need of grief counseling, it is the disenfranchised griever.

Disenfranchised Grief and Grief Counseling

What is grief counseling? It is a process of helping people work toward a healthy completion of the tasks of grieving (Worden 1982) by providing a type of general support that offers human comfort and care *and* that accepts and encourages appropriate grief (Raphael 1983).

A grief counselor is someone who assists the griever in developing the suitable skills and supports him in his completion of the requisite tasks of successful grief resolution. The uniqueness of disenfranchised grief creates a situation in which the grief counselor becomes a social and familial surrogate for the griever. In addition, it requires that the counselor focus on his own issues of concern and acceptance around painful, potentially frightening and embarrasing life-styles and resulting loss experiences. When the counselor has begun to get in touch with her own feelings and reactions, genuine support is possible.

The role of the counselor is to:

Support the griever as he goes through the grief process

Design intervention strategies that will compensate for the absence of necessary supports and deficient coping skills

Assist the individual in grief to achieve a realistic perspective on what resolution of grief will mean to him: changed life-style; new social roles; and possibly a new identity.

Examine appropriate ways in which the person will be able to maintain a realistic memory of the deceased

Assist in the creation of the adjusted life, helping the griever to identify how he may survive and grow in a life without the deceased

Throughout the whole counselor/client relationship, the counselor should

Be straighforward

Ask simple direct questions

Be empathic

Stay with the griever even when frightening experiences are being described

The initial step in counseling in all types of grief experiences is to conduct an assessment of the affected individual and his response to the loss. To understand and counsel a person in grief, the counselor must know

In what specific ways the object was important to the individual

The typical coping patterns of the individual

Her social and cultural milieu

Her attention toward loss and death

The special resources or disabilities the individual possesses for coping with loss (Schoenberg et al. 1970).

In a disenfranchised grief experience, the nature and intensity of the grief must be assessed accurately with the specific issues of disenfranchisement being defined. The counselor should assess:

1. The nature of the relationship:

   How long did the relationship exist?

   How did the relationship begin?

   What were the dimensions of the relationship?

   Who are the others who might be affected by the relationship and/or the death?

2. The death event:

   When, where, and how did the death occur?

   How did the griever first learn of the death?

   From whom was the information of death received?

   What were the griever's affective responses to the event?

3. The styles of coping:

   What was the griever's initial response to the death?

   How did the griever attempt to cope with the loss?

   What was the result of these actions?

   What would the person want to do?

4. The support available:

   With whom, if anyone, did the person share his thoughts and feelings about death?

   What was the griever's predeath social support system like?

5. Personal state:

   What, if any, prescription, over-the-counter or illicit drugs, and/or alcohol are being used?

   Is there any history of medical (physical or mental) problems that may influence the griever's ability to perform necessary grief work?

   What does the griever hope to achieve in counseling?

The answers to these assessment questions will provide the counselor with the necessary data to design a strategy for intervention. Worden (1982) describes ten principles and procedures that should be the foundation of any grief counseling strategy:

1. Help the survivor actualize the loss

2. Help the survivor identify and express feelings

3. Assist the survivor to learn how to live without the deceased

4. Facilitate the withdrawal of emotional ties from the deceased and encourage the formation of new relationships

5. Provide time to grieve and give the survivor permission to grieve

6. Interpret normal behavior

7. Allow for individual differences in the response to grieving

8. Provide continuing support over the most critical periods at least for the first year following the death

9. Assist the survivor in examining her defenses and coping styles

10. Identify any pathology and refer the person to an appropriate therapist

Insomuch as disenfranchised grief occurs when there is an absence of social recognition and/or social sanction of the grief is nonexistent, the unique consequences of the disenfranchisement must be addressed in designing a counseling strategy. The counselor must pay additional attention to (1) the absence of others with whom the griever can share feelings, and (2) a lack of active participation by the griever in any ritual employed around the death.

A complete description of the techniques of grief counseling is beyond the scope of this chapter. Therefore, the suggested strategies for counseling the disenfranchised griever which follow assume a concurrent use of accepted grief counseling techniques. (The sources identified in the references at the end of this chapter include a number of excellent texts on grief counseling.)

Encourage the Griever to Talk. The counselor should help the griever develop the ability to identify, understand, and verbalize the full range of feelings being experienced. Special attention should be focused on the potential for anger, guilt, jealousy, and frustration previously described. The counselor should help the griever to examine how he functions when these feelings are being experienced and what techniques he uses for coping with or resolving the feelings. This may be the first opportunity for the griever to share his feelings. The counselor should ask what the person wants to do about his guilt, anger, or other feelings. The responses may provide clues to how and why the griever is functioning, especially if he indicates a desire to act on the guilt or anger. Having the client focus on the positives that existed in the relationship may help in guilt and anger reduction. Even in relationships that existed for very short periods of time, there are positive qualities that may be found and shared.

The griever should be encouraged to make note of the feelings experienced during the day, the events or activities that prompted the feelings, the ways he copes when these feelings surface, and how he evaluates the effectiveness of the coping attempts. This note taking may be in the form of a diary or an audiotape. This format may enable the survivor to remember and share with the counselor the feelings that arise between counseling sessions. This procedure may serve to legitimize and validate the grief. In addition, it communicates to the griever that it is all right to grieve. It tells him that it is normal to have these feelings.

Resolving the Loss. Disenfranchised grief, as has been frequently stated, excludes the griever from active involvement in the death-related rituals and ceremonies. In the absence of involvement in the rituals, there need to be events or experiences that occur at the appropriate times in the grief process to permit an expression of the significance of the loss, a willingness of the individual to accept the loss, and a preparation to move on. The counselor should assist the griever in finding ways to say goodbye and to express the necessary feelings associated with this goodbye statement.

To help, the counselor might have the survivor talk through an "imagined" funeral. The counselor might also suggest that the griever write a eulogy to the deceased, indicating what he would want to have said if he had attended and participated in the funeral rituals. After the writing, the survivor might be asked to share the euology with the counselor. This sharing may serve as a ritual substitute. It may permit the griever to express his feelings and say the goodbye he was not permitted to because of his exclusion from the rituals.

A visit to the grave side after the internment may also provide the griever with an opportunity to make a final statement and begin the process of emotional disengagement. In the absence of a grave, the griever might use some personal item or photograph of the deceased as a grave substitute. This item should be something that will enable the griever to focus his attention on the mental image of the deceased, making it easier to complete disengagement.

Internalizing the Memory. Rando (1984) suggests that in normal uncomplicated grief the counselor encourage the griever realistically to review and talk about the deceased and their mutual relationship. It is recommended that the counselor have the griever repeatedly review the entire relationship, back to its earliest origins, and to include a description of the hopes and fantasies that helped form the relationship. It is as if the griever is creating a mental scrapbook.

The griever should be encouraged to express the memories creatively if he feels comfortable in doing so. This may include photographs or drawings of shared experiences. The counselor may encourage the griever to tell the story of the picture and what occurred that day. It may be a sharing through music that helps the griever identify feelings, events, and experiences within the relationship. A goal of this technique is to provide stimuli that will help the bereaved tell a complete story of the deceased (Schoenberg 1980).

It is imperative that the counselor accept the reality of the relationship by referring to the relationship and its meaning as described by the griever and by using the deceased's name when talking with the survivor. Not to refer to the relationship or not to use the deceased's name may be perceived as an indication of further rejection of the relationship and/or the survivor's grief response.

Taking Control. Disenfranchisement in grief often results in feeling completely out of control in one's life. Pressing needs, intense desires, future hopes and plans cannot be realized. Nor can the frustration and emptiness brought on by the death be shared. Skills for coping, efficient in past stress experiences, do not resolve the current problem. Self-worth may be questioned. A sense of helplessness begins to infiltrate one's thoughts.

The counselor should have the griever enumerate those problems that she perceives to be the most stressful. This list should include a brief description of what coping behaviors the survivor has tried. Using a stress rating scale similar to the one developed by Holmes (Doyle 1980) will help in identifying stressful life events and their impact on the individual. Holmes's scale lists a number of life events, both positive and negative, that are likely to create a stressful situation. Such a scale attempts to quantify the amount and intensity of stress one is experiencing at a specific time. The goal of such a scale is to identify very stressful times so as to motivate the individual to search for ways that will reduce the stress. This, in turn, may reduce the sense of crisis the griever is experiencing. The counselor, with the scale results, is better able to assist the griever in evaluating the appropriateness of his coping behaviors and in his search for alternative ways to cope.

One way to evaluate coping is to examine its outcome. If the coping behavior results in the person's feeling inspired (a deep, visceral feeling of well-being and personal satisfaction), the behavior choice was a good one. If the outcome results in a dispirited feeling (an overall sense of dissatisfaction with self, a feeling of depression, and a lessening of self-worth), the choice of coping behaviors was not a good one. A good way to begin this search for more positive ways to act is for the counselor to ask what the griever feels is most necessary and appropriate to do in taking control of his life.

The Counselor as Surrogate. In disenfranchised grief the counselor is a surrogate standing in for those family members and social supports that are present in sanctioned grief. The counselor is the significant other with whom the survivor may cry, sit in silence, question, yell, reminisce, feel hurt, plead, pray, and generally seek understanding and strength. The counselor's task is to help the griever move away from the need for counseling and to create the needed intimate relationships with others in her life. The griever needs to feel comfortable with her feelings and to work toward the development of intimate relationships with the knowledge of the pain that one experiences when an intimate relationship is lost.

The definition of intimate relationships, as used here, is not limited to the narrow concept of physical or sexual intimacy. It refers to a relationship that is so open and sharing that all parties to the relationship are completely free to be themselves. No roles, limitations, camouflaging, or pretense is necessary. There is no need to impress, to feel or be shamed, to disguise or to hide. It is a relationship built on total and complete trust, honesty, and equality.

The counselor providing care for a person in disenfranchised grief should assist the griever to move toward and create intimate relationships with at least two different people, lest one die and leave the other alone in grief.

A last recommendation refers to the use of community self-help support programs. Since disenfranchised grief is brought on by a lack of social recognition and support, it is important that the griever return to the social environment and receive this needed recognition and support. The creation of or referrals to self-help support groups may ameliorate the pain and distress of disenfranchised grief. These groups, modeled on programs like Widow-to-Widow, Parents of a Murdered Child, and Survivors of a Suicide, may provide support to lovers of AIDS victims, individuals who have suffered pet loss, perinatal loss, or abortion, as well as any number of other types of disenfranchised loss. In short, these groups can provide the support the rest of the society fails to. The counselor should survey his community to identify those support groups to whom he may refer. This resource listing should include name of the group; the location of the group; the telephone number and the best time to call for information; the name of a contact person; fees, if any; and any information about the individuals who are responsible for the group's activities.

It is imperative that the counselor know when to remove herself from the life of the client and when to refer or recommend intensive therapy to the client. As with the community groups, the counselor should have a list of therapists he feels comfortable using as his referrals.

In conclusion, disenfranchised grief is a difficult or complicated grief because it is socially unrecognized and largely unsupported grief. The major problems arising from this category of grief are related to this lack of familial and social support so desperately needed at this time. The essential task for the grief counselor, then, is to assess the nature of the lost relationship and any apparent deficiencies in recognition and support. In this way the counselor will be able to design more effective counseling strategies to assist the griever in coping with and surviving the loss of a significant other.

References

Barton, D., ed. 1979. *Dying and Death: A Clinical Guide for Caregivers*. Baltimore: Williams and Wilkins.

Doka, K.J. ed., 1989. "Disenfranchised Grief." In *Disenfranchised Grief*. Lexington, Mass.: Lexington Books.

Doyle, P. 1980. *Grief Counseling and Sudden Death*. Springfield, Ill. Thomas.

Maslow, A.H. 1969. *Toward a Psychology of Being*. Princeton: D. Van Nostrand.

Osterweis, M., F. Solomon, and M. Green. eds. 1984. *Bereavement: Reactions, Consequences, and Care*. Washington, D.C.: National Academy Press.

Parkes, C.M., and R.S. Weiss. 1983. *Recovery from Bereavement*. New York: Basic Books.

Rando, T.A. 1984. *Grief, Dying, and Death: Clinical Interventions for Caregivers*. Champaign, Ill.: Research Press.

Raphael, B. 1983. *The Anatomy of Bereavement*. New York: Basic Books.

Schneider, J. 1984. *Stress, Loss, and Grief*. Baltimore: University Press.

Schoenberg, B., A.C. Carr, D. Peretz, and A.H. Kutscher, eds. 1970. *Loss and Grief: Psychological Management in Medical Practice*. New York: Columbia University Press.

Schoenberg, B.M., ed. 1980. *Bereavement Counseling: A Multidisciplinary Handbook*. Westport, Conn.: Greenwood Press.

Stroebe, W., and M.S. Stroebe. 1987. *Bereavement and Health: The Psychological and Physical Consequences of Partner Loss*. New York: Cambridge University Press.

Weizman, S.B., and P. Kamm. 1985. *About Mourning: Support and Guidance for the Bereaved*. New York: Human Science Press.

Worden, J.W. 1982. *Grief Counseling and Grief Therapy: A Handbook for the Mental Health Practitioner*. New York: Springer.

Part VI
Conclusion

As was stated earlier, a book such as this has a certain sense of incompleteness. Since beginning research in and conceptualization of disenfranchised grief, I am constantly reminded of the many circumstances and situations that can lead to unsanctioned loss. The chapters in this book seek to explore some of the dimensions of such loss, recognizing that numerous other contexts exist. It is hoped that the exploration of these dimensions will encourage further speculation, research, and application of the concept of disenfranchised grief.

Nevertheless, it does seem fitting, at the conclusion, to draw together the central themes. Perhaps, upon reflection, there are four.

1. People exist in multiple relationships and have a tremendous capacity to form meaningful, significant, and multifaceted attachments in their environment.

Certainly this book has emphasized that people can form significant attachments in different kinds of relationships. We are involved in webs of relationships that include not only family (in the broadest sense, including stepparents, stepchildren, half siblings, and so forth), but also lovers, friends, colleagues, and caregivers. Though this point seems obvious, it is often ignored in a society that emphasizes the primacy of the dyadic relationship and the nuclear family, extending to those relationships an almost exclusive monopoly to mourn.

There is also an ironic paradox. Through television, movies, and books, popular culture has often portrayed the diversity of human relationships. In the media, for example, friendship is often celebrated. But on the rare occasions when the media shows grief, it is almost always in the content of a few, select family roles.

And human attachments extend into time. Past relationships, such as those of ex-spouses, may still hold a degree of attachment and thus there may be a residue of grief. Attachments may extend into the future as well. An unborn child may still engender the dreams, hopes, and love of significant others, so that when such promise is terminated grief is the result.

Attachments too are specific, in that people attach themselves to the particular characteristics of the other. When these characteristics change, a sense of loss can result.

And finally, human attachment can extend beyond its species. In our society, especially as it has become more urban, animals have developed more than utilitarian value, and significant pet-human bonds develop. This too is celebrated in the media, as in the favorite old TV program, *Lassie*. The loss of this attachment can bring grief. This bond also illustrates, however, that humans are not only attached to other humans or even animals but to many aspects of their environment: homes, possessions, jobs, organizations, ideals, and beliefs.

In short, then, people are capable of a great capacity for relationships and attachments, so naturally they become vulnerable to grief when these attachments and relationships are severed. The problem results only when that fact is forgotten, when the natural resultant grief is minimized or ignored.

2. We need to broaden our definitions of loss.

Since people are capable of great diversity in attachment, it follows that we need to recognize those attachments and broaden our definitions of loss. Every society has "grieving roles" or norms that indicate who, how, for whom, and at what length people should grieve. Though these norms are supported informally, in interaction with others, they also may be codified in everything from personnel policies governing time off for grief to contractual arrangements that specify the legitimacy of varied losses as they affect contractual compliance (for example, "nonrefundable" airline tickets). As indicated in the chapters throughout this book, these norms disenfranchise, or fail to recognize and validate, grief in many situations.

Western industrial society is achievement oriented and individualistic, and in it these norms tend particularly to disenfranchise in two broad categories. First, as has been stated, the individualistic nature of society tends to disenfranchise those who do not have recognizable kin-based relationships. Second, the allowance for grief often reflects an underlying utilitarian bias. The extent to which grief is recognized reflects both the perceived social value of the deceased the griever.

The perceived social value of an individual has long been recognized as a factor in the treatment of the dying patient (Glaser and Strauss 1964, Roth 1972, Sudnow 1967). It seems clear that it is a factor in grief as well. There is an expectation that one will grieve less for individuals who are less socially valued, such as, for example, an older parent of an adult child. And there is also a sense that socially devalued persons such as the old or developmentally disabled have less legitimacy to grieve.

Beyond these two factors, there are whole categories of loss that are simply not socially recognized or legitimized. Perinatal losses, pet lossed, and psychosocial losses are but a few of the categories in which the right of the bereaved to mourn is, at best, only partially acknowledged.

In recent years, there has been increasing sensitivity on the part of the caregiving community, particularly among those regularly dealing with the dying and bereaved, toward the need to recognize such losses. And while that sensitivity is both welcome and essential, there is also a responsibility to increase and enhance public education.

3. The central theme in counseling the disenfranchised is to validate loss.

Since the disenfranchised griever is dealing with a loss that is not socially recognized, one of the critical interventions of the counselor is to validate loss. Often the griever shares that same sense that his or her grief is inappropriate and nonlegitimate. Thus, although numerous interventions are suggested in this book they can be succinctly summarized by the victim: help grievers recognize and explore their loss, and find meaningful and appropriate ways to mourn.

Yet there is one caveat here. The counselor needs to explore a client's loss fully. One of the dangers inherent in the conceptualization of disenfranchised grief is that by legitimating certain losses, counselors may fail to explore fully other, underlying losses. For example, grief over pet loss may be a legitimate response to the death of a valued companion animal, or it may be the manifestation of an earlier unresolved loss. In one case, a middle-aged clergyman sought counseling because he was having a difficult time resolving the loss of a dog. In counseling it became clear that he was really responding to a series of losses that had occurred within the past five years. This was the first loss that was "his"; it was the first loss in which he did not feel that he had to take care of the mourners.

The caveat also works the other way. Even in counseling persons who have clear, recognized losses, the counselor needs to be careful to explore other losses that may be complicating present grief. Often clients may even be unaware of delayed grief reactions from earlier unresolved losses that were disenfranchised. For example, in taking histories from widows in her program, one therapist makes it a point to ask clients whether they have had a pregnancy terminated. Her clinical experience has been that many times the women who have had intense grief reactions to the loss of a husband may have never resolved, or even recognized, these earlier losses.

4. Rituals are critical tools for the resolution of grief.

There has been both empirical (for example, Carey 1979, Doka 1984) and clinical (Rando 1984) affirmation of the critical role of ritual in resolving loss. The chapters here support that observation by indicating that one of the most difficult aspects of disenfranchised grief is the absence of or exclusion from mourning rituals. Certainly this remains an important area for exploration.

This also suggests that one of the more powerful interventions counselors can use is helping participants, when there is need, to plan, develop, and perform rituals that will facilitate grief resolution. Absence of or exclusion from predeath or funeral rituals does not preclude participation in personalized, significant, and meaningful therapeutic or postfuneral rituals (Rando 1984, Doka 1984).

Finally, it seems fitting to emphasize the vital importance of continued research, education, and resource development. One of the most positive aspects over the past two decades or increased death awareness has been the development of many support groups. These self-help groups provide an essential service to the bereaved. They offer opportunities for ventilation and support, exploration of coping styles, education, and finding role models. Still, many are organized around recognizable losses and sanctioned roles— those of the parent, child, sibling. The losses described here suggest a need for other forms of groups or perhaps broader criteria for invitation and inclusion.

The development or redefinition of support groups is but one of the ways our society will have to recognize the effect of diverse life-styles on patterns of loss. Personnel policies may have to become more flexible. Counselors may need to become more aware.

Death education courses at any level can have a significant enfranchising role. For example, children can consider in nonthreatening ways pet or friend loss. In professional death education courses, material can be incorporated describing other aspects of disenfranchised grief. For instance, nurses might consider the role and needs of lovers in patient care plans, or funeral directors might discuss the issue of ex-spouses and funerals. At any level, students can be made aware that where there is attachment there is loss, and where there is loss there is grief.

And there is also a considerable agenda for research. Most of the chapters here reflect that need. Extensive studies, with larger and national samples, of disenfranchised grief are few. In almost each situation, there is research that should be done documenting the extent and manifestation of grief, the variables that complicate or facilitate grief, and the strategies that seek to ameliorate grief.

Ernest Becker concluded his massive treatise, *The Denial of Death*, with this observation: "The most that any one of us can seem to do is to fashion something—an object or ourselves—and drop it into the confusion, make an offering of it, so to speak, to the life force" (1972; p. 285). It is sage advice. And perhaps nowhere is that contribution more needed, although perhaps even that is neither recognized nor acknowledged, than by the disenfranchised griever.

References

Becker, E. 1972. *The Denial of Death*. New York: Free Press.

Carey, R. 1979."Weathering Widowhood: Problems and Adjustments of the Widowed during the First Year." *Omega* 10, 163–72.

Doka, K.J. 1984. "Expectation of Death, Participation in Funeral Arrangements, and Grief Adjustment." *Omega* 15, 119–30.

Glaser, B., and A. Strauss. 1964. "The Social Loss of Dying Patients." *American Journal of Nursing* 64, 119–21.

Rando, T. 1984. *Grief, Dying and Death: Clinical Interventions for Caregivers*. Champaign, Ill.: Research Press.

Roth, J.A. 1972. "Some Contingencies of the Moral Evaluation and Control of Clientele: The Case of the Hospital Emergency Service." *American Journal of Sociology* 77, 839–56.

Sudnow, D. 1967. *Passing On: The Social Organization of Dying*. Englewood Cliffs, N.J.: Prentice-Hall.

Index

Abortion, elective: description of maternal-infant bonding, 137–139; factors that affect the grief process, 142–145; maternal-infant bonding and, 139–142; previous research on, 135–137

Abramson, L.Y., 164

Addis, M., 189

Adolescents. *See* Young adults

AIDS, bereavement patterns in survivors of, 304–307; current social climate, 38–39; disenfranchised grief and, 303–304; effects of on, on the concept of love, 33–34; familial support, 35; grief following death of the loved one, 35–38; legal unpreparedness, 37–38; loss and grief prior to death, 34–35; psychosocial support, 39–40

AIDS, foster parenting children with: description of foster parents, 46–49; discrimination of children and foster parents, 48; legal unpreparedness, 44–45; role of foster parent, 43–44; sources of support, 48–49, 52; statistics on, 45; types of grief associated with 49–52

AIDS, health care professionals and their relationships with patients: attending funerals, 59–60; dealing with grief, 60; mortality, 61, 63–64; personal values, 61; sexuality and love, 61–62; social values, 61; sources of support for, 62–64; stigmatization, 57–58

AIDS, hospice workers and: guidelines for, 307–311; overview of hospice movement, 301–303

Aisenberg, R., 206, 219

Albert, E., 33, 34, 36

Aldrich, C.K., 163

All Our Losses, All Our Griefs (Mitchell and Anderson), 246

Allistair, M., 80

Alzheimer's disease, 187, 188, 189. *See also* Psychosocial loss

American Association for Suicidology, 101

American Psychiatric Association, 242

Anderson, H., 243, 245, 246

Angle, C., 206

Antelyes, J., 148

Anthony, S., 205

Anticipatory grief, children with AIDS and, 51

Antonucci, T.C., 217

Archov, P., 149

Association for Death Education and Counseling, 101

Atchley, R., 9

Averill, J.R., 148

Barbuto, J., 34

Barley, Kenneth, 34, 38

Barton, D., 313, 315

Becker, E., 203, 204, 332

Bell, R.R., 77, 79

Benfield, D.G., 117

Bennett, M.B., 191

Bennett, M.I., 191

Benoliel, J.Q., 287, 296

Bereavement: Studies of Grief in Adult Life (Parkes), 17

About the Contributors

Rita A. Aber, M.S., is a graduate of the College of New Rochelle's Gerontology Program. She was formerly Activities Therapist at the Dementia Day Program at Burke Rehabilitation Center in White Plains, New York.

John L. Abraham, M.Div., an Episcopal Priest and Thanatologist, is Rector of the Episcopal Church of St. Matthew, Tucson, Arizona. He is a bereavement consultant, hospice founder, and the initiator of university death education. For the past decade John has been a member of the Association for Death Education and Counseling and he authors "Jest Death," a nationally distributed newsletter column about death-related humor.

Gary R. Anderson, Ph.D., is an Associate Professor at Hunter College School of Social Work. He has authored numerous articles on children and AIDS. His forthcoming book, *Responding to the AIDS Crisis: Innovations in Child Welfare Services,* will be published summer, 1989. He has served as a consultant to numerous child welfare agencies.

Edith S. Deck, R.N., M.S., a nurse and sociologist, is Associate Professor of Nursing, University of Vermont. A noted writer on Assertiveness Training, she and Dr. Folta collaborated on research in the United States, Norway, Nigeria, and Zimbabwe where they studied health care workers and dying patients, impact of children's death on mothers, friends in grief, widows, and cross-cultural grief.

Lois Chapman Dick, death educator and counselor, is a member of the Foundation of Thanatology and on the Board of Directors of the international organization, the Association of Death Education and Counseling. She has served as a clinical associate to the School of Medicine, University of Washington and lectured at colleges and universities in Canada and the United States. Lois resides in Kirkland, Washington, a suburb of Seattle.

Richard R. Ellis, Ed.D., is an Associate Professor and Chairman of the Department of Counselor Education at New York University, in New York. He also is director of the department's M.A. degree programs and is founder of its M.A. program in thanatological counseling. At this time he is developing a new M.A. comprehensive program in thanatological counseling and education. He has a small private practice.

Jeanette R. Folta, R.N., Ph.D., FAAN, a nurse and sociologist, is Professor and Chairperson of Sociology, University of Vermont. Involved in research on death and dying, she is the first nurse to systematically study the topic. She and Ms. Deck collaborated on research in the United States, Norway, Nigeria, and Zimbabwe where they studied health care workers and dying patients, impact of children's death on mothers, friends in grief, widows, and cross-cultural grief.

Ruth L. Fuller, M.D., a psychoanalyst and child psychiatrist, is an Associate Professor, Department of Psychiatry, University of Colorado Health Sciences Center. She is the Director of the Pediatric Psychiatry Consultation Liaison Service, University Hospital, a national consultant on minority mental health, and a periodic advisor to hospices.

Sally B. Geis, Ph.D., sociologist, is Director, Iliff Institute for Lay and Clergy Education (Denver), and a Clinical Associate Professor, Department of Psychiatry, University of Colorado Health Sciences Center. She is an international consultant on education and has done work with the bereavement team of the Hospice of Metro Denver.

Phyllis Gurdin, M.S.W., is Director of the AIDS Specialized Foster Care Program at Leake and Watts Children's Services, one of the earliest and largest programs of its kind. A long-experienced social worker, Dr. Gurdin has lectured widely on the needs of children with AIDS.

William V. Hocker, a practicing funeral director in New Mexico, is currently the President of the National Funeral Directors Association. He is a frequent contributor to symposia and grief workshops across the United States.

Jeffrey Kauffman, M.A., M.S.S., is a psychotherapist with a specialization in bereavement, in practice in suburban Philadelphia. He is Director of the Center for the Care of Community Institutions, a staff support and bereavement consulting service to hospices, hospitals, nursing homes, schools, police departments, social service, and mental health agencies.

Nathan Kollar, S.T.D., is Professor of Religious Studies and founder of the Gerontology Department at St. John Fisher College. An internationally recognized scholar of the relationship between death and religion and the rituals associated with death, his most recent book is *Songs of Suffering* (Winston, 1982).

Dale Kuhn, M.A., S.T.M., is Program Director of Care and Counseling, Missouri. Rev. Kuhn, a Lutheran clergyman, has been involved in pastoral counseling for the past fifteen years.

Louis LaGrand, Ph.D., a professor of Health Science at Potsdam College of the State University of New York, is the author of *Coping with Separation and Loss as a Young Adult* and *Changing Patterns of Human Existence*. He is the President of the Board of Directors of Hospice of St. Lawrence Valley and is a member of the Board of the Association for Death Education and Counseling.

Claire Lavin, Ph.D., a clinical and school psychologist, is an Associate Professor in the Graduate School at the College of New Rochelle. The author and former director of CNR Graduate Programs in Special Education, Claire has worked extensively with the mentally retarded and emotionally handicapped.

Elise Lev, R.N., Ed.D., a nurse-researcher, is a post-doctoral fellow in psychosocial oncology at the University of Pennsylvania, School of Nursing, Philadelphia. She is currently on leave from her associate professor position at the College of New Rochelle, School of Nursing, where she developed and taught a course in hospice nursing. In addition she is a co-founder of the Hospice of Stamford, CT.

Terry L. Martin, Ph.D., is an Assistant Professor of Psychology at HooD College in Frederick, Maryland, and a counselor in private practice. Dr. Martin consults with nursing homes, hospitals, hospices, and schools on issues related to aging, loss, and death. He has been a death educator for twelve years and has convened workshops on death, loss, and aging for professionals throughout the United States and Canada.

David Meagher, Ed.D., is an Associate Professor in the Thanatology Program of Brooklyn College. He is the coauthor of *Death: The Experience* and editor of the Newsletter, *Death and Life*. Dr. Meagher has been a consultant to school districts, boards of education, and medical examiner's offices.

Miriam S. Moss, M.A., is a Senior Research Sociologist at the Philadelphia Geriatric Center. She has been Project Director in a broad range of behavioral research in gerontology. She and her husband, Sidney, have written extensively on family separation and reunion across the life cycle.

Sidney Z. Moss, ACSW, is Senior Family Therapist in the Family and Children's Unit, Northwest Center (Philadelphia). He also has a private practice in family therapy.

Jane A. Nichols, is the bereavement consultant to the Regional Neonatal Intensive Care Unite of Children's Hospital Medical Center of Akron (Ohio). Ms. Nichols entered the field of thanatology through funeral service where she was one of the pioneers of the adaptive funeral and ongoing supportive care for bereaved persons. Since joining Children's Hospital stasff in 1978, she has researched parental reactions to the death of a newborn and developed a responsive bereavement program. Author of numerous articles and chapters, Jane has also lectured nationally.

George S. Paulus, Ph.D., is Professor of Social Science at Michigan State University. His current research interests are in the area of sudden and multiple loss of significant attachment objects.

Larry G. Peppers, Ph.D., a sociologist, is an Associate Professor of Sociology at Clemson University. He has published two books, *Motherhood and Mourning* and *How to Go On Living after The Death of A Baby*. Dr. Peppers has consulted with numerous hospitals and parent support groups.

Vanderlyn R. Pine, Ph.D., a sociologist, is a Professor in the Sociology Department of The State University of New York, College at New Paltz. A national consultant on dying, death, and bereavement, he is the author of four books, the editor of four, and has published over fifty articles.

Elliot J. Rosen, Ed.D., a family therapist, is a senior faculty member of the family Institute of Westchester in Mt. Vernon, New York. He writes and lectures extensively on issues of loss and grief in the family, consults to a number of hospice organizations, and serves as consulting psychologist to Jansen Memorial Hospice in Tuckahoe, New York.

Julian Rush, M.Div., a minister, is executive director of the Colorado AIDS Project and Associate Pastor, St. Paul's United Methodist Church, Denver.

Dennis Ryan, Ph.D., has his degree in Comparative Religions from Fordham University in New York, and is an Associate Professor of Religious Studies at the College of New Rochelle. In 1971, he traveled to India to do research for his doctoral thesis on the Indian Epic, the Mahabharata. More recently, in 1986, he lived for a year in the Peoples Republic of China where he did research on their religious beliefs and practices.

Alexis J. Stein, M.Ed., C.D.E., is Executive Director of TO LIFE, a non-profit education and counseling organization specializing in grief and loss issues. She has written numerous articles, columns, and books on grief, coping, and teen suicide. Alexis is a nationally and internationally recognized speaker who lectures on a wide variety of issues.

Cyrus S. Stewart, Ph.D., C.S.W., is Professor of Social Science at Michigan State University and Vice President of Meridian Professional Psychological Consultants in East Lansing, Michigan. He maintains an active clinical practice, specializing in marital and family therapy. His research interests are in the area of adolescent suicide and the establishment of Community Crises Response Teams.

Ann E. Thomas, M.S.W., is a clinical Social Worker at Queens Medical Center in Honolulu. She has worked for ten years with the terminally ill and bereaved.

John C. Thrush, MPH., is Chief of Health Surveillance Section, Michigan Department of Public Health. His current research interests are in the area of suicidology and health risk behaviors.

Howard R. Winokuer, M.Ed., C.D.E., a counselor and Certified Death Educator, is the co-founder and Chief Executive Officer of TO LIFE, a non-profit organization that provides counseling services in the areas of grief, loss, and life enhancement. He has worked as both a national and international consultant in the field of grief and has recently served as a member of the North Carolina Governor's Youth Study Commission.

About the Editor

Kenneth J. Doka, Ph.D., is a professor of gerontology at the Graduate School of the College of New Rochelle and a Lutheran Minister. Dr. Doka has taught, researched, spoken, and written in the area of dying, death, and grief for the past eighteen years. His articles have appeared in *Omega, Death Studies,* and other journals and trade magazines.